IN THE SHADOWS OF GIANTS

IN THE SHADOWS OF GIANTS

KEVIN JOHNSTON ∾

Gill & Macmillan

Gill & Macmillan Ltd
Hume Avenue, Park West, Dublin 12
with associated companies throughout the world
www.gillmacmillan.ie

© Kevin Johnston 2008
978 07171 4435 8

Index compiled by Cover To Cover
Typography design by Make Communication
Print origination by Carole Lynch
Printed and bound in Great Britain by MPG Books Ltd,
Bodmin, Cornwall

This book is typeset in Linotype Minion and
Neue Helvetica.

The paper used in this book comes from the wood
pulp of managed forests. For every tree felled,
at least one tree is planted, thereby renewing
natural resources.

A CIP catalogue record for this book is available
from the British Library.

5 4 3 2 1

The author and publishers have made every effort
to trace all copyright holders, but if any has been
inadvertently overlooked we would be pleased
to make the necessary arrangement at the
first opportunity.

To Maura

CONTENTS

PROLOGUE IX

1. After the Famine 1
2. The development of Belfast Harbour and the growth of shipbuilding 24
3. Diverging communities: Belfast after 1850 50
4. Edwardian Belfast 81
5. The White Star trinity 100
6. The Third Home Rule crisis 132
7. The Great War 153
8. The war at home and the war at sea 185
9. Birth pains of a new state 194
10. The slide into depression 233
11. The Second World War 258
12. Brave new world 286
13. A terminal condition? 311

BIBLIOGRAPHY 344
INDEX 346

PROLOGUE

To begin with, Belfast was simply on the way to somewhere else. It was the lowest ford in the River Lagan, where a sandbank had developed. The woods around it grew on a mixture of floodplain and unstable clays, unsuitable for settlement. The ford had a strategic value, however, and was captured by the kingdom of the Ulaidh as it expanded at the expense of the kingdom of Dál Riada and its people, the Cruithin. The Ulaidh established themselves on the northern slopes, and there are linguistic traces of them in Benmadigan, the old name for Cave Hill, in MacArt's Fort, and even in Glengormley.

There were other conquerors to follow, most notably the Normans. William de Burgh, the 'Brown' Earl of Ulster, was murdered in 1333. There was an inquiry into the circumstances of his death, and the report mentions that there had been a castle, probably built about 1250, and a borough town, which had been destroyed in 'John Logan's War'. On drier ground, further up the hill, was the White Church, the parish church of the Shankill, built on the Farset River. There was a chapel near the castle and near the ford, on the site now occupied by St George's Church in High Street.

There are several hypotheses about the site of the ford, but it may well have changed over the years to cope with changes in the bed of the river.

Not all travellers used the lower ford at Belfast. It was subject to the tide, and there are accounts of travellers having to swim with their horses if they judged matters wrongly, as did Lord Deputy Sidney in 1575. The Normans seem to have preferred to travel further upriver, at Belvoir Park and Edenderry, where there were also fords, beyond the reach of the tide. They had a series of mottes or small forts along this route, which would have had the effect of making the lower Lagan a safe haven. It seems to have been within this area that some of the Normans from Carrickfergus set up their base. The castle was probably built somewhere around present-day Castle Lane or Castle Place. From here it would dominate the peninsula formed by the Farset to the north, the Blackstaff to the south, and the Lagan itself to the east. It would have been raised above the surrounding ground, probably on an artificial platform. Its purpose was to house a garrison to watch over the ford, though it may also have come to fulfil some of the functions of a manor.

The report of 1333 talks of a borough town, which means that it would have had some form of charter. It would have had a market, as rents were paid in cash and money had to be earned; but Belfast's valuation was near-ly the lowest in the area. It was probably seen as a rural borough rather than a proper town. There are signs of buildings of that time in the area of the present-day Cornmarket and High Street. This would support the idea of a road leading along the line of Ann Street from the ford.

The next reference to Belfast comes in the Annals of Ulster for 1476. By then it was controlled by the Clandeboy O'Neills. During a war between Henry O'Neill, one of the Tyrone O'Neills, and Conn O'Neill, Henry attacked and took the castle at Belfast. Ten years later Feidhlimidh O'Neill, who may have been Conn's son, captured the castle in his turn. A few years later Hugh O'Donnell captured the castle in the course of an extended raid in the north-east of Ulster. That he took the trouble to do so suggests that it had grown enough in value to make it worth attacking. It is possible that the O'Neills levied a toll for the use of the ford, or may even have had a quay. There seem to have been development and land grants to the west and south, in the Falls, Malone and Derryvolgie, bringing increased pros-perity to the area.

There are indications that the O'Neills may have rebuilt the chapel at the ford to show their growing power. This was sufficient to attract the attention of Gerald Fitzgerald, Earl of Kildare, who brought his army north to capture Carrickfergus and destroy Belfast Castle, yet again, in 1503. Nine years later he was back, this time attacking Belfast as a prelude to leading a punitive expedition through the Glens of Antrim. He took a son of Niall O'Neill with him as hostage. Fitzgerald was an ally of the Tyrone O'Neills, doubly linked to them by marriage. Both were allied to the English king, Henry VII, who was supporting O'Neill in his effort to bring all the Ulster clans under his control.

After 1550 the Scots became a serious factor in County Antrim. At first allied with the Clandeboy O'Neills, they later assassinated the clan chief. There were stirrings of discontent, different clan groupings had different ambitions, and the inclusion of the Scots may have been the catalyst that blew Gaelic Ulster apart in the late sixteenth century, culminating in the Nine Years' War and the Flight of the Earls.

In the early years of the seventeenth century a sea change came over Ulster, as the most Gaelic of Ireland's provinces became the most closely controlled by the English throne. During those years of war a final atroci-ty was committed in Belfast. At that time the lord of the castle at Belfast was Sir Brian MacPhelim O'Neill. Walter Devereux, Earl of Essex, invited himself and his entourage for a short stay. After three days of pleasant dalliance he gave his soldiers the order to put O'Neill's entire household to the sword as traitors. O'Neill, his wife and his brother were taken to Dublin and hanged, drawn and quartered. Devereux was pleased with a job well done and an example that would make the Irish think twice about future uprisings, little knowing that it would be another twenty years before Ulster would be brought to its knees. Before he left Belfast he noted that it would be suitable for development into a town, as it had 'all the commodities,' a good harbour, plenty of wood, and land suitable for cultivation.

After the Flight of the Earls—so romantic in name, so craven in nature —another Lord Deputy of Ireland, Sir Arthur Chichester, was granted Belfast and its hinterland as a reward for his services during the wars. He determined to destroy any possibility of a future rising by the Irish through the means of granting the land forfeited by the rebels, and some more as well, to English and Scottish settlers who would clear the land and make it not only safer but profitable for its overlords. It was an ambitious scheme and was never carried out in its entirety. In the meantime Chichester went about the process of making Belfast into a model plantation town. When the King's commissioners visited in 1611 they were impressed by the progress made on the castle and the number of craftsmen who were being employed. Another fortification had been built further upriver, on the plains of Malone, near the present-day site of Shaw's Bridge.

Although the Irish may have seemed cowed, it was somewhat early to take things for granted. Protestant suspicion of the native Irish seemed to be justified by the rebellion of 1641, when the remaining Irish lords rose up against the settlers. There were tales of massacres, not diminished in the telling, from as near Belfast as Portadown and Newcastle.

The town of Belfast had come a long was since its garrison days and now returned two members to the Irish Parliament in Dublin. What it had not gained was a rampart, or any defences other than the castle. Faced with the possibility of disaster, many of the leading citizens sought refuge at Carrickfergus. One man, Captain Lawson, a retired soldier who now owned an ironworks in the Old Forge area of Malone, beat a drum through the town, looking for volunteers who would stand and fight. About twenty came forward, and he marched them to the ironworks, where he was joined by more men, bringing the total to about 160. These he led to Lisburn, where they successfully held the town against the vanguard of the Irish army under Sir Conn Magennis until reinforcements arrived. When they got back to Belfast a few days later they set about building a rampart and improving the town's defences.

The rest of the decade passed in chaos and confusion. General Robert Munro brought a Scottish army to Belfast to support the settlers. They were welcomed at first, but tensions developed when civil war broke out in England. The Scots supported Parliament, but Colonel Chichester remained loyal to King Charles. They both decided to let sleeping dogs lie, as by now the rebel Irish had been joined by the Old English, who were still Catholic. Any weakening of the forces defending Belfast might lead to the town's capture.

Even the arrival of reinforcements from Scotland did not lead to open hostilities. It was only when the Scots began to administer the Covenant 'to extirpate Popery, Prelacy and Heresy' that Chichester felt compelled to move, as the Covenant attacked the Church of England as well as the Catholic Church. Chichester tried to prevent the Scots from proselytising, but they reacted by seizing Belfast and expelling him. Perhaps encouraged by this, Munro went on to lead his men to Tyrone, to attack the Irish. He was routed at the Battle of Benburb on 5 June 1646, where he lost half his men and all his guns before managing to scramble back to Belfast.

By this time the Parliamentarian forces had won in England. They thanked the Scots for their help and politely asked that Belfast be returned to their jurisdiction. The Scots refused, and they now found themselves at war with their erstwhile allies. In late 1648 the Parliamentarian general George Monck arrived with his army outside the gates of Carrickfergus. The officer of the watch seems to have had no hesitation in opening the gates, and Munro was arrested. Shortly afterwards, Belfast also surrendered. When Monck returned to England, however, Belfast was taken over by Montgomery of Ards and Sir George Munro, who had led the Scottish army in England. They declared that they were holding the town on behalf of King Charles.

Soon after, Cromwell came to Ireland to clear up the loose ends. He dealt ruthlessly with the citizens of Drogheda, which had held out against him, then sent Colonel Robert Venables to Belfast to bring it to heel. There was a little fighting and a siege that lasted four days before the town surrendered. The townsfolk were lucky: as they were all Protestant, Cromwell thought he might have need of them in the future.

During the period of the Protectorate, when Cromwell was king in all but name, the practice of religion was severely regulated. Catholic priests were exiled or put to death, and those who did not attend approved services were fined. The pressure, particularly on those of higher degree, was relentless, and it is no surprise that many decided to conform to the Protestant creed. It is perhaps more surprising that so many did not.

When Cromwell was gone and Charles II was restored to the throne, Belfast entered a period of expansion and prosperity. Ships traded with the Low Countries and Spain. An iron industry developed, which might have lasted longer if the woods around Belfast had been properly managed. In the twenty-five years of Charles's reign the population of Belfast doubled, from one thousand to two thousand. To begin with, the fact that his brother, who became King James II, was a Catholic did not seem to worry the people of Belfast, who declared their loyalty to him. Only two years later Richard Talbot, Earl of Tyrconnell, who was also a Catholic, was made Viceroy, and he began a policy of recruiting Catholics to the army and allowing them to practise law. Though the town refused to build a

Catholic church for the use of Irish soldiers, it was granted a new charter in 1688. This removed it from the control of the Chichester family but doubled the number of burgesses. Half of these would have to be Catholic.

This was only a temporary respite, because William of Orange landed in England and was soon in effective control of Britain. James, deciding that Ireland would be a better venue in which to continue the struggle, landed with his army at Kinsale, County Cork. His soldiers came north to tighten his control over the country. In Derry the citizens embarked on their famous resistance; in Belfast they opened the gates, hoping that there would be no looting. The Jacobites left Belfast and Carrickfergus in August 1689, when Frederick, Duke of Schomberg, landed at Ballyholme, less than twenty miles away. There was a long wait of almost a year before William and his main army were able to land, and during that time Schomberg's army manned the Gap of the North, protecting Ulster from the Jacobites. When William and Schomberg joined forces it was only a matter of time before James's supporters were driven out of Ireland.

William came from a country that was used to minorities, and tolerated them. The original terms of the Treaty of Limerick, which ended hostilities, reflected this; but Parliament was not in such a forgiving mood and replaced the treaty with much harsher terms. Unable to do anything about this, as he had undertaken to respect the will of Parliament, William tried what he could personally to alleviate the conditions of his subjects. He even awarded an annuity to the Presbyterian ministers of Ulster out of his own purse. This was very welcome in Belfast, where most of the towns-people were Presbyterian and there was a Presbyterian majority on the corporation.

When William died, in 1704, and Queen Anne took the throne, the penal laws were extended to all non-Anglicans. All office-holders under the Crown had to take the Anglican Communion. The majority of Belfast's people no longer had any say in the running of the town. The Presbyterian clergy had their annuity revoked and were constantly harassed by the Vicar of Belfast, William Tisdall. It was not until King George I succeeded Queen Anne that things returned to normal.

It may have been the shared experience of those years at the sharp end of the penal laws that maintained the good relations between Presbyterians and Catholics in Belfast that characterised most of the eighteenth century. It helped that the town was prosperous, and that there were not many Catholics—seven in the town and fifty in the barony, according to one contemporary estimate. They were a threat to no-one. The parish priest was allowed to say mass on an oak table in a sandpit at Friar's Bush. There were Catholic churches at Derriaghy and at Hannahstown. As the century progressed and the Catholic population of Belfast grew, they were allowed to attend mass in a derelict building in

Castle Street. Although this provided welcome shelter during the winter, compared with Friar's Bush, it was so dirty that worshippers had to bring with them a piece of board or a brick on which to kneel.

Belfast made its money through commerce and trade. By 1700 it was already the fourth-busiest port in Ireland. By the 1750s there was a thriving banking industry. The Chamber of Commerce was founded in 1783, and soon afterwards there was a Harbour Corporation and a White Linen Hall. Manufacturing began in the second half of the century, much of it taking advantage of the fast streams that flowed from the Antrim hills. The first linen mill was built in Greencastle in 1776, and more were built in the town itself. Some of the mills were built to produce cotton. In 1786 Arthur Chichester, Earl (later Marquis) of Donegall, bought the district of Ballymacarret, just across the river. A glass factory began production there the same year.

There were occasional frights. The American War of Independence arrived on Belfast's door when the American admiral John Paul Jones raided the lough in 1778. Then France entered the war on the side of the colonists. There were few regular soldiers in Ireland, and it looked as if the country was open to invasion. The gentry set up a number of Volunteer corps. Although throughout the country roughly equal numbers of Catholics and Protestants volunteered, in Belfast there were no Catholics wealthy enough to afford the uniform, and so the Volunteers were exclusively Protestant.

The Catholic Relief Act was passed in the same year as the American raid, allowing Catholics to buy property. The Catholics of Belfast were able to obtain a lease on a house in what is now Chapel Lane. Protestants contributed more than half the costs of the chapel that was built there, St Mary's, and two companies of Volunteers in uniform attended the opening service.

Prosperity was beginning to seep downwards in Belfast society, so that even individual weavers were prospering. Both the linen and the cotton trade were thriving during the French wars, and supplementary yarn had to be imported. There were problems in the countryside, however, with Catholic and Protestant secret societies committing murder and mayhem in the fight for land. An Insurrection Act was passed in 1796, aimed at removing these furtive movements, but it was also used against elements among northern Presbyterians who called themselves the United Irishmen and were agitating for a parliament that would include Catholics. The following year more than five hundred political arrests took place in Ulster, mostly in Belfast. Then, in 1798, there was a series of un-coordinated risings throughout Ireland, each easily put down but causing a fright at the time. In Antrim and Ballynahinch it had been Presbyterians who had been slaughtered, and the feeling was growing that helping Catholics was costing Protestants too much.

To the government in London, and in particular the Prime Minister, William Pitt, it was obvious that the only way to succeed in introducing measures to alleviate the hardships of the Catholics was to ensure that Protestants did not feel that they would become a minority in the country, forced to live under the control of the Catholic majority. The only way forward was to create a political unit in which Protestants would be in a permanent majority; and the only way to do that was to bring about a union of Great Britain and Ireland. It took a lot of arm-twisting and a lot of bribery, but the Act of Union was passed by the British and Irish Parliaments in 1800 and came into effect in 1801. The second half of the bargain, full Catholic emancipation, was to be introduced in the near future; but King George refused to agree to the legislation, and the matter was let slide.

A profound change also took place in Belfast. The Marquis of Donegall died in 1799 with debts of £200,000. His heir was forced to sell and lease large areas of the town, which led to the building of more houses. Up to then the town had ended at Donegall Square, South, with nothing but green fields stretching from there to the Sandy Row. Although Belfast was still very much a Protestant town, enough Catholics had moved in to have their own district, known as the Pound, attracted by the many mills in the district. At the same time smaller Catholic enclaves grew up, most around mills, as in York Street and Whitehouse, or near factories, as in the Short Strand. As the years went on, publicans, shopkeepers and dealers moved into the Pound, and parts of it began to improve in quality and value. Well-off shopkeepers began to live in Barrack Street, and butchers set up shop in Hercules Street, later replaced by Royal Avenue.

An equivalent Protestant area grew up to the south of the Pound, in the Sandy Row. Originally it had been a brickfield, serving the builders of Belfast, but in the early nineteenth century a number of mills were built in the district. For migrants from the counties to the south and west of Belfast this was the first part of the town they saw; and with the availability of work and housing—though there were no churches or schools—most of them stayed. Catholics among them tended to press on to the nearby Pound, and so, almost by default, the Sandy Row became a Protestant district.

A great number of those who settled in the district were handloom weavers, and they brought with them to Belfast the prejudices of the countryside, of Orange Order or Ribbonmen. While in the country Protestants may have known their Catholic neighbours, and even trusted them, in the town there were no such niceties. There was even a grievance built in to the situation. Catholic migrants had arrived in Belfast first and had claimed the dry ridge between the Blackwater and the Farset on which to live. The Sandy Row was built in the floodplain of the Blackwater, and its inhabitants were liable to severe outbreaks of fever and cholera.

The first sign of things to come occurred on 12 July 1813, when an Orange procession tried to make its way along Hercules Street. In the ensuing riot two people were shot dead. Two Orangemen were found guilty of murder, while four Catholics were found guilty of riot. The fact that the Catholics had tried to resist the Protestant parade shows an interesting change in their self-image about this time.

The number of Catholics in Belfast had increased fourfold in the previous ten years. A second Catholic chapel was being built in Donegall Street, largely paid for by Protestants. Other chapels and schools would follow later. In the first forty years of the nineteenth century the Protestant population of Belfast trebled, but the Catholic population increased by a factor of approximately 20. Many of the newcomers were described as raw and uneducated. It was as these reinforcements changed Belfast's Catholics from a tiny, unobtrusive, even self-effacing minority to a well-established community that reports of sectarian strife became more common.

Some of the animosity was based on religious prejudice. Much of it also derived from economic rivalry, coupled with political unrest and with a leavening of old-fashioned bigotry. By 1814 the French war was more or less over. Prices for cotton fell and prices for food rose. Rents also became more expensive. There was still plenty of work, but a weaver might have to work twenty hours a day to feed and clothe his family.

Unrest crossed sectarian boundaries in the food riots of 1815. The boundaries were re-established when Catholics, under the leadership of Daniel O'Connell, began campaigning for emancipation in the 1820s. A branch of the Catholic Association was formed in Belfast in 1824, and a 'fighting fund' was collected after mass on Sundays. The fact that this was supervised by the priest widened its appeal to Catholics but alarmed Protestants, who invoked pictures of the massacres of 1641 in their opposition. In the end the government suppressed the Catholic Association; it was unable, however, to suppress the upsurge of Catholic political awareness throughout Ireland. The pressure led to the introduction of a Catholic Emancipation Bill in 1829. O'Connell had succeeded in defining a national Catholic identity in Ireland. Unfortunately, in doing so he had felt the need to make speeches that were crudely sectarian in content. Protestants were listening, and in creating one nation he defined another.

Violence centring on Orange parades returned to Belfast in 1825. The government had banned processions, and the district master of the Orange Order in Belfast assured the local magistrates that there would be no 12th of July parade that year. But several lodges defied the ban and marched from Smithfield to Carrickfergus. On their way back, fighting began with Catholics in York Street, and rioting spread to the town centre and lasted all evening. In the aftermath the police arrested twenty-three Catholics for rioting, while not one Protestant was charged with rioting or taking part in an illegal parade. The next Orange parade held in Belfast was after the passing of Catholic Emancipation in 1829. The day ended in violence.

Catholics too had their parades. On St Patrick's Day in 1830 a crowd of them marched through the town. They cheered as they passed the houses of people they supported and groaned outside the house of a well-known Orangeman. He appeared to fire a shot at the mob, though no-one was hurt, and the crowd wrecked his house, and nine or ten others. Sixteen Catholic rioters were arrested.

The Representation of the People Act (1832)—commonly called the Reform Act—extended the vote to a wider electorate. The property qualifications still meant that there were few votes in the working-class areas: the Sandy Row had about thirty voters, while the Pound had about sixty. This was enough to persuade the rest of the working class in both areas that there was entertainment value in elections. Candidates recruited supporters by buying them drink in public houses. The resulting mob could be used to intimidate voters or to drown out the speeches of opponents.

Because Belfast's Conservatives were closely aligned with the Orange Order, while the Liberals had at least some sympathy for Catholics, mobs tended to form along sectarian lines. After a noisy and unruly campaign on both sides, the result of the first election held under the new system was that two Conservative members were returned for Belfast. It was estimated that only two hundred Protestants voted for the Liberal candidates, the rest of their votes coming from Catholics. Not a single vote in the Sandy Row was cast for the Liberals. When the results were declared, a few days before Christmas, a triumphant mob attacked Hercules Street. Beaten back, they gathered outside the Conservative committee rooms. After listening to speeches they decided to chair the successful candidates through the streets. They tried once more to enter Hercules Street and once more were beaten back. As they retreated, some police came into the street and, without authority, fired on the Catholics, killing two elderly men and two boys. No charges were ever brought.

Daniel O'Connell, at about this time, began campaigning for the repeal of the Act of Union. As Protestants believed that their liberties were guaranteed by the union with Great Britain, this was an alarming development. Rumours circulated in Protestant circles of oppression in the south carried out by Catholic priests. A Christ Church Protestant Association, led by the Rev. Thomas Drew, was so focused on keeping up the fight that he refused to allow middle-class Protestants outside his Durham Street catchment area to become voting members, in case they diluted the intensity of his drive. He argued that the battle of the Protestant working class was with Catholics, not the middle class. His church, Christ Church, on the corner of College Square, North, became a focus of resistance to Catholic expansion.

Against such a background, sectarian violence was almost inevitable. There were riots on Christmas Day, 1833, and a man was bludgeoned to death in Waring Street. In 1835 the 12th of July was a Sunday, and there were special services in Christ Church. Orange arches had been erected where they could be seen from the Pound. Both Catholics and Protestants had the advantage of Saturday evening to indulge in drink and were in the mood for trouble. Catholics erected a green arch, and stone-throwing began. The police, unable to do anything, sent for the military. The soldiers dismantled the green arch and then moved on to do the same to the Orange arch. The inhabitants of the Sandy Row resisted, tearing up cobblestones and throwing them at the police and soldiers. One of those hit was the magistrate, who, not unreasonably, read the Riot Act and then ordered the soldiers to open fire. A man and a woman were killed. Rioting became general. In the wake of the riots many people moved house, anxious to have the security of their co-religionists about them. The week effectually defined the boundaries of the Protestant Sandy Row and Catholic Pound.

A new Under-Secretary for Ireland, Thomas Drummond, was appointed in 1835. Convinced that the troubles in Ireland stemmed from the pernicious attitude of the ascendancy, he set about curtailing their powers. He set up the Royal Irish Constabulary, though local police forces in Belfast and Dublin were retained. He began a campaign against the Orange Order, led by stipendiary magistrates appointed by Dublin Castle, who had authority over local magistrates, appointed by landlords. Both Orange and Ribbonmen parades were banned, and there was a series of peaceful St Patrick's Days and Orangeman's Days for the rest of the decade. This did not eliminate violence in Belfast, but at least it was curtailed and kept under control.

When Drummond died, in 1840, O'Connell relaunched his campaign for the repeal of the Union. To Belfast Protestants this was proof of the continuing machinations of Rome, and even liberal Protestants resented the campaign. When O'Connell visited Belfast in 1841 his speech was drowned out by the jeering and catcalling of the crowd. A riot developed, involving mobs from both communities, and many windows were broken. O'Connell left Belfast in a closed carriage the next day, with a large RIC escort.

The campaign for repeal continued in Belfast, however, and a huge meeting was held in Berry Street. Catholic priests were involved, though forbidden to take part by their bishop. There were probably up to three thousand supporters. Perhaps the most important thing that was happening was that working-class Catholics were receiving a much more subtle form of political education than that obtained in election riots or sectarian battles. They were learning that it was possible to focus on results, and that there were many ways to get those results. When it did not suit the association to be identified with violence, its members learnt to ignore provocation. After it was discovered that there were Ribbonmen among the membership, any who were identified had to take an oath renouncing their former allegiance. Eventually the movement split, as most monoliths do, on whether or not physical force was an acceptable tactic, and whether nationhood or religion was the more fundamental.

There was serious sectarian strife in the 1840s on a number of occasions. In 1843 the troubles lasted several weeks, and many houses were damaged. A distasteful development was the rise of Protestant attacks on Catholic funerals—an easy target, as funeral processions had to pass the Sandy Row on their way to Friar's Bush Cemetery. This objectionable practice would be reversed in the 1920s, when Protestant funerals had to travel along the Falls Road. Another thing that was becoming apparent was the partiality of the Belfast police, who seemed to be beyond the control of the magistrates. There is a story that when a policeman discovered that he had arrested a Protestant by mistake he released him and replaced him with a passing Catholic.

There were riots after every Orange parade for the rest of the decade, though none of the intensity of 1843; but when the tribulations of famine and disease were added to those of civil strife, the authorities once more banned Orange marches, and for a number of years special church services were held in their place.

Protestants had seen their privileges wane. Once undisputed masters of Belfast and Ulster, they were now confronted by Catholics who saw themselves as equals. Their protection from the tyranny of a Catholic majority was the Act of Union, and they did not want it repealed. They were unionists, though the term might not be widely used.

Catholics, who had clung on for years as victims, inconspicuous but useful, had gained in confidence as they had gained in numbers. They had seen how the power of numbers could force concessions from the authorities. They knew what they were: Irish nationalists.

| AFTER THE FAMINE

Queen Victoria had planned to visit Ireland in 1845, but the Great Famine intervened and made it impolitic for her to do so. Instead she came in 1849, when the government had declared that the famine was over, and she made a somewhat curtailed visit to Cork, Dublin and Belfast. It was on Friday 11 August 1849 that she arrived, the royal yacht *Fairy* sailing at the head of the Royal Yacht Squadron, together with a review of local boats that had sailed out to greet her, warned of her arrival by a telegraph that the Town Council had installed on the Copeland Islands. Providing a musical accompaniment was the Young Men's Total Abstinence Society Band, on the *Erin's Queen*. The ships anchored in the Garmoyle Pool, where the River Lagan flowed into Belfast Lough.

The overnight passage from Dublin had been rough, and the Queen and her husband, Prince Albert, had suffered from seasickness. Here in the calm of Belfast Lough she may have wanted to spend the morning recovering, while crowds gathered in the town. However, shortly after nine o'clock various dignitaries came on board to express their loyalty. The mayor, William Johnston, accompanied by his council, was the first to arrive. Having heard their declarations of affection and loyalty, Victoria showed her gratitude by knighting the mayor there and then on the deck of the *Fairy*.

Other parties took turns to assure the Queen of their loyal affection. The Catholic clergy of Down and Connor declared: 'We yield to no class or portion in warm attachment to your Majesty's person, or devoted loyalty to your Majesty's throne.' The General Assembly of the Presbyterian Church, referring to the fact that this was the first visit of a monarch to Belfast since William III had passed on his way from Carrickfergus to the Boyne, declaimed: 'Your Royal predecessor came to assert our liberties in time of war; your Majesty comes to perpetuate them in time of peace.'

There was one sour note. The Queen had been emphatic that she would not honour any establishment that was restricted to Protestants. She was aware of the sectarian strife in Ireland and was determined to do nothing that would in any way encourage it. Part of the original programme had been a visit to the Deaf and Dumb Institute, but this had been cancelled when it was discovered that no Catholics were helped by the institute and that it was opposed to integrated education. As a gesture, the royal route would still pass the institute but it would not stop. Among the delegations came one from 'the loyal inhabitants of County Down.' Presenting the address was Lord Roden, who had been publicly reprimanded by the Viceroy shortly before because of the prominent part he took in the massacre of Catholics at Dolly's Brae. In choosing him the landlords and gentry of County Down were showing their defiance of the administration in Dublin Castle.

At two o'clock the royal yacht weighed anchor for the short journey to a pavilion that had been erected on the site of the old Town Dock, only recently filled in. (The site is now occupied, precariously, by the Albert Clock.) Here they disembarked, the Queen, Prince Albert and their young son Edward, Prince of Wales, who was resplendent for the occasion in a sailor suit. They were greeted by representatives of town and province, then boarded a coach that had been lent by Lord Londonderry and began their tour. They passed under a triumphal arch that bore (in mis-spelt Irish) the message that their majesties were accorded a hundred thousand welcomes. To reinforce the message, thousands of well-wishers, some on galleries while others simply lined the streets, shouted their acclamations 'like the roar of the wind in the forest.' Trainloads had come from the towns of the Lagan Valley and County Armagh. Shopkeepers in Armagh had gained kudos by closing for the day and allowing their assistants to travel to Belfast. Their banner declared that 'such gestures demonstrate the moral worth of the community.'

When the cavalcade reached Donegall Place, just before three o'clock, the royal anthem was played and the Queen and her party entered the White Linen Hall, where there was an exhibition demonstrating every stage in the production of linen, from flax in the field to damask on the table. The Marquis of Londonderry, a patron of the Linen Hall, conducted the royal party around; then it was back to the carriage and on with the tour.

The route now took them up Wellington Place, along Great Victoria Street and out the Lisburn Road as far as the workhouse, opened in 1841 on the future site of Belfast City Hospital. Here the workhouse children, dressed in humble attire but clean and neat, gave three loyal cheers before the party went on to the Botanic Gardens and visited for a few minutes the recently opened Queen's College, built in what was at that time an almost rural location. Here the couple disappointed the Rev. Thomas Drew, whose anti-Catholicism was already well known in Belfast. He had declared publicly that his loyalty was conditional on the Queen not visiting Queen's College, as religious education was not on its curriculum. (It is interesting to note that the Catholic diocesan authorities in Belfast also opposed the college, and for precisely the same reason.)

The rest of the tour took Queen Victoria north to the Clifton Street poorhouse, where some of the boys formed a brass band that played 'God Save the Queen' as the cavalcade passed. Next was the huge York Street Spinning Mill, after which they were escorted back to the end of High Street, where the Queen and her family re-embarked at six o'clock.

That night the mayor hosted a magnificent banquet in the Donegall Arms. There were fireworks on Queen's Island, which lasted till midnight. The country folk around the town showed their appreciation by lighting bonfires on the surrounding hills. The visit had been a triumph, and Belfast had been enchanted by the tiny Victoria. It was a day when troubles could be forgotten.

Belfast, however, had problems that some wished they could forget. Behind the decorated route of the day's parade lay streets that were among the worst in the United Kingdom. This was in a town that had received favourable comments in a report on poverty in Ireland printed after a government inquiry in 1836. Belfast had a tradition of looking after its poor. The Clifton Street poorhouse had been operating since 1774 and was caring for more than two hundred old people and almost two hundred children. A house of industry near Smithfield had distributed bread to more than a hundred people a day and gave out rations to as many as six hundred families in distress. It had also given spinning-wheels and flax to nearly eight hundred women so that they could earn money producing linen yarn. It ceased operations in June 1841, considerably in debt.

Since the extension of the Poor Law (Amendment) Act (1834) or 'New Poor Law' to Ireland in 1838 there had been a crisis in the charities. Most inhabitants of Belfast who had a little money to spare felt that it was their duty to contribute to the welfare of the poor. This had been true since Belfast began to accumulate wealth in the eighteenth century. But that was different, because the help was voluntarily given and because there was an element of choice on the part of the donor. He could choose a charity that helped people he felt needed it, in a manner of which he approved. There was no flexibility in the new Poor Law. The Board of Guardians determined on an amount that all ratepayers must pay, and the money could be used only to help paupers within the workhouse: it was not allowed to intervene outside this establishment, which was designed to be as austere as the human body and soul could endure. Citizens resented paying this compulsory rate while they were still helping people who were experiencing hard times but not absolutely destitute. Quite often people would expect to be unemployed for part of the year and would need help only for that period. One remedy had been tried by the house of industry; another was to collect enough money to help a distressed group to emigrate. The important thing was that the donor could decide, with knowledge of the local situation. When the donation became compulsory and its use constrained by regulations, the middle classes of Belfast began to quibble, looking for escape clauses. Some insisted that a pauper had to have lived in Belfast for three years in order to qualify.

Unlikely allies opposed the law. Archbishop Crolly preferred 'outdoor relief' (payment to the poor outside the workhouse), believing that good supervision would eliminate fraud. The Rev. Henry Cooke, an argumentative Presbyterian, warned that any move to put poor people together in a workhouse would inevitably lead to immorality. In this he was supported by Dr Tennant, who had worked in the house of industry.

The workhouse opened in May 1841 and was designed to care for (if that is the right phrase) up to a thousand inmates in conditions so harsh that there was no chance of anyone choosing to go there except as a last resort. A selection of the paupers who entered the establishment in the late winter of 1841/2 gives an idea of how desperate people were before they would appeal to the charity of the Poor Law Guardians. A 67-year-old widow, badly clothed and dirty, was admitted on 16 January and died on 12 March. A twenty-year-old female beggar, infirm and in rags, was admitted on 13 February and died six days later. A fifty-year-old labourer, ill clothed and infested with vermin, was admitted on 8 March and died on 13 April. To be fair, not all died. A hungry servant girl of twenty-two was admitted with filthy ragged clothes on 5 March; she was discharged in good health on the 20th.

In spite of a slight recession, the Belfast economy was sound, and Belfast could probably cope with Belfast's poverty. The 'hungry forties' in Belfast were not simply a result of famine. There was a series of recessions in the cotton industry, with some weavers in Belfast reduced to a state of total destitution. The worst-hit area was Ballymacarret. Here, weavers were not employed by the Belfast mills but produced cloth for Glasgow manufacturers. More than half were unemployed, and many of those still in employment suffered when Gilbert Vance, one of the Glasgow manufacturers, reduced their wage to a pittance, pleading economic necessity. Some worked for as little as 4 pence for a fourteen-hour day. The only way any of them could be helped through the Poor Law was if they sold all their property and became paupers, a point of no return that few were prepared to pass.

In the end, concerned citizens set up a Relief Committee. There were heated discussions about the best way to alleviate hunger. Some felt that relief had to be earned and that able-bodied men should be put to stone-breaking; others believed that food should be given without any attendant conditions. In the end there was a compromise. Soup kitchens were set up in Ballymacarret and Smithfield, the two districts in most need, and enough meals were distributed to feed some nine-tenths of the population of the two areas. Meanwhile about five hundred men were employed breaking stones on Corporation Island and on the banks of the Lagan. A thousand pounds was raised by subscription, while some of the local rural landlords contributed any vegetables they could spare. Donations were even collected from the workers of Falls Mills and Ardoyne Weavers, of £5 and £2 3s, respectively.

Even with this charity there were many who had no other resort but the workhouse. In 1841 the average number of inmates was 450. By July 1842 the average was nearly 900. In January 1844 it was overcrowded, holding more inmates than it was built for. This was before the potato blight had reached Ireland.

The Great Famine changed everything in Belfast, both the nature of its poverty and the way in which relief was managed. The newspaper-reading public would have become aware of the potato blight in the summer of 1845, when there were reports of a mysterious disease affecting the potato crop. In August there were outbreaks in England, and the authorities, knowing of the reliance the Irish had on potatoes as a staple diet, worried about the disease spreading to the western island. There was nothing that could be done, and the disease reached Ireland in September, reducing much of the staple foodstuff of the Irish people to a black, sticky mess. There is a belief in the north-east that this area was relatively untouched, but some authorities report that blight was particularly virulent in County Antrim. It was only the fact that the disease had arrived so late in the year that enabled farmers to save three-fifths of the crop.

There is also a belief that the English did not concern themselves about Ireland's troubles. This also is not true. The Prime Minister, Sir Robert Peel, moved at once to find exactly how much was lost. As he knew that enough of the crop was saved to maintain the people until the early spring, he had time to make sure that the correct relief measures were adopted and properly co-ordinated. He even ordered Indian corn, but this had to be kept secret in case the move was considered too interventionist. There were things he did not do that earlier governments had done to ameliorate the effects of famine. Against the advice of many town councils, including that of Belfast, he did not suspend the distilling of whiskey and other spirits, which used up grain, nor did he limit the export of food from Ireland. In this way he alienated himself from the very people who would have to administer his policies in Ireland. Already upset about the workings of the Poor Law, they felt they had been through similar situations before and that they knew best. Several councils, again including Belfast's, tried to persuade the Lord Lieutenant, Lord Heytesbury, to prohibit distilling on his own authority. In spite of agreeing with them, and in spite of having tried to persuade Peel of the necessity of the measure, Heytesbury refused to act.

Some philanthropists simply accepted the situation and tried to get on with it. Everyone was urged to try to recover every edible piece, even from diseased potatoes. A recipe was printed and distributed, entitled *Plain Directions for Making Good Bread from Unsound Potatoes.* More radical individuals felt that these recommendations about obtaining nutrition from rotten potatoes were merely an attempt to camouflage the fact that grain was being exported that could be used to feed the people.

In the meantime potatoes had doubled in price by March 1846. It would have taken one of Gilbert Vance's weavers twenty-two hours' work to earn enough to buy a stone of potatoes. The position of the weavers was made even worse by the fact that the cotton industry was suffering from yet another depression. On 27 March 1846 the *Banner of Ulster* claimed that out of 411 looms in Ballymacarret, 206 were not being used, and the rest would be idle within a week. Approximately a thousand people were subsisting on one meal a day and could not afford to light a fire. The owner of the newspaper established a relief committee, which would use what donations it got to feed about ninety families for as long as it could. It bought in 1½ tons of Indian corn. It also approached Belfast Town Council with the request that it petition the government for further help. The council demurred on a point of geography: the district of Ballymacarret was in County Down, they said, while by far the greater part of Belfast was in County Antrim. Conditions in County Antrim were not bad enough to justify asking for extra help. No account was taken of the unique position of the Ballymacarret weavers, in that they were working for Scottish employers. In June the relief committee did receive a grant of £100 from the Relief Commissioners in Dublin.

Things looked brighter in May, and there was evidence that oats were doing well and that the potato crop seemed healthy. The outlook was sufficiently promising for some of the people of Belfast to return to a more traditional concern: sectarian politics.

It is important to understand the antipathy felt by the great majority of Belfast's Protestants to the idea of repealing the Union of Great Britain and Ireland. The Union was the Protestants' guarantor that they would not end up as a beleaguered minority in a country whose government would be under the undue influence of the Catholic Church. It was the fact of the Union, and the trade it allowed, that gave them their relative prosperity, compared with the rest of Ireland. Protestants resented what they saw as the favouritism shown to Irish Catholics and the perfidious nature of the Catholics themselves.

In 1836 the Grand Lodge of the Orange Order had dissolved itself as a response to accusations that it had been involved in stirring up sectarian violence. In 1845 it reinstated itself and now, in 1846, there was a feeling that Protestants should use the 12th of July celebrations to send a message to the government. Although they had not taken place for some time, the tradition of marching was going to be reintroduced. Most of the gentry and the upper middle class were against the move, and many stayed away. Most newspapers in Ulster also spoke out against the marches; but it was to no avail.

As the 12th of July was a Sunday that year, the marches were held on the next day, Monday. In Belfast there was a special service on Sunday at St George's Church, conducted by the Rev. William McIlwaine. His theme was the Rising of 1641, when Catholics had risen and killed their Protestant neighbours. The gathering for County Antrim was to be in Brookehall, near Lisburn, and on Monday the lodge members travelled there by train. They had been warned to be sober and decorous, and so they were. From the platform there were complaints about mill-owners who had refused to allow workers to attend the celebrations, and of landlords who had stayed away from the marches, as well as Protestants who were 'indifferent' to the current threat. Estimates of how many attended the field at Brookehall varied according to the politics of the newspaper printing them, from as low as 14,000 to as high as 85,000.

When the Orangemen returned to Belfast the lodges marched off to their various districts. There were some clashes when one lodge met a group of Catholics parading to the sound of drums and carrying the green branches of liberty. Some of them were also carrying more aggressive agricultural implements, but no-one was seriously hurt, and the police arrested a few Catholics, leaving the Orangemen to proceed.

In the lodges afterwards it was agreed that the day was a triumph and that more of the same was needed. A Grand Lodge of County Antrim was formed, and more lodges were established within Belfast. As Ireland approached the catastrophe of famine, Orange heroes were riding high in Ulster.

In the month of the marches, July, signs of blight were seen on the potato crop, earlier and more extensive than they had been in 1845.

There is an Irish superstition that bad things arrive in threes. The year 1846 seems to support this. The blight was universal, leaving no district untouched. The cereal harvest, which was vital to many farmers as a cash crop that allowed them to pay the rent, was also below average. Even market vegetables, such as turnips and carrots, suffered. The flax yield was down, with implications for the linen mills. Also bringing the problems into the towns was the continuing economic recession in England, the effects of which were beginning to bite in Ireland. There was a new government in England, headed by Lord John Russell, and his approach to relief would be very different from that of Peel. He recognised that Peel's measures had fended off the worst of the famine's effects, but they were considered ruinously expensive by the new ministry. Russell made two decisions, one of which seems to contradict the other. In future, relief in Ireland would be based on public works. At the same time, financial support for landlords or committees that instigated public works would be reduced or withdrawn. It was also made harder for anyone to receive assistance, even through employment on public works. The coming winter, with its disease, starvation and emigration, marked the real start of the Great Famine.

To begin with, the local press reported the problems of the poor as if the poor were the cause of them. Durham Street was flooded by sewage each year when the Blackstaff broke its banks, even in good times, and nothing was done about it. Manure heaps, described in reports as 'nuisances', were so numerous that they nearly blocked some streets; Donegall Street alone had 341. Clearing these away was one of the less pleasant tasks of the Town Police Committee. Their excuse for not doing so was that farmers were not buying manure that year, because of the potato failure.

Some of Belfast's leading papers, including the *Northern Whig* and the *News Letter,* reported stories of the distress in the south and west of the country while ignoring the suffering within the town. To their credit, the *Banner of Ulster* and the *Vindicator* attacked the indifference shown by the comfortable few towards the wretched conditions in which many struggled to survive. The mansions of the rich were insulated from the scenes of distress. Hunger stayed within Ballymacarret on the east of the Lagan and in the twin districts of Smithfield and the Pound on the west; but as the year progressed other areas began to suffer, and the rapidly increasing numbers of the poor and distressed made it impossible for even the most sheltered citizen to hide from the problem. As happened in other towns, many people from the countryside came in hope of getting work or receiving charity. As Belfast was a port, there were even some who hoped to get a passage out of the country. This continued to be true throughout the famine years, and the record shows that on 12 April 1847 more than a thousand people embarked for Québec.

There were people who tried to help. The butchers of Hercules Street set up a soup kitchen, donating food and even giving money to maintain it. In contrast to their generosity, even now some people were complaining that food should be sold to the poor rather than given to them, in case Belfast got such a good name for charity that paupers would arrive from all over the province. Worse, some of the merchants were brought before the courts in November, charged with adulterating the Indian meal that was becoming the staple of the poor.

Now the effects of the poor flax crop began to be felt. For want of material, the mills were working short-time. Even the most reluctant of merchants now recognised their duty. At a meeting to discuss what could be done it was decided that soup kitchens were the cheapest way of getting food to the largest number of people. Further, running soup kitchens entitled them to a grant from the Relief Commissioners.

Perhaps it was not quite as simple as that. Normally the Commissioners would give a grant equal to the amount donated locally, allowing twice as much food to be bought. This did not apply if the food was going to be given away free or even below cost: in that situation, no grants were available. In spite of this, people gave anyway. The master bakers of Belfast gave the Relief Committee a donation of £111 just before Christmas.

Ironically, the day after this donation was made a group of about two hundred men attacked bakers' shops around Belfast. They had just been laid off temporarily by the Belfast to Ballymena Railway, because the extreme cold was interfering with operations. They went first to Bernard Hughes's Bakery in Donegall Street, where they demanded bread. When it was refused they refused to go away. Two 'gentlemen' bought loaves, which they distributed among the men, who then left the bakery. They did not go home, however, but to the Public Bakery in Church Street. Here they dispensed with politeness and said simply that they would take bread from the shelves if they were not given any. They were given bread to the value of £1. Inevitably, such a large crowd moving through the town drew the attention of the police, who were waiting when the crowd arrived at Elliott's Bakery in North Street. The leaders were arrested and the rest dispersed quietly. Although the incident ended quietly, it seems to have been a symptom of a crumbling social structure within the town.

The *Northern Whig* condemned what it described as the men's greed and went on to argue that Belfast, the industrial capital of Ireland, was immune to the effects of the famine. It was a minority view, and a town meeting held on St Stephen's Day once again called on the government to ban distilling and to use the grain saved for bread. Someone had estimated that the grain saved from the closure of the distilleries would be enough to give a 1-pound loaf each day to 4½ million people. Again the administration in Dublin met them with polite phrases but little else. Someone at the town meeting had anticipated this, saying that nothing would be done till England itself was suffering from famine.

With the intense cold of that winter, the distress was spreading to new parts on the outskirts of Belfast. In Merville the old and infirm were suffering. A soup shop was set up at Whitehouse, and £100 was raised to set up a relief station in Dundonald. People were stewing and eating turnips that had been grown as animal fodder. In Holywood a soup kitchen was open on Tuesday, Thursday and Saturday afternoons to sell soup at 1 penny per quart.

In Ballymacarret things were becoming desperate. Although the district was within the town boundaries, there was a growing sense of resentment at the fact that the Belfast Poor Law Union insisted on treating it as a separate district. Just how desperate things were is shown in the pages of the *Banner of Ulster*. In the past, an article said, the people of Ballymacarret had said they would accept help only if it came from a Protestant source. The crisis was now of such proportions that the people would accept potatoes if they had been grown by the Pope himself. They did have some help from the Society of Friends, which released two tons of Indian meal from their Belfast depot.

As the spring of 1847 came it seemed as if nothing could be done even to maintain the status quo. The public works system could not cope. The humane institutions were 'filled to inconvenience,' according to the *News Letter*. At the General Dispensary the staff awaited what they saw as an inevitable epidemic. A group of women had set up the Ladies' Association for the Relief of Irish Destitution in January. In February another group of ladies decided that charity began at home and set up an Association for the Relief of Belfast Destitution. They sought to provide clothes and blankets for the needy. To help them in their planning they asked for reports from local medical attendants working in the district dispensaries. All the reports emphasised the extent of the destitution. The worst cases were not seen, because they were huddled in damp straw in dark houses, unable to go out because of cold or hunger or sickness or even because they were ashamed to go out in their wretched clothing. These people died in desolation and misery.

The Relief Committee also had its pride, and a sense of shame. Confronted with the hardship that existed in the wretched buildings of Carrick Hill and North Queen Street, they did not wish to apply for government aid, because it would spoil the good name of the town, which saw its reputation as one of manly independence. Nevertheless, no matter how difficult the committee tried to make it for someone to qualify for relief, the number that did qualify simply grew and grew. The level of dependence in areas such as Ballymacarret was as high as in some of the most notorious unions along the west coast. Three hundred families were receiving donations of coal. Eight hundred quarts of free soup were being distributed daily.

Some people tried to make their help more constructive. A school for girls and a workroom for women were opened in the House of Correction. At the same time more novel ways of raising funds were introduced, and Shakespeare readings and amateur dramatics attracted huge crowds. One Belfast market levied a halfpenny on the price of every pig bought, to be paid by the purchaser. This raised £150 for Dock Ward Soup Kitchen.

In spite of the fact that government assistance in most of Ireland after the spring of 1847 was directed through soup kitchens financed by Poor Law taxes, rather than public works, Belfast held out against the changes. There was a certain amount of mutual congratulation on Belfast's self-reliance before people got on with the business of financing and administering relief. It was difficult, even physically, to keep up with demand. New apparatus was introduced to speed up the preparation of soup, but up to fifteen thousand people were totally reliant on this diet, and the numbers seemed likely to rise. It was estimated that about a thousand families did not have a stick of furniture in their rooms. Clean straw for bedding was distributed, but a feeling of pessimism was growing in the hearts of members of the various committees, as all their efforts seemed to be inadequate in the face of the increasing misery.

The number of vagrants coming into Belfast was a cause for concern. Lacking the residential requirement for claiming Poor Law relief, they immediately became a strain on Belfast's charitable resources. Medical authorities also saw them as a potential vector for the various diseases that accompany famine. The Rev. Thomas Drew of Christ Church argued that such vagrant paupers should simply be driven from the town and a watch set up to prevent any incursions in the future. Others countered that this was no Christian reaction to the problem, saying that the incomers should not be prevented from begging in the streets.

What was decided on was the establishment of a Day Asylum, where the poor could be fed and receive industrial training. Suitable accommodation was found in a disused weaving factory made available by Andrew Mulholland, the linen magnate. Three days after it opened it had 650 inmates, only 100 of whom came from Belfast, while nearly 500 had come from the south. This reflects the scale of the influx that Belfast was receiving. To try to deal with the crisis, inmates were allowed to remain only for one week. Night shelter was completely overwhelmed, and it was becoming increasingly common to find the bodies of those who had died overnight in the streets or in the fields around the town.

People weak from hunger and cold were open to infections and contagions, and it was not long before smallpox, diarrhoea and dysentery were common in Belfast, both among the paupers in the workhouse and in the streets and among the poorest people in the town. Poor housing, overcrowding, poor or no sanitary facilities and a lack of medical facilities contributed to the spread of disease. The winter of 1846/7 had been the coldest on record. Many of those who came to the workhouse were ill before they arrived. Naturally, the rate of mortality within the institution began to rise. The greatest rate was among the young, who were cared for in cold, damp wards: half the deaths were of children under the age of seven. Problems with the equipment in the laundry meant that patients' clothes could not be cleaned or fumigated properly. The clothes could not even be dried properly and so were passed on to the next wearer while still damp. The medical officer suggested that boarding over the bare earth floors of the workhouse, and building some fireplaces, would help to contain the spread of disease.

Dr Andrew Malcolm, who worked among the poor, knew that the town was open to an epidemic of fever, and the Fever Hospital, near the

workhouse, was already overcrowded. The fever that concerned the Board
of Guardians most was typhus, also known at the time as famine fever. In
the days before antibiotics this was a terrifying disease, the symptoms of
which included vomiting, delirium, gangrene, swelling, and blackened
features. Even nowadays, if it is not diagnosed early and treated, the death
rate from this disease can be as high as 40 per cent of those infected. It is
at its most deadly when it infects the heart muscle, causing myocarditis,
or the brain, where it causes encephalitis. For such victims, death was a
genuine release.

Typhus is spread by body lice and finds free expression in crowded,
unhygienic conditions where people have few opportunities to wash. The
lice feed on infected blood and may deposit their infected faeces on a fresh
person. The typhus bacteria in the faeces can then enter the body by the
sort of wound that occurs where someone scratches an area irritated by
louse bites. It can also be contracted by breathing in dried faeces.
Symptoms may not appear till two weeks after exposure, so the disease can
be well established even before the first person has begun to show any
signs of the illness.

Typhus seems to have arrived in Belfast from an unexpected direction.
Many of those refugees still able to do so had tried to emigrate from
Ireland; indeed it has been estimated that the number of famine deaths in
Ulster was almost equalled by the number of emigrants. England and
Scotland were popular destinations. America, however, was the place that
most emigrants wanted to reach. The United States had strict controls on
passenger ships arriving there, so it was an expensive destination. Canada,
on the other hand, could be reached for as little as £3. The reason, apart
from the lack of regulation, was that many ships were employed in bringing from Canada to England such products as salt fish, oil, timber and
flaxseed. On their return voyage they often did not have enough cargo
even to act as ballast. Although these ships were in no way suitable for
transporting passengers, unscrupulous owners made them available for
the desperate wretches who needed to get away. The Irish were treated as
cargo, stuffed into holds on ships that were ill provided with the basic
necessities of food and clean water. In such conditions there was no
defence against typhus. These were genuine coffin ships, and there are
heart-rending descriptions of their arrival at Grosse-Île, the isolation
centre in the St Lawrence River, where many died within sight of what they
had hoped would be their new home. In 1847 alone, 5 per cent of those
who embarked for Canada died at sea; another 3½ per cent died at Grosse-
Île, while 8 per cent died in Canadian hospitals. The total death rate was 17
per cent—almost one in five.

In March 1847 the sailing ship *Swatara* left Liverpool for Philadelphia,
full of Irish emigrants, most of them from Connacht. When the ship was

several days into its voyage the first signs of typhus began to show themselves. Someone—passenger or crew member—had brought it on board.
In the cramped conditions on board, lice and, with them, typhus spread
rapidly through the ship. Unkind winds drove it into Belfast Lough, where
several sick passengers were transferred to the Fever Hospital. Some
medical examiners visited the ship and found it very poorly ventilated.
The passenger quarters were so dark that the doctors had to borrow a
lantern before they could be inspected. The passengers had been living on
the government allowance of 1 pound of bread per day. Accommodation
was found for them in Waring Street, while the *Swatara* was towed to a
remote part of the harbour and fumigated. The Relief Fund provided £30
for buying food. The ship was reprovisioned and put to sea again but this
time only got as far as Derry, because the disease had spread rapidly
among the passengers. When the ship left Lough Foyle the winds once
again drove it back, and it returned to Belfast a second time. In harbour,
the disease jumped ship and was soon spreading through the town. The
epidemic the Board of Guardians had dreaded was upon them.

In May a group of concerned citizens organised a Board of Health, setting
themselves the specific task of finding additional accommodation that
would be suitable for typhus sufferers. There had been a cholera outbreak
in 1832, and some buildings used at that time were still available. Sheds
were erected in the grounds of Belfast Infirmary in Frederick Street. The
infirmary at the workhouse was enlarged. A hospital was even improvised
at the Academical Institution. Not even these preparations were sufficient,
however, and at its peak, in July, the epidemic was sending an average of
660 people per week to hospital. To provide for them, tents had to be
erected in the grounds of the workhouse. These were to be used for those
lucky patients who were convalescing, allowing the main hospitals to treat
patients who were at the acute stage. The workhouse piggery, stables and
strawhouse were converted to accommodate six hundred paupers.
Galleries were added to dormitories where the ceiling was high enough. By
the end of the year 13,678 fever admissions were recorded in Belfast, and
Dr Malcolm wrote that he considered that 20 per cent of Belfast's population
had been infected. He reported seeing people falling in the street, too weak
from hunger or disease to go any further.

Long before this the town was running out of space in which to bury
its dead. The Charitable Society had to close its small graveyard by 1 July.
By that time the Shankill Cemetery was also full, with some coffins
covered by only a few inches of soil, and it was estimated that the Catholic
Friar's Bush Cemetery would be full within a month. To save space, the
sextons in Friar's Bush created deep, square graves capable of containing
forty coffins. It was further decided that the bodies of unclaimed paupers
should be buried in the grounds of the workhouse. Here too, before long,

there were multiple burials, with the first coffin eight feet deep and the last with only two feet of soil covering it.

Today it is impossible to estimate with any certainty the number who died of fever. Using modern estimates of the virulence of typhus, a rough guess might be that somewhere between 1,400 and 2,800 succumbed. To compound Belfast's problems, many towns in England and Scotland were repatriating Irish refugees to the town, it being the most convenient port for much of Britain. These unfortunates had fled the famine but had not had enough property or savings to pay even the modest fare to Canada. Having made their way, using the last of what money they had, to Britain, they were unwelcome in towns and cities that were having their own problems in dealing with poverty. By 1849 the parochial authorities in Glasgow alone were sending their Irish, no matter where in Ireland they originated, back to Belfast at the rate of a thousand per month. These arrived without food or money, and undoubtedly many of them brought disease with them. In many cases the Poor Law Guardians sent them back again, and there are cases of women being returned to Glasgow with 'a six-penny bun to share among four of them.'

All this was long before the days when a government felt it had to inter-vene on the people's behalf when a national disaster such as famine occurred. The Prime Minister, Lord John Russell. said as much: 'It must be thoroughly understood that we cannot feed the people.' That was a matter for private charity.

In August 1847 an amended Poor Law was introduced that made the Poor Law Guardians responsible for famine relief as well as general distress. To meet their extra responsibilities they leased several establish-ments, which they converted into auxiliary workhouses. They also built a permanent extension to the workhouse capable of housing a thousand children, together with a school and training rooms.

A fund was opened in January 1847 for which £7,000 was eventually raised. Mill-owners gave as much as £200 each. As the central authorities in Dublin were by now paying for the treatment of anyone suffering from famine fever, this was enough to provide soup from kitchens in Howard Street and York Street to as many as fifteen thousand people a day. There was even enough to provide outdoor relief in the wider countryside. The great and the good of Belfast could reflect that they had done much to relieve the hardship of their fellow-citizens. They could not do everything, however, and the hardship and dying continued.

Even as the typhus epidemic died away, only months before the visit of Queen Victoria, an epidemic of cholera struck Belfast. It had been expected, as there had been reports of the disease spreading through Europe in 1848. A Belfast Sanitary Committee was formed in March 1848 to try to prepare for this next plague. During the summer, notices were posted around the town emphasising the need for high standards of cleanliness and ventilation. In October health visitors were employed to go to the homes of the poor to advise them on what steps they could take to escape infection. Once again, it was not enough.

Cholera came to Belfast with a man who had been returned with his family to Ireland from Scotland. His death in December 1848 was the start of the plague.

At the dispensary alone, 2,282 cases of cholera were recorded in 1849, reaching a peak in March and again in July. Of the cases recorded, 997 died—a mortality rate of 33 per cent.

This was not the first time that cholera had struck Belfast. There had been an epidemic in 1831–2, but at that time the mortality rate had been only 16 per cent. It has to be assumed that the standards of hygiene among the poorest in Belfast at the end of the 1840s were substantially worse than they had been seventeen years previously, and that the cholera bacteria found it easier to kill victims whose constitution was already at a low ebb after the trauma of the previous years. It was not until October 1849 that the medical authorities could announce that the epidemic seemed to be over.

Cholera is a particularly unpleasant disease. Like typhus, it is caused by a bacterium that is present in infected faeces. Unlike typhus, however, it is human faeces that it uses. It is transmitted in a population when infected human faeces get into the drinking-water supply, something made easier because the victims' faeces take the form of watery diarrhoea. For many the disease progresses no further than this diarrhoea and vomiting, accompanied by leg cramps; but for some—about one in twenty—the diarrhoea and vomiting are profuse. These people lose bodily fluids so rapidly that it leads to dehydration and clinical shock. Unless they are treated promptly, victims can die within hours.

The key to preventing the spread of cholera is maintaining the purity of drinking water, combined with personal cleanliness and the prompt removal of filth of every description. Yet a report produced by the Sanitary Committee in 1849 spoke of streets in a 'filthy, flooded, neglected state,' of areas full of open drains, many of them full of 'semi-liquid filth.' Cromac Street had huge cesspools, and the dark courts of the Smithfield area were as neglected as it was possible to imagine. Worst of all, however, was Ballymacarret, where the rural habit of establishing a dung heap outside the farmhouse door had been brought to the city, and behind the houses there were 'extensive accumulations of liquid manure.'

It was Dr Malcolm who was forcing the better-off people of Belfast to take account of what was happening in the meaner streets of the town. The main sewers flowed directly into the tidal River Lagan. Malcolm demonstrated that at high tide the water from the river flowed right into these sewers, holding back the normal flow of sewage and allowing solid matter, that is to say, faeces, to settle on the bottom, all through the system, right back to the homes even of the wealthy. An act of Parliament had set up Water Commissioners as far back as 1840, and work had been done to collect water from Carr's Glen, but by 1852 only three thousand of the ten thousand houses in Belfast had piped water. Not all these houses had a cistern, which would allow impurities to settle. This 30 per cent of houses with piped water did not represent 30 per cent of the town's population, as they were houses of the relatively wealthy and therefore were not as densely populated. One hundred and eighty streets were unpaved, so filth soaked into the ground rather than drained away. Three thousand houses did not have even the smallest of yards. There were not enough street-cleaners in the poorer areas of the town, so 'offensive remains' were allowed to accumulate.

Dr Malcolm went on to demonstrate the correlation between such living conditions and the spread of the typhus epidemic of 1847–8. In the first year, the fever struck in seven out of every ten houses that did not have an efficient sewerage system but fewer than one in five houses in the better-drained areas. In the second year of the outbreak there were no cases of typhus in the first-class streets, 22 in the second-class streets, and 81 in third-class streets, while in the lanes, entries, alleys and courts there were 156. Seventy per cent of the total number of cases occurred where there was the worst housing.

It was not simply a matter of poverty. Dr Malcolm mentioned one address where, because the landlord was insistent on the need for cleanliness, there had not been a single case of cholera in 1849. He felt that he left 'death and pestilence' behind when he crossed the Blackstaff River. People, even poor people, who lived in suburbs like Sandy Row were luckier, because they had healthy fresh air from the mountain and still had views of the countryside.

Dr Malcolm acknowledged that some improvements had been made. The town dock and the quays along High Street had been covered in. The construction of Victoria Street, and of Corporation Street to the north, had cut through a warren of these mean streets, and the new, wide thoroughfares were letting light shine in areas where there had been a permanent gloom. He pointed out, however, that the improvements in the main streets also increased the contrast with the remaining poor areas, where there were still narrow lanes often less than twenty feet wide, or dark courts accessible only through a covered archway. Traces of some of these are to be found in the entries off High Street and Ann Street in contemporary Belfast.

The good doctor's work gained further force in 1853 when the Rev. W. M. O'Hanlon, minister of the Congregational church in Upper Donegall

Street, published *Walks among the Poor of Belfast*. In this small book, written in the form of twelve letters, he described the conditions in which the poor were forced to live. In one room he found seven people living and sleeping 'in the lowest stage of social degradation,' their beds the floor. There were no windows. Four were women and three men; two of the women were mother and daughter but not related in any way to the others. Of Barrack Lane he said: 'No pure breath of heaven ever enters here; it is tainted and loaded by the most tainted, reeking feculence, as it struggles to reach these loathsome hovels.' Most houses had at least two families living in them. He was also concerned about the immorality that, he felt sure, such conditions encouraged. He worried about incest and further worried that girls, to avoid incest, would become prostitutes. In one short street he found five brothels, abodes of 'uncleanliness and vice.' Someone had told him of this, but when he went to verify the report he discovered that there were another two, less well known.

O'Hanlon, like Malcolm, did not think that poverty alone was to blame. He acknowledged that poverty existed and was aware of women working for as little as 7 pence per week. Alcoholic drink, he thought, was the principal reason that the poor were trapped in their poverty. He counted twenty spirit stores in Smithfield, all of them doing a good trade. One owner told him that he had sold 9,380 gallons of whiskey in 1852, without counting any other alcohol. O'Hanlon counted worst those places where drink and sexual promiscuity were combined. In spite of his condemnation of alcohol, he knew there were other factors at work. He preached that property had duties as well as rights. Condemning slum landlords, he commented that 'principle seems to be lost sight of in such squalid nooks.'

It is hard to believe that, through much of this time of trauma, there were those who still found time to indulge in politics. In 1848, during the pause between the plagues of typhus and cholera, such politics centred on the possible repeal of the Act of Union. There had been a rising the previous year, the script for which might have been written by Samuel Becket. The Orangemen of Belfast asked only to be armed and they would protect the town from Irish outrage. To show their readiness they marched on the 12th of July, walking 'with the proud step of men conscious of their moral and physical superiority,' according to the *News Letter*. God had shown that they were in the right by visiting the worst of the effects of the famine on the Catholic south and west of Ireland. Even in Belfast more Catholics had died than Protestants, they said, ignoring the fact that Catholics had the worst housing and the greatest poverty. Now, in the Field at Carrickfergus, they listened to speakers condemn agitation for repeal while they drank the whiskey thoughtfully provided by Mr Robinson, who also owned the meadow in which they stood. One speaker said that they should not merely defend the Union but should campaign for the repeal of the Catholic

Emancipation Act. The encroachments that Catholics had made over the previous years had to be reversed.

It is scarcely surprising that when the lodges returned to Belfast there was trouble, for fiery talk and fire-water are a dangerous combination. A Catholic girl was attacked in Sandy Row. It was claimed that she had been carrying a green bough, which had become the symbol of the repeal movement, but it is difficult to believe that even a lunatic would enter a notoriously violent Protestant area, on her own, carrying such a provocative object. Whatever she was or was not carrying, it was Orangewomen who attacked her, stripped her to the waist, pulled out all her hair, and would have killed her if some of their menfolk had not intervened. Later guns were fired in the border streets separating Sandy Row and the Pound, but things were quiet by nightfall.

Fear of a Catholic rising fed on itself, and through the winter of 1848/9, while the poor of Belfast died of cholera, newspapers that supported the Orange tradition kept up the pressure. One, the *Warder*, which proclaimed itself the guardian of Protestantism in Ireland, anticipated Hitler by nearly a hundred years when it warned of the dangers of the 'Papal project and Roman-led Jew plot.' There were a number of seemingly malicious fires in Belfast that winter, all blamed on Catholics. When two Protestants were killed when they attacked a St Patrick's Day parade in Crossgar, County Down, the Protestant press called the marchers 'Ribbonmen' and said that the Orangemen who had attacked the march had been acting in self-defence. The nationalist press responded with the assertion that all parades should be banned so as to end the party riots that disgraced the country.

In such a charged atmosphere, people looked forward to the 12th of July with mixed feelings. Even the press in England showed an interest. The *Times* described the Orange Order as 'that rather impracticable body . . . who are resolved upon celebrating the twelfth of July with all its ancient mummeries.'

When the Belfast lodges gathered in the Massareene estate in County Antrim—it took thirty-eight railway carriages to get them there—they were once again congratulated on the role they had played in defeating the nationalist rising and were warned against the threatened ascendancy of the Catholic Church. They were reminded that theirs was a growing organisation and that, with twenty thousand people attending, this was one of the biggest gatherings yet held. Best of all, from everyone's point of view, was the fact that it had passed off peacefully. Or nearly did. That evening, two men drove horses decorated with orange lilies through Ballymacarret. Presumably they strayed too close to the Catholic enclave of Short Strand, because they were attacked by local railway workers. A general fight developed as local Orangemen joined the fray, but the crowds were dispersed by the police without trouble. One of the horsemen later died of his injuries, and in the days after the funeral there was widespread rioting in the area around Barrack Street.

What happened in Belfast was nothing compared with the trouble in County Down, from an incident whose reverberations went far beyond the county and Belfast. Dolly's Brae was a small village in a defile in the townland of Magheramayo, inhabited almost exclusively by Catholics. The gathering place for the Orangemen of County Down that year was at Tollymore, near Castlewellan. Rathfriland Orange Lodge decided that they would march through Dolly's Brae, even though they had never taken this route before and it was out of their way. The *Warder* claimed that the decision was taken in response to the killing of the two Protestants at Crossgar on St Patrick's Day. The authorities felt that they could not ban the march, as the Party Processions (Ireland) Act (1844) had lapsed. They hoped that by sending enough soldiers and magistrates they could prevent a clash from taking place.

The first part of the day passed peacefully enough. Approximately 1,300 people marched from Rathfriland, all armed to the teeth, according to the *Newry Telegraph*. They were escorted by dragoons and magistrates; other dragoons had taken up station at Dolly's Brae, because there had been trouble there the previous year. The dragoons, under the command of Major Wilkinson, were accompanied by a magistrate, Captain Skinner. Soon afterwards some Ribbonmen appeared, presumably with the intention of guarding the tiny village. They were surprised to find the position already occupied. They were, possibly, just as surprised when the Orange procession passed through Dolly's Brae in an entirely disciplined and orderly manner, went down the road to Castlewellan and on to Tollymore. The numbers of the Ribbonmen had by now built up to nearly a thousand, and they celebrated their delivery by firing shots in the air; but Captain Walker was satisfied that no breach of the peace occurred.

Meanwhile, in Tollymore, the usual speeches were being made. Lord Roden, who was a grand master of the Orange Order as well as being host for the day, had ensured that alcohol was available in quantities sufficient to match the thirst of the tired marchers. He also reminded them of the threats to their freedom, religion and laws by making a virulent attack on Catholics, and called on those present to do their duty as loyal Protestants. By the time the demonstration was over, at about five o'clock, the Orangemen of Rathfriland knew where their duty lay.

As they left the estate the officers commanding the dragoon escort were surprised when the magistrates made no effort to persuade the marchers to go home to Rathfriland by the direct route. Instead they made once again for the mountain road to Magheramayo. Feeling some disquiet, the dragoons followed. Ahead of them the assembled Ribbonmen moved away from soldiers guarding Dolly's Brae and moved to a position on the hill overlooking the road, about a mile beyond the narrow pass.

As the Orangemen reached the village, someone at the head of the procession was heard to say, 'Now, my boys, not a shot is to be fired.' This injunction was emphasised by Sub-Inspector James Hill of the constabulary, who asked each file of Orangemen as it passed 'not to fire a shot, even for fun.' Then there was a shot. Major White thought it came from the head of the Orange procession. Almost at once there was an exchange of shots. Hill chose to lead his constables against the Ribbonmen. When the police began to fire, the Ribbonmen decamped. Hill called on the Orangemen to cease fire, but instead they blazed away, ignoring the fact that there were police on the hill as well as nationalists. One of the magistrates, George Fitzmaurice, rode along the line of Orangemen, calling on them to cease fire in case they hit a policeman. When he got to the tail of the procession he found that some of the marchers had attacked houses in the village, and one householder was lying wounded. He called on some of the Rathfriland men to go to the wounded man's aid, but they refused, saying he 'wasn't of their party.' The dragoons, who could not interfere because none of the magistrates had called on them to do so, cooled their anger by trying to put out the fires. It was too late for some of the buildings, including the church and the priest's house, but it was, as Major Wilkinson said, the best they could do.

The results of the skirmish were variously reported. The *Newry Telegraph* said fifty Ribbonmen had been either killed or wounded, while not a single Orangeman had been even wounded. The *Warder* put the deaths at six, including one Orangeman. It noted that one of the dead was a ten-year-old boy, while another was a woman of eighty-five who had been stabbed with a bayonet. Finally, it justified the incident by claiming that the Orangemen had been 'roused beyond endurance.'

The 'Battle of Magheramayo' was debated in Parliament. John Bright, member for Birmingham, argued that the incident had occurred because both Orangemen and police saw Catholics as a common enemy, and that the only crime in the north of Ireland was to be born a Catholic. He demanded that the inquiry that was to be set up should be searching and impartial. It was. The magistrates who had accompanied the procession were reprimanded for allowing the affair to get out of hand. Lord Roden had his magistracy withdrawn. Most significantly of all, the Party Processions (Ireland) Act was back on the statute book before the marching season of 1850.

As the famine and its attendant epidemics passed, Belfast gradually returned to its own normality. Work has been undertaken to compare the experience of Belfast in mid-century with port cities in Britain, particularly Bristol, Liverpool, Edinburgh and Glasgow. These cities had the same medical support system and the same philanthropic support from the better off. Housing conditions in Belfast may not have been as bad as cellar dwellings in some English cities, but Belfast wages were lower. Belfast mortality rates, however, were worse than any comparable town or city in Britain. Using the figures of the 1841 epidemic and comparing them with the rest of Ireland, it is seen that the mortality rates of the young, those under forty-five, were twice as high as the country as a whole. In 1852, a year without plague or famine, Dr Malcolm calculated that the average life expectancy in Belfast was nine years, because of the extremely high infant mortality rate.

The force that allowed Belfast to rise from the after-effects of the famine to the great city it was in 1900 was the textile mill. The first of these had been opened in 1779, when eighty people were employed in a factory in which newly installed machinery was spinning cotton. The Napoleonic Wars began soon after this, and the government was buying as much cotton cloth as it could lay its hands on. Although the wars ended in 1815, the factories continued working with cotton and increasing the prosperity of their owners until 1825, when 3,500 workers were employed in more than twenty mills around the town. The following year, however, there was a recession in the British cotton industry, and the goose seemed to have laid her last golden egg.

By a happy accident, however, the spinning industry had a new opportunity open for it at this crucial time. It was literally an accident, for in the summer of 1828 Mulholland's Mill in Henry Street burned down. Rather than rebuild it as a cotton mill, Thomas Mulholland did some research into the mechanical spinning of flax, sending his brother to Lancashire to investigate. As an experiment, he had some flax spindles put in his mill in Francis Street. He was so pleased with the results that he had the mill adapted to work exclusively with flax and renamed it the York Street Mill. The success of the product was so great that for a while it seemed as if every person who had enough money to invest was opening a linen mill. Bleachers, doctors, even printers went into the business. By 1834 there were nearly as many people spinning flax as there were spinning cotton, and by the time Queen Victoria visited Belfast there were twenty-nine mills spinning flax and only four spinning cotton.

Such a rapid change in production was a disaster for hand spinners throughout the country, as they could not produce yarn as cheaply as the mills. It also proved a disaster for handloom weavers, because it became difficult for them to obtain yarn. For many, the only answer was to move to Belfast and to bring their looms with them. Here they could still find employment, as their wages were so low that there was no incentive, at least for the time being, for mill-owners to introduce power looms. Now in the years of famine their numbers were hugely increased, as weavers who had remained in the countryside were faced with ruin and starvation. The winter that followed the disastrous summer of 1846 was the harshest in a generation, and in their despair people came from all over the country, even from west of the River Bann, pulled in by Belfast's reputation for prosperity. Starving wretches flooded into the town, sought refuge in dark lanes, huddled in rags for warmth.

At about this time another upheaval was occurring in the linen trade. Up till then power looms for linen were capable of dealing only with the coarsest cloth, rather than the quality material that Belfast was producing. It was cheap anyway to pay hand weavers a modest sum to make the cloth. There are stories of men working hours that must have led them to an early grave, because they were paid by the yard and the rate was so low that some had to work a hundred hours a week to feed their family. It was believed by the mill-owners that a reasonable rate for a hand weaver was one shilling per day. Earnings were so low that speculators did not think it worth while to build houses for linen workers, as the rent they would be able to pay would not give a sufficient return. Mill-owners themselves had to provide housing, and this was done as cheaply as might be. This was one of the reasons that the housing stock was so poor and so crowded.

After the devastation of the Great Famine and its accompanying plagues, however, there was a shortage of handloom weavers, many having died or emigrated. As they now had something to bargain with, the weavers were able to force up their wages. Nothing motivated a mill-owner more than a threat to his profits, and to counter this threat more investigations were undertaken in Lancashire, where there had been recent improvements in looms that managed to deal with the problem of linen's lack of elasticity. Straight away, Belfast linen mills began to have power looms installed, at such a rate that there were 1,691 by 1857. In spite of the unfortunate repercussions of this for the handloom weavers, it was an important step for Belfast, and it came at just the right time.

In the United States trouble was fermenting over the issue of slave-ownership. The northern states saw a great moral abhorrence, and little economic value, in a system that allowed one man to own another. In the southern states there were people in positions of authority and prestige who felt that their way of life would be destroyed if they lost the right to keep slaves. Cotton and the plantation estates it supported were labour-intensive industries, and plantation-owners claimed it would be impossible to pay their workers and still make a profit. When war broke out between the states it seemed at first a catastrophe for Belfast. Two-fifths of Belfast's linen was exported to the United States. Most mills put their workers on short time. As expected, exports to the United States fell by more than half. Something else happened, however.

The northern states had the better navy of the combatants, and they used it to blockade the Confederacy ports. The result was that little cotton was getting through to England, and the little that arrived became very expensive. Linen was the closest material to cotton, and now suddenly there was a huge gap in the market. Belfast moved to fill it.

Chapter 2 ∾

THE DEVELOPMENT OF BELFAST HARBOUR AND THE GROWTH OF SHIPBUILDING

Belfast man with romance in his heart and a woman on his arm, living at the time when the horrors of 1798 were over and the prosperity brought about by the French wars was just beginning, could have done worse than stroll on a spring evening to the Long Bridge over the River Lagan. He would need to be a man who checked things in advance, however, or who had a working knowledge of the movements of the sea around the shores of Belfast Lough: he would need to know that he would arrive on the bridge at the same time that the highest part of the tide passed under it. Then he could turn his lady to face northwards, and together they could appreciate the view.

Before them was spread the full beauty of Belfast Lough. To their left Cave Hill dominated the line of hills that marked the edge of the Antrim Plateau and stretched down to Carrickfergus. On their right the gentler hills of Castlereagh pointed the way to the Ards Peninsula. Three miles away, on the lough itself, a cluster of ships' masts showed where the Pool of Garmoyle gave safe anchorage in all weathers. It was surely a sight to stir the bosom of all but the most cynical.

But the view depended on the man's timing. If he had been unfortunate enough to arrive at low tide it would have been a very different scene. The hills would still have framed the lough, and the ships would still have been turning at anchor in the Pool of Garmoyle; but the river would have disappeared, or almost so. A faltering stream would be making its way towards the sea, winding among sand and mudbanks, no more than two feet deep in the centre. The smell of the rich slob deposited by the Lagan would be augmented by the faecal smell of the detritus of Belfast, emptied into the nearest stream by busy housewives or maidservants and now drying out at the side of the river, because the Lagan's flow was so slight in this part of its course that it did not have the strength to carry its rubbish into the sea. But it was not the smell that distressed the merchants of Belfast.

As the nineteenth century got under way, Belfast seemed blessed with a combination of circumstances. There was a growing number of cotton mills producing material for which the logistical needs of the French wars offered a ready market. Even when the wars ended, in 1815, there was sufficient home demand to keep the industry in Belfast in a very healthy state. This continued after protection was removed from Irish cotton in 1824, as raw material was the same cost everywhere in the United Kingdom; and if coal had to be imported into Belfast, the cost of transporting it could be offset by the employers by the simple expedient of paying Belfast workers smaller wages. There was a setback in the 1830s when there was a decline in the cotton market, but Belfast enterprise was up to that, and mill-owners, following the example of the pioneer Thomas Mulholland, converted their mills to the production of linen. Prosperity continued throughout the century, with only a few minor set-backs in the 1850s.

The great financial investment needed was provided in great part from within Belfast. At the turn of the century the Bank of Ireland held a monopoly, and no other bank could be established except as a private partnership. This meant that anyone setting up such a bank would be personally liable for any debts the bank incurred and would not receive the protection that a limited liability company offers. Nevertheless three Belfast banks were established in the first decade of the new century: the Belfast Bank in 1808 and the Northern Bank and Commercial Bank in 1809. Each partner invested £10,000, and there was enough capital for all three banks to survive the financial crisis of 1820, when many other Irish banks collapsed.

The Bank of Ireland's monopoly was removed in 1824, and the banks of Belfast formed joint-stock banks, each with a capital of half a million pounds. The Belfast Bank and the Commercial Bank united; but with the establishment of the Ulster Bank in 1836 there were three major banks drawing substantial deposits from investors all over the province. There was also a Savings Bank, which provided for the needs of less wealthy customers.

The fact that there was money to invest as well as products worth investing in should have meant that openings for making money were practically limitless. There was a problem, however. Raw materials had to be imported freely, and exports had to be equally freely shipped out of the town. The River Lagan was neither particularly large nor particularly fast-flowing. Belfast had been built at the lowest point in the river at which it was practical to build a bridge. Below the bridge the flow of the river decreased even further, and it meandered through a vast mudflat of its own creation. The channel, as we have seen, was shallow, and even small ships could pass through it only at high tide. Larger ships, and smaller ships awaiting the tide, had to anchor in deep water in the Pool of Garmoyle, opposite present-day Holywood. Goods from the larger ships had to be transferred to smaller vessels, locally called gabbards, to complete the three miles to the town.

As far back as 1785 the Chamber of Commerce had petitioned the Irish Parliament in Dublin for £2,000 towards the cost of excavating a channel from the Town Docks to Belfast Lough. The Parliament did not release the funds but did something that was much more useful to an enterprising town like Belfast: a Corporation for Preserving and Improving the Port of Belfast was established. Belfast, faced with a mouthful like that, renamed it the Ballast Board. Whatever it was called, almost all its members were merchants who were keen on improving the facilities of the port.

They started off with great enthusiasm. They did some deepening of the channel, within the limited methods that were available at the time. They also insisted that all ships using the channel, whether incoming or outgoing, had to carry a qualified pilot. This cut down on the number of occasions when the channel was blocked by a ship stuck on a mudbank. They also went about improving the facilities in the town itself. They obtained a lease from the Marquis of Donegall of ten acres near Ritchie's shipyard and began work at once on building a quay and a graving-dock in the area now known as Clarendon Dock. Other improvements were carried out by private individuals, and the trade passing through the port increased to almost twice what it was before the improvements. By this time the balance of trade (the excess of exports over imports) was £900,000 in Belfast's favour.

For all the efforts of the Belfast Ballast Board, which included the building of a second graving-dock, where repairs to ships could be carried out, and improvements to the town's docks, the condition of the channel remained an impediment to the expansion of Belfast's trade. It is unlikely that Belfast's industrial growth could have continued after about 1830 without substantial improvements being made to the harbour. One of the driving forces behind the harbour improvements was a man whose name we shall come across later, William Pirrie. A sea captain who had gone ashore in middle age, Pirrie came to Belfast from Scotland to look after the local interests of his father's shipping company.

The introduction in 1830 of steam dredgers that had the power to excavate to the depths necessary to accommodate an ocean-going ship meant that Pirrie's hopes could become a reality. But even when the Ballast Board decided to go ahead with a plan to cut a new channel in the river, with the option of cutting a second later if that turned out to be necessary, it took six years for the enabling act to be passed by Parliament. Vested interests made things difficult. The act would give the Ballast Board the right to deepen the channel and to buy out private quays. The Marquis of Donegall, whose family had originally owned all of Belfast, complained that this would give too much power to such a group, comprising as it did mere merchants. His nominees in Parliament argued vehemently. This caused great anger in Belfast, where the marquis was not a popular figure. He had come to Belfast with a reputation as a spendthrift and gambler whose word could not be trusted. Nor could he be trusted with ready cash. The hunt in Doagh, of which he was patron, had a collection taken up with which to buy claret. The money was passed to Lord Donegall, but neither the wine nor the money was ever returned to the members of the hunt.

The marquis was not, however, the only one to cause the board problems. Lord Templemore wanted the channel dug on the County Down side of the river, so that he could develop the foreshore and improve access to his land at Ballymacarret. Also, the owners of quays on the County Antrim shore looked for compensation at a much higher rate than the board could pay. It was not, therefore, until 1839 that work began on the project. Raising the capital needed was something of a problem, though people saw the advantages that the work would bring to Belfast industry and were keen to invest in it. The Treasury had to provide a loan of £25,000 to get the project started. The improvements came just in time, for by 1841 Belfast was Ireland's principal port, based on the value of its exports.

The project was in two parts. A channel was dug through the slobland, cutting off the first bend in the river below the Long Bridge. Its depth was to be such as to allow nine feet of water even at the lowest tide. At the same time the river was deepened along the dock. The resulting spoil was dumped on the slob to the south of the new channel, creating what was in effect a new island. This was known at first as Dargan's Island, after the contractor in charge of the project; the name was changed to Queen's Island in honour of Victoria's visit in 1849. The Ballast Board went on to buy all the private docks and quays downriver from the Long Bridge, which was in a bad state of repair and had to be replaced in 1841 with the Queen's Bridge. This gave the board full control of how the harbour would develop in future. Instead of trying to recoup its investment by raising prices, it reduced dock and pilotage charges to encourage trade.

It was so successful in this that the Harbour Commissioners, who took over in 1847, were able to begin straight away on the second cut, which came to be called Victoria Channel. This was ready for the Queen's visit. William Pirrie, who by now was chairman of the commissioners, presided at the opening. A small flotilla of ships, led by the tug *Superb*, started down the new channel. The Royal Mail steamer *Prince of Wales* carried the main party, including the commissioners, the pick of Belfast's establishment, as well as General Bainbrigge and the officers and men of the 13th Regiment. The *Prince of Wales* was followed by the *Whitehaven,* loaded with fare-paying pleasure-seekers, while the tug *Erin's Queen* came last, towing the *Fawn* and *Gannet.* Pirrie, by way of naming the Victoria Channel, emptied a bottle of champagne into the waters, to the cheers of the crowds. Cannons sounded, and 'Rule Britannia' was played. A good day was enjoyed by all.

While the channel was being dredged, some of the spoil was also used to fill in the old docks. These became Queen's Square, Albert Square and Corporation Square. In front of these the commissioners built Donegall Quay out into the river, so that the very biggest ships could come alongside without having to leave the dredged channel. The smaller ships, which were mainly colliers, were given alternative facilities at Queen's Quay on the County Down shore, where there was a coal dock late into the twentieth century. In the middle of the nineteenth century almost half a million tons of coal was landed there each year.

Once again, the timing of these improvements was perfect. During these years Belfast was being joined to its hinterland. The Lagan Navigation, which connected Belfast with the whole of mid-Ulster, was the first of these links. It was later supplemented by the railway, which made it easier for goods to be brought to the port for shipment. Passengers were also carried, of course, but the fact that trains ran on a Sunday meant that they were not equally welcomed by all sections of society. Those who considered that the Sabbath was sacrosanct were outraged. One clergyman told his flock that he would rather join a company for theft and murder than invest in the Ulster Railway, which was sending souls to the Devil at sixpence a ride; every blow of the railway whistle was answered by a cry from Hell. Businessmen from North Armagh and as far away as County Fermanagh comforted their conscience with the thought of how much faster, easier and more reliable the train was over the old system of horse-drawn wagons.

Another industry to take advantage of the improved harbour facilities was shipbuilding. There are records of shipbuilding form at least 1636, when Belfast's importance as a settlement began to grow; and there is a probability that shipbuilding on some scale had taken place before that. The Lord Deputy had reported to Queen Elizabeth in 1538 that Belfast was a suitable place for the industry. The Lagan Valley was heavily wooded, and there were small fishing hamlets along the shores of Belfast Lough. There was also great demand on the wood for making charcoal for a local iron industry.

The two industries—shipbuilding and iron—demanded different ways of managing woodland. The people of the Lagan Valley did not want to manage it at all, as there was a tradition of Irish outlaws, known as 'wood kerns', living in the deep groves and coming out to raid English and

Scottish settlers. The woods were allowed to disappear by about 1730, and the iron industry died.

Not the shipbuilding. The normal wear and tear on small wooden boats that had to make their way along the coasts of Ireland and Britain and continental Europe meant that there was always the need to have facilities for repairing or even replacing damaged ships. For most of the time the vessels built were between five and twelve tons, with crews of two or three. As ships became bigger, shipbuilding became more of a science than previously, and the specialist equipment and facilities needed went beyond the small-scale craft that it had been. Although a ship of 150 tons, the *Eagle's Wing,* had been built in 1636, and one of 250 tons, the *Loyal Charles,* some time later, shipbuilding in Belfast was moribund by the end of the eighteenth century. There were only six jobbing ship-carpenters in Belfast, not properly organised and without any leadership. Almost all ships that had suffered damage had to be sent to Scotland or England for repairs. This was not a satisfactory situation at a time when Belfast's trade was expanding rapidly.

As often happens in the story of Belfast, there was an enterprising individual who saw an opening and moved to take advantage of it. For all the problems that the lack of a yard caused traders, the situation of Belfast caused even more for shipbuilding. The river was crowded—even more crowded than the Thames, though on a smaller scale. All supplies had to be brought in by sea, and, though sea transport was the cheapest available, this still added to the cost. This mattered even more later when ships were being built of iron and steel.

Nevertheless William Ritchie of Ayrshire visited Belfast in March 1791 and arrived back in July, bringing with him ten men, some apparatus and some materials from his existing shipyard in Saltcoats. He had been asked by the Harbour Board to set up a shipbuilding business and to build a graving-dock (more usually called by laymen a dry dock). Both this dock and a second one that the Harbour Board commissioned in 1820 are still to be seen at Clarendon Dock, off Corporation Street, on the north side of the river. It is a tribute to the skill in construction of those early engineers that the second of these docks, completed in 1826, is still operational and is used to carry out service and repair work on the *Victoria,* a ship used by Belfast Port Authority to carry out survey work and to maintain navigation lights on the approach to the harbour.

Ritchie did not wait even till the first dock was completed but started immediately on building ships. His first Belfast ship, the *Hibernia,* of 300 tons, was launched on 7 July 1792, almost exactly a year after he had set up shop. Ten years later Ritchie recorded that he had working for him 44 journeymen-carpenters, 55 apprentices, 14 sawyers, 12 blacksmiths, and several joiners. His total wage bill was £120 a week.

Ritchie built ships of between 50 and 450 tons. A brother set up another shipyard beside William's and this was also successful. But it was William who was the real innovator. His shop cast anchors for his ships. He reclaimed land from the shore and built his own stone-fronted docks. Many of his oak-built ships traded with the West Indies, and an admirer wrote of them in 1811 that 'for elegance of mould, fastness of sailing, and utility in every respect they are unrivalled in any ports they trade to.'

Another Ritchie brother, Hugh, entered into a partnership with Alexander McLaine, and it was the firm of Ritchie and McLaine that launched in 1820 the *Belfast,* of 200 tons, the first steamship built in Ireland. The engines were provided by Coates and Young of Belfast. Eighteen years later, in 1838, this firm launched the first iron steamship built in Ireland, the *Countess of Caledon.* This ship was built to tow lighters, or barges, on Lough Neagh.

William Ritchie had died by this time and his firm was taken over by Connell and Sons. Also in 1838 this firm launched the *Aurora,* at 750 tons Ireland's biggest ship of the time and the first passenger steamship to be built in Ireland. An interesting addition to the launch ceremony was the band of the 22nd (Cheshire) Regiment, lined up on deck playing appropriate tunes as the ship slid into the water.

The bend of the Lagan below the Long Bridge must have been crowded by this time. It would have been more crowded by the time the Victoria Channel was completed, because bigger ships needing more space alongside were coming right into Belfast. The crowding was exacerbated by the closure of the old Town Docks, so that even smaller ships were being moored along the river. The building of Donegall Quay was probably the final nail in the coffin as far as the long-established shipyards were concerned. The Harbour Commissioners decided to develop the County Antrim shoreline as trading docks, while encouraging shipbuilding to move to the County Down side. To start the process they laid out a shipbuilding yard and a patent slip on Queen's Island. One of the smaller shipyards, Thompson and Kirwan, moved across the river and established its business in the new yard in 1851. Shortly afterwards a new Harbour Office was built on the site of William Ritchie's yard, a symbol of the change in use.

The move to Queen's Island was not universally popular among the workers. As the men worked a twelve-hour day, for a large part of the year they had to catch the ferry that took them to and from work in the dark. Nevertheless, two years later Robert Hickson expressed interest in establishing an iron shipyard on the island. The *Great Britain* had been aground in Dundrum Bay for most of 1846 yet had suffered very little damage, demonstrating how strong an iron ship could be. The commissioners obliged and laid out another yard. It cost them £1,116, and it included equipment for shaping and boring iron plates and angles. Hickson had started business as an ironmaster and had set up a foundry in Eliza Street in the Markets area, reclaiming scrap iron. Discovering that the extra expense of importing much of his raw materials meant that he could not compete with English or Scottish foundries in selling iron plates, he decided—as almost every foundry in Belfast eventually did—that the only solution was to sell his iron in the form of a finished product. Other firms built engines or ventilation equipment. He would build iron ships.

Queen's Island was still an island at that time, but the fact that the main flow of the river no longer went along its old course meant that the old river bed would gradually have become shallower and eventually become a marsh. Recognising this, the authorities filled in the old river, claiming the island for County Down. Belfast was now ready for one of the most important figures of the nineteenth century to enter the scene.

Edward Harland was born in Scarborough, Yorkshire, in 1831, the sixth child in a family of eight. His father was a doctor who was interested in local politics and enjoyed tinkering in mechanics. Dr Harland had taken out a patent in 1827 for an early steam-driven horseless carriage. The scale-model prototype worked perfectly, but the pressure on his time meant that he was never able to complete the full-sized carriage. He was Mayor of Scarborough for three terms and also served as a justice of the peace. He was on friendly terms with George Stephenson, builder of locomotives. Somewhere he found time to practise as a doctor.

Edward's mother came from landed stock. She was very good with her hands, as well as being artistic. She put this to practical use. Instead of having their toys bought for them, the children made them, under their mother's supervision. In the circumstances it is not surprising that Edward grew to have a fascination with watching skilled men at work. He made friends with many of the town's craftsmen, picking up tips in a number of fields. He particularly enjoyed visiting the shipyard of William and Robert Tyndall; here he learnt the elements of shipbuilding and became skilled in applying his lessons to building the 'neatest and swiftest' of model yachts.

At grammar school he did reasonably well in drawing and geometry, and at the age of twelve he went to Edinburgh Academy, remaining there for two years. This was a school of more traditional values, where the classics were considered the most important subjects. Edward's brother was a medical student at the University of Edinburgh, and they spent a lot of time together. The younger boy learnt to make models of all sorts of machines and buildings. When their mother died in 1844 Dr Harland wanted Edward to study law and become a barrister. Showing the strength of will and the determination that would later serve him well in Belfast, son persuaded father that a career in engineering would be a better choice, and he became an apprentice at the Stephenson Engineering Works in Newcastle.

The young Harland would spend four years in the workshops and finish with one year in the drawing office. He worked from six in the morning to a quarter past eight in the evening, six days a week, with an early finish at four on Saturdays. Before he was eighteen he was trusted to build one side of a locomotive. After this he worked on a brass-turning lathe. In his auto-biography he writes that he spent all his free time eating or sleeping.

One notion caught his mind during one of his rare visits home to Scarborough. The north-east coast of England is a dangerous place for shipping, and there were many occasions when sailors' lives depended on the reliability of the ships' lifeboats of the time. Harland set his mind to designing one that would be more or less unsinkable and that could be launched from a ship's deck even in the roughest seas. By coincidence, the Duke of Northumberland offered a prize in 1850 for the maker of the best design and model. Harland worked long and hard at the drawings and in the construction of the model. He even took the finished product out in a dinghy so that the sea trials would be realistic. When he eventually submitted his work he was confident that he had fulfilled the required specifications. There were 280 entries, and his model did not win. He consoled himself with the belief that the judges were not prepared for his innovation and did not have the imagination to understand how it would work.

Back in Newcastle, Harland was chosen by the manager as his assistant in designing caissons for Keyham Dockyard in Plymouth. Other engineer-ing projects were being carried out in the north-east, and Harland tried to visit as many of these as he could, which gave him the opportunity to pick up knowledge and skills he knew he would need in later life.

By the time he had finished his apprenticeship, in 1851, the firm was happy to take him on its books at the full adult rate of £1 per week. It was a slack time for railway engineers, and by this time, aged twenty, Harland seems to have been a driven man. He left the firm and, after a break to visit London and the Great Exhibition, went to Glasgow, hoping to get employ-ment there. He got a start with a firm that built marine engines. For him this was paradise, with all the great shipbuilders along the Clyde. Saturdays after work were spent walking around the yards, looking at the great liners being built for Cunard Steamships Ltd and the Peninsular and Oriental Steam Navigation Company (familiarly known as the P&O Line). He managed to get on board most of these and studied their relative advantages and disadvantages. Above all, he enjoyed watching engineers overcome problems.

Harland was delighted when his firm, J. and G. Thomson of Glasgow, began to build its own ships. Although a naval draughtsman had been taken on, Harland was given much of the routine work to do. When the senior draughtsman left for another position on the Tyne, Harland was promoted in his place. He was not given any increase in wages, but the experience was useful, and he was soon offered a new contract and a pay rise.

Good things, like buses, come in flocks, and very shortly afterwards Harland obtained, through the recommendation of George Stephenson, a managerial position in Thomas Toward's shipyard on the Tyne. He claims he was reluctant to leave Thomsons' yard, but that did not stop him conducting a piece of industrial espionage. He would need a new angle and plate furnace built on the Tyne. He fed Glenlivet whisky to 'the best man at this job' on the Clyde, questioned him judiciously, and went off to the Tyne with detailed notes on how to build what turned out to be 'the best furnace on the Tyne.'

A new offer came to him, this time as manager of Hickson's shipyard in Belfast. Hickson knew nothing of ships, and he was looking for someone with shipbuilding experience to guide that side of the business. Harland saw the advertisement in a newspaper and applied for the position. He was accepted, and at Christmas 1854 one of the greatest driving forces of Belfast's prosperity in the nineteenth century arrived on the Lagan.

Harland soon realised just how little Hickson knew about the business, and discovered that the previous manager, a man called Jordan, had been sacked because he was not up to the job and had spent much of his time ingratiating himself with the workers. Harland decided that his first priority was to instil a sense of reality in the men, who were being paid above-average wages for below-quality work. He cut their wages and demanded a higher standard in their work. He also imposed a smoking ban.

The response of the workers, as Harland had expected, was to strike. He sensed their antipathy and realised that they would try to frustrate his work in the hope that he would resign. Instead he went to Scotland and recruited skilled hands from the Clyde. These strike-breakers were subject to serious intimidation by the old hands. To compound Harland's difficulties, the former manager of Hickson's had leased the old yard of Thompson and Kirwan's on the County Antrim shore and had recruited some of Hickson's leading hands. This threat faded away, however, because the man's incompetence was such that the new yard never got beyond the laying of one keel. Hickson's creditors were becoming impatient, and at one point Harland had to guarantee personally the wages of the workers. Friends advised him to put the whole thing down to experience and to leave Belfast for friendlier climes. He was determined to succeed, and gradually those working for him, together with the more realistic of the men on strike, began to appreciate the strength of that determination. More men returned to work. Harland was able to appoint competent foremen, and gradually the business began to gain momentum. One pleasant surprise was when the foreman of Toward's shipyard on the Tyne came to work for him.

By now the firm was making money. It was building large sailing ships as well as propeller-driven steamships. There was even some salvage work done; wrecked ships were raised and brought to the yard for repair. It began to strike Harland that all his hard work was only making money for Hickson, who was the sole owner. The yard manager was paid a salary, and no more. After three years Harland decided that he would be better off working for himself and determined to start his own shipyard. The place he chose was Birkenhead. For those who are interested in decisive moments in history, it is interesting to speculate about what would have happened to Belfast shipbuilding if Liverpool City Council had granted the necessary land to Harland. Instead, it turned him down.

He might still have left Belfast but for the fact that Hickson offered to sell him the Queen's Island yard for £5,000, as he had not completely satisfied his creditors, and the Ulster Bank had foreclosed on the iron-works. This left the younger man with the problem of finding what was a substantial amount of money in 1858. His benefactor was a Liverpool businessman named G. C. Schwabe, a native of Hamburg. He was described by Harland as an old and esteemed friend, but he was more than that: he was a man with money to invest and the contacts to ensure that the investment would be a success. Part of the deal seems to have been helped by the fact that Harland had taken on one of Schwabe's nephews, Gustav Wolff, as personal assistant. Wolff was not required at once, as Harland had agreed to finish those ships that Hickson still had on order before starting business on his own. In the meantime the young German went to sea as an engineer, to broaden his experience.

Harland was not idle on his own account and was busy looking for orders. His first came through the Schwabe connection. He received an order for three steamers from James Bibby and Company of Liverpool, of which Schwabe was one of the partners. At this time, and for some time to come, there were no facilities in Harland's shipyards for making engines, and these had to be ordered from Greenock, on the Clyde. Even so, this was a large order, especially for a new shipyard-owner. Harland wrote to Wolff, at that time in the Mediterranean, asking him to come back to Belfast to take charge of the drawing office.

In 1859 Harland took over the yard of Thompson and Kirwan. The order for Bibby's was completed early the next year and he received further orders, this time for two larger steamers. Pressure of work and the fact that he had to travel away from Belfast quite often made him decide that he needed a partner who could ensure that work, and the five hundred workers, would be as carefully supervised when he was absent as when he was doing it personally. The man in whom he had most confidence was Wolff, who was delighted at the invitation. Harland brought £1,916 to the new firm of Harland and Wolff, while Wolff contributed £500. A further

£12,000 was lent by Wolff's mother and by Schwabe. The partnership began officially on 1 January 1862.

Although there had been shipyards in Belfast for at least two hundred years, the scale on which Harland and Wolff worked, together with the level of innovation the firm brought to shipbuilding, meant that there was a quantitative difference between the new yard and what had gone before. Harland brought all the ideas about ships that he had garnered over the years and began putting them into practice. The first ships he had built for Bibby and Company had been conventional in design, but he had to prove that he was capable of building such ships before ship-owners would have the confidence to allow him to experiment with their orders.

Bibby's must have felt that confidence, because they allowed him to set his own dimensions for the two ships in the second order. He made the ships much longer than usual, without increasing their beam, or width. As the top speed of a ship is a function of its length, and the narrow beam made the new ships streamlined, they could carry more passengers or cargo while using little or no extra fuel. To ensure that the increased length did not make the ships any weaker, the main deck was made of iron. The result was a vessel shaped like a box girder, very strong and very safe. There was a great deal of scepticism when the new ships reached Liverpool, but the sceptics were confounded when the ships made repeated voyages across the Bay of Biscay on their way to and from the Mediterranean with a speed and level of comfort that other companies envied.

This was not the only innovation that Harland and Wolff made to increase the operating efficiency of the new ships. In those days ships' engines were not very efficient, and long voyages were impossible without calling at intermediate ports to take on more coal. To economise on fuel, ships still had sails, so that they could take advantage of suitable winds. This had the disadvantage that sails required many sailors to adjust them, especially on the big square-rigged ships of the time. These new ships had fore-and-aft sails, as can be seen on modern yachts, which reduced the number of men needed. Steam winches were placed at convenient places on deck so that they could be used for heavy lifting and for handling cargo, once again allowing the owners to cut back on the number of men they had to employ.

The partners also looked at the ships' engines. Originally, sea water had been used to produce the steam to drive the engines. The problem with this was that salt formed in the boilers and along the pipes, so reducing their efficiency as well as causing damage by corrosion. Working in close co-operation with some of the senior captains in Bibby and Company, Harland and Wolff developed a system whereby pure water could be used instead. Spent steam from the engine was passed through pipes that were kept cool by being surrounded by salt water. The steam condensed as water, which could be reused. This saved on costs of repairs and maintenance as well as making the engines much more efficient: Harland estimated that there was a 20 per cent saving in coal from this one improvement.

Some changes were minor but had profound effects. Most ships still had a bowsprit, which is essentially a mast sticking out from the bow of the ship; underneath this was the figurehead. By removing these, and by making the bow nearly vertical, Harland and Wolff made it possible for the longer ships to manoeuvre in harbours that might otherwise have been too small to be used. Ease of manoeuvre in tight spaces was also helped by the introduction of powered steering gear, and by moving the steering position to the centre of the ship.

There had always been problems in working with the combination of wood and iron, so Harland and Wolff simply used iron wherever possible. Where iron could not be used they experimented with other materials, including concrete.

There were other problems to be overcome. The increased range of their ships encouraged Bibby and Company to widen their markets. When the Suez Canal opened they ordered the very large steamers that would be capable of trading with Australia and New Zealand. For these very large ships, which would need to have as large a cruising range as possible, Harland in his design reintroduced some square-rigged sails. To ensure that this was not a retrograde step with regard to the size of crews he designed special 'travellers' so that the yards (the horizontal spars from which the sails are hung) could be raised and lowered quickly. The combination of these square-rigged sails with the fore-and-aft sails meant that a ship's captain could be very flexible in his use of the wind.

Before the ships could be built, work had to be done on lengthening and strengthening the slipways, as well as installing new machinery. This cost the firm £1,500, but the year still ended with a small profit. A further three ships were ordered, even longer, at 400 feet, yet still with a beam of only 37 feet. These were not used, as originally intended, on the Australian run. At first they were used in the Mediterranean, but they were later put on the Liverpool–Boston run, carrying immigrants when travelling west and exchanging these for cattle for the home run.

All in all, Harland and Wolff built twenty ships of various sizes for Bibby and Company between 1861 and 1870. To have such a consistent order book, building innovative and successful ships for a successful company was the best start that the yard could have wished for. The shipping world saw strong ships that were different to look at, economical to run, and constantly working without showing any signs of weakness. In every harbour that they entered they advertised the achievements of the Belfast shipbuilders.

These were not the only ships built during the decade. There was one order from the Admiralty for a gunboat. HMS *Lynx* was built at a loss of £5,000, but the partners considered it an investment. Foreign governments tended to place naval orders only with shipyards that had already completed Admiralty contracts.

Those years in the 1860s were not without their problems. At the beginning of the decade the Harbour Commissioners had intended to build a large graving-dock on the County Antrim shore. Following submissions by Harland and Wolff and others, they decided in 1862 to build it instead on Queen's Island. Early in 1863 it looked as if they were going to change their minds yet again. Harland and Wolff threatened to shut down their Belfast yard and move to Liverpool. How serious this threat was is hard to judge, given Harland's previous experience with Liverpool City Council, but the commissioners treated it seriously enough and came up with a compromise. They undertook to build a floating dock on the County Antrim shore, while building the graving-dock on the County Down side. They also excavated part of the old course of the river to form the Abercorn Basin. The work was completed by 1867.

In that year there were serious riots in Belfast, in which the shipyard workers took a prominent part. The partners were forced to face down demands that Catholic workers should be expelled from the yard. Harland himself put up notices to the effect that if any Catholic was forced to leave the yard, the yard would close until the man was allowed to return.

The firm also took on some risky projects. It recovered the *Earl of Dublin* off the rocks at Ballyhalbert. At its own expense it repaired and lengthened this ship, at a cost of £16,000. Together with the loss on HMS *Lynx,* this put the company books seriously into the red for 1868. It took the final Bibby and Company order for three very large ships, made the following year, to return the partnership to profitability.

One problem in any labour-intensive, highly skilled industry is keeping the workers gainfully employed. While it is possible to lay men off at slack times, there is always the danger that they will go elsewhere for a job or that, if the period of unemployment is extended, the edge will be lost from their skills. Either way, the skill pool will be diluted. A steady run of orders, as had happened with Bibby and Company, is the ideal solution. If each order completed has a modest but guaranteed profit it will allow a firm to build its economic strength and allow its capital to grow so that it can invest in new developments and keep up to date in its plant, perhaps even expanding into new income-producing initiatives.

The opportunity to do this came to Gustav Wolff early in 1868, when he was visiting his uncle at the latter's home, Broughton Hall, Liverpool. There he met the thirty-year-old Thomas Ismay, a director of the National Steam Navigation Company (familiarly known as the National Line).

Ismay had just bought the White Star Line for £1,000. This line, which specialised in the Australian trade, had gone bankrupt the previous year, with debts of £527,000. Its fleet consisted of clipper ships (fast multi-mast square-rigged sailing ships) and would need replacing. Schwabe had suggested that Ismay forget about the Australian route and look instead at the North Atlantic. The American Civil War was over. Commerce with North America was making up for lost time and was being supplemented by a huge increase in emigration from Europe to the United States and Canada. Already the Cunard and Inman Lines were making huge profits, and Schwabe was convinced that there was room for another shipping company. He offered to organise the finance for the new line if Ismay would change to the North American trade and if he would buy his new ships from Schwabe's nephew's company, Harland and Wolff. In return, Harland and Wolff would agree not to build any ships for White Star's rivals. The arrangement was that the ships would be charged at cost plus a fixed 4 per cent. Costs would cover only material and labour, with no allowance for overheads. There were penalty clauses for late delivery.

Ismay began realising the value of his old ships straight away. Those he could sell he sold; the rest he leased or chartered, allowing his capital to accumulate until he could order new ships. In 1869 he formed the Oceanic Steam Navigation Company (familiarly known as the White Star Line, from the design of its house flag), with £4,000 in capital and £1,000 in shares. Harland and Wolff each became major shareholders, with Harland contributing £21,000 between shares and loans. For the time being the market was allowed to believe that this capitalisation was to improve the White Star Line's routes to Australia. Later in 1869 White Star ordered its first ship from Harland and Wolff, the *Oceanic*. Sixty more would follow, the last, the *Georgic*, being built in 1932.

Although some profit was guaranteed on each of these ships, it was not always what profit on the open market would have been: for such large and prestigious ships a profit of 10 per cent might have been expected. It was safe, however, and it was supported by the fact that these ships were built on the understanding that future contracts and repair work would be done by Harland and Wolff. Even so, the official profit margin was increased to 5 per cent in 1882.

The criteria Ismay set for his new ships were that they should be capable of carrying a large cargo as well as a large complement of passengers, both cabin (first-class) and steerage (third-class), and that they should be able to make the crossing between Liverpool and New York in at least as short a time as any liner in the Cunard and Inman lines. At 420 feet they would be the longest that Harland and Wolff had built, as well as being the widest, with a beam of 41 feet. The partners felt they were ready to take up this new challenge, as they had been building their staff and work force over the years. All their foremen had been promoted from among the workers. The key personnel—the manager, Walter Wilson, and the head draughtsman, William Pirrie—had been trained at the yard as gentlemen-apprentices, paying £100 for the privilege, and had worked in every department, proving themselves at every stage men of great ability.

The firm was very thorough in its preparations. Four berths were built, facing the new Abercorn Basin. The yard by now had six slips. More land was taken over behind the patent slip. A new platers' shop and a new smithy were built. The partners even built a ship at their own expense, the *Camel*. It was built very strongly and had very big hatchways, being primarily designed to bring completed engines and machinery from wherever they were made, but they also used it to experiment with some of the mechanical innovations they intended to use on the new White Star ships. The manager's younger brother was sent to make several voyages in ships that were fitted with the sort of compound engines that were being considered for the new liners. When these proved to be satisfactory three were ordered from Maudsley, Sons and Field of London and three more from George Forrester and Company of Liverpool. The intention was to build the hulls while the engines were being built, and to bring the engines to Belfast in the *Camel* as they were completed.

Although the hulls of these ships were essentially of the same pattern as the ships that had been built for Bibby and Company, Harland and Wolff were extremely thorough in the design and introduced several new features. Many of the changes they made arose from discussions with Ismay, who concerned himself mainly with the passengers' comfort and convenience. First-class passengers were accommodated amidships. Up to this time all passengers had been housed at the stern, though this suffered from rough seas much more than the centre of the ship. To make matters worse, on a propeller-driven ship the drive shaft produced a very disagreeable vibration. This area in future would be left to steerage passengers.

The move to the centre of the ship allowed other improvements to be made for those who could pay for them. There was a smoking saloon that extended the full width of the ship, allowing first-class passengers somewhere roomy and comfortable to meet and socialise when the weather was inclement. For better days there was a promenade deck above the saloon; this could be reached by a grand staircase rising from the saloon. All passenger accommodation was lit by gas, which was made on board, though this was later replaced with electricity. Cabins were double the normal size, and their portholes were also larger, allowing in more natural light.

It was not only the first-class passengers who benefited. Although steerage passengers were still housed in the stern, a great deal of effort was put into improving standards of accommodation, sanitation and convenience.

The sailors were also looked after, with well-lit and ventilated quarters in the fo'c'sle (the front of the ship). Many of the work areas on deck were protected from the worst of the elements. On the foredeck there was a shelter deck known as a turtle-back, designed to protect sailors from water breaking over the bows in rough weather. There were steam winches to perform the hardest work, and even the wheel was power-assisted, with its own steam engine. The engineers and firemen had their quarters near their place of work, so they could get to their meals or come off watch without having to go on deck in dirty weather. The whole ship was designed with the idea that an ocean voyage, even on the unreliable North Atlantic, could be an enjoyable experience rather than simply something to be endured.

The first ship completed was the *Oceanic*, which made its first trip from Liverpool to New York in May 1871. Its speed was at least a knot faster than any of its rivals, and the rough weather it experienced gave it little trouble. Even when it was heading straight into a swell it did not have to reduce speed, as the turtle-back meant that it would not take sea over the bows. The only problem was a technical one. The high waves caused the safety valves of the boilers to move slightly, allowing some steam to escape. To allow this to go untreated was to waste fuel and power, but Board of Trade rules meant that the safety valves could not be modified while the ship was carrying passengers. The solution was to be found in the *Camel*, which had the same type of engine as the *Oceanic*. An experiment with spiral springs proved successful. When this was demonstrated to the Board of Trade, the modifications were allowed to be made on the *Oceanic*.

It was not surprising that rival companies decided to answer the White Star challenge. The Cunard Line even placed an order with Harland and Wolff to lengthen four of its ships.

The drive of the senior partner meant that the Belfast yard did not rest on its laurels. Two larger ships were built for White Star, the *Britannic* and the *Germanic*. This time the main innovation was a second funnel; and the ships were so much faster that they cut an entire day off an Atlantic crossing, the *Germanic* covering the distance in seven-and-a-half days. These ships were built not only for speed but also for endurance. The *Germanic* was later sold to a Turkish firm, and during the First World War it was torpedoed by a British submarine. It was salvaged and repaired and continued a long working life till it was broken up for scrap in 1951, seventy-seven years after being launched.

During 1872 conditions in the yard were improved when the working week was reduced to fifty-one hours. This did not prevent five hundred workers stopping work early on 15 August to take part in protests against home rule. The management took as strong a stand as possible against sectarianism in the yard, but it was unable to prevent Catholics being turned out of their homes in Protestant districts.

A more positive development that year was the founding of the Belfast Ropeworks. This began in rather a small way, with a hundred workers. There was almost no limit to the amount of rope a shipyard needed, especially in the days when even steamships carried sailing gear. Wolff bought shares in the ropeworks in 1873, with the intention of having a say in its affairs. In 1876 it became a limited liability company, with Wolff as chairman. Someone with a good eye for publicity persuaded Blondin, the famous tightrope walker, to use Belfast rope. The firm soon diversified beyond the expected rope and twine. By 1900 it employed three thousand workers and was producing sash cord, binder twine, fishing lines and fishing nets as well as ropes for ships.

In 1878 Harland, working with the shipyard manager, Walter Wilson, discovered something that might have seemed very insignificant but for the fact that it saved a great deal of money over the years. In the early days of propellers, corrosion caused a number of problems. Not only did it impair the efficiency of the propeller but it destroyed its balance. This would set up a vibration that at best was unpleasant and at worst could destroy the propeller shaft. Harland and Wilson discovered that the simple process of attaching a plate of zinc to the hull of the ship near the propeller meant that the zinc would corrode instead. This device is still used throughout the world.

The shipyard was expanding to meet all the challenges of the era. Two thousand four hundred men were employed by 1870, and the numbers were growing. In 1880 the Harbour Commissioners allowed the firm enough extra land to increase the size of the yard to forty acres. It now had ten building-slips. The same year Harland and Wolff took advantage of the extra land to establish a new engine works, thus reducing the firm's reliance on outside agencies. The company was now, for all practical purposes, self-reliant. It was also becoming very large. In 1882 it took over the northern half of Queen's Island, which until then had been open to the public as a pleasure garden. The firm was also too unwieldy to be managed effectively by the two men who had brought it all about, who were now in early middle age and were beginning to look for a life beyond Queen's Island. Harland went on to be Mayor of Belfast and a Conservative member of Parliament for North Belfast until his death in 1895. Wolff also went into politics and was Conservative member of Parliament for East Belfast from 1892 until 1910.

Continuity in the firm was ensured by the nature of the man who took over. Although he had been born in Canada, William Pirrie had come to Belfast, on the death of his father, early enough in childhood to be considered a native of the town. His grandfather, Captain William Pirrie, had been one of the driving forces in the development of Belfast Harbour and had been given the honour of officially opening the Victoria Channel.

The younger William had joined the firm as a boy and had worked in almost every position of responsibility over the years. Harland spoke highly of his character, perseverance and ability, and the young man had been made a partner by the age of twenty-seven. He was now effectually in charge, although he was lucky enough to have as a lieutenant Walter Wilson, who had joined the firm as its first gentleman-apprentice in 1857, when it was still owned by Hickson. Wilson was an 'engineers' engineer', whose creative ideas, based on practical experience, were the basis of many of the firm's innovations.

The firm's expansion came at the wrong time, just before a depression that lasted from 1881 until 1885. Harland and Wolff did what employers did at that time: they cut wages. Riveters and platers were the first to suffer. In January 1884 they were locked out until they would accept a cut in wages. There was a strike of boilermakers two months later, protesting against a cut of 10 per cent in their wages. There was no chance of their succeeding while men were being laid off, and a further 10 per cent was cut off trade wages the following year. By 1886 the work force had fallen from a peak of 5,000 to approximately 3,500. It would have taken an optimist to point out that this was still an improvement on 1870. Such an observant person would have been right to be optimistic. The yard was on the edge of the biggest expansion in its history.

Depressions in trade or otherwise end eventually, and the quiet period in the early 1880s helped to cloak a sea change in the construction of ships. After 1882 a greater tonnage of steamships than sailing ships was being built in the United Kingdom, and developments that came in the next few years increased the advantages of steam over sail. Steel was beginning to be used for the hull and superstructure, and Harland and Wolff had launched their first steel-hulled ships at the end of 1880. As steel is much stronger for a given weight than iron, ships were lighter while still being stronger. Engines were becoming smaller and more efficient, so neither they nor the coal that was used as fuel took up as much space, leaving more room for passengers and cargo. The older ships were no longer viable, and shipping firms had to invest in new vessels or go out of business. Harland and Wolff had established a reputation for looking at ships from the owner's point of view, and for being in the lead with innovation. The company was flooded with orders.

Two of the most significant orders were completed in 1889 for White Star when the *Teutonic* and the *Majestic* were launched. The designs were not new, as they had been submitted to White Star by Harland as far back as 1880. Being drawn up by Harland, however, they had the usual surprises. There were new, triple-expansion engines in place of the less efficient four-cylinder compound that had been used up to then. The new engines gave greater power yet were more efficient, cutting back on the operators' expenses. Instead of both engines driving a single propeller there were twin propellers. The ships were about 10,000 tons and could carry 1,275 passengers, 300 of whom would be first class, where a lot of money could be earned. In keeping with the burgeoning reputation of White Star for luxury, the twin funnels were placed far enough apart to allow all first-class passengers to be seated together for meals in one great dining saloon. The *Teutonic* completed its first transatlantic voyage in 6 days, 17 hours and 25 minutes, a new record.

One of the interesting facts about shipbuilding in Belfast is that there were only two yards, compared with the forty-five on the Clyde and seventeen on the Wear. Yet the two yards were among the biggest producers of shipping. For the rest of the century Harland and Wolff launched an average of 100,000 tons of shipping per year. By 1900 it was employing nine thousand men. When combined with the 'Wee Yard' of Workman Clark, their growth rate outstripped all other shipbuilders in the United Kingdom up to the outbreak of the Great War. The rate of growth was at its highest towards the end of the century. In 1899 Harland and Wolff launched four ships for White Star alone, the biggest of which, the *Oceanic II*, was the largest ship afloat. It had become the greatest shipyard in the world.

Harland and Wolff had worked alongside a number of lesser shipyards for most of its existence. When, in 1879, 23-year-old Frank Workman, who had been trained as a premium apprentice, left the firm to take over a four-acre shipyard on the County Antrim bank, which had better facilities, the older firm for once had a genuine rival. The Harland and Wolff management were not very pleased, particularly as Workman took with him a gifted member of the shipyard's staff, William Campbell, to act as his yard manager. It is probable that Workman had the courage to take this step because family connections were likely to send some business his way, as he was linked by marriage with the owners of the City Line of Glasgow. The orders, however, did not come rushing in. Most of the winter of 1879/80 was spent in getting the yard into shape. An injection of much-needed capital was brought to the new business when Workman was joined by another product of the Harland and Wolff system, nineteen-year-old George Clark. Clark was Scottish; his father part-owned a thread manufacturing business, while his maternal grandfather was the founder of the City Line. The partnership of Workman, Clark and Company was registered in April 1880, and the firm soon had 150 men working on its first orders. Although the City Line ordered a barque (a type of sailing ship), the *City of Cambridge,* from the firm in 1881, the line was not prepared to put all its eggs in one basket. Two sister-ships were ordered from other firms, and the workmanship of the completed ships compared. The Belfast ship compared well enough with the others for further orders to follow.

It was perhaps lucky that Workman Clark was operating on a site with little scope for expansion. It meant that it could not over-extend itself and forced it to work within the limits imposed by a dearth of capital. It had no room for an engine works to begin with and had to buy in its machinery. It tried Rowan and Sons of Belfast but does not seem to have been satisfied, because it tried several other firms before settling on the Glasgow firm of J. and J. Thompson. Although the site was limited, the company was building ships 400 feet long by 1882, and an adequate cash flow meant that it could add to the site as more space was needed. In 1883 it built the *Teelin Head* for the Head Line, built in steel rather than iron. (The Ulster Shipping Company was familiarly known as the Head Line, as its ships were all named after promontories on the Irish coast.) The Star Line, another Belfast shipping firm, ordered the *Star of Austria* in 1886 and later ordered further steamships. Workman Clark had built 114 ships by 1894—a surprising number of them sailing ships. These were the bulk carriers of their day and were designed to be used on routes where they could take advantage of the trade winds, sacrificing speed for economy.

But it was obvious that the future was in steamships, and in 1891 Workman Clark decided that the firm needed its own engine works. It recruited Charles Allen as engineering director, and his first task was to establish the new facilities.

Whether by accident or design, Workman Clark was developing a speciality in ocean-going cargo ships. Some of the biggest of these were cargo-passenger vessels, which optimised the owners' ways of earning money. In 1892 one of these, the *Southern Cross*, proved that the firm could deal with the largest and most complex of ships but at the same time emphasised the restriction that the small size of the yard imposed. In 1894 the opportunity to overcome these difficulties arose when the firm of McIlwaine and McColl on the County Down shore, which had specialised in inshore and coastal ships, went bankrupt. By buying this concern Workman Clark was able to extend its capacity to ten building-slips, one of which was capable of building ships up to 700 feet long. There was also an engine works in the new yard. The firm rationalised its production by having the County Antrim works (now known as North Yard), which had been built to its own specifications, make engines and boilers for all ships, while the newly acquired works (South Yard) concentrated on repairs and making auxiliary machinery, such as pumps, windlasses and other ancillary equipment.

The breakdown of operations between the two yards gives some indication of why a shipyard needed so much space. In the North Yard was the administrative block. Here negotiations were made with shipping lines and the criteria laid down for the building of individual ships; put simply, it was the commercial heart of the business. The partners had suites of offices here, and within easy reach were the managers of the individual departments, each with his own consulting rooms. So important was this aspect of the business that a fireproof building was specially built to house the plans, estimates, tenders, company books and other important documents.

Nearby was the drawing office. It was here that the ideas discussed in the consulting rooms were given shape. (It is significant that all the great chairmen of Harland and Wolff were outstanding draughtsmen; for the really important orders it was the chairman who produced the original drawings.) As one of the most important buildings in the yard, a great deal of attention was lavished in its design and construction. It was light and airy and was kept at a comfortable temperature all year round. It was important that there was nothing to distract the draughtsmen from their work, as the devil was in the detail. A simple mistake at this stage might well multiply itself as work was transferred to the building-slip.

A long, two-storey building, 200 feet long and 70 feet wide, held three very important departments. First was the model shop, where each ship was built as a scale model before construction began. In this way any obvious mistakes or design faults would show up before too much money had been expended. On the first floor of this building, and stretching its full length, was the moulding shop, where the plans of a ship were reproduced at full scale, ready for work to begin. On the ground floor was the riggers' shed, where the wire hawsers and stays were worked on, together with all the equipment to use with them, blocks and gears for lifting heavy weights. This was a much more cluttered area than the moulding shop above.

Vast quantities of paint were needed, and their flammable nature meant it had to be stored very carefully. The paint shop not only had elaborate protection against fire but actually had members of the city's fire brigade on stand-by, in direct telephone contact with the Central Station.

Timber was another flammable substance that had to be stored carefully. In the days of sailing ships, shipyards had 'timber ponds' where trees and timber would be floated until required. The move first to iron and then to steel meant that less timber was needed, and it was usually bought in ready cut. It still had to be kept until it was thoroughly seasoned, usually under cover in well-ventilated sheds. As ships' accommodation became more luxurious, more exotic and more expensive, wood was bought for the fittings of the cabins and drawing-rooms.

Between the timber yard and the fitting-out basin was the joiners' shop. This too was a large building, 200 feet by 130 feet, fitted with electrically powered machinery for making the furnishings of the ship. It contained nearly three hundred joiners' benches. The reason for its positioning so near the fitting-out basin is that the furnishings could be transferred directly to the ship, with little danger of their being damaged.

Although by this time only steel ships were being built by Workman Clark, a significant amount of woodwork was still required. This was carried out in the carpenters' shop. Specialist work, such as the making of wooden masts, spars and other specifically maritime work, was carried out in the spar shed, which is beside the carpenters' shop.

There were two platers' sheds. In the first, steel bars were heated in the furnace and bent to shape. When that was done the bars were taken to punching machines and the holes made in preparation for the riveting. The second platers' shed contained punching and planing machines as well as rollers for flattening steel plates. One set of these rollers was more than 30 feet long and capable of cold-rolling steel 1½ inches thick; the top roller in this set weighed 40 tons. Also in the platers' shed were furnaces to deal with plates and frames. The plate furnace was capable of heating a sheet 30 feet by 7 feet. The furnaces were heated by gas, and there was a light railway system in the shed for moving the plates and frames about. A bevelling machine near the furnaces bent the frames while they were hot, working to much tighter tolerances than manual labour would be able to do. One hydraulic machine punched manholes in plates. Another 'joggled' them, putting in a lip that would allow plates to overlap, creating a better join. This process saved a great deal of weight in ships, which could then be used to carry more cargo. The plate was then finished off to size. Among other machines in the shed was a set of shears that could cut the heaviest girders to length.

In an annex to the platers' shed was the beam shed. Here the heaviest T-beams could be bent and cut to shape. When they were ready the beams would be riveted to skids before the self-powered cranes lifted them and moved them to the vessels. By the use of machinery it was possible for these very heavy loads to be moved by two men.

The smiths' shop had forty blacksmiths' furnaces operating, powered by large electric fans, as well as steam hammers. Jib cranes using hydraulic lifts were used to move the forgings about.

The building berths were the places where the ships gradually took shape. There were five of these in the North Yard. Because the ground in both yards consisted of deep deposits of clay, it was necessary to sink many piles deep into the mud to make sure the berths were completely stable. Beside each were a number of derricks, each about 150 feet high, which allowed heavy weights to be loaded into the ships while they were still being built. The vessel took shape as plates were attached to the internal frames. Each 'strake', or line of frames, stretched from the bow to the stern; to this each plate was attached with rivets. In the old days, when ships were much smaller, rivets would be heated and then hammered tight by a man with a hammer. By this time plates had become so heavy that this work was beyond the strength of most men. Hydraulic riveters had to be used, particularly with the 'sheerstrake' or top strake, which was attached to the deck.

Almost all the machinery in the works was electrically driven, and to provide the power for this, together with the lighting that was needed, the North Yard had its own power station. The engines driving the two generators were both made by the firm. To power them were five boilers, which produced enough steam to have some left over for general use around the yard.

The South Yard duplicated many of the facilities of the North Yard but had a few additional ones. The sawmill was close to a timber unloading jetty and had all the equipment needed for converting raw wood into the timber needed for ships. The main difference with the North Yard was the concentration on repairs. At the beginning of the twentieth century the 820-foot Alexander Graving-Dock was in operation, but the other docks were much smaller. Another dock was at the planning stage. The crane on the jetty was large for the time, capable of lifting 100 tons.

The last major feature in the South Yard was the building that housed the engine and boiler works. Here too there was good headroom and an adequate supply of cranes to ensure that very heavy weights could be moved around safely. It had its own generation plant, also made by the firm, capable of producing both reciprocating and turbine engines.

Fittings to be used on the hull, such as winch piping, steering gear, steam heating and so on, were made in the fitters' shop. The arrays of lathes, boring and planing machines were also used to maintain and repair other machinery used in the shipyard.

When ships were launched they consisted of little more than the bare hull and decks. Tugs brought them to the fitting-out basin, which was about 1,000 feet long, 200 feet wide, and deep enough to take even the biggest ships. Its wharves had to be very strong to take the weight of the cranes and the machinery that had to be transferred to the ship during the fitting-out process.

By now Workman Clark was producing nearly half the tonnage of its larger neighbour and was number six in the list of the United Kingdom's shipbuilders. The soubriquet 'Wee Yard' was only relative.

A problem for all the shipbuilding firms operating in Belfast was finding skilled labour, and this persisted well into the twentieth century. Although there were large numbers of unemployed men in Belfast, there were few who had a background in engineering. The rest of Ireland was much the same, and so it was to Scotland and the north of England that the Belfast shipbuilders had to go to recruit men with the requisite skills. It was not easy to do, as most people in Great Britain saw Ireland as a foreign and a hostile land and did not take the time to differentiate between Ulster and the rest of the country. The recent history of riots in

Belfast saw to that. Also, the fact that there were only two employers meant that security of employment was even more tenuous than usual. Yet they came, and they came in such numbers that when Harland and Wolff established its own engine works it was called the 'English' works, because of the number of Englishmen employed in it. The wages were no better than in other shipbuilding areas, but the cost of living was much lower. Because of the housing problems earlier in the century, Belfast now had a stock of quality houses at reasonable rent. Food was cheaper for Scottish workers moving to Belfast but about the same for English workers. The main difference was the amount of work that was available for women. By having his wife work in one of the linen mills, a riveter could enjoy a much higher standard of living than he would have on Wearside.

There was one lasting legacy of this influx of skilled workers. Skilled workers were hard to come by and were paid very good wages. Unskilled workers were everywhere and could be recruited locally, and they could be paid a pittance. The resentment of the home-grown labourer for the mollycoddled blow-in was inevitable, and persistent. It was the cause of much unrest in the early twentieth century.

In 1884 William Pirrie took effectual control of Harland and Wolff, of which he had been a partner for ten years. One of his first acts was to extend the arrangements that had existed with the White Star Line—whereby ships were charged at cost plus a fixed percentage—to other favoured customers. This select group became known informally as the Commission Club, and it operated within an increasingly complicated system of mutual shareholdings and directorships between shipbuilder and customer that culminated in Harland and Wolff becoming part of the International Maritime Marine Syndicate in 1902. This may have ensured enough of the work in which the yard specialised but it had within it a worm that threatened to destroy Harland and Wolff forty years later. Because there was a guaranteed profit in every contract, there was no need to keep a tight grip on costs. When costs got out of hand in the 1920s there was no culture of limiting expenditure, and the effect on fixed-price contracts would be very nearly fatal.

Between 1880 and 1914 Harland and Wolff frequently expanded the yard and re-equipped to meet the needs of larger and more luxurious passenger liners. It invested in huge gantries for the Olympic-class liners. Even then demand outstripped the ability of Queen's Island's to meet it, and the firm would find it necessary to set up repair facilities in Liverpool and Southampton, as well as building yards on the Clyde.

The century ended as it began, with a clamour for improvements in the harbour. By 1894 all available land along the Victoria Channel was being used for docks or for shipbuilding. That there was need for more land was universally agreed, but there was a great debate about its location. There were sloblands that could be reclaimed on both sides of the river. It had been policy to site commerce on the County Antrim shore, where quays would be convenient for the heart of the city. On the County Down shore, on the other hand, the remains of the old river bed made a good start to a new channel, and this time the County Down advocates won the argument. The Musgrave Channel was begun in 1899 and completed in 1903. Its spoil was used to create 140 acres of new land.

The Ballast Board could look back on a century or more of local achievement. Belfast was not only the largest port in Ireland but was the world leader in shipbuilding. Thousands were directly employed in the docks and the shipyards. Belfast firms owned two hundred ships, totalling 300,000 tons, and keeping these operational was a task that provided employment not only for sailors but for chandlers and agents. Lubricating it all was an excellent banking service. Middle-aged businessmen could smoke their cigars after dinner and drink the best of port while looking forward to the twentieth century. They had come a long way from the man on the Long Bridge.

Chapter 3

DIVERGING COMMUNITIES: BELFAST AFTER 1850

Part of the reason for good relations between Catholics and Protestants in the late eighteenth century and into the nineteenth century was that the Catholic community in Belfast was relatively small. This changed as the nineteenth century went on and an increasing number of Catholics moved to the town in search of work.

The presence of the Orange Order and the political tensions caused by such issues as Catholic emancipation and, later, the debate about the repeal of the Act of Union sparked several incidents and might have caused more but for the fact that the Catholic clergy worked hard in the cause of community relations. An example was Bishop William Crolly, who was appointed Bishop of Down and Connor in 1825. He was an original supporter of the non-denominational Lancaster Street and Brown Street schools. Even when he was voted off the governing committee and started his own denominational Sunday school in St Patrick's Church he felt that there was a value in religiously integrated schools. When in 1831 the National Board for Education was set up to establish non-denominational schools he welcomed the development. Catholic and Protestant communities supported one another in their appeals to the board. When the Rev. Henry Cooke attacked the new system in 1832, Bishop Crolly came to its defence. There was an acrimonious exchange of letters in the columns of the local newspapers.

Even before the influx of refugees from the Great Famine, the Catholic Church in Belfast had not the organisation to care for its flock. The most populous Catholic district, the area around Smithfield and the Falls Road known as the Pound, did not have a church building of its own, and residents of the Pound, if they wished to attend mass on Sundays, had to make their way to St Mary's in Chapel Lane or St Patrick's in Donegall Street. The Catholic Bishop of Belfast in 1841, Bishop Cornelius Denvir, claimed that so many people wanted to go to church on Sundays the chapel yards and even surrounding streets were crowded with worshippers, who had to kneel in the open air during the service, no matter how bad the weather.

The situation was relieved somewhat in 1844 when St Malachy's Church was opened in Joy Street. Although it alleviated a little of the crowding in the town, the church was built to serve the Markets area. The Pound still had no church of its own.

The town's Catholic population needed more than buildings. As late as 1856 there were still only four priests in Belfast, to serve a Catholic community estimated at forty thousand. It may be that Bishop Denvir was a poor organiser; it is certainly true that he was reluctant to do anything that might provoke a Protestant backlash. He allowed only one religious order into the diocese, the Sisters of Mercy, who were running a girls' school in Callender Street, near the town centre. From 1854 they also ran evening classes for girls and young women working in the mills. Within the Pound itself there were no Catholic schools. Even by 1859 there were only two Catholic-managed schools in the district, both of them run by lay people connected with the Society of St Vincent de Paul, although there were three other Catholic schools on the periphery. Some children attended the non-denominational Model School on the Falls Road or even Protestant-managed schools elsewhere. Some simply attended Sunday school, also organised by the Society of St Vincent de Paul, where there was some basic secular education as well as religious instruction.

When attendance figures for the schools are examined it becomes obvious that education was not seen as a priority in most families. Of the two Catholic schools within the Pound, one had an attendance of less than 43 per cent, while the rate for the second, a boys' school, was 24 per cent. It can only be assumed that parents had a greater need for their children to be at home or at work.

Taking Belfast as a whole, the situation was not much better, either in enrolment or attendance. The Primate of Ireland, Archbishop Joseph Dixon of Armagh, complained in 1861 that only 2,370 Catholic children out of the estimated 12,000 in Belfast were enrolled in Catholic-managed schools. There was a feeling that great numbers of the Catholic community were being lost to the church. As we shall see, there was some substance to this fear. Cardinal Paul Cullen, who had been Archbishop of Armagh before being transferred to Dublin in 1852, used the influence he had gained from being rector of the Irish College in Rome to send Redemptorists and other missionary orders into pockets where there had been conversions to Protestantism. One reason given for these small communities falling away was that during the years of hunger the price of soup was the renouncing of the Catholic faith. In Catholic Ireland, accepting a bribe or taking the easy way out was known until recently as 'taking the soup.'

Cardinal Cullen did not limit his efforts to countering conversions. He said that Protestants could never be trusted, and that he had never dined with one. Later he relaxed this policy to some extent and shared a meal with the Prince of Wales; but most Protestants viewed him askance and considered his comments a threat to their freedoms.

Meanwhile Belfast's Protestant community, after some years in which it had to come to terms with the after-effects of famine and plague, was entering a period of spiritual renewal. That is not to say that the years since the epidemics of typhoid and cholera had been altogether quiet. One of the less pleasant aspects of rural life that had been brought to the town with economic migrants was the organised bigotry that had been a feature of Ulster country life since the late eighteenth century. On the Protestant side this manifested itself in the growth of the Orange Order. There were riots on 12 July 1852, mostly at the interface between Sandy Row and the Pound. There were other incidents, however, involving people expelled from their homes and workers attacked in mills or on their way between work and home. These activities of the 'lower classes' were not supported by the Protestant middle class.

There was substantial support for the Orange Order, and by 1856 there were forty-two lodges in Belfast. It was an Orange parade on 12 July 1857 that led to serious rioting. The parade was unofficial, as such demonstrations were prohibited by the Party Processions (Ireland) Act (1850). Orangemen, wearing no regalia and accompanied by their womenfolk, made their way to Christ Church, close to the notional boundary between Sandy Row and the Pound, where the congregation was addressed by the Rev. Drew. His sermon had two themes. Firstly, Protestants had been and still were being tortured and killed by Catholics, at the instigation of the Pope. Secondly, the needs of business should not be allowed to interfere with the overriding duty of every Protestant to support Protestantism. He urged wives to ensure that their husbands lived up to this principle.

Outside, things were quiet. Across the way, a large group of Catholics watched as the congregation filed out of the church. A substantial detachment of police stood between them, ready for trouble. And there might well have been trouble, but for a moment of drama that descended into farce. Out of nowhere a man rode his horse straight at the Catholic crowd, waving an orange lily about his head. Instantly he was dragged from his horse, and he might well have been beaten to death if the police had not reached him in time. It was only when they got him clear that they discovered that he was a Catholic, named Logan, who was very drunk. Both crowds went home.

The rest of the day was quiet, although there was a great deal of firing of guns in the air. This went on all the next day, the 13th, and by that evening crowds had built up on both sides of the boundary. Finally, on the evening of 14 July, attacks were being made by both sides and shots were being fired on both sides. It became obvious that both had made preparations. Each had made firing platforms, with loopholes for aiming through, from rubble lying around. All the street lighting was extinguished. In spite of the belligerent nature of these tactics, or perhaps because one cancelled out the other, this long-range sniper fire was completely ineffective. The only casualties caused by firearms occurred when a man from Sandy Row managed to get past the Pound's defenders. He found two children playing in the street and shot them both. One, a girl, was shot through the eye but survived. Her friend, a boy, was shot in the leg, which had to be amputated.

Most damage was done where one community impinged upon the other. Protestant tenants of the Catholic landlord William Watson were forced by their co-religionists to leave their houses in Albert Crescent. As soon as they were clear the Sandy Row mob attacked the houses and tried to destroy them. The mob then turned its attention to May Street, where they tried to wreck the house of every Catholic. The mob from the Pound retaliated, not by protecting the Catholics of May Street but by attacking the homes of Protestants living in Lemon Street, all of which were destroyed.

In some of these affrays people from the Pound felt that the police were excessively lenient towards the Sandy Row mob and began to see them as targets as well, and by the end of the week the police would not enter the Pound without military support. Several Catholics who lived in Sandy Row were intimidated out of it; others were attacked on their way to work in the area. Most of those intimidated gave evidence to the commission of inquiry that was set up after the riots. There were claims that similar incidents of intimidation had taken place in the Pound, but none of these victims were named, nor did they give evidence before the commission.

At about this time the Rev. William McIlwaine announced his intention of preaching a series of 'sermons for Catholics' on the steps of the Custom House. His theme was to be the errors of Rome. Although he had begun his preparations before the riots, some people of influence persuaded him that, in the circumstances, to go ahead with the sermons would be inflammatory. He agreed to postpone them.

The riots died down after a week or so. Belfast was quiet until the end of August, when the Rev. McIlwaine announced that he would now deliver his sermons at the Custom House Steps and that he would be accompanied by the Rev. William Drew of Christ Church. Once again pressure was put on them by the leaders of the Protestant community and they decided to postpone them further. The Rev. Hugh Hanna—'Roaring Hanna'—took the opportunity to step into the breach. The gentry and magistrates of the town were horrified, and Hanna too was persuaded to stand down. This was not to the liking of the Protestant crowd, who expected more from him. He was greeted by hoots and catcalls and, preferring the displeasure of the gentlefolk to the derision of the mob, he changed his mind yet again and decided to go ahead with the sermons. In the final report on the riots this decision was said to prove that the Rev. Hanna danced to the tune of the extreme Protestant faction and was not—as he liked to portray himself—their leader and defender.

The expected resurgence in rioting lasted for the rest of the month and continued well into September. There were fights at the Custom House Steps, where Catholic crowds were opposed by workers from the shipyards armed with staves. Even at this early stage there was an identification of the men from the yards with the Protestant cause. There were also the usual disturbances at the boundaries of the Pound and Sandy Row.

These riots were different from those in July in one particular way. Both sides had more middle-class support, although at this point it was usually moral support. The Protestant middle class felt that the open-air sermons were religious services and therefore should have been allowed to go ahead. Men of means on the Catholic side were dismayed at the lack of protection that the police and the authorities gave to the Catholic minority. They took up collections to pay the fines of Catholic rioters; £90 was collected in July, while £60 was collected in one day in September.

At a distance of 150 years it is difficult for someone who has come through the liberal education of the late twentieth century to understand the intensity of the language used by the Protestant clergy at that time. At a time when religions other than Judaeo-Christian orthodoxy were the sole preserve of the scholar, it was presumed that Catholicism and Protestantism stood in direct opposition to one another. Perhaps the most prominent church still to espouse the cause of Protestantism in this way is the Free Presbyterian Church in its Ulster manifestation. The Rev. Ian Paisley, its head, believes that God speaks directly to him in the words of the Bible and that he helps others by preaching the word of God to them. He believes that the Pope is the Anti-Christ, in the sense that the Pope has usurped the position of Christ. (Interestingly, the Pope gives himself the same title in words that imply a different judgement: he is the Vicar of Christ, where 'vicar' means 'acting in the person of'.) For Paisley, the Pope and Rome do not simply offer false teaching: they persecute true Christians. If there is no evidence of them doing this it simply means they are getting better at it. Worse, the religion practised by Rome is not Christian but Babylonian in origin. Paisley takes the words of St Paul, 'Abstain from all appearance of evil,' to mean that born-again Christians must avoid the contamination and confusion of the mind by keeping themselves separate from the polluting hand of Rome.

These views may seem extraordinary, but they were widely held in Belfast in the 1850s. England was no more liberal. In the popular novel *Lorna Doone*, published only in 1869, the proof of the evil in the Doone clan is that they are Catholics. The Protestant clergy of Belfast were men of their time.

The growing solidarity between the Catholic middle class and working class expressed itself in other ways. This was the year that saw the opening of the Catholic Institute in Hercules Place, whose aim was to provide for the educational and recreational needs of Catholics at rates even the poorest could afford. In it there were concerts, and an annual St Patrick's Day dinner. There were even rooms for visiting clergy. It was representative of the whole spectrum of Catholic society in Belfast.

Two years later, in 1859, there was a significant development. Among Protestants there was a religious revival, with people accepting the belief that salvation was the result of the sacrifice of Jesus Christ, who chose whom he wanted to save; and for those who accepted this offer, Heaven was their reward. The same thing had happened in America and had come to Ulster at Kells, County Antrim, where prayer meetings had become revival meetings. From there it came to Belfast. The congregation at revival meetings were urged to make themselves open to a personal conversion experience and to bear in mind those things that showed the difference between Protestant and Catholic. Although there were some Catholic converts, the revival probably succeeded because of the extent of its anti-Catholicism. The services were held in churches, but the conversion experience itself was independent of clergy and beyond the control of the churches.

One important influence was the Rev. Hugh Hanna. He conducted daily services in his Berry Street Church and was 'adulated by women.' Many women who had experienced conversion asked him to come to their home so that they could get his advice and pray together. The *Banner of Ulster* reported that Hanna was 'most assiduous in his attendance on them,' and it is a matter of record that the majority of conversion experiences in Belfast in 1859 happened to women.

The Catholic clergy were concerned about the claim that Catholics were being converted. They were already worried that there were not enough places for Catholic children at Catholic schools, and that membership of the church would be eroded if Catholic children went to schools where the ethos was Protestant. As well as this, Catholic authorities have always been wary of enthusiasms, because, although they can encourage piety, they are very difficult to control. The *Banner of Ulster* claimed that Catholic priests were being brought in by the families of converts to persuade them to remain Catholic. There were reports that a girl had sent for Hanna but that a priest was brought instead. The girl sent him off, the newspaper noted with approval. Another such convert was allegedly told by her Catholic family that she would have water thrown over her if she continued to show signs of heresy. Finally, it was claimed that Catholic managers in places of work would dismiss workers who were reading the Bible. Some of these reports may have been true, because at least one such case came to court. A girl who was eleven days short of the the age of consent was ordered by the court to stay with her mother rather than go to the Rev. Hanna's church, where she had converted. The mother put her in a Dublin penitentiary. When the girl was released she made her way to Berry Street, where Hanna found her a position with a respectable Presbyterian. The girl's mother organised a gang to recapture her. They attacked the respectable Presbyterian but did not get the girl. The mother was sentenced to a month in prison.

One positive aspect of the revival for the Catholic community was that it took place during the summer. During June and July that year public houses were almost empty, and Protestants concentrated more on their souls than on their sashes. It was illegal anyway to march on the 12th of July, and the season passed without trouble.

The Protestant churches gained as well. Congregations became much bigger, in some cases too big for their church buildings, and a number of new churches were built in the early 1860s. There was a Primitive Wesleyan chapel in Mill Lane, off Sandy Row. The following year Presbyterians opened a new church in Great Victoria Street. Among all the churches there was a growing sense of the unity of the Protestant cause.

Whatever the reason, the next four years passed peacefully, and it was not till 1864 that the next serious trouble occurred. The Orange Order had continued to grow in strength, as it had done since the time of the Great Famine. During the year the decision was taken that the order was ready to form a Belfast Grand Lodge. Meanwhile the Catholics of Belfast were becoming more openly nationalist, in that they saw their future as part of the entire island of Ireland. When the foundation stone for a monument to Daniel O'Connell was to be laid in Dublin, on 7 August, many Belfast Catholics took advantage of the Ulster Railway, which had its terminus in Great Victoria Street, to join in the celebration.

Daniel O'Connell was not popular among Belfast's Protestants. Less than a generation before he had had to leave the town under the protection of the Royal Irish Constabulary. Protestants saw no reason to celebrate his memory. The fact that there was going to be a parade in Dublin also rankled, as Belfast had not been able to have an Orange parade for several years. Some people from Sandy Row decided that they would ruin the Catholics' happiness by welcoming them as they returned from their excursion. The train from Dublin had to pass under a road bridge (appropriately named the Boyne Bridge) just before it arrived. The Sandy Row group prepared a large effigy of Daniel O'Connell; around its neck they hung a rosary and on its breast they put a cross. As the Dublin train passed underneath and drew in to the station, the effigy was burned. A large crowd of Protestants, estimated by the police at five thousand, cheered as the flames rose. Reluctant to let the matter go at that, the crowd now began to make their way towards the Pound but were stopped by the police.

That might well have been an end to the affair, but the group from Sandy Row preferred to take the joke a stage further. They organised a mock funeral from Sandy Row to Friar's Bush Cemetery, the Catholic cemetery on the Stranmillis Road. In front they carried a coffin containing the ashes of the burnt effigy, and they told everybody they were going to bury Daniel O'Connell. The gatekeeper at Friar's Bush was having none of it, and they retreated under the threat of his rifle. The fact that they retreated before one man seems to indicate that they were in good humour still and that they viewed the affair as an extended joke. On their way home they emptied the ashes into the Blackstaff River, and most of them dispersed. A few, however, made another attempt to get to the Pound but again were prevented by the police.

Whatever the inhabitants of the Pound thought of the burning of Daniel O'Connell's effigy, they did not consider repeated attempts to invade their territory as a joke. On Tuesday they spent the day preparing their defences. Sure enough, on Wednesday there were skirmishes between Catholic and Protestant groups, though they were confined to Durham Street. In spite of the fact that the police made arrests, these skirmishes went on the next day. Then the Catholics did something that raised the stakes by attacking the Methodist chapel on the Falls Road.

Friday saw the worst trouble so far, with mill girls being assaulted in both districts. Houses were damaged, and a Protestant crowd attacked the Catholic Penitentiary for Fallen Women. Catholics retaliated by attacking the Rev. Cooke's church in Great Victoria Street. In many of the mills work had to be suspended because workers could not get through. At the end of the day some Catholic mill girls who had been at work in Sandy Row were attacked as they tried to go home. Some policemen were there, but they refused to help, even when entreated by the girls. As usual, people were also being intimidated out of their homes.

Not all Protestants were involved in these attacks. The Rev. Isaac Wilson tried to protect some of the Catholic poor who were being driven from the district. He later told the commission of inquiry that he had had to face down a 'hatchet-bearing mob' to allow the refugees to escape. Not all of these were able to find shelter, even in the Pound, and some had to spend the night in the fields beyond the town.

The intimidation of the workers, with the consequent threat to the livelihood of people who had little or no disposable income, raised the stakes once again. The rioting and shooting was the fiercest yet, continuing until first light on Saturday morning.

The weekend remained quiet, but the next day was 15 August—the Feast of the Assumption or Mary Day, an important feast day for Catholics. A large number of navvies, who were not Belfast men but had been brought to Belfast to work at digging the new docks, gathered outside St Malachy's Church in Alfred Street. They then went on the rampage, making for the Protestant district of Brown Square, where they attacked the national school. Workers from Thompson's iron foundry, which was also in Brown Square, saw what was going on and spilled out into the street to defend the school. The navvies retreated towards the Pound; here they encountered men from Sandy Row, but they rallied and soon had the upper hand. But it was now late afternoon and the mills were closing, and Protestant reinforcements arrived, carrying firearms.

The police eventually managed to separate the two factions, but the rioters refused to disperse. Small groups kept making sallies into 'enemy' territory. One large group from the Pound broke away and went towards the town centre, throwing stones as they went. They attacked the Rev. Cooke's church for a second time. Meanwhile a group from Sandy Row was making for St Malachy's. Expecting this attack, men from the Pound had already taken up defensive positions around the building. The Protestants also attacked a nearby convent and the Catholic bishop's house. Open warfare began, and firearms were used freely. There were wounded on both sides, and one of the Catholic casualties died some days later. The shooting continued into the night.

In the morning a group of policemen attempted to escort Catholic workers into Sandy Row. They were met by a stone-throwing mob and forced to retreat. As the police retreated, shots rang out from the Protestant side. The police fired back and two rioters were killed. One was John McConnell, a leading figure in Sandy Row, whose wife had been prominent in preparing the Daniel O'Connell effigy the previous week. By now there was also shooting in the Millfield district, and both sides suffered casualties before the military opened fire and dispersed the mobs.

At this point the shipyard workers entered the picture once more. Several hundred left work and went to Brown Square. The crowd that had already gathered there joined forces with them and attacked Malvern Street National School, which they demolished. They went on into the centre of the town, to High Street. Here they raided gun dealers, although some said that they would return the guns when they were finished, as they knew the dealers were 'the right sort'. Others among them raided hardware shops and armed themselves with spades and shovels. Their target was the docks, but a combination of police and soldiers prevented them getting through.

Back in Great Victoria Street a mob from Sandy Row was waiting for the Dublin train. Someone had spread a rumour that Catholic reinforcements were arriving from the capital. Whether the rumour was true or not, no attempt was made to distinguish between friend and foe, all the passengers being attacked indiscriminately. There were local police on the scene, but they did nothing to intervene.

Next morning police and soldiers saturated Sandy Row and the Pound. Houses were searched, and some guns were found. The trouble was that most guns were in the hands of the shipyard workers, most of whom lived on the other side of the river, in east Belfast. That afternoon they returned to the docks while police and soldiers were busy elsewhere and attacked the navvies. Caught by surprise and overwhelmed by numbers, the navvies were driven into the river. One of their number, who had been hit on the head with a carpenter's adze, died a few days later.

Now that there were deaths on both sides there was a pause until the funerals. There were great contrasts in the way the two communities dealt with these. On the Catholic side, the priests insisted that they would officiate at funerals only if the mourners were restricted to relatives and friends. In every instance this condition was met. For the funeral of John McConnell the arrangements were very different. In spite of the fact that he was involved in starting these riots, his funeral procession was followed not only by Sandy Row residents but by many representatives of the middle-class areas of Belfast. Many were openly, and illegally, carrying firearms. The middle-class residents of Donegall Place, considered one of the better areas in the town, urged the funeral to divert to Castle Place, where a crowd of Catholics was watching. The magistrate supervising the funeral, a man named Lyons, made no effort to insist that the hearse follow its intended route, nor did he order the police to disarm anyone in the funeral procession. Not surprisingly, a riot ensued.

There was no definite end to the riots. A Catholic was shot dead during a sectarian raid in Smithfield the next day. People were exhausted, however, and a peace committee was formed that helped negotiate a return to what passed for normality in Belfast. The authorities were still worried about middle-class involvement in the riots. As McConnell had been killed while he was part of an armed crowd attacking the police, did attendance at his funeral indicate a secret sympathy for mob rule?

As was usual after riots of this nature, a commission of inquiry was set up. (In his testimony, the chairman of Belfast's Police Committee claimed that he could tell a man's religion simply by looking at him.) The commission came to a number of conclusions. The magistrates, who were Conservatives, were criticised for not taking prompt action against the Protestant mob. In a sense, the magistrates only represented the views of the Town Council, which was in the hands of Conservatives. The ruling party was anti-Liberal in politics, anti-liberal in practice and anti-Catholic in intent. The town police were also declared to be sectarian, with 154

Protestants in an establishment of 160. The commission recommended that the force be disbanded and that it be replaced by the Royal Irish Constabulary. Much greater numbers of police were needed, and the figure settled on for Belfast was 480.

This was a momentous decision, as the RIC was an all-Ireland force, with a majority of Catholic members. Many of those to be stationed in Belfast would be from the south of Ireland, and this was resented not only by the Town Council but by most of the local Protestants. It introduced a level of distrust between them and the forces of law and order.

Catholics now began to get on with their lives. Until recently they had been a community defined by nationality rather than religion. The poor organisation of the Catholic clergy and the lack of places in Catholic schools left religion as something to be desired before death rather than something that had a daily relevance. A new bishop was appointed, one who was very different from his predecessor. Bishop Patrick Dorrian was not prepared to maintain a low profile, or to worry about upsetting his Protestant neighbours. He was an ultramontanist, believing in extending the power of the Pope over Catholics; the method he used was to increase his own control over the Catholics of his diocese. He remained unconcerned that this extension of the Pope's powers was exactly what Protestant pastors had been warning their flocks about.

All over Ireland the Catholic clergy had been at work extending their control over the faithful. It has to be remembered that the Catholic Church that arose out of penal times and Catholic emancipation was a very different establishment from that which had co-existed with the native Irish lords for centuries. That earlier Church had been tied to the system of septs and brehon laws. It did not even have a role in matrimony, which remained a civil arrangement in Ireland till Cromwell's time.

The new Church was taking charge, and it fought hard against any link with its old, inferior position; and nowhere had it to fight harder than in Ulster. What might be called 'folk religion'—a combination of superstitions and a belief in the magical powers of the statues and shrines of saints—was prevalent at all levels of Catholic society. Sermons were preached against unseemly practices at wakes. In County Donegal the complaints were against the 'unbounded mirth and festivity'; in County Armagh the priests were against 'tricks and pastimes quite unbecoming,' which could be sexually suggestive or could involve the corpse being dealt a hand of cards, having a pipe stuck in his mouth or even being taken onto the floor for a dance. Efforts were made to substitute hymns for the keening that was traditional at funerals. Pilgrimages were stopped or strictly controlled. The pagan fires of St John's Eve, around which people danced at Midsummer, were described as an occasion of sin (and may well have led to occasional sins). Dancing at the crossroads and the dubious sport of cock-fighting were condemned from the altar in Duneane, near Toome. In Rostrevor 'gatherings for the purpose of amusement' were stopped by the clergy. Rates of 'illegitimacy' among Ulster Catholics were much higher than among Catholics in the other three provinces, and the priests were determined to do something about it.

The Catholic Church was becoming puritanical. Puritanism, indeed, was a feature of both the Protestant religious revival of the 1850s and the later Catholic revival. They were alike in more ways than this. Both laid a great emphasis on the primacy of faith; both were triumphalist in nature and encouraged a spirit of religious fervour. Regular prayer and regular attendance at services were encouraged. They were against promiscuity in sexual matters and intemperance in the consumption of alcohol. Both sets of clergy saw it as their duty to condemn pernicious books, just as Pope Pius IX condemned pernicious thinking in his encyclical of 1864, *Syllabus of Errors*. Both sides even accepted the idea of infallibility, though one group vested it in the Bible while the other gave it to the Papacy. Even the Catholics accepted the literal truth of the Bible. Sadly, however, it was what divided them that the two communities concentrated on, rather than what they had in common.

Bishop Dorrian quickly demonstrated his energy. In May 1865 he organised a general mission for the Catholics of Belfast. Twenty-four extra priests were drafted in and heard confessions ten hours a day. By the end of the month it was estimated that twenty thousand confessions had been heard—and that many of those who made confession had done so for the first time. Catholics of the town were made to feel that they were members of a confident, growing congregation.

The next thing to be addressed was the lack of church accommodation. In the past it had been impossible for everyone wishing to go to mass to find room in a church. Bishop Dorrian commissioned the building of St Peter's Cathedral near the Falls Road, capable of seating three thousand people. It had a grand opening in 1866. Haydn's Mass No. 3 was sung with full orchestral accompaniment, while two cardinals and twelve bishops officiated. Entry was by subscription, at 10 shillings for seats in the nave, with cheaper seats in the aisles costing 5 shillings. Although few residents of the Pound could have afforded these charges, there were special trains to bring people from as far away as Cookstown and south Derry. The local people were more likely to attend the evening service, when the charge for admission was 2 shillings and 6 pence or 1 shilling. Several hundred had to be turned away for lack of room.

Cardinal Cullen presided, vespers were sung and a sermon preached by Bishop John Pius Leahy of Dromore. For people whose lives were bounded by drab streets, the scale of the building, the glory and colour and the majesty of the rituals were a revelation. A means of escape from the pressures of their everyday lives was being shown to them.

Bishop Dorrian kept up the pressure. St Mary's in Chapel Lane and St Patrick's in Donegall Street were replaced by larger, much more ornate buildings. He introduced many Italian devotions to try to embrace a broader section of the population. There was more emphasis on adoration of the Eucharist. People were encouraged to pray to the Virgin and to popular saints for their intercession on the supplicant's behalf. Regular processions were introduced, particularly on the feast of Corpus Christi. The faithful were encouraged to make approved pilgrimages and to make participation in the sacraments a regular part of their lives. Catholic societies were formed. A branch of the charitable Society of St Vincent de Paul was set up in the Pound as early as 1865.

There was one organisation working within the Catholic community of Belfast that Bishop Dorrian was not prepared to tolerate. This was the Fenian movement. The Fenians derived from the Young Ireland revolutionaries, who had made an abortive rising against British rule in 1848. Some of the Young Irelanders had escaped and in 1858 set up an organisation in America that called itself the Fenian Brotherhood. (They adapted the name from that of the Fianna, the mythical warrior bands of ancient Ireland. In choosing this name they were attempting to derive their legitimacy from a time before Ireland was conquered by the English—before, indeed, Ireland had become Christian.) One of the escaped revolutionaries, James Stephens, who had returned to Ireland in 1856 and had kept low to begin with, set up a parallel secret organisation in Ireland at the same time, which later adopted the name Irish Republican Brotherhood, made up of men who were prepared to use violence in the cause of Irish independence. Because of the methods they were prepared to use, they considered it necessary to maintain secrecy. This secret organisation would be the driving force in bringing about the Easter Rising in Dublin in 1916.

The wider Fenians numbered about a thousand in Belfast in 1865. How many of these were in the secret brotherhood it is harder to estimate. Certainly, when *habeas corpus* was suspended and Fenians were interned in 1866, the rate of arrest in Belfast was among the highest in Ireland, exceeded only by Dublin and Cork. Before that happened Bishop Dorrian had already moved against them. He denounced them from the pulpit, and he made it a condition of absolution that those making confession who were in the society should leave it. These and other pressures did work, and many did leave the society, though a strong nucleus remained. The arrests in 1866 and further arrests in 1867 finished the movement off in Belfast, as many of those who escaped arrest fled to America. There was no Belfast involvement in the Fenian rising of that year.

Strangely, another organisation that Bishop Dorrian disliked was the Catholic Institute. The problem, as he saw it, was that the institute was under the control of lay people; he described such initiatives as 'Presbyterian' and would have none of it. When he judged the moment right he went on the attack. He demanded that the committee hand over to him complete control of the institute's contents and activities. If they did not comply he offered them two options: they could dissolve the institute, or he would excommunicate each individual member. The institute was dissolved.

Bishop Dorrian's other preoccupation was the provision of Catholic education. Under his predecessor the Sisters of Mercy had opened a girls' school near the town centre, which also arranged evening classes so that young women working in the mills could become literate. The Christian Brothers now opened a boys' school in Barrack Street, near the charity school that already existed there, familiarly known as the Ragged School.

The Protestant community was also changing. In response to the signs of the Catholic Church flexing its muscles, the differences among the Protestant denominations, particularly those between Presbyterians and Episcopalians, were being minimised. A good example of this occurred at the end of the decade, in 1869, when the Church of Ireland, heretofore the state church, was disestablished. All Protestants viewed this as an insult to Protestantism. There were several religious organisations in existence, including self-improvement societies, temperance societies and the Young Men's Christian Association. It is interesting that many of these organisations, whatever their declared aims, most often heard lectures on anti-Catholic themes. The evil of the Papacy had been foretold in the Bible; the watch-word was 'Death rather than the Mass.' The doom of Popery was drawing nigh, the YMCA was told, and Italy would be free of 'Popery, tyranny, priest-craft, Jesuits, monks, nuns, traditions, indulgences, masses, wafer gods and holy water.' The Banner of Ulster recorded that there was great applause when this was announced.

The principal Protestant organisation in Belfast, however, was the Orange Order. Its importance in Ulster's countryside was diminishing, but within Belfast it was going from strength to strength. Between 1850 and 1870 its membership in Belfast increased by 300 per cent, with more than a hundred lodges and four thousand members. Although often thought of simply with regard to anti-Catholic rhetoric and actions, it also performed an important social function within its various districts. During the year a lodge would organise social evenings for its members and their wives. (Membership of the Orange Order was, and is, confined to men.) The occupations of the masters of the lodges make a list of ordinary jobs: spirit grocers, labourers, clerks, mill workers, painters and porters. Members might expect help in finding a job.

The Twelfth of July celebrations were at the core of the lodge's year. The build-up lasted for months, with band rehearsals, and arches to be paid for and erected, while marching in or watching the parade involved the whole community. It was a community festival involving only part of the population, however, based on religious and political conflict. For the rest of Belfast's inhabitants it was 'Croppies, lie down!'

For most of the century Belfast politics reflected the politics of the United Kingdom rather than the rest of Ireland. The Town Council was a contest of Conservative against Liberal, with the Conservatives having a regular majority. In spite of the Catholic population being almost a third of Belfast's total, they played no effectual part in local politics. Up until mid-century they had had a sort of working relationship with the Liberals, but the increasingly sectarian nature of community relations in Belfast was putting even that under strain. The Representation of the People (Ireland) Act (1868)—commonly called the Irish Reform Act—was intended to increase Catholic representation throughout Ireland by extending the franchise. Up till then the property qualification that would entitle a man to vote in parliamentary elections was £8; this was reduced to £4. In Belfast the parliamentary constituency was also extended to match the municipal boundary; this increased the parliamentary electorate from five thousand to approximately twelve thousand. The property qualification for municipal elections remained at £10.

Whereas in the rest of Ireland the Reform Act produced the desired effect and increased the Catholic electorate, Belfast turned out to be an anomaly. The majority of new voters were skilled working men with a tradition of voting Conservative and of supporting the Orange Order. They were vehemently opposed to any arrangement that embraced Catholic voters. By increasing the strength of the Conservatives, the result of the act was to increase sectarianism in Belfast rather than to diminish it. To begin with, however, there was a a hiccup for the Conservatives. The new voters were from the working class, and they were concerned that the gentry who ran the Conservative Party in Belfast did not do enough to advance the interests of the Protestant working class. They decided to form an association to appoint a candidate specifically to look after their needs, and the Belfast Protestant Working Men's Association was formed.

The specific issue on which they wanted action was the Party Processions (Ireland) Act (1850). This had been introduced in response to the massacre of Catholics by Orangemen in the incident dignified in Orange song and mythology as the Battle of Dolly's Brae. To prevent provocative marches by Orangemen, Orange marches were banned altogether. This was much resented by the Protestants of Belfast, whose leading social institution was the Orange lodge and whose central social event of the year was the Twelfth of July procession. Most working-class

Protestants felt that their leaders, both in the Grand Orange Lodge of Ireland and in the Conservative Party, were too eager to comply with government diktat. They found their candidate in a man who has gone down in history as William Johnston of Ballykilbeg. The previous year he had defied the act by organising a Twelfth of July procession. When brought to court he had refused to compromise and was sent to jail by a local aristocracy and Conservative leaders who said it was their intention to enforce the act. Johnston immediately became a local hero.

The Conservative establishment was horrified at the new organisation and at Johnston's presumption. The Ulster Protestant Defence Association, which had been formed to defend the Church of Ireland as the established church, claimed that Johnston's candidature was a Papist and Liberal plot to divide Protestants. They mobilised their support as best they could, but they were fighting a losing battle, in several ways. Firstly, they chose the wrong issue on which to fight. Although working-class Protestants viewed the disestablishment of the Church of Ireland with distaste as a slur on Protestants, it was a theoretical issue, not one that would make any change in the everyday life of Sandy Row. Johnston's message, in contrast, was unashamedly populist. He claimed that the Orange aristocracy was out of touch with the ordinary Orangeman and was more concerned with position and privilege than with the wishes of the people. His supporters compared them to those who, before the Siege of Derry, had wanted to come to an accommodation with the Jacobite forces. By the end of his campaign it was said that there was not a voter in Sandy Row who was not pledged to Johnston.

The second mistake the establishment made was to underestimate Johnston's political cunning and ruthlessness. Lacking money himself, he approached the Liberal candidate, Thomas McClure, and they came to an agreement: McClure would finance Johnston's campaign, and Johnston would use his influence to get McClure elected.

It is tempting to think that the Protestant working-class voice that was the Belfast Protestant Working Men's Association might have been the first step towards working-class solidarity in Belfast. In Britain at this time many liberal workingmen's organisations were being formed, whose primary care was for the economic well-being of their members. In Belfast this was not to be. Even with Johnston's support, McClure was despised by working-class Protestants as too soft towards Catholics. Johnston's supporters even attacked McClure's rooms; and Johnston, when he saw he way the wind was blowing, repudiated any links with McClure. It is probably truer to say that the BPWMA was not really set up in opposition to the aristocratic end of the Orange Order but rather was to remind those aristocrats of the necessity for pan-Protestantism, of the necessity to accommodate all Protestants, including the working class, within the establishment. The Conservative Party in Belfast, realising this, later came to an agreement that the BPWMA would in future be consulted about the choice of candidates for parliamentary elections.

After Johnston was elected, many of his supporters gathered in Sandy Row, ready to invade the Pound. The police and a timely shower of rain dissuaded them from doing so.

It is not altogether certain that Johnston himself would have supported the attack on the Pound. He was something of an enigma. Although he detested Popery, he had many Catholic tenants and was a good landlord. After being elected to Parliament in 1868 he declared:

> My Catholic fellow-countrymen have not misunderstood me. My conduct was not an insult or a scorn to them. It was a defence of the Protestants of Ireland.

It seems likely that he believed in equal marching rights for both communities. Certainly, for some years after his election there seem to have been improved community relations in Belfast, with neither side doing anything to provoke the other. This is particularly noteworthy as, in 1869, the Church of Ireland was finally disestablished, something that would normally have fired Protestant anger. Similarly, the mass demonstrations of Catholics demanding an amnesty for Fenian prisoners that were held in the same year did not provoke a reaction.

In 1870 two Catholic newspapers, the *Northern Star* and the *Ulster Examiner,* asserted that the improvement in relations was the result of the influence of William Johnston and the BPWMA. In the same year Johnston successfully introduced a private member's bill to repeal the Party Processions Act. He was to remain in Parliament for some years before resigning in 1878 to take up the post of Inspector of Fisheries and was subsequently involved in many issues that went beyond the confines of Belfast politics (one of these, interestingly, the introduction of the Plimsoll line).

Back in Belfast, however, the calm did not last long. The Party Processions Act had lapsed in 1872, and in that year the Twelfth of July procession passed off peacefully, though heavy rain that caused flooding in Sandy Row may have dampened the day's enjoyment.

There were many new developments among the Catholics of Belfast. A Belfast Home Rule Association was formed that year. Many of its early leaders had been involved with the Fenians, but Fenianism had been a broad church, and membership did not necessarily mean that an individual supported violence. Also during the same year the Catholic Young Men's Association was set up. Although this was a non-political organisation, with a reading-room for its members and an ethos of self-improvement, its first president was John Duddy, who was also involved in the Belfast Home Rule Association.

A third organisation that became prominent at this time was the Ancient Order of Hibernians. This organisation is almost a mirror image of the Orange Order, complete with sashes (green rather than orange) and banners. It was it that organised what was to be the town's first nationalist parade, out to Hannahstown, on 15 August. The numbers of those who marched suggest that there were more than Hibernians taking part. The man chosen to lead the parade was James Biggar, a town councillor, chairman of the Board of Water Commissioners and president of the Belfast Home Rule Association. His presence allowed various authorities to describe the occasion as a 'home rule march'. Certainly some banners displayed the slogan *Remember 1798,* while others showed the Irish harp without a crown, symbolising independence from British authority.

Huge crowds gathered in the Pound, at the town end of the Falls Road and in Hercules Street. Their plan had been to start from Carlisle Circus. The Rev. Hanna objected, saying that he feared for the safety of his new church, St Enoch's Presbyterian Church in Berry Street. It was eight years to the day, after all, since navvies had attacked nearby Brown Square School. Encouraged by Hanna, a Protestant crowd gathered in Carlisle Circus and attacked the parade. The police asked Biggar to change his route, and he complied. The Catholics moved to the Linen Hall and left from there to go along Divis Street, making for the Falls Road and Hannahstown. At the top of Divis Street, where it becomes the Falls Road, there was an open area dividing the Falls from the Shankill Road, known as the Brickfields, roughly where Durham Street now stands. Here there was an ambush by Protestants, who attacked the parade with clubs, bricks, bottles and guns. But the parade was too large to be stopped, and at least thirty thousand people made it to Hannahstown. Here they heard Biggar speak in favour of an amnesty for Fenian prisoners and of a government of Ireland that was independent of Britain.

Guns were brought out and distributed, so that the parade could be defended on its way back. In the excitement of distributing and arming them, one man wounded himself fatally.

While this was going on, the town centre was still experiencing difficulties. Some five hundred shipyard workers had left work early and were now making for Carlisle Circus, for the ostensible purpose of guarding St Enoch's. Prevented from getting there, they rampaged through the town and attempted to attack Hercules Street. In a running battle, the police beat them back, but Head Constable Irwin was seriously injured when he was hit by a cudgel.

The Hannahstown parade, flanked now by armed men ready to defend it, made it back unmolested to Belfast, where it dispersed quietly. The mob around Carlisle Circus did not. The Rev. Hanna was carried shoulder-high through the Shankill area, on the northern edge of the town. The town itself was quiet for most of the evening, but about ten o'clock a group emerged from Sandy Row. They brought tar barrels with them, which they lit on the top of the Boyne Bridge, with the intention of rolling them into the Pound. There were clashes near the terminal of the Ulster Railway in Great Victoria Street. The police intervened, and the mob turned its attention to the police barracks, where they managed to break most of the windows. By midnight the casualty wards of the General Hospital were full.

Next day was Friday. It began with shots being fired at people going to their places of work, and several were wounded. Around noon Catholics were driven out of their homes in Malvern Street, off the Shankill Road. By early evening about three thousand men were involved in sectarian stone-throwing. Later in the evening Catholics wrecked St Stephen's Church in Millfield. At Trinity Church in Stanhope Street the sexton decided that the building was under threat and tolled the church bell for reinforcements. Thousands of Protestants came to the scene. It took several charges of mounted police, during which at least two men were killed, before order was restored to an acceptable degree.

Overnight it became obvious that order had not been completely achieved. Catholic-owned public houses on the Shankill Road were looted, and a man was found shot dead on the Falls Road as Saturday morning dawned. Police in the Shankill area fired two volleys in an attempt to disperse the looters, but it required the military to clear the road with a sabre charge. After the mills closed at midday there were many reinforcements to both Protestant and Catholic crowds. By three o'clock the streets were crowded. Magistrates had ordered the public houses closed, but this had little effect, as rioters simply broke into premises and helped themselves. Fighting went on in many places around the town, and the weapons used were various: sticks, stones, spear-headed walking-sticks, skull-crackers, pointed irons, cleavers and bludgeons. The police were forced to discontinue arresting rioters and to concentrate instead on saving life and property.

The worst fighting took place at the Brickfields, where the rival crowds fought with guns. Here the military had the unenviable task of inserting themselves between the combatants. With fixed bayonets, the 78th (Highland) Regiment forced the Catholics back, while the 4th Dragoon Guards charged the Protestants again and again. It was evening before the soldiers managed to disperse the crowds.

Sunday was not a day of rest. One potential flash-point was avoided early on when the priest officiating at the funeral of the man who had shot himself at Hannahstown held the service two hours earlier than the advertised time. There was trouble in Lettuce Street in the Pound, where there was an incursion by an armed gang of Protestants. Shots were exchanged and there were casualties on both sides before the police arrived.

This became the main pattern of rioting over the next few days, of small armed gangs moving around quickly, of quick encounters before one side withdrew or the police intervened. When they were not making incursions into 'enemy' territory these gangs roamed their own areas, intimidating people of the other religion and wrecking their homes so that they could not return. Most of this wrecking took place in the streets in the border areas of the Shankill and Falls districts, where most of the mixed Catholic and Protestant housing was.

By the end of the rioting the religious dividing lines of Belfast had become abrupt. It was as if two separate organisms had developed defensive skins in case one contaminated the other. The correspondent of the *Daily Telegraph* (London) reported that the streets themselves looked as if they had been sacked by an invading army. The evictions, on both sides, caused much suffering. There are descriptions in newspapers of families moving aimlessly about the town, carrying all they still possessed in a handcart or across their shoulders.

The seriousness of these riots underlines the importance of the subject that would dominate religious rivalries in Belfast and throughout Ulster for the next fifty years. Home rule was a desire by the Catholic and nationalist people of Ireland to have a devolved parliament sitting in Dublin that would have roughly the same powers as the present Scottish Parliament. At this early stage it was no more than that. There was no clamour, for example, to remove the monarchy, or to have a separate Irish army. There were some, like the Fenians, who wanted complete independence, but they were still in a minority. The feeling of most Catholics was that an Irish parliament would do no more than allow Irishmen to concentrate on Irish affairs, while providing a certain sense of national identity.

The Protestants of Belfast saw home rule as something much more threatening than that. They took no comfort from the fact that the movement had been begun by a Donegal Protestant, Isaac Butt, who was also a loyal Orangeman, nor that another Protestant, this time from County Wicklow, Charles Stewart Parnell, was the current leader of the movement for home rule. Their position within Ireland was as a permanent minority; it was only within the United Kingdom that they became part of a Protestant majority, and it was only within that position that they felt that their 'freedom, religion and laws' would be safe.

But it was more than simply this. Belfast's commercial needs and ambitions were different from those of Dublin or Cork. It had been so since Belfast had established itself as a commercial centre. In the eighteenth century, when Dublin had advocated protection, Belfast had wanted to take its chances in the rough and tumble of free trade. Now more than ever the town saw its commercial and trading future—the wealth of its people, indeed—as being closely linked with Great Britain. To increase the political distance between Britain and Ireland was to risk increasing the commercial difference, and that would be to Belfast's detriment. The importance of this point is that it gave political and commercial rationale to Belfast's anti-Catholicism. From this time on, Protestants became more rigorous in their opposition to any political development that threatened their position in Ulster. They attacked any Catholic procession, of whatever nature. The Protestant mob saw the words *Catholic, nationalist, Fenian* and *home-ruler* as interchangeable, as if they were synonyms. To allow Catholics to march was to allow them to make a claim on the territory that they covered. In Belfast, they were allowed to claim nothing. Every attempt to parade would be opposed.

Shocked at the violence of the August riots, many Catholics were particularly outraged at the fact that there was no *quid pro quo* for the non-interference of Catholics with the Twelfth of July Orange parade. The Protestants had shown that there was going to be no toleration of any Catholic parade. Before the end of the decade even processions by the Holy Family Confraternity were being attacked.

As a response to the riots of 1872 concerned Catholics formed the Ulster Catholic Association. Its name recalled the organisation set up by O'Connell, and its aim was to secure full civil rights and privileges for Catholics. The association was based on parishes and was open to Catholic men aged sixteen and over who were of good character. The *Daily Examiner* supported the campaign. It was necessary, it said, because people felt that all the royal commissions in the country could not protect Catholics from riots. Worse, it seemed as if nothing could prevent discrimination in employment. A Protestant merchant might deal almost exclusively with the Catholic community, yet it was a very rare one who gave a job to a Catholic, even as lowly a job as porter. The newspaper hoped that the new association would build enough clout to bring about change. It proved to be another false hope, however, and the association changed little.

Talks between the mayor and Catholic clergy also seemed to promise an improvement in the condition of Catholics. Although he was a Conservative, James Henderson was aware of the negative publicity the rioting was bringing to Belfast, particularly when it was reported by London newspapers. The clergy were also worried about the riots—not simply because of the harm being done to their flock but because the act of rioting put some of their congregations beyond clerical control. It was agreed that future marches should be outside the town boundaries. This agreement lasted for three years, but in 1875 it broke down. There was nothing Catholics could do about it. Now that Orange marches were legal, they were gaining support even from Protestant liberals and had influential local support. Their numbers were simply too great for Catholics to do anything about it.

Catholics were in an invidious position. Previously, parades on both sides had been illegal, and each side took its chances with the police in arranging one. After 1872 the law protected the right of Protestants to parade. In principle Catholics had the same right, but the reality was that Protestants would react and there would be bloodshed. Catholic leaders, and in particular the clergy, kept a tight rein on any Catholic organisation that might want to exercise its right to march. There were no parades that year. Some commentators suggest that the reason for Catholic docility was that those who lived in the Catholic enclaves had been cowed by the violence of 1872. A more likely reason is the grip that Bishop Dorrian and his priests kept on the faithful, and particularly on their wives. There was also the sense that momentous things were happening beyond Belfast. It was not in Belfast, Bishop Dorrian felt, that the future of Belfast's Catholics would be decided.

The campaign for home rule was becoming more organised, as the resistance of Orange and Conservative to change ensured that it would. The declared aim of the Belfast Home Rule Association was to strengthen the Union of Great Britain and Ireland by granting Ireland a limited measure of self-government within a federal system. An Irish parliament would provide the heart that would develop resources, stimulate trade and stop the tide of emigration, according to the association's president, John Duddy. After the events of 1872, Belfast home-rulers became somewhat less moderate, and by 1876 they were demanding more active measures than were being offered by the Irish Party under Parnell. Belfast wanted more agitation and more obstruction. To that end the Belfast association organised a Home Rule Rally, whose aim was to encourage members of Parliament to greater activity in the next parliamentary session. At the rally they mocked Orange opposition to home rule and pointed out that Orange opposition had not been able to prevent the disestablishment of the Church of Ireland. They neglected to point out that Orange pressure had led to the repeal of the Party Processions Act.

At a rally held later in the year, on 15 August, Duddy demanded that the Irish Party '. . . change their strategy at once, assume the offensive, strike some bold and decisive blow at the power of England which would bring her to a sense of her duty.'

This was a challenge to Parnell's leadership. Parnell responded by coming to Belfast in September 1877. At a meeting of the Belfast Home Rule Association he advocated the tactic of restricting obstructionism to activities within Parliament. If that failed, the members of the Irish Party could return to their constituencies and report that all constitutional methods of righting Ireland's wrongs had been tried and had failed. The responsibility would then be with England. Other methods might then be justified.

Resolutions in favour of obstruction in Parliament were passed unanimously. Although the *Belfast Morning News,* a moderate paper, felt it was wrong to consider all Englishmen as the enemy, there were still elements of the Fenians in Belfast who felt that Parnell was not going far enough. At a home rule meeting in October 1879 the speeches were interrupted by calls of 'Irish republic!' and 'Use the rifle!' Parnell felt that such voices would be more easily controlled inside the movement than outside; he came to an agreement with the Fenian leader, John Devoy, that Fenians could enrol in the Home Rule Association as individuals.

To make it possible to make speeches at home rule meetings without interruption by Fenians, Parnell now adopted the ruse of blurring the degree of self-government that he would accept. It was now possible for an extreme nationalist to imagine that Parnell was working for an Irish republic while others thought he worked towards more limited aims. Several Fenians became active in home rule agitation.

They may have been more active than Parnell intended. In July the Belfast leadership organised a convention of Ulster home-rulers at which two of the motions seemed to be critical of Parnell's leadership. One demanded the nationalisation of land, rather than having it turned over to peasant ownership. The second implied that the national organising committee was not working with as much energy as it might. Parnell wrote to Belfast complaining that he had to be careful, otherwise coercive legislation could be introduced in the south. The Belfast leadership replied that they were used to facing violence for their political beliefs. Parnell was not to be moved: he sent a circular to all Ulster branches of the Home Rule Association condemning the convention. It did not take place.

The Irish National League, which was the all-embracing home rule organisation at that time, organised a meeting in Belfast in January 1885. The purpose was to consider the new distribution of parliamentary seats in Belfast. The Belfast leadership was not consulted. Duddy asked people not to attend the meeting but was ignored. That same month the entire council of the Belfast association resigned, leaving Belfast without a home rule organisation. The gap was soon filled when a branch of the Irish National League was set up early the following year. Father Patrick Convery, who was administrator at St Peter's, was elected president.

The Belfast organisation was now in the safe hands of the Catholic Church and the Dublin home rule establishment. None of the old Belfast leadership would join the branch, and there are indications that memories of the rift hindered recruitment. In 1886 the new leadership got round the problem by allowing three hundred 'ladies' to join, the first branch in Ireland to admit women.

It is an indication of the strength of the grip the clergy had on the Catholic laity that by 1885 there were the following organisations in St Peter's Parish: the Women's Total Abstinence Society, with 1,700 members; the Holy Family Confraternity, with 1,600 members; St Peter's Total Abstinence Society for Youth, with 2,500 boys and 2,400 girls; and St Peter's Mutual Improvement Club, which met every Saturday. The clergy also kept firm control of the activities at St Mary's Hall, which had been built to replace the Catholic Institution. They had even contrived inter-mediate classes at the Christian Brothers' School, so that Catholic boys could now prepare for white-collar jobs or even for the priesthood.

Political Belfast was trying to come to terms with the Representation of the People Act (1884) (commonly called the Third Reform Act). Belfast now had four parliamentary seats. In addition, the franchise had been extended, and members of the Irish National League were active in registering voters and in organising transport to take the old and the infirm to polling stations.

There were elections in November 1885 after the Irish Party brought about the defeat of the Conservative government in London. The Home Rule candidate was Thomas Sexton, a barrister living in Dublin and now standing for West Belfast. The constituency was almost equally divided between the Protestant Shankill area and the Catholic Falls. Sexton lost to the Conservative candidate by thirty-seven votes. In an election the following year he defeated the Conservative, James Horner Haslett, and became Belfast's first home rule MP.

The results of the 1885 election were the more significant. In the House of Commons there was a hung parliament. Although the largest party was the Liberals, no single party could govern without the support of at least one other. It was now that W. E. Gladstone, leader of the Liberal Party, announced that he had been converted to home rule for Ireland. He did this although nearly a hundred MPs in his own party were ideologically opposed to it. Gladstone ignored this opposition and became Prime Minister, with the support of Parnell and with a commitment to home rule.

For almost the whole of the nineteenth century Belfast's Protestants had viewed the activities of their Catholic fellow-citizens with distrust, if not outright suspicion. For much of the time this distrust was atavistic: it was a re-enactment of the religious and ethnic wars of the sixteenth and seventeenth centuries. The matter of home rule was different. As we have seen, Belfast Protestants saw their prosperity and religious freedom as best protected by the continued Union, with one parliament in London. Until now the home rule debate had been a theoretical one, as any form of self-rule for Ireland had been opposed by the leaders of both major parties in Parliament. This cynical betrayal by Gladstone changed matters, as supporters of home rule now had a theoretical majority in the House of Commons. Protestant reaction was swift. There was a spontaneous revival in the Orange Order, with representatives of all levels of society joining the organisation.

In January 1886 Colonel E. J. Saunderson MP formed the Ulster Loyalist Anti-Repeal Union. One of the organisation's first guest speakers was the Conservative Randolph Churchill (father of Winston Churchill). He had spent a time in Dublin as a young man and was sympathetic to the idea of Irish nationalism, and as a member of the Conservative government he had opposed the use of coercion in Ireland. Now that he was in opposition, however, he was determined to get his party back into power, and to use any lever he possessed in doing so. He felt now that Gladstone had given him just the weapon he needed. He wrote to his old friend Lord Justice Fitzgibbon:

> I decided some time ago that if the GOM [Grand Old Man, i.e. Gladstone] went for Home Rule, the Orange Card was the one to play. Please God it may turn out the ace of trumps and not the two.

Churchill was not long entering the affray. In February he was invited to speak to a gathering in the Ulster Hall, Belfast. He said that the Home Rule Bill would plunge a knife into the heart of the British Empire and told the crowd that if they chose to fight they would find many supporters in England. As he had said on landing at Larne on 22 February, 'Ulster will fight, and Ulster will be right.'

He was not the only politician to speak in apocalyptic terms, and, as the date of the vote approached, Belfast Protestants worried about the outcome as if it were the Battle of Armageddon. Orators and newspapers fed the fear that Protestants would become a minority in Ireland, that they would lose both employment and religious freedom. The atmosphere was so tense that it required only a spark to set it off. Belfast is one place where sparks are easily found.

On Friday 4 July, in an otherwise routine fight between a Protestant and a dock labourer who was a Catholic, the labourer allegedly taunted the Protestant that when home rule was passed there would be no work for 'his sort' in Belfast. The exchange probably took place, as it is quoted in the report of the subsequent commission of inquiry. The statement shows how poor an understanding of home rule the Catholic labourer had; the reaction shows how wound-up Protestant nerves were. When workers at the shipyard heard of the taunt, about a hundred of them downed tools and made for the docks. Without hesitation they attacked the dockers, who, spread out as they were along the quays, could not marshal their forces. Attacked piecemeal, they were routed, with ten of them injured seriously enough to require hospital treatment. Some were trapped and had to jump into the water to swim to safety. One, a youth named James Curran, was drowned.

When the rumour of battle reached the Catholics of the Pound and Hercules Street they rallied in support. The police prevented them from attacking those shipyard workers who had to pass close to the Catholic district on their way home to the Shankill Road. Saturday seems to have been quiet, but Curran's funeral on Sunday had to be protected from a Protestant mob. On Monday the mayor, Sir Edward Harland, contacted Dublin Castle with a request for extra soldiers and police. Police were stationed in the Shankill district to protect Catholic public houses, and there were several clashes with excited crowds.

The next day, Tuesday 8 June, the Irish Government Bill (commonly called the First Home Rule Bill) was put to the vote in the House of Commons. Not unexpectedly, ninety-three Liberals defied the leadership, and the bill was defeated by thirty votes.

News of the result was telegraphed to Belfast almost at once. The reactions of the two communities, again not unexpectedly, were very different. Catholics had been warned by their priests to stay indoors. They did so, but many of the residents of the Falls Road deliberately set their chimneys on fire, to lament the result of the vote. Ironically, jubilant Protestants were setting fire to tar barrels and lighting bonfires in celebration. The resulting pall was described as being as thick as a London fog. That evening a crowd attacked the small group of police protecting a Catholic public house near the Brickfields and forced them to retreat. A group of four hundred police reinforcements had just arrived in the station at Great Victoria Street and were sent immediately to support their beleaguered colleagues. Facing a mob throwing stones and window glass, the magistrate read the Riot Act, and the police opened fire with buckshot. There were screams from the crowd of 'Murder the Fenian whores!' Nevertheless the police were able to disengage and retreat to look after their wounded.

The epithet used by the crowd is significant. There was a general belief among Belfast Protestants that the RIC was composed almost entirely of southern Catholics. While this was true for the majority of the rank and file, the officers were almost exclusively Protestant. That cut no ice with the inhabitants of Sandy Row and the Shankill. From this point in the 1886 riots the main enemy became the police. There were still encounters with Catholics, but the main target of violence and invective was now the RIC.

The violence certainly increased, and the cause of peace was not helped by the fact that many of the police on the street were unfamiliar with

Belfast. On the Wednesday there were disturbances in Donegall Street, and most of the available police were sent there. In the Bower's Hill Barracks on the Shankill Road most of the police left were strangers. A liquor store was broken into and people began looting its contents. The police moved to prevent this. At about the same time a group of Protestant workers from Coome's foundry on the Falls Road, who seem to have left work early, came on the scene and were baton-charged by the police. The mob built up to about two thousand. Women brought broken paving-stones to the rioters, carrying them in their aprons. If the stone-throwing waned, women and girls brought more stones to the front and threatened any man who looked as if he was going to stop. Two clergymen, William Johnston and Hugh Hanna, had been trying to calm the crowd. They spoke to the magistrates and arranged that the police would retire to their barracks. The district inspector on the scene reported that as soon as the police began to move towards the barracks the crowd decided that they were retreating and attacked again. The police were forced to take refuge in the barracks anyway, and from here they opened fire on the crowd. The shooting seems to have been indiscriminate. As well as shooting two of the rioters, they killed a serving girl, Mary O'Reilly, who was watching from an upstairs window. James McCormack was killed as he drank in a public house. Minnie McAllister, a clothing worker, was shot as she went about her business, and James Kyle was killed as he ran to her assistance. The firing seems to have gone on after the crowd dispersed.

Another police barracks, this time in the Sandy Row district, was also attacked. The executive committee of the Belfast magistrates had a crisis meeting. It was agreed that the police should not be deployed in Protestant districts and that their place should be taken by the military. This did not prevent disorder the following day, Thursday. Houses were attacked in Great Victoria Street and the Dublin Road. Public houses were attacked in York Street. Worryingly, Bower's Hill Barracks was attacked again. This time some Protestant clergymen and two local men formed a living wall, protecting the barracks until the military arrived. The soldiers were made welcome by the crowd, and the matter seemed to be settled, at least for the time being. In his sermon that Sunday the Rev. Hanna described those shot by the police as martyrs, and blamed both police and government.

The restored peace lasted for more than a month. Even the Orange parade on 12 July passed without serious incident. On the 13th, however, there were clashes on Grosvenor Road, and by evening rival mobs had formed up at the Brickfields. Shortly after the fighting began the Catholics were urged by their clergy to disperse; when police and soldiers arrived and it was obvious that their district would be protected from Protestant invasion, most of them complied. The field was now left to the police and military on one side and the Protestants on the other. One policeman,

Head Constable Gardiner, was deliberately shot and mortally wounded by looters. A soldier of the West Surrey Regiment was also killed. Two rioters were shot dead by the police using buckshot.

There were still angry crowds on the Shankill and Falls the following day, but the Catholics were kept under control by their priest, Father Magee, and the bluster came to nothing. Once again there was a period of peace, but this lasted much less than a month. The Rev. Hanna organised the annual excursion for his Sunday school to take place on Saturday 31 July. The magistrate asked that no bands should accompany the excursion, and Hanna agreed. Unfortunately, two Orange bands turned up at the station to greet the children when they arrived back, and this provoked serious rioting in Carrick Hill. Even before they had got as far as High Street the police were having trouble with some of the drunks who insisted on accompanying the parade. Catholics made matters worse by throwing stones over the police at the bands. From a Protestant point of view it looked as if the police were holding them steady so that they would make an easy target for the Catholics. Rioting developed into looting, and the police once again opened fire in Boundary Street that evening; and yet another Catholic public house was attacked in the Shankill.

On Sunday large numbers of police and military were unable to prevent an attack on Catholic children from St Joseph's parish in York Street as they returned from an excursion. Catholic dockers counter-attacked, and riots involving up to a thousand people raged around York Street for hours. Street lights were extinguished and there were desperate fights in the dark. One observer remarked that the rioters were masters of the tactics of street fighting and that the only way to control them would have been to use artillery. Much of York Street was sacked that night, and when the weekend was finally over, thirteen people had died.

Rioting continued all that week in the Shankill, Ballymacarret, Sandy Row and the Pound. It reached a new intensity the following Saturday, when most of the Catholics working in Harland and Wolff were driven out of the shipyard. The police were trapped in Dover Street, off the Shankill Road, and had to shoot their way out, leaving three Protestants dead. On Sunday the fighting centred on the Springfield area. A total of twelve people were killed that weekend.

The following weekend one of the few Catholics who had remained in Harland and Wolff was seized by Protestants and covered in tar. Rioting broke out again and developed into another gun battle at the Brickfields. The final serious incident occurred when a Catholic crowd attacked Divis Street RIC barracks. The police fired into the crowd, killing one person and injuring others. Shortly after this heavy rain began and lasted for days. The riots, as they did so often, petered out.

A worrying development from the Catholic point of view was that there now seemed to be deliberate connivance by some employers in the intimidation. The Harland and Wolff management made no real effort to help Catholic workers to resume their employment. Equally, known mob leaders were not disciplined. In Ewart's mill, Catholic women were intimidated at their place of work. When the police came to identify the women's attackers they were refused admission by the management and were attacked in their turn by people from inside the mill throwing 'bolts, coal cinders and stones.' There also seems to be evidence of connivance among employers that anyone giving evidence against an attacker would be blacklisted and denied employment anywhere. Some employers stood out against intimidation, but these were a minority. The Society of St Vincent de Paul administered welfare to those Catholics who lost their jobs through intimidation.

An equally worrying development for the authorities was the legitimacy that the Protestant rioters received from the support of many of the middle class. This support seems to have derived in the main from the fact that the Protestant mob was facing the RIC. There was a general belief— openly stated in sermons by Hanna and others—that the administration in Dublin Castle had deliberately drafted in a constabulary of southern Catholics with the intention of crushing any opposition to home rule. This antipathy towards the RIC was also expressed by a Belfast MP, Samuel Wesley de Cobain, in a speech that was widely reported in the press. He said that he had received intelligence from the south that the police had let it be known that they were going north 'to carry a war against a certain class of inhabitant.' He also called the RIC 'liveried assassins'. Even during the riots the Rev. Kane of Christ Church in Sandy Row had told his parishioners that the 'foreign police' wanted an excuse to shoot them. The fact that the local magistrates prevented the RIC from patrolling the Shankill area shows that they did not trust them, as the final report noted. In early August a statement was issued that pointed out that movements of the constabulary were decided by the Constabulary Inspector and not the Chief Secretary in Dublin, but that was too late.

The legitimacy afforded to the rioters by their 'betters' had two results. Firstly, the riots lasted much longer than might have been expected. Secondly, classes of people joined in the fighting who in the past would not have gone near a riot. Foremen from factories and shopkeepers from respectable establishments threw stones at the police with the same enthusiasm as drunks and corner boys, the well-dressed standing shoulder to shoulder with the ragged.

The riots of 1886 were the worst of the century. They were also the last serious ones. The image of the Protestant mob attacking a royal constabulary did no good for the loyalist cause in Great Britain. For six years, however, the danger of home rule seemed to have been averted. The Belfast political establishment made no inflammatory statements. The home rule movement itself was disastrously split when it became known that Parnell had been having a love affair with the wife of one of his fellow-MPS. The Conservative Party treated Irish Catholics with kid gloves. It was only when a general election was called in 1892 that the spectre of a Dublin government was revived. Gladstone let it be known that he would introduce a new Home Rule Bill if he was elected.

Once more the Conservatives reached for the Orange card. More importantly, Ulster's Liberals and Conservatives buried their differences and, in a show of unity, organised a Grand Ulster Unionist Convention to be held in the Botanic Gardens on 17 June 1892. The numbers attending were huge. What was now the Great Northern Railway, which served southern and western Ulster, ran fifteen special trains to Great Victoria Street Station. The Northern Counties Railway, which served Counties Antrim and Derry, brought more than twenty thousand people through York Street Station. Many businesses, including the shipyards, stopped work at eleven o'clock. Great efforts had been made by the organisers to avoid trouble. Remarkably, there were no bands, just people making their way along the streets to the part of the Botanic Gardens closest to the River Lagan. Here the ground is very level and a huge hall, covering more than an acre of ground, had been erected in only three weeks. It has been claimed that it was the biggest structure ever used for a political purpose in Ireland or Britain. The men who entered did not sing; as far as they were concerned, the matter was too important for song.

The Protestant Archbishop of Armagh said the opening prayer, a former Moderator of the Presbyterian Church read the 48th Psalm, and they all sang 'God is our refuge and our strength.' The Duke of Abercorn was the first to speak; but it was Thomas Sinclair's speech that was received best. He predicted that Unionists would ignore a Dublin government if one was to be set up and would continue to run their own affairs. No speaker made a hostile remark about Catholics.

Such self-discipline was to no avail, however, and Gladstone was returned to power. Sure enough, the Irish Government Bill (1893) (commonly called the Second Home Rule Bill) was passed by the House of Commons, a fact that was celebrated in some Catholic areas by the burning of bonfires. When the bill was blocked by the House of Lords, the Unionist establishment, the Orange Order and employers enforced strict discipline to ensure that there was no repeat of the disgraceful behaviour of 1886. Lord Pirrie let it be known that he would not tolerate the expulsion of Catholic workers from the shipyard, and the workers believed him. The Gladstone government did not last very long in any case, and the Conservatives were back in power by 1895.

The rest of the century passed quietly. Belfast was booming, and there was employment for all. A symbol of the future was the White Star liner *Oceanic,* the biggest and longest ship ever built, as elegant as a thorough-bred and with a design speed of 21 knots (24 miles per hour). A stand to hold five thousand spectators was built for its launching ceremony in 1899, and the money raised was donated to the Royal Victoria Hospital. Catholics and Protestants had built it. The question now was, could such co-operation continue into the twentieth century.

Chapter 4 ⌇

EDWARDIAN BELFAST

In 1901 Belfast had a population of 349,000 and still growing, although the rate of growth was beginning to slow down. It was a city of women—188,000 of them, compared with 162,000 men. A surprising number of women headed households—a quarter in Protestant homes, as many as a third in Catholic homes. Among young people who had moved into the city the imbalance was even more striking: there were ten women for every seven men in the Protestant population, and ten women for fewer than six men among Catholics. The reason is probably that the surest source of employment in Belfast at that time was the linen industry, where women did most of the work. The factories that employed these women were mostly in the west of the city, as the original textile industry had relied on the streams there to provide the power for spinning.

The characteristic view of west Belfast was of huge factories surrounded by tightly squeezed industrial housing, the whole overshadowed by the towering mill chimneys. Smoke from these chimneys gradually drove the wealthy from their homes in Donegall Square out to the leafy suburbs of Malone, beyond where the unruly Blackstaff River could still overflow and cause a nuisance by flooding the streets.

The other great provider of employment was shipbuilding, and the various industries that supported it. These were in and around Ballymacarret, close to Queen's Island. Thousands of men streamed over the bridge to and from work, while cranes and gantries rose high in the sky, and the noise of hammering rivets was loud enough to be uncomfortable in the city centre if there was an east wind to carry it.

Although the noise might have led a listener to believe that building a ship was an ensemble performance, a shipyard was a hierarchical place, and everyone knew his place. Leaving aside the management, the most important to the firm were the highly skilled tradesmen. In Harland and Wolff there were at least twenty-three broad categories in which apprenticeships were served, with another number of categories of roughly equal stature occupied by leading hands. These two groups added up to about 55 per cent of the work force.

One problem that men in this category faced was the possible erosion of their status if the firm introduced technology that would allow their job to be carried out by semi-skilled and therefore cheaper workers. To help maintain their position as an elite, which was self-perpetuating, because their sons tended to be taken on as apprentices, they were extremely union-minded, and the unions spent much of their time fighting other unions and making sure that demarcation disputes were settled to their members' advantage. Even within unions there might be problems with different categories, such as engine-smiths and ship-smiths, about who had the right to perform a task where there might be some overlap.

This is not to say that the skilled workers were cosseted. Their jobs were often harsh and dangerous. In 1912 seventy workers were killed by falling objects alone on the Lagan, Clyde, Tyne and Wear. This did not include those killed by drowning, fire, explosions or traffic accidents. The sound of an ambulance was a regular one on Queen's Island. Seventeen men died on the *Titanic* before it had even left the Lagan. Life expectancy for some trades could be anything between forty-eight and fifty-nine, and there was always the danger of an accident resulting in a man no longer being able to work. There were also hazards that at the time were considered minor ones, such as boilermakers and riveters becoming deaf at an early age.

It was difficult to get an apprenticeship unless you were the son or at least the nephew of a skilled man already working in the firm. The length of an apprenticeship varied between five and seven years, beginning at sixteen. Parents had to pay a deposit of up to £5 to guarantee their son's good behaviour, in addition to buying his tools, which could cost more than £17, or the equivalent of more than three weeks' full wages for an adult. What the apprentices got for their money is not so clear. They did acquire a skill, but while they were indentured they were considered second-class citizens and could not even become full members of their union.

Harland and Wolff refused to consider workers such as stagers, crane-drivers and machinemen as skilled but regarded them instead as semi-skilled. The reason is that the firm did not require them to complete a formal apprenticeship: the idea was that they 'picked it up' as they went along, and their wages reflected the value the management put on their work. Stagers, for example, earned only about half a pattern-maker's weekly wage, in spite of the fact that the 'staging'—the wooden scaffolding they erected—had to support the weight of men and machinery working around a ship. Men's lives depended on them. Harland and Wolff paid slightly better than Workman Clark, but by 1913 the rates for the two firms were the same.

At the bottom of the shipyard heap were the unskilled workers. Little value was placed on their work, as they could easily be replaced, and their wages were about the lowest in the United Kingdom. As well as that they were employed casually and had no job security. Their union, the National Amalgamated Union of Labour, existed to protect them from being exploited by skilled workers rather than from employers. Because it was able to organise so many members in the Belfast yards, the union was treated with respect but was not included in the articles of agreement between Harland and Wolff and the skilled unions.

About 5 per cent of the Harland and Wolff work force worked in the office; and although that included everybody from messengers and porters upwards, all considered themselves a step above those in the yard. Within the office, however, there was a definite hierarchy, once again defined by pay. The 'managers' actually ran the yard, and there could be up to sixty of these. Below them was the supervisory level—head foremen and assistants and storekeepers—seen as the backbone of the yard. There were more than 300 draughtsmen and 150 timekeepers. All were supported by a clerical staff of more than 450. Dining-room workers, porters etc. totalled another 125.

At this time there were few women in the firm, other than those working as waiters and cleaners. This would change by the end of the Great War, when tracers in the drawing office and typists in the front office became part of an increasingly female work force.

Although there is a general belief that industrial relations on Queen's Island were very good, this might be an over-simplification. In fact there were several industrial disputes in the last twenty years of the nineteenth century, some of them involving lock-outs. The most serious was in 1895 when, in a rare display of co-operation, the two Belfast yards joined with the Clyde yards in introducing joint bargaining procedures for both centres. When the Belfast men went on strike the Clyde employers began laying off men at the rate of 25 per cent per week. There was great bitterness in Belfast when the Clyde workers voted to accept the employers' offer. As there were twice as many workers on the Clyde as on the Lagan, the vote was automatically carried.

The fact that neither of the Belfast yards joined the Shipbuilders' Employers' Federation, which was vehemently opposed to trade unions, is often put forward in support of the belief that they had excellent industrial relations. Records show that there was a constant correspondence among all shipbuilders, including those on the Lagan, identifying the movements of 'troublemakers' and ensuring that they were blacklisted.

As some trades declined in importance, demarcation disputes arose as unions tried to create or retain monopolies. Shipwrights, so important for wooden ships, had refused to adapt to the needs of working with iron. By 1900 the trade had shrunk so much that it had to fight a desperate rearguard struggle against the carpenters, who were encroaching on work traditionally done by them. In every dispute between then and the Great

War the shipwrights lost work to the carpenters. There were other conflicts resulting from two unions representing the same group of workers, especially when one union was in dispute with the employers while the other was not. If at such times the second union offered to put in extra tradesmen, it gained strength in the yard at the first union's expense. There is one example that shows that Harland and Wolff at least could deal with a problem in an imaginative way. When the firm signed a memorandum of agreement in July 1914 with the unions representing its skilled workers, one of the signatories was the Amalgamated and General Society of Carpenters. As no such union existed, it is likely that it was a catch-all title combining the General Union of Carpenters and Joiners and the Amalgamated Society of Carpenters and Joiners. This alliance of convenience lasted till 1921, when the two unions amalgamated at the national level.

The most common area for disputes was the relationship between skilled and unskilled workers, usually with the tradesmen's helpers complaining about conditions imposed on them by skilled team leaders. One complaint was voiced about the conditions in which unskilled workers laboured at about the time of the Great War:

> [The craftsman] hadn't the broad human touch of the other fellow who carried the mud to him, carried the mortar to him, carried the machine . . . got into the hole and with the seat of his pants cleaned that part of the boat and got threepence for cleaning it. And when the skilled man got in after it was cleaned he got a shilling for working in a dirty corner.

Belfast was a city of young people. Three-quarters of the population was under forty. There was a high marriage rate—almost twice the rate for Ireland as a whole. The corollary was that Belfast's birth rate was high: 30.4 births per thousand population, compared with 23.1 for Ireland as a whole.

And it was a city with a recognisable social hierarchy. At the pinnacle was the city's official aristocrat, Anthony Ashley-Cooper, ninth Earl of Shaftesbury, Lord Lieutenant of Belfast from 1904 to 1911 and Lord Lieutenant of County Antrim from 1911 to 1916. His mother, as the only surviving child, had inherited the estate of the Marquis of Donegall in 1883. The Chichesters, Earls of Donegall, had been the first owners of Belfast, granted to their ancestor at the end of the Elizabethan wars. They were demanding landlords and were not always popular with their tenants. When the original Belfast Castle was burned to the ground in 1708 they had moved themselves to London and to Fisherwick in Staffordshire. When the second marquis inherited in 1799 he spent his fortune—an income of £30,000 per year—and then spent other people's money as fast as he could borrow it. When he owed so much that he could get no further credit (£250,000, or about £4 million in today's money) he decided to come to Belfast, which at least would make it less convenient for his creditors to chase him.

As it turned out, he chose the right sanctuary. With him he brought his wife and sons. His wife brought her family. When the young Lord Belfast (as he was then known) had been in debtors' prison in 1795 a man named Edward May contrived to get him released. Whether it was a condition of the transaction is not known, but he was then persuaded to marry May's 'illegitimate' daughter, Anna. The May family stuck close to the Donegalls for the rest of their lives and were even given the honour of being buried in the Donegall vault in Carrickfergus. The younger members of the family stayed close as well. Among other rewards, they got long leases on parts of the Donegall estate at low rent, building up considerable estates of their own. Their name is remembered in May Street and in Maysfield.

When creditors did follow the second marquis they found the sheriff unwilling to seize the property of the landlord, and when they got him to court they found that local juries decided that the May family, Donegall's in-laws, had prior claims. Even the furniture in his house seemed to belong to someone else and could not be seized. But there was hope on the horizon. In 1818 Lord Belfast was to marry a daughter of the Earl of Shaftesbury, and financial troubles might be forgotten. Unfortunately an anonymous 'well-wisher' informed the earl that there was an error in the special licence granted in 1795 on the occasion of the marriage to Anna May and that the marriage was illegal. Lord Belfast and his six brothers were illegitimate.

That was an end to the rescue plan, and ruin beckoned. There was even a rival heir to the estate. In circumstances like this, however, it is a great help to know the right people. In 1821 the King signed into law an act of Parliament that changed the legislation retrospectively. Lord Belfast was legitimate after all, and the following year he married his new bride, Harriet Butler, daughter of the Earl of Glengall. Unfortunately, the match did not provide enough money to pay off his father's debts, and the marquis was forced to desperate measures. He granted leases in perpetuity at the existing rents in return for ready cash, and almost all the ground in Belfast was granted away in the next few years. In County Donegal too, and in County Antrim, thousands of acres went the same way. He lost all his influence in Belfast. When he died, in 1844, his heirs discovered that he had not paid off the debt, as he was supposed to, in the 1820s. He had managed to get rid of at least half a million pounds in ten years, and there was little to show for it. His son, George Hamilton Chichester, third Marquis of Donegall, who had maintained the family tradition by building up debts of his own, must have been sick to the pit of his stomach.

In fact there was evidence of where at least some of the money went. When the family came to Belfast they had lived in Donegall Place, just opposite the site that would become Robinson and Cleaver's department store. They had moved from there in 1807 to a modest country house known as Ormeau Cottage. The marquis was not satisfied with this, and in 1823—the year after he was supposed to pay off his debts—he began work on a 20,000-square-foot mock-Tudor building, to be known as Ormeau House. His maintenance costs on this establishment were horrendous: he was paying £1,600 a year for fodder alone, not to mention expenses ranging from veterinary fees to wine bills. He was popular with the citizens, giving lots of employment even if he was slow to pay his bills. When he died there were effusive expressions of regret, but talk of erecting a statue to his memory came to nothing.

Lacking inheritance, the third marquis made a career in the army and afterwards at court, and let Ormeau House. The estate was an encumbrance. During the Great Famine many landlords throughout Ireland found themselves effectually bankrupt. The government set up the Encumbered Estates Court, which took over estates and sold as much as was needed to cover debts, the new titles to the land being guaranteed by Parliament. The Donegall estate was one of the first, and nearly the largest, to be dealt with. When the necessary land was sold, very little was left other than the Ormeau demesne and the Deerpark high on the slopes of Cave Hill. The annual income from Belfast was now only £1,300.

The family lost not only its land but its only son. Frederick Richard Chichester, Lord Belfast, who had composed a waltz for the visit of Queen Victoria in 1849, contracted scarlet fever on a visit to Naples four years later, at the age of twenty-five, and died. Unlike his grandfather, Frederick Richard was well enough liked for talk of a statue to go beyond mere talk, and it was erected in College Square, East. The direct Donegall line was now restricted to one daughter, Harriet. In 1857 she married the heir of the seventh Earl of Shaftesbury, known as 'the Great Reformer'. The Shaftesbury connection had not been cancelled, merely postponed for thirty-eight years.

The third marquis was married twice. His first wife's sister had a house in County Tipperary in the Scottish baronial style, which he admired. When he married a second time, in 1862, he decided to leave Ormeau House, which he detested, and to build a new house in the now-fashionable Scottish style. This was built between 1867 and 1870, close under the cliffs of Cave Hill, and was named Belfast Castle. The demesne at Ormeau was let and the hated house, now empty, allowed to decay. In 1869 the City Council was allowed to rent the land at £10 an acre, an annual cost of £1,750, and it became Belfast's first public park. Ormeau House and its out-offices were flattened, and the council financed the project by selling the land that is now North and South Parade and Park Road for building. The little that was left was leased to Ormeau Golf Club in 1892.

This was not the end of the Donegall involvement in Belfast. Lord Shaftesbury no longer owned or had influence in the city, but his County Antrim estates were large enough to justify an annual visit, and he seems to have maintained very good relations with his tenants. The improvements in transport and in particular the improvement to Belfast Harbour made these visits more convenient. He maintained a staff of nineteen indoor servants at Belfast Castle. The Shaftesburys subscribed to the tradition of *noblesse oblige,* paying money to local charities and opening the grounds of Belfast Castle to good causes. Lord Shaftesbury played an active part in public affairs, becoming Lord Mayor of Belfast in 1907. When Queen's College became Queen's University the following year he was the university's first chancellor. His final gesture was to donate the castle and its grounds to the city in 1934.

Whereas Lord Shaftesbury was undoubtedly a 'proper' aristocrat, there were many others who would have been seen in Belfast as virtual aristocrats. In other parts of the United Kingdom it was common for very successful businessmen to 'gentrify' themselves by withdrawing from business and living on their investments. There was no tradition of this in Belfast, where people like John Dunleath, owner of the York Street spinning mills, ennobled as Baron Dunleath in 1892, remained in harness until he died in 1895 with a personal fortune of almost £600,000. William Pirrie, chairman of Harland and Wolff, was granted a peerage in 1905. He too was fabulously wealthy, and was prepared to let it show. He lived in Ormiston House, where he could entertain more than 150 guests to dinner. When giving a banquet in honour of Lord Dufferin he chartered a ship for the occasion, which sailed from London to Belfast equipped with all the cutlery, linen and staff of the catering firm. Finding Belfast lacking as a suitable milieu in which to show off his airs and graces, he and his wife moved to London in 1898 and took a house in the fashionable Belgravia district. Later he moved to an estate in Surrey, where he continued his lavish entertaining. Among his guests there were at times employees of Harland and Wolff. He did not stop working, however. The head office of the firm was moved to London for his convenience, and he continued to visit Belfast, though less frequently as he grew older. He left more than £1 million in his will.

This level of society in Belfast has been described as 'this thinly inhabited stratosphere of the seriously wealthy.' Below that, at a more human level, were the ordinary well-to-do. This class consisted of about two to three hundred families that formed a tightly knit community. The ties that bound were business and family interests. Family relationships led to interlocking companies, while shared social, sporting and educational establishments (most of the children being sent to the same boarding-schools in Britain) led to a sort of freemasonry of favours performed or owed. As they tended to live in the same suburbs, well away from the sounds and smells of industry, in large villas with extensive gardens, they often formed the congregation at the same church. Wives and daughters worked together in the same charities. Husbands and sons were members of the same clubs, the Reform or, more often, the Ulster Club. With them lived their indoor servants, many of whom worked for little more than their keep. Though most of these were women, there were 283 butlers, valets and footmen employed in Belfast in 1911.

The middle class is hard to define, because it ranges over such a wide spectrum of occupations and incomes that it is almost a class defined by aspiration rather than anything else. In the Edwardian age anyone earning between two and five hundred pounds a year might have considered that his family was middle class. This income would have allowed him (most likely *him*) to rent a comfortable house in one of the better parts of the city or suburbs. The location would be chosen as much for health as for social status. The centre of the city was an unhealthy place to be, with atmospheric pollution from the mills and from thousands of coal fires and the risk of disease every time the flooding of the Blackstaff interfered with the town's sewage. The family would almost certainly have at least one maid, as this was not a great expense and would have relieved the wife of most of the drudgery of housework. They might even have had a cook.

One of the most important characteristics of middle-class families is that they would have sent their families to fee-paying schools. These would have been grammar schools rather than public schools, and the fees might not have been very high. The importance of continuing education was that it showed that the family was in a position to postpone the income that an extra worker in the house might bring. The deferred income would be much greater when the child had higher qualifications. Finally, after all these outgoings, the middle class would have had enough disposable income to be able to save for sickness or holidays, and even have something to put away for retirement.

The institutions of the middle class moved out of town with them. Although the Academical Institution remained on its original site, a preparatory department was set up on the Malone Road. Victoria College was built near the junction of the Lisburn Road and Malone Road, safely above the level of the Blackstaff's floodplain. Even Fisherwick Church abandoned its site in Great Victoria Street and moved to a more salubrious site, following its congregation to the suburbs. Although the Malone Road was an area of choice, good land was becoming available in the old Deerpark, on the slopes of Cave Hill, and was developed into Oldpark and Newpark. North along what is now the Antrim Road villa-sized parcels of land were developed into housing for the lower middle class in Mount Vernon, Parkmount, Duncairn, Fortwilliam and Skegoneill. In the east of the city what had been the estates of Ormeau, Ravenhill, Annadale, Knock,

Belmont and Stormont were developed as neat rows and avenues of villas. These were more modest than their south Belfast counterparts, because they were among the last to be developed and were occupied in the main by shopkeepers and merchants who had been made wealthier by the general increase in spending power.

The houses in the city centre that had been abandoned by the middle class were soon replaced by commercial premises. No less than five department stores were opened in or near Donegall Place. Brand's provided ladies' tailoring. Sawers' premises in High Street provided best-quality fish and meat for those who could afford it, while the firm of S. D. Bell in Ann Street provided groceries from the top end of the market. For more modest spenders there were four branches of Lipton's and six branches of Home and Colonial Stores. The Belfast Co-operative Society had 2,500 members and eight branches. There were branches of English multiple stores, such as Tyler's shoe shops, which had eight city-centre shops. Over them all, the City Hall presided from its opening in 1906.

Access to the city centre from the suburbs was by tram, a service that was taken over by the corporation in 1904. The maximum fare was 2 pence, and there were cheap fares for workmen at appropriate times. The trams had originally been pulled by horses. There were more than a thousand of these, and their management and stabling gave employment to many of the lower working class. These jobs went, however, when the corporation took over and introduced electrification, at a cost of £1 million.

The working class could not be defined as a single group. There was an extremely sharp division between the skilled artisan class on the one hand and the huge semi-skilled or unskilled working class on the other. Those who had served an apprenticeship in shipbuilding, engineering or building were able to earn enough to allow their wives to stay at home rather than go out to work. Pay rates were at least as good as in the rest of the United Kingdom. They would live in a terraced house with five or more rooms. (The five was important, for it took them above the 'two up and two down' houses that the less fortunate inhabited.) There was enough money to allow their sons to stay on after national school and go to the Technical College. Money might not stretch to a fortnight in Portrush, but there would be day trips to Bangor or Whitehead. The father's privileges would be jealously guarded by trade unions that existed as much to guard against encroachments from below as to safeguard against imposition from above. No young man, however well qualified, could get a job at this level unless he was 'spoken for' by someone already in the firm, usually a father or an uncle. The artisan was a pillar of the community and would have spent some of his spare time on union business or as an elder of his church. He would almost certainly have attended regular meetings of his Orange lodge. On Saturday afternoons he might have cared for an allotment, where he would show his thrift by growing vegetables for his family. On Sunday he would have worn a stiff collar and tie and have had a regular pew in his church.

The craftsman's wife could afford to shop in the Home and Colonial, where she could buy mutton chops from New Zealand at 9 pence per pound, or in Lipton's. Danish butter was cheaper than Irish, at 6 pence per pound. She probably paid cash, as these establishments, run by managers rather than owners, did not encourage credit without a banker's reference. (This would not have been a problem, because her husband was providing enough money to manage the house without hardship yet not enough to encourage a habit of extravagance.) New co-operative stores were opening around the city, and these had the reputation of selling the best bread. They also had a reputation for quality and hygiene in the milk they sold—important at a time when milk was still being sold from open cans on carts. Some families, especially on a Friday night, might treat themselves to fish and chips. On special occasions there might even be ice-cream, bought from Macari's on Peter's Hill or Fusco's in Great Victoria Street. More often than not there would be meat for Sunday dinner.

There were still two-fifths of Belfast's population who stood a real chance of ending in a pauper's grave. When they could find work at all, the semi-skilled and unskilled of Belfast earned rates of pay that were very much lower than in the rest of the country and often less than half that earned by the artisan. Their numbers were continually being added to by people moving in from the rest of Ulster, so it was easy for employers to play them off against one another, especially as they had the extra card of sectarianism to play. These men and women of the lower working class had no effective trade union, and it was not until the dock strike of 1907 that they were able to make a heroic, if ultimately unsuccessful, stand against the ruthlessness of the employers. A few were lucky enough to have steady employment, but for most of them work was obtained from day to day. A group of men would stand outside the gates of a firm, or near a ship in the docks. The foreman would come out, pick as many men as he needed, and turn his back on the others. For many, the foreman became as much a figure of hate as the Pope.

These people had little spare time, other than unemployment. If a man was working with a craftsman, in the shipyard for example, he only had to work a 54-hour week. For that he would be paid between 16 and 19 shillings—less than half what the craftsman was earning. A tram conductor worked 60 hours per week. A carter was outside in all weathers for 68 hours a week. Yet these were the lucky ones, because they knew on Monday morning that they would have a pay packet at the end of the week. Casual workers did not even have this and may have been dependent on their wives and daughters working in the linen mills. Even at the docks work was casual, with men being brought in as needed to unload ships as they came in. They were paid 5 shillings for a ten-hour day and would have thought themselves fortunate to get work on four days of the week. Even on the cross-channel coal docks on Queen's Quay, where the men unloading coal from the ships at least had permanent work, the most that could be earned was £1 4s per week. It might be tempting to say that these were the Catholics, and that their sufferings were the result of religious discrimination. Like many easy answers, there is an element of truth in it. Most Belfast Catholics were in this bottom social group, and Catholics were under-represented at every level above this. But the dockers on Queen's Quay were Protestants, and the majority of semi-skilled and unskilled workers were Protestants, and yet there seems to have been little effort on the part of their 'betters' to improve their conditions.

Women in work were an important element in the family income, though they were even less well paid than their menfolk. Women who worked at sewing machines embroidering linen handkerchiefs were paid the equivalent of 1½ pence per hour. For a sixty-hour week they could earn 7 shillings and 6 pence. They would have had to work almost forty-seven hours to earn enough to buy a dozen of these handkerchiefs in a shop.

The staples for these families were tea, white bread (bought stale from the bakery by the poorest families), sugar and tinned condensed milk, as opposed to the wheaten bread, buttermilk, potatoes and broth that a rural family might expect. A treat would be bacon, imported from America, or the less attractive joints of pork, such as cheek, trotters or hock, bought directly from the slaughterhouse. There was little time for a wife who spent her days in the linen mills to cook a nourishing dinner, and she had few facilities with which to do it. The houses that families such as this could afford to rent did not have cookers, and they cooked on open fires. It was only when the Gas Department undertook the free installation of penny meters that people got gas into their homes. Even then, many were limited to a single ring burner, or a single gaslight. Philanthropic owners of bakeries would open their ovens on Christmas Day to allow poor families to have at least one properly cooked meal in the year.

Taking housing conditions as a whole, there are indications once again of the relative advantage of being a Protestant. Fixed baths were much more common in Protestant households (one in six) than in Catholic households (one in sixteen). The remainder had to make do with a zinc bath in the kitchen. Although by-laws had been passed requiring every house to have a water closet (flush toilet), many still had to rely on pits where the human waste was covered with ashes from the fire. Some of this was poverty, but there was also the problem of getting an adequate supply of water. There was also a problem with maintaining the pressure of the water system, as much of the water was taken from low ground near the level of the river. For getting rid of the waste, a man would come round the streets every few weeks and collect what was euphemistically called night soil, in an open cart. Although these houses each had a 9-foot-square back yard, they did not have back access, and so the nauseating material had to be carried out through the house. Only in houses built after 1878 could one be certain of having rear access.

The problem with water persisted for most of the century, and it was not till 1893 that it was treated seriously. An act was passed that allowed the corporation to bring into Belfast water from the Annalong Valley in the Mourne Mountains. The water did not arrive until 1901, but even before this the corporation passed by-laws that would deal once and for all with the problem of night soil. All owners of properties containing cess-pits, ash-pits, pail closets and privies were required to replace them with water closets. The corporation undertook the necessary sewerage works. Loans were available from the corporation, and almost all the old unsanitary devices were replaced by water closets in the back yard within the next twenty years. This was not possible for those houses that were literally back-to-back and had no yard. Luckily, this was the time of Belfast's building boom, during which some fifty thousand houses were built. Though few of them were planned with water closets, at least the conversion was straightforward. This did not immediately relieve the city from the scourge of typhoid fever, however, which actually increased during the 1890s. In 1906 it was still so prevalent that a report claimed that no other city in the United Kingdom had nearly so bad a rate of occurrence.

Having made a start by solving the problem of importing enough fresh water, Belfast now had to tackle the other half of the equation: how to export its waste. Although there had been voluntary groups that concerned themselves with health problems in the years during and after the Famine, it was not till 1865 that Belfast appointed a Sanitary Committee, and it was another fifteen years before the post of medical superintendent officer of health was established. Dr Samuel Browne, a former naval surgeon, was appointed. He was seventy-one when he took up the post. In 1887 an act of Parliament was passed to allow the construction of a drainage system. This merely carried untreated sewage out into the deep water of the lough by means of a wooden 'shoot', as it was called. Within a few years the shoot was leaking and bursting regularly, and there were complaints of the smell at low tide. Belfast Lough does not have a great tidal range. Although this was useful in the development of the harbour, it did little to disperse the sewage.

In a city that depended so much on horses there was also the problem of animal waste. Where the environment allowed, many of the poorer people tried to supplement their diet by keeping pigs or poultry. It was reported in 1896 that one small yard in Percy Street contained sixty pigs and thirty cows. The sewage was allowed to seep into the street. Even though the corporation had powers to regulate dairies and cowsheds, little seems to have been done.

Dr Browne died in harness in 1890 and was replaced by Dr Henry Whittaker, another elderly man. He was poorly qualified but tried to make up for this by supplying many reports. He thought typhoid was caused by 'miasma' or polluted air. Another culprit, it was thought, was the shellfish trade. Poor people would collect shellfish from the lough shore and sell them from barrows. This trade was eventually forbidden by by-law.

An even more difficult killer to eradicate was tuberculosis, generally called 'consumption' at the time. This was a particular killer of women aged between twenty-five and forty-five and seemed to attack workers in the linen industry, where conditions were ideal for the incubation of the disease.

The oldest houses were around the sites of the original mills of Smithfield. Even the best of these houses had only three rooms: two bedrooms upstairs and a single kitchen and scullery downstairs. Rent was from 2 shillings and 6 pence to 3 shillings and 6 pence per week. Demolition was only beginning here at the turn of the century, and it was progressing at a very slow rate. Many speculators were building three-bedroom terraced houses for the middle-income market. What houses were being built for lower-income groups came in two varieties. Both were small, with four rooms, 'two up and two down,' together with a small scullery built as a lean-to at the back. In the scullery was the tap that provided cold water for the house. Beneath it would have been a 'Belfast' sink, capable of bathing a good-sized child.

Though both varieties were exactly the same size, the different layouts echoed the social aspirations as well as the income of the families occupying them. The more basic was the 'kitchen house', in which the front door opened on a small hallway. There was a kitchen at the front of the ground floor, while at the rear were a bedroom and the scullery. The stairs led up to a small landing, off which were two bedrooms, a small one to the rear and a slightly bigger one in front. The rent for a house like this was between 3 shillings and 6 pence and 4 shillings. In a 'parlour house' the upper floor was exactly the same but the rooms on the ground floor were arranged differently. At the front was a parlour, generally reserved for Sundays and important family occasions. The kitchen was at the rear, along with the scullery. For the privilege of having a parlour rather than a third bedroom the tenant had to pay between 6 pence and a shilling extra each week. In two-bedroom houses it was usual for the parents and the girls to sleep in the front room, while the boys squeezed into the much smaller back bedroom. Not surprisingly, the kitchen house was more popular than the parlour house.

There were some houses with five rooms, where the third bedroom was built in the back 'return' over the scullery. These were very expensive to rent, from 5 shillings to over 6 shillings a week, and could be afforded only by those whose skilled trade gave them a good wage.

In the years after 1900 the cost of living rose at a higher rate than wages. People who were most vulnerable became more reliant on the pawnbroker to cover the gap between the last of the money and the next, and in some areas this dependence became part of folklore. Sam McAughtry, who lived in Tiger's Bay in the 1930s, wrote amusingly of the regular Monday morning visits to the pawn, and of the jokes and epithets that were used to cover the humiliation. The standard joke became the one of Father's Sunday suit, redeemed every payday, only to be returned to the pawnbroker a few days later, neatly wrapped in brown paper.

The hundred or so pawnbrokers in Belfast at the time could not save everybody, and an increasing number of families had to turn to the Poor Law Guardians for help. Although the Guardians were entitled to give relief to people without necessarily admitting them to the workhouse, they did not enjoy doing this. It seemed to them that the fewer who received this outdoor relief, and the less that was given, the more righteously they were doing their work. An example of their thinking was that travel on trams was a luxury that need not be included when the amount of poor relief to which a family was entitled was being calculated. In case a family might not be inclined to express the credit due to the Guardians for their magnanimity, the names of all who were receiving outdoor relief were publicly displayed in each area. The desire to avoid such humiliation meant that many people who needed it did not apply for help, and Belfast gained the honour of having the lowest pauper rate in the United Kingdom—888 for 1914, while the Glasgow figure was 18,000.

One innovation that helped relieve absolute poverty was the old-age pension, introduced in 1908. A person had to be seventy years old to receive it, at a time when average life expectancy was considerably less than this, and to have other income of less than 10 shillings per week. The amount granted was minimal: 5 shillings per week—half the amount paid in England. Nevertheless it was enough to keep the wolf from the door and the pensioner from the workhouse. Seven thousand people qualified for it in Belfast.

At the other end of the age scale, conditions for children who came to the workhouse were improving. They no longer had to spend their time in work but were found foster homes if at all possible. Some older children were placed in apprenticeships, while others were sent abroad to one of the dominions. This last practice was continued at least up to the 1950s in orphanages of the Sisters of Nazareth; the shame of sending a child to the workhouse was still too much for most families. Under a by-law of 1903 workhouse children could be licensed as street traders, errand boys or flower-sellers. For many, this was no more than a euphemism for begging. Several missions provided shelter, and there were even doss-houses where those with some funds could stay in what were often filthy conditions. Others were forced to sleep rough. One gang haunted the area of the Brickfields, between the Falls Road and the Shankill. The Central Mission tried to help these, providing meals, and calculated that there were about sixty-five gang members, of an average age of twenty.

It was easy for such boys to get sucked into the soft, sticky edges of crime, and many of them appeared before the courts. Betting shops were illegal, and libraries blacked out the racing pages of newspapers, but there was a great deal of street betting, and many boys acted as runners for the bookies. Although there were more job opportunities for girls than for boys, short-time working and low wages in the linen mills meant that there were still girls desperate enough to take their chance in brothels. Other girls became pregnant outside marriage and in those extremely judgemental times were ostracised by their families. Some felt that their only hope was in prostitution. This proved no easier to eradicate than the illegal gambling. When a brothel was closed by the police in the city centre it would soon reopen in a street further out.

There was always alcohol. In the early part of the nineteenth century the major public holiday was Easter Monday. It was traditional for the people to make their way up to the caves of what was formerly called Benmadigan and was now Cave Hill. Here the revellers could dance and 'quaff the cup of glee,' probably poitín. Items reminiscent of the Lammas Fair at Ballycastle could be bought for food: cockles and mussels, with dulse (edible seaweed) or yellow man (toffee) to follow. At first these entertainments had been enjoyed by Catholics and Protestants alike, but in 1828 some Orangemen from Carnmoney started a tradition by having a demonstration. After that the Catholic bishop, Bishop William Crolly, asked his flock to stay away.

The public mood even among Protestants was moving away from such demonstrations of excess anyway, and in the years leading up to the great revival in 1859 clergymen were declaring that they were positively sinful. Churches began to organise excursions to Belvoir or Stranmillis, which would incorporate soft drinks, a meal al fresco and at least one sermon. The excesses on Cave Hill did not stop at once, but by mid-century there were alternatives, even to someone who did not find soup and a sermon an attractive way to spend a day in the country. For those who had the money it was possible to go to Bangor on the steamer, or to any of the resorts that the railways were developing around the coast.

The real alternative to Cave Hill was Queen's Island. Belfast's first zoo was established there, as well as an amusement arcade. This became popular for more than just Easter, but at busy times the fun would be optimised and the chance for the management to make a profit increased with a programme of sports, games and displays. There was even music, played by a blind harper called McIlvenna, who in earlier days had serenaded the crowds on Cave Hill. The coming of the shipyards to the island first curtailed and then closed the pleasure gardens, but about the same time the Botanic Gardens, visited in 1849 by Queen Victoria, became available to the public. More moneyed people came here, so the *hoi polloi* were expected to behave themselves. Police and pickets of soldiers ensured that perfect decorum was maintained.

As the town's prosperity increased, people began to look for other means of entertainment. The opportunity to spend money was offered when some drinking saloons began to offer entertainment in the form of annexes where music and singing would be performed. To pay for the singing, the customer was required to drink at a rate that satisfied the proprietor. Some of the saloons were rough, and women singers were popular. At first these saloons were the exclusive haunt of the working class, but some enterprising owners added 'snugs' where a daring young gentleman might drink with a few friends without subjecting themselves to the common gaze. When this proved viable some proprietors set out to attract this wealthier clientele and began to bring in well-known singers from England. The next step was to increase the audience by providing establishments where a respectable man and his friends could listen to the performances without being distracted by the noise of the drinkers. The Alhambra was built to meet this need.

This brought even more of the rising stars of England and Scotland to Belfast. The entertainment was not always sophisticated, however. A favourite act was to have small boys dipping in barrels of tar to try to extract sixpence. The combination of small boys, tar and a meagre prize attracted a wide range of customers while keeping expenses down. It was still not a place to take a mother-in-law or a sister. Bernard, who opened the Olympia Palace in 1891 on the site of the present Grand Opera House, tried to raise the tone. Essentially what he offered was music hall with the worst of the vulgarity taken out. The new fare was called 'variety', and it proved so popular that the Empire Theatre of Varieties soon followed in Victoria Square. Admission prices for the new theatres were low enough to attract the middle class but too high for most of the working class. The problem now faced by the Alhambra was that its income was not sufficient to allow it to compete with the others in offering fees that would attract the most popular stars. The management adapted by showing the first films in Belfast in 1896, in a hint of what was to come.

The theatre in Belfast had a troubled history in the nineteenth century. Plays were ignored if they were considered immoral, or were heckled if any attempt was made to present a new version of a well-loved classic. Local productions became rare, and most of the shows were staged by travelling companies. Opera proved popular with the well-to-do, but the theatre also managed to win a working-class audience. This new group was particularly fond of pantomime. When the Olympia Palace became the Grand Opera House in 1895, the future of theatre in Belfast was safe.

There were those who could not afford any of these entertainments yet still attended. This put a strain on family finances that it might take months to make good. There were others who simply did not have the cash to attend; for them the temptation was to take advantage of the anti-depressant and analgesic effects of strong drink, which was still readily available. Whiskey was 1 penny per tot. Public houses were there for the men, while women might use the snug or buy drink in the off-licence and take it home. For most victims there is no possibility of hiding their vice, and the sight of drunk and incapacitated men and women was an offence to the sensibilities of respectable citizens and troubled their imaginations with the further debaucheries that drink could lead to. Many of the initiatives that were introduced to ameliorate the situation were connected with the Church. A Jesuit priest established the Pioneer Total Abstinence Association in 1898. The idea behind this was that respectable Catholics would voluntarily abstain from alcoholic drink and would make their 'heroic offering' to God in the hope that he would intervene to protect alcohol's victims from themselves. Combining the idea of sacrifice and prayer, it proved very successful, though it may be that it was most successful with the sort of Catholics who were least likely to become drunkards anyway. The Prime Minister, David Lloyd George, put a duty of 8 shillings per gallon on whiskey in his 1908 budget. An Armagh Presbyterian minister began the Catch-My-Pal movement in 1910, whereby friends supported one another in their efforts towards abstention. It was so successful that Orange processions that year were remarkable for their sobriety. The North Belfast Mission campaigned for restrictions to be put on the sale of alcohol. The coming of the Great War brought this about. Even the City Council had temperance posters printed.

The pressure told on the licensed vintners, who complained that they were the victims of a vicious campaign. It is interesting that no-one suggested that misery was the cause, as well as the result, of excessive alcohol consumption; and no-one suggested that improving living conditions might help to curtail the desire for drink.

Although there was still a substantial Catholic minority, Belfast by the early twentieth century had taken on the character of a Protestant city. The total number of Catholics was not reduced but had declined as a proportion of the city's population. Moreover, most Catholics lived in carefully defined enclaves and were effectually excluded from the decision-making process. The increase in population in the second half of the nineteenth century was almost exclusively Protestant, coming from Counties Armagh, Antrim and Down. Those Catholics who did come to the city tended to be women looking for a position in domestic service or employment in the linen mills. Catholic men tended to emigrate altogether rather than move to Belfast. This attitude is understandable, given the sequence of anti-Catholic riots that had persisted through the century.

The biggest Catholic area at the beginning of the twentieth century was the one stretching from the Pound out along the Falls Road. The shape of this is reminiscent of a Catholic salient pushed into the front lines of Protestant Belfast. Just as in the Ypres Salient some fifteen years later, the occupants were vulnerable to attack from the north (the Shankill) and from the south (Grosvenor Road and Donegall Road).

One result was that this area took on an identity of its own and, rather than civic pride, had a perverse pride in its neighbourhood. Half the Catholic families in the city lived here. The area had the poorest housing, with fewer rooms than average and fewer amenities. Half the residents had a gas supply to their houses, as opposed to 70 per cent of Protestants. The corporation did remedy this by installing in every house a penny meter, one light bracket and one gas ring. It is perhaps churlish to wonder whether they were concerned more with tapping another source of income than with ameliorating living conditions along the Falls Road. It was the sharing of common hardship that built up the community spirit of the Falls and other Catholic enclaves in Belfast.

Another contribution was the sense that Catholics were permanently excluded from all that was good in Belfast. Fourteen per cent of the engineering, iron manufacture and shipbuilding work force was Catholic, while 21 per cent of the male work force in the linen industry was Catholic. Even these figures disguise the fact that Catholics were almost totally unrepresented at the skilled and semi-skilled levels. Foremen in the linen mills were almost exclusively Protestant.

The cream of the jobs—in the shipyards, in James Mackie and Sons' engineering works or in the Sirocco Works—could pay up to £2 a week in the early years of the century. Access to these jobs was restricted to the children or friends of those already working there. What began as an informal arrangement developed into a unionised system administered by the Belfast and District United Trades Council. Even lower-working-class Protestants needed to have somebody on the inside. There was no hope for Catholics.

Pervading all public life was the influence of the churches. The clergy were permitted, even expected, to comment on all aspects of society. A handful of people may have been atheists or agnostics, but few of these would have admitted it openly. Church attendance was almost universal in

Catholic areas and among the upper and middle classes, as well as among the respectable working class in Protestant areas. Among Protestants of the lower working class, however, church attendance was a more fickle thing, and it has been estimated that only one in fifteen of its parishioners attended Ballymacarret Parish Church. The last dying echoes of the Year of Grace, 1859, had died away, and there was not the same enthusiasm for building churches.

In education the influence of the clergy remained as strong as ever. The new College of Technology was staffed exclusively by Protestants. In a sense this was inevitable, given the Protestant grip on the skilled industries in Belfast. It meant, however, that this Protestant monopoly would be bound to continue, as few Catholic students would be tempted to enrol. The Catholic diocesan authorities set up a rival trade school in Hardinge Street, run by the Christian Brothers. This quickly paid dividends in a number of apprenticeships. It is worth noting that Catholic distrust of the municipal college seemed to be justified in the Home Rule Crisis of 1912–14, when the college's resources were made available to the Unionist side; there was even a UVF bakery set up, presumably to satisfy the needs of Protestant digestive tracts unable to cope with the 'Fenian' bread of Bernard Hughes's Bakery.

Chapter 5 ～

| THE WHITE STAR TRINITY

W hen Bruce Ismay decided to order what would be the three largest liners in the world he was not simply making a grandiose statement of the self-confidence of the White Star Line: he was making a calculated bid for a section of the travel market that promised huge profits for whoever controlled it. He wanted the jet-setters of the early twentieth century, the rich and the beautiful of Europe and America, to gravitate towards his ships. His would be the fashionable ships of the North Atlantic run, Grand Hotels of the sea, where every luxury was available for those who could pay for them. It was to be a subtle change of emphasis but one that, he believed, would gain him the crown.

Within the United Kingdom, Ismay's only real rivals were the Cunard Line, and it had recently introduced two fast liners, the RMS *Lusitania* and RMS *Mauretania*. (A Royal Mail ship was a liner qualified to carry mail under contract to the Royal Mail.) There are troubles with speed, however. One problem is that a ship designed for speed is not designed for passengers' comfort. Both Cunard ships had a reputation for dipping and rolling, and there was talk of vibration from the powerful turbines making parts of the ships uncomfortable. The second problem is that speed is expensive, and it is a continuing expense, persisting through the life of the ship. A direct comparison between the *Lusitania's* coal consumption, 1,000 tons per day, and what was to be the coal consumption of the *Olympic*, the first of the new giants, at 650 tons per day, shows a saving of 35 per cent. Luxury, on the other hand, was a one-off cost, paid when the ship was built and to be paid again only in part at any future refits.

Savings in the long run were all very well, but the capital cost of these ships would be tremendous, even allowing for the generous 'costs-plus' terms offered to White Star by Harland and Wolff. Fortunately, White Star had found itself a fairy godfather in the unlikely shape of John Pierpont Morgan, an American financier who had made his millions in coal, steel and railways. At the beginning of the twentieth century he saw an opportunity to broaden his portfolio and make more money. A price war was taking place on the North Atlantic route, and the only people benefiting were the passengers. The cut-throat competition was hurting all the companies involved. Morgan began to buy these companies—Dominion Line, Red Star Line, Leyland Line and Atlantic Transport—to organise them under a controlling group, the International Mercantile Marine Company, and to impose uniform shipping charges on them. The ships he bought continued to be registered as British and to have British crews. This enabled Morgan to avoid higher American taxes and to escape the net of America's anti-monopoly laws.

When Cunard introduced the *Lusitania* and *Mauretania,* the two largest and fastest liners the world had ever seen, White Star had to respond appropriately, and this was the essential factor in encouraging the line to accept Morgan's buy-out offer, which was ten times what the line had earned in 1900: £10 million. Part of the agreement was that White Star ships would be available to the Royal Navy in case of war. The deal was completed in late 1902, with Bruce Ismay remaining as chairman and managing director of White Star and later president of IMM.

This was great news for Harland and Wolff, and for Belfast. Under the agreement signed between Bruce Ismay and Lord Pirrie in 1899, Harland and Wolff would have the building of all the ships for all the lines controlled by IMM. More particularly, when the decision was made in 1907 to proceed with the giant Olympic-class liners, at an estimated cost of £1½ million, Belfast would become the focus of the shipbuilding world.

It is important to consider the scale of what was being undertaken. These ships were going to be more than 100 feet longer and 15,000 tons heavier than the *Lusitania* and *Mauretania.* There was no dockyard in the world big enough to accommodate their construction. There was no pier in New York long enough for them to tie alongside.

Steps were taken immediately to ensure that the infrastructure would exist to accommodate these ships when they were ready to operate. Ismay approached the New York Harbour Board to negotiate the installation of a pier long enough for the giant vessels. In the shipyard itself Pirrie had to arrange that three construction slips be converted into two gigantic slips— which meant that only two of the new ships could be built at a time. At the same time work began on two enormous gantries, at 220 feet the largest in the world, to operate over the slips. It was also necessary to consider arrangements at Cherbourg, where passengers travelling to and from France were exchanged. Passengers there had to be transferred from the shore by tender. The one then in service was an old paddle steamer, considered unsuitable for use with the *Olympic* and *Titanic.* It was decided to build two new tenders. The larger, *Nomadic,* would be designed for transferring first-class passengers to and from the lines; the other, *Traffic,* would deal with the remainder of the passengers, together with the mail.

It is interesting that no thought was given to upgrading the tenders at Queenstown (Cóbh) Harbour, County Cork, where the ships would pick up passengers from Ireland. There is a photograph of tenders approaching the *Olympic,* small paddle steamers whose decks are crowded. Perhaps it was decided that the only passengers likely to be picked up there would be emigrants travelling in steerage and that upgrading would be a waste of money.

Architects and draughtsmen from Harland and Wolff were soon working on concept drawings and initial plans for the ships. A preliminary set of drawings was ready by 29 July 1908, when Ismay, Pirrie and Thomas Andrews of the draughting department met to consider the ideas being put forward. Pirrie liked what was put before them, and two days later a contract was signed for the first two ships of the Olympic class.

Work now began seriously on the designs for the ships. From the start, the ideas were that the ships would be more or less identical, although, as one was going to be completed before the other, there was always the option of modifying the second one in the light of the experience of building and operating the first. The basic design, the ships' length and beam and the modelling of the hull, was the responsibility of Pirrie himself. The general construction of the ship, its equipment and its decoration were the responsibility, to begin with, of Harland and Wolff's general manager, Pirrie's brother-in-law and cousin, Alexander Carlisle. Carlisle had designed the *Oceanic,* launched in 1899. The hull of the new ships would be based on this plan, suitably expanded and with the modifications necessary for their extra weight and size. The ships' superstructure and navigating bridge were built to give a high degree of rigidity. This was necessary because each ship would be so long that great stress would be put on it by waves as it passed along, trying to flex the ship one way as it rose to the top of one wave and to flex it in the other direction as the ship went into the trough between waves.

Some of the parts that were to be ordered in from other firms were of staggering proportions. The stern-frame, used to hold the propeller shafts in place, made up of various castings done by the Darlington Forge Company, weighed a total of 190 tons. The rudder, also made at Darlington, was built in five sections of solid cast steel. The top section was made of steel of the same quality as that used in naval gun-jackets. When assembled, it weighed 101 tons and had a length from top to bottom of 78 feet 8 inches and a breadth of 15 feet 3 inches. The main anchor, which was carried on the deck, weighed 15½ tons, while the side anchors weighed 8 tons each.

The engines were of great importance. Nobody had ever tried to design a propulsion unit capable of pushing so much weight through the water at an acceptable speed, and it was here that Harland and Wolff once again produced an elegant solution. They used two traditional reciprocating engines, one on each side, and in the centre an additional low-pressure turbine capable of producing 16,000 horsepower from a pressure of a mere 9 pounds per square inch. This combination of engines proved to be more economical than simply having reciprocating or steam turbines. At 21.7 knots (25 miles per hour), the *Olympic,* as the first ship was to be called, would use about 650 tons of coal per day, contrasting with the 1,000 tons used by the *Lusitania* and *Mauretania.*

An extremely important aspect of any ship is the safety of its passengers. This was particularly true in this new age of super-liners, carrying more people than would have been thought possible only a decade or two previously. The British Board of Trade had regulations concerning the number of lifeboats to be carried, but these were based on much older ships and had not yet been updated. Alexander Carlisle, whose task it was to address such matters, felt that there should be many more lifeboats than the regulations demanded: in fact the twenty lifeboats that were eventually carried by the *Olympic* and *Titanic* exceeded the minimum demands of the Board of Trade. Carlisle felt that the ships should carry up to sixty lifeboats. The problem was that they took up valuable space. It was to save space that four of the lifeboats ultimately fitted to the giant ships would be collapsible, so that they could be stored flat.

There was a solution. Lifeboats hang from davits along the side of a ship. Our mental picture of ships normally has one lifeboat to each pair of davits. Carlisle, however, was aware of an innovative davit that had been developed by the firm of Welin in London, called the Welin quadrant davit. The design of this allowed more than one lifeboat to be stored on a pair of davits. They had already been adopted by the Union Castle Line, where they carried two lifeboats per pair. When Carlisle realised how big the new ships were going to be he wrote to the inventor, Axel Welin, and asked whether it would be feasible to design davits that could carry up to four lifeboats on each pair. The reply was in the affirmative, and he was sent a set of drawings of the proposed davits.

Right from the start, Ismay seems to have been against the addition of any extra lifeboats. It is interesting to speculate about why this should be. Perhaps he felt that the appearance of so many lifeboats might put doubts into the minds of the very passengers he wanted to attract, those who would look on a ship as a mobile Grand Hotel, moving between America and Europe while offering standards of comfort and care equal to anything to be found on land. Perhaps he felt that the number of lifeboats was irrelevant. After all, in the entire history of the White Star Line the firm had suffered only one fatality among the hundreds of thousands of passengers carried; why should things be different in these new and most up-to-date ships?

One reason that was taken seriously at the inquiry into the sinking of the *Titanic* was the possibility that so much extra weight so high on the ship, perhaps 100 tons, might make it less stable. Carlisle, in his testimony, stated that if during testing a ship was not as stable as the design required it could be rectified by extra ballast near the keel.

There seems to have been a stalemate, but Carlisle got at least some of his way by suggesting that the Board of Trade might change the regulations about the number of lifeboats to be carried, and that White Star would be at a commercial disadvantage if it had to delay the introduction of its ship, or to withdraw them from service, while new davits were fitted. There was in fact an Advisory Committee at the board that would deal with this question and would sit in 1911. Ismay agreed to finance the new quadrant davits but refused to do more. Although Carlisle was still concerned that the ships would go to sea with too few lifeboats, he was not able to force his point of view, because of the way meetings between the owners, White Star Line, and the builders, Harland and Wolff, were managed. A review meeting might last all day, but only one person spoke on each side, Ismay for White Star and Pirrie for Harland and Wolff. The others spoke only if requested to do so by their principals. It was a long way from the brainstorming sessions that characterise modern business meetings.

Strangely, Carlisle left the yard to which he had dedicated all his adult life, and what was undoubtedly the greatest shipbuilding challenge of the time, when he resigned from the yard in June 1910 and moved to London. He gave no reason for this, then or later, but it might be reasonable to think that he did so because he could no longer put up with the imperious ways of Pirrie. He took up a position with Welin, the company whose davits he had installed in the new liners. His place at the yard was taken by another relative of Pirrie's, his nephew Thomas Andrews.

Another device that was used to increase the safety of a ship was the installation of waterproof bulkheads. Bulkheads are barriers built from side to side of a ship and that divide it into a number of compartments. If the shipbuilder makes each bulkhead waterproof they can isolate any compartment in which there is a leak and prevent the water spreading to the rest of the ship. To be truly waterproof a compartment must reach as high as possible in the ship, preferably to the weather deck, and must have a waterproof top, so that water cannot spill over the top of the bulkhead into the next compartment. Naval ships are designed like this, as Carlisle stated in his testimony, because they go out expecting to be damaged. A presumption is made by shipbuilders that a cargo or passenger ship is designed to float, not to collide with rocks or icebergs. Because they occasionally do so, an effort is made to provide some waterproofing, but it cannot be of the standard incorporated in warships.

There are many reasons for this. The most obvious is the need to move about the ship. At that time truly waterproof doors were not available.

This meant that in the lower decks of warships the bulkheads were solid, not pierced in any way. In a merchant ship this was impossible. The lower decks were where the engines lay, with all their ancillary machinery, and engineers and stokers had to be free to move about here. This meant that a merchant ship's waterproofing had an area of weakness right in the centre. To some extent this was compensated for by the waterproof compartments at the bow and stern, where most collisions were likely to occur in large ships, but it was a weakness nevertheless, though one that shipbuilders felt it was possible to live with.

These were not the only problems. Even when the keel of the *Olympic* was laid, on 31 March 1908, agreement had still not been reached with the New York Harbour Board about extending the piers allocated to the White Star Line. Even when the Harbour Board had agreed on the value of extending the piers, that was not the end of the affair. Ultimate control of New York Harbour was vested in the War Department, but the Harbour Board agreed to intervene on White Star's behalf. Eventually, permission was given for the extension, but it was so late that only a temporary extension had been completed by the time the *Olympic* arrived in New York on its first crossing.

The length of the ships had caused problems in England as well. White Star had had to change its port of embarkation from Liverpool to Southampton, where there was ample berthing even for ships as big as the *Olympic* and *Titanic*, although the ships would continue to be registered in Liverpool.

The construction of the *Olympic* proceeded well, considering the scale of the ship and that a sister-ship, the *Titanic*, which would turn out to be even bigger, was being built at the same time. The *Olympic's* hull was ready for launching by the early autumn of 1910, and on 20 October, in front of guests who included the Lord Lieutenant of Ireland and the Lord Mayor of Belfast, the 26,000-ton hull (painted off-white for the occasion, as this was considered more suitable for photographs) took sixty-two seconds to slide into the water. As it went, the guests saw revealed the hull of the *Titanic*, huge beneath its giant gantry.

The launch of any ship is not the end of the story, as most of the ship's fittings have still to be installed. The hull was towed to the fitting-out basin, where the next stage of construction started immediately. The four giant funnels, so typical of the Olympic class, were manoeuvred in place with a crane that had been bought from Germany at a price of £30,000. Three of these funnels acted as exhausts to the three engines, but the fourth was, in a sense, a dummy. Pirrie had been anxious to maintain the elegance of the ship as much as possible. He wanted to avoid having to place a great number of the traditional pipe-shaped ventilators all over the deck and instead used a fourth funnel as the main ventilation system, thus eliminating what he saw as one of the main threats to the clean lines of the ship.

Much of what Ismay saw as the most important work for his vision, the fitting out of the passenger accommodation, was carried out at this stage. Although he was determined that both steerage and second-class passengers would travel in greater comfort than would have been provided in previous ships, it was on first class that most of the creativity was lavished. There were thirty suite rooms on the bridge deck and a further thirty-nine on the shelter deck, just below. These were designed to be let in groups. Each suite room had an adjacent room that was fitted as a sitting-room or dining-room. In addition to these there were 350 first-class cabins, 100 of which were single-berth. To move between decks in first class there were two grand companionways or stairs, the forward one extending from the boat deck to the upper deck, the one aft extending from the promenade deck to the shelter deck, the stairs and landing decorated in the style of a great house in Restoration times. The promenade deck was enclosed, with windows that could be raised or lowered at will. First-class passengers also had exclusive access to the open boat deck, where more invigorating open-air promenading was an option.

There were also many public rooms. The first-class dining saloon was decorated in Jacobean style, with oak furnishings, and had accommodation for 532 passengers. These passengers would gather before meals in the reception room, also fitted out in the style of a Jacobean hall, with panelled walls. If anyone felt that the saloon was not quite what was wanted there was an *à la carte* restaurant. Here friends could dine in groups of between two and eight on French walnut furniture, in a room fitted out in the style of Louis XVI, while listening to the ship's orchestra. There was a lounge in the style of Louis XV, where bridge or whist could be played; a reading and writing room designed primarily for ladies, with an atmosphere of 'refined retirement'; and a smoking room, which gave through a revolving door onto the veranda, with views of the sea and tables for coffee or absinthe. For the more active there were the swimming pool and the squash courts, while for those who liked to feel healthy without too great an expenditure of energy there were the Turkish baths. Attached to this last was the cooling room, where patrons could regain their strength in a relaxing ambience of Cairo or Damascus.

Decoration extended to the first-class staterooms ('cabins' would be too demeaning a word to describe them). In the suite rooms there were the following styles: Louis XVI, Empire, Adam, Italian Renaissance, Louis XV, Georgian, Regency, Queen Anne, Modern Dutch and Old Dutch. All staterooms had a cot bed; in the suite rooms these were four feet wide.

Second-class cabins were two or four-berthed, and they had available to them a smoking room and a library. Even the *hoi polloi* were cosseted, compared with other liners. Steerage class had 84 two-berth cabins, although the remaining 960 steerage-class travellers had to sleep in 'enclosed bunks' in large dormitories. They did have access to a smoking room and a 'general room', under the poop deck, well away from first class.

The extent to which the designers of these ships went to protect their passengers, at least those in first class, from unpleasant sights is amazing. A special corridor was built from the stokehold to the crews' quarters so that stokers, notoriously unkempt at the end of the watch, could be kept away from the passengers.

When all this had been done, the *Olympic* was moved to the Thompson graving-dock, built specially for the new giants, and the water was removed so that final work could be done to its hull. When that was done it was ready to undertake its sea trials, which began on 28 May 1911. These passed without incident, and the ship returned to Belfast. When the *Titanic* was launched, on 31 May, the *Olympic* was there to transport Ismay and Morgan to Liverpool. After remaining only a day there it went to Southampton to prepare for its first voyage.

The ship arrived on 3 June and immediately began loading the vast quantities of food, linen, coal, china and the thousand other things it would need *en route*. By Wednesday 14 June it was ready. There had been worries about a seamen's strike, but these were averted on 10 June, and the *Olympic* got under way for New York, under the command of Captain E. J. Smith, early in the afternoon of Wednesday. It was missing one passenger who might have been expected to travel: Pirrie had decided to remain in London for the coronation of King George v. He intended to join the *Olympic* for its second transatlantic voyage.

Although the number of first-class passengers was only 450, it was a record for a westward passage in June. Many of them were Americans, for whom a coronation would have been of little interest.

Bruce Ismay travelled and spent most of the voyage moving about the ship, taking notes as things struck him. He saw, for example, that the bridge-deck promenade was little used by passengers, who preferred to use the promenade deck. On the principle that space should be used, he ordered changes in the final design of the *Titanic*. This involved adding extra first-class accommodation on both the bridge and promenade decks, putting a new restaurant on the bridge deck and rearranging the promenades. Eventually these would also be fitted on the *Olympic*, but for the time being these were the only internal differences between the ships.

For the crew, and for the paying passengers, the trip across the Atlantic passed without incident. Captain Smith found to his delight that his ship's speed exceeded prediction: it was travelling at an average of 21.7 knots (25 miles per hour). It was off Fire Island by a quarter past midnight on Wednesday 21 June, and it was estimated that it would be alongside Pier 59 in New York by 8:30. There was some concern about the fragility of the temporary extension to the pier, as a knock from the *Olympic* could dislodge it and send it floating downriver. The *Celtic* had already bumped into it, but without doing serious damage. Just in case, it was reported that twelve tugs would be waiting to guide the huge ship gently to its berth. One tug, the *O. L. Halenbeck,* had an interesting moment when it was sucked under the *Olympic's* stern, its flagstaff was carried away, and $10,000 worth of damage was done to its superstructure; but that was the only untoward incident in the hour that it took to make the great ship fast. Even then there was a delay in unloading, as the ship was so long that only one first-class gangway could be used. In spite of these teething problems the crossing had taken only 5 days, 16 hours and 42 minutes. Ismay telegraphed to Lord Pirrie the message 'Olympic is a marvel, and has given much unbounded satisfaction,' although he was later quoted as saying that the combination of spring bed and spring mattress 'accentuated the pulsation of the ship to such an extent as to seriously interfere with passengers sleeping.'

The voyage ended with only one sour note. As the *Olympic* came upriver from quarantine it had met the *Lusitania* on its way to sea. It was, and is, tradition that a new ship is saluted by the old, and all manner of craft saluted the *Olympic* by dipping their ensigns or sounding whistles. The *Lusitania,* it was noticed, did not. Some people suggested that Captain Charles of the Cunard liner was so caught up in taking his ship to sea and in receiving congratulations for his coronation honour (being made a commander of the Order of the Bath) to remember his manners. Others thought otherwise.

The rest of the summer passed in a total of four round trips across the Atlantic. When the *Olympic* left Southampton on 20 September to begin its fifth crossing, things began to go wrong. The waters between the Isle of Wight and the coast of Hampshire were, and are, extremely congested. The constricted entrances to the area east and west of the island mean that tides are particularly strong, while the presence of the Brambles Bank in the middle of the western approaches, dividing the water into two channels, increases the need for precise navigation and ship-handling skill. It is an area where many maritime collisions occur. Nowadays there are strict regulations for separating ships, with larger ones having what is effactually an exclusion zone extending 1½ kilometres ahead of them and 1 kilometre behind. In those days, with a plethora of small working boats plying their trade along the Channel coast, such niceties would have been impractical and, before radar, unenforceable.

The day of departure was a typical misty autumn one. The harbour at Southampton had been used by the crew only a few times. (It will be remembered that the company had moved there only because of the great length of the *Olympic*.) It would be reasonable to assume that the ship's officers would be particularly careful in manoeuvring through unfamiliar channels, but that would be to forget that the ship was under the command of Captain E. J. Smith, whose cavalier attitude to hazard was to play a central part in a tragedy that would happen less than a year later. In the event the *Olympic* reached the end of the Thorn Channel, north of Cowes, without incident. At West Bramble Buoy, which it reached at 12:43 p.m., it began a turn to port (the ship's left). This would take it down the east coast of the Isle of Wight, still the route used by ships making the passage from the Solent to Cherbourg. While making this manoeuvre it sounded its whistle twice, to alert nearby shipping of the change in course. It also increased speed from 10 to 16 knots (12 to 18 miles per hour). It was just then that a ship appeared behind it. This was HMS *Hawke*, an armoured cruiser, which was making its way at speed on a clockwise circumnavigation of the island. The cruiser must have been travelling at more than the *Olympic's* 16 knots as it passed Egypt Point, the northernmost point of the Isle of Wight, because it began to overtake the great liner on the starboard (its right-hand side). Its bow was at least as far forward as the *Olympic's* third funnel, though one witness claimed that it was level with the liner's bridge, when the cruiser's captain, Commander W. F. Blunt, seems to have realised that the two ships were making for the same channel and that there was not room for both of them. He ordered a reduction in speed, and the *Hawke* began to fall back.

Then disaster happened. As with the tug in New York Harbour, the huge propellers of the *Olympic* made their influence felt, and their suction began to pull in the much smaller *Hawke*. There was little the cruiser could do to avoid the collision. By reducing speed it had lost some of the effectiveness of its rudders, as these are at their best when the pressure of the water from the propellers is operating directly on them. To increase speed now would simply drive the cruiser harder into the *Olympic's* side. Commander Blunt did the only thing he could by stopping the port engine and by going hard astern on the starboard one. This would normally be enough to pull the bow of the cruiser to starboard, away from the liner. In the event, however, the suction was too great and the armoured bow of the *Hawke*—designed to sink ships by ramming them—crashed into the *Olympic's* starboard side, in the area of second-class cabins towards the stern, and holing it above and below the waterline.

Luckily, the accident happened during lunch, when all the passengers were in the dining saloons, and nobody was seriously injured. There was considerable damage to some of the cabins, however, and as the *Hawke* struggled to free itself, losing its battering-ram prow and almost capsizing as it did so, much cabin furniture and luggage was pulled into the sea. Among these was a leather bag containing clothes, surgical instruments and other things belonging to a Dr Downton. The bag was picked up by a passing boatman and handed in to the Customs at Cowes.

The waterproof compartments meant that the *Olympic* was in no danger of sinking, although two of them were full. The ship was brought to a standstill and the anchor dropped while Captain Smith reviewed the damage. There was a hole 25 feet high and 10 feet wide in his ship's side, 85 feet from the stern. The *Hawke's* ram had gone in far enough to bend the *Olympic's* starboard propeller shaft and fracture the engine's crankshaft, and damage had also been done to the starboard propeller. Worse, the main turbine was inoperable, possibly because of the shock of the collision. There was no possibility of the vessel continuing its journey; and because it was lower in the water it was not able to return to Southampton till the next day, when there would be a suitably high tide. In the meantime about one hundred passengers who wished to return to London were taken off that evening by the Isle of Wight ferry *Duchess of York*. The remaining passengers, possibly feeling quite adventurous, were happy to remain on board until the next day, when, assisted by tugs, the injured giant was brought into the Harland and Wolff repair yard and the crew released.

The same day White Star issued a writ for the costs incurred in the accident against Commander Blunt (as, for most of the twentieth century, the Royal Prerogative meant that government institutions were immune from prosecution). The Royal Navy countered with a writ against the White Star Line for the expenses incurred in the repair of its cruiser. Two inquiries followed. The first, convened by the navy, began hearings on 22 September. It exonerated Commander Blunt of any fault. The Court of Enquiry, which delivered its judgement on 19 December, agreed with the naval inquiry and found against White Star, saying that the accident was solely due to the faulty navigation of the *Olympic*.

Years later Captain Bertram Hayes of the White Star Line would say that the Admiralty must have had the better lawyer, because it didn't have the better case. Although the company appealed all the way to the House of Lords, it was unable to get the verdict overturned. This may seem a perverse judgement in the light of modern maritime 'rules of the road', whereby an overtaking ship must give way at all times to the ship being overtaken, and where a ship moving in a restricted channel must keep to the right of that channel as much as is safe, as the *Olympic* was doing— hence the *Hawke's* inability to pass it on its starboard side. The Admiralty argued, however, that there had been room for the *Hawke* to pass when it began the manoeuvre but that Captain Smith had closed the gap by moving the *Olympic* to the right. The Admiralty used expert evidence to argue that the suction of the *Olympic* on the *Hawke* would have caught the cruiser on its way forward if the ships had been travelling on a parallel course. On the other hand it could be argued that Captain Smith could have averted disaster by stopping his engines once he saw the effect his propellers were having on the *Hawke*. He had already had the problem in New York but seems to have made no attempt to learn from it.

The result was a financial disaster for White Star. Its business plan would have required the income from the *Olympic* to help pay for the completion of the *Titanic*. It was necessary, therefore, to get it back in service as soon as possible. To that end it was transferred to Belfast, where the *Titanic* was cannibalised to provide parts that the *Olympic* urgently needed, for example its propeller shaft. Work was done quickly enough for the *Olympic* to be back in service by November.

This was not the last time, however, that the *Olympic* had need of its younger sister. The following February it lost a propeller blade and purloined a replacement from the *Titanic*.

The *Hawke* incident may have been a problem financially, but the publicity it gained was probably worth every penny. Amazed that any ship could remain afloat with the amount of damage done to the *Olympic*, people began to talk of it as 'unsinkable', and they were encouraged to think that a crossing of the Atlantic could be considered 100 per cent safe. It was unwise of them to think so. Nevertheless White Star felt sufficiently reassured by public opinion to go ahead with ordering the third great ship in the trinity, the RMS *Britannic*.

Meanwhile the *Titanic* was nearing completion. It is a comment on the efficiency of the Belfast shipyard workers that in spite of the setbacks caused by its use as organ donor to the *Olympic* it was ready for its first voyage in April 1912. Much of its story had taken place in the shadow of its older sister. It had been ejected from its graving-dock when the *Olympic* had needed it after the *Hawke* incident. Even its launch, though well attended, was not quite the glamorous affair that the *Olympic's* was: its hull was sent into the Lagan in workaday black, with no concessions to the convenience of photographers. For that matter, its very name put it in second place. It was named after the Titans, the original giants of the Earth, who had been consigned to oblivion by the Olympic gods, under the leadership of Zeus.

For anyone of a superstitious nature the scheduling of the *Titanic's* sea trials for 1 April seemed inauspicious, but bad weather meant that they were postponed to the following day. When its trials did take place it passed them with no difficulty. It reached a maximum speed of 23.5 knots (27 miles per hour) and at high speed had a turning circle of just under three-quarters of a mile. Some idea of the momentum built up by a ship of this size is given by the fact that, from travelling at a speed of 20 knots (23 miles per hour) it took half a mile to come to a stop.

The *Titanic* now sailed for Southampton, where it tied up just before midnight on 3 April. The following day the remaining officers and men came aboard. Stewards familiarised themselves with the interior of the ship so that they could assist passengers to find their way about. Cargo came on board and was stowed. All was ready, but for one thing. There had been a coal strike in Britain since February, and many ships could not sail. White Star would not tolerate any more delays. Coal was scavenged from the bunkers of every ship in the International Mercantile Marine group that would not be sailing. As sailing day approached, the *Titanic* acquired its full load of coal.

The voyage itself was due to start on 10 April, at midday. During the morning passengers wandered around the ship. Second-class passengers had an opportunity to see how the other half lived, as they were allowed to visit all the first-class public rooms while the ship was alongside. No doubt they also hoped to have glimpses of the rich and the beautiful, because Ismay's vision of a floating Grand Hotel had now become reality. Once at sea, class divisions would be rigorously enforced.

On schedule, tugs began to manoeuvre the *Titanic* from its berth at noon. Its outer engines started, and its side propellers began to revolve. In a ghastly replay of the *Hawke* incident, the suction created by the *Titanic's* movement began to drag the liner *New York,* on the *Titanic's* starboard side, away from its berth. So great was the suction that the *New York's* mooring cables were snapped and the smaller ship began to drift free. Captain Smith, who had transferred from the *Olympic* to the *Titanic,* had learnt his lesson by now. He had his port engine go astern to increase the distance between his ship and the *New York.* One of his attendant tug-boats got the smaller liner under control and moved it out of the way. The *Titanic* was free to proceed.

At Cherbourg more passengers came on board, including one of America's richest men, John Jacob Astor, who was returning from his honeymoon. Not all of those embarking were glamorous or fashionable. One of the two tenders, the *Traffic,* brought steerage passengers as well as mail. After Cherbourg, the final port of call before the crossing proper began was Queenstown (Cóbh), County Cork. Here most of those embarking were emigrants, travelling in steerage on their way to a new life in America.

The *Titanic* now continued south-west. The weather became much colder, and there were occasional patches of fog. As darkness approached on the evening of their fifth day at sea, Sunday 14 April, the wireless operators on board were kept busy sending private messages to Cape Race radio station, to be forwarded by cable; but among the incoming traffic was a growing number of ice warnings. One of these, from Masaba, which Captain Smith may not have seen, gave almost the exact position of the iceberg that was to be the *Titanic's* nemesis. At about 11 o'clock the liner *Californian,* only ten miles away, sent a warning that it had been forced to stop at 10:30 because of icebergs. The *Titanic's* senior radio operator, John (Jack) Phillips, was busy with messages for Cape Race and had replied: 'Shut up, shut up! I am busy; I am working Cape Race!'

The previous year, 1911, had been a particularly warm one in the northern hemisphere, and the high temperatures had caused more icebergs than usual to break off from the Greenland Ice Shelf. Some of these had been caught in the Labrador Current, a cold-water flow that travels south along the coast of Canada and the north-eastern United States. Several ships were even concerned enough about the number of icebergs to stop for the night. The *Titanic* did not but continued on its course at about 22 knots (25 miles per hour).

It is difficult to work out the thought processes of Captain Smith on that fateful evening. He was aware of the ice warnings, as some of them were posted on the bridge. He was not in a race for New York: there were no records that he was in a position to break. If the reports of ice had worried him there were at least two options open to him. He could have taken his ship further south, beyond the icebergs, before crossing the Labrador Current, rather than sail directly to New York; alternatively, he could have slowed the ship down, giving the lookouts a better chance to spot any danger ahead and the crew more time to react. He did neither. Had he too come to believe that his ship was unsinkable?

It was the worst sort of night for spotting an iceberg. There was no moon, so there would be no reflection off the ice. The sea was without a ripple, so there would be no breaking water to show the base of the iceberg. Worse, there was a slight haze, so they could not even pick out the horizon. Even so, at about 11:40 p.m. the two lookouts saw a huge shape looming out of the haze. One of them rang the ship's bell three times, the standard warning that there was an object dead ahead. He then telephoned the bridge with the information. First Officer William Murdoch reacted quickly. To slow the ship down, he ordered all the engines to go hard astern. He then ordered a turn to port and closed the ship's watertight doors, isolating the sixteen compartments from each other. His manoeuvre almost worked, and it looked as if the *Titanic's* starboard side would pass harmlessly alongside the iceberg. There was a collision, but it did not seem very violent. Indeed one of the lookouts commented to the other, 'That was a narrow shave.' An old iceberg is a twisted and jagged thing, however, and under the water a spur of ice had slashed its way through 300 feet of the hull, popping rivets and twisting steel plates like paper.

Captain Smith was wakened and made his way to the bridge. His first task was to establish the extent of the damage, and he sent Fourth Officer Joseph Boxhall forward to make a preliminary survey. When Boxhall came back and reported that the mail room was flooding, Smith ordered him to calculate the ship's exact position, just in case. Bruce Ismay arrived, a suit pulled over his pyjamas. He was told that the *Titanic* had struck an iceberg and that it looked as if it was seriously damaged.

Smith now asked Thomas Andrews, on board with a small team from Harland and Wolff, to join him on the bridge. Lord Pirrie would normally have been on board but was recovering from illness; his doctors had forbidden him to travel, and his nephew had taken his place. After Andrews arrived on the bridge the two men set out on a tour of inspection. They were shocked to find that five watertight compartments were flooding already. The damage exceeded their worst fears, and Andrews's calculations showed that the ship would sink in less than two hours.

Smith knew what had to be done. He ordered the lifeboats to be prepared and then went himself to the wireless room, where he gave the operator, Phillips, a note of the ship's exact position and asked him to send what was then the international distress signal, CQD, together with the *Titanic's* call sign, MGY. Ironically, the wireless officer on the nearest ship, the *Californian*, had finished duty at 11:30, still annoyed at the rebuff he had received from the *Titanic*.

The engine rooms were a hive of activity. The engines were stopped, but there was the danger of an explosion if the water reached the furnaces, and these were now being raked out. Already the crew had had to abandon the foremost boilers, which had flooded quickly. Some of the passengers also had to move quickly. The steerage-class accommodation for single passengers was far forward, and deep below the waterline; water was already coming under the cabin doors. Other passengers, in first and second class, noticed little; some even returned to their beds after being told that the ship had struck ice. On the well deck, near the bow, some steerage passengers had discovered large amounts of ice that had broken off the iceberg.

It was not only passengers who thought nothing serious had happened. Quartermaster George Rowe, on duty on the poop deck, right at the stern of the ship, had seen a tall shape pass in the night and thought there had been a close encounter with a sailing ship. It was almost an hour later, when he noticed a lifeboat in the water, that he contacted the bridge and found out what was happening.

Long before this, however, a list had developed on the ship, at first sensed rather than seen, then definite enough to be measured. Smith ordered the passengers to be mustered, the boat assignments to be brought, and the remaining officers to be roused. Throughout the ship, crew members were being roused from their bunks, and they gradually began to realise the seriousness of the position. Even among the passengers there was a growing awareness of their predicament, although no alarm had been sounded. Men from the steerage quarters near the bow of the ship came aft to warn the single women in their quarters.

One problem that became obvious was that the seamen did not know their assignments. There had been no lifeboat drill on the journey, and notices allocating crew members to lifeboat stations were either not posted or not read. No attempt had been made to allocate passengers to boats—perhaps because it would have become obvious that there were lifeboat places for only half those on board that night. Not that anybody was anxious to board the lifeboats. There was an understandable tendency to trust to the bulk and brightness of the ship rather than take a leap into the unknown by trusting oneself to the darkness of the ocean in a tiny rowing boat. There seemed no rush to get people into the boats, in spite of Ismay's urgings, and it was not till 12:45 on the Monday morning, more than an hour after the collision, that the first, Boat 7, was lowered away. It was this boat that Quartermaster Rowe spotted and reported to the bridge. He was ordered to come to the bridge himself and to bring some rockets with him. These he gathered from a locker nearby and carried in their tin box.

The reason for the rockets was that the lights of the *Californian* had been spotted, and it was hoped that its crew would recognise the *Titanic's* distress signals. An attempt had already been made to contact it by Morse lamp, but the distance was just too great for it to come to anything. One rocket was fired every five or six minutes. These were seen on the *Californian,* but the officer of the watch, Second Officer Herbert Stone, merely wondered why a ship would fire rockets so late at night.

The operators at their station were having a little more luck. The *Frankfort* answered at 12:18 but gave no indication of how far away it was. Other ships followed; but the first real moment of hope was when the Cunarder *Carpathia* almost accidentally contacted the *Titanic* at 12:25. When told the news, its wireless operator reported to the captain and soon came back with the information that it was only fifty-eight miles from the stricken liner and was 'coming hard.' The *Olympic* was 500 miles away but was also coming with all speed.

At about this time Captain Smith called in to the radio room for an update. While he was there the second operator, Harold Bride, suggested that they send the new international distress signal, sos. In Morse code this was dot-dot-dot dash-dash-dash dot-dot-dot, so easy that the rankest amateur could recognise it. At 12:45, just as the first lifeboat settled in the water, the first sos ever was sent out by an ocean liner.

As people began to accept that they were in danger, sad partings began to take place all around the ship. Because of the shortage of lifeboats, Captain Smith had ordered that women and children be allowed leave first. Some women refused to leave their husbands, but most got into the boats. Things were becoming more urgent, as the slant of the deck had now become steep enough to create unease in even the most sanguine of passengers. The work had to be done more quickly, and, under pressure, more mistakes were made. Boats were lowered without a full complement: Boat 1 had only twelve people on board, although its capacity was forty. Even when this was happening Second Officer Herbert Lightoller, in command on the port side, refused to allow any man to enter a boat, even if there was space. He made only one exception, when he allowed a Canadian yachtsman to join a boat that had only one seaman aboard.

On the starboard side First Officer William Murdoch was more pragmatic, allowing men to board any boat in which there was space if there were no women around to take their place. It was from this side that the almost empty Boat 1 had been lowered. People had moved further aft, however, so there was no-one around. Below decks, on the other hand, there were many people who did not have a chance even to see Boat 1. Many steerage-class passengers were kept below, and only women were allowed on deck, in small parties, to be conducted to individual boats. Steward John Hart brought two groups on deck, to Boats 8 and 15, and the latter was waved away at 1:30 a.m.

Not all the emigrants were so lucky. Some found themselves in a cul-de-sac as they tried to reach the upper decks. More chillingly, some found themselves up against barriers manned by sailors who refused to let them through. Many of these passengers gave up, and some went to their dining saloon, where they began to say the Rosary.

On deck, eyes were still fixed on the *Californian*. In the still night its lights were so clear that it seemed only a short distance away, and it must have been unbelievably frustrating to be ignored, in spite of continued attempts to attract its attention with rockets and Morse lamp. In fact the watch on the *Californian* were examining the spectacle with great interest. Its officers simply could not make sense of what appeared to be a list on the *Titanic,* nor of the fact that its red (port) navigation light had disappeared. Other ships did not seem any more capable of understanding what had happened. Even the *Olympic* asked, at 1:25: 'Are you steering south to meet us?' At 1:45 Phillips sent to the *Carpathia*: 'Come as quickly as possible, old man; engine room filling up to the boilers.'

There was now no reluctance to enter the boats. Some men disguised themselves as women; others hid themselves under the seats; some simply leapt into boats as they were lowered. Guns were fired and culprits hauled out, where possible. Many men, on the other hand, seemed to have accepted their fate. There were small groups of men talking in various parts of the ship. Ismay seemed to be one of them, moving calmly as C Boat, one of the collapsible lifeboats, was prepared for lowering. Then, just as it was about to be lowered, he stepped on board and sat among the passengers.

Only two boats remained, both under Lightoller's supervision. Boat 4 was lowered so that passengers could enter it through a window from A deck. The second officer examined everyone boarding to ensure that no men were sneaking away. When that was done they moved to D Boat, where again only women were allowed on board. At 2:05 this, the last boat, was lowered. There were two more collapsibles lashed to the roof of the officers' quarters, but it was obvious that efforts to release them were hopeless.

A 2:05 Captain Smith told the radio operators that they were released from their duties, and he then moved among those members of the crew still standing beside the empty davits and told them it was every man for himself. Some of the crew chose to take to the waters at this stage, although the seamen among them must have known that they would not survive long before succumbing to the cold. Most of the remaining passengers seemed to be awaiting their fate. A steward saw Thomas Andrews at about 2:10. He was stretched out on a card table, looking strained and drained of energy. He did not react when spoken to.

Now the *Titanic* began to sink more quickly. Survivors describe seeing a wave sweeping up the deck. Some jumped; others waited till they were level with the water and stepped in. One thing all of them felt was the desire to be clear of the ship, free from the suction as it sank and from the tangles of rope and other debris that might drag them into the depths. Those watching from the boats sat in horrified silence, not sure what they were seeing in the dim starlight. None reported the hull breaking in two.

Finally, it was gone, fast enough in the end to cause a gulping sound as it sank. It was 2:20 a.m.

For those unfortunates now floundering in the water the end was relatively quick. The temperature of the water on that April night was 28 degrees Fahrenheit, lower than the freezing point of fresh water and low enough to induce hypothermia within a few minutes. The more the swimmers struggled, the more quickly they would have lost heat. Shivering would have disabled them, and then a slight sense of inebriation. From that to a desire to sleep would have taken a very short time, and from sleep to death would have been almost instantaneous. Only those who were extremely fit, and who had an overwhelming drive to live, would have survived for any length of time; and even then survival was not an open-ended process. It depended on being lifted out of the life-sapping sea while there was still a sufficient vital spark burning within their bodies. Some clung to the overturned Boat B. As the only other things clear of the water were the remaining lifeboats, these were the swimmers' only hope of salvation. Yet they provided little help.

Fifth Officer Rowe did his best. He rounded up Boats 14 (his own), 10, 12, 4 and D and tied them together. He divided the passengers among the other boats and then, with a hand-picked crew, took Boat 14 back in among the flotsam. All this took time, however, and it was after 3 o'clock before he picked up his first survivor. He picked up four in total, of whom one died within the hour.

In Boat 5, third Officer Herbert Pitman gave the order to go back to the wreck site, but his women passengers demanded that he not go, and so the boat, with a capacity of sixty-five and only forty on board, sat in the low Atlantic swell and listened to people dying three hundred yards away.

It was different in Boat 6. Here the women wanted to return but Quartermaster Robert Hitchens refused. Boat 6, with a capacity of sixty-five yet only twenty-eight on board, also floated motionless on the swell. Boat 1, under the command of Lookout George Symons and in which there were only twelve people—only two of them women—continued rowing away from the scene. On the upturned Boat B, thirty men balanced precariously on the boat's bottom, trying to counteract the swell in case they were thrown into the water and listening to the ominous hiss of air as it escaped from the hull.

Altogether, only 13 of the 1,600 people who were still on the *Titanic* after all the boats had gone were plucked out of the water, and most of them were rescued by boats that were still close to the scene. Only Boat 14 returned to look for survivors.

As the last despairing cries died down, the night became strangely peaceful. The stars were bright, and some in the boat spoke of showers of meteorites. After a while Fourth Officer Boxhall began firing off green flares. As the night went on, however, and there was still no sign of rescue, the early composure was lost and people began to bicker. On Boat 1 this took an ironic turn. Fireman Robert Pusey complained to Sir Cosmo Duff Cooper that passengers, even though they had lost everything, at least had the wherewithal to start over again. Sailors, on the other had, had not only lost their kit but had their wages stopped from the moment the ship had sunk. In an impatient gesture that he was afterwards to regret, Duff Cooper promised the crew of the lifeboat £5 each towards the cost of a new kit. When news of this got out later, it seemed uncommonly like a bribe.

At about 3:30 a.m. there was a distant flash in the south-west, followed by a distant boom. Soon afterwards the lights of a distant steamer became visible. The *Carpathia* was coming.

Even now, life was not guaranteed. Spirits that were ravaged by shock and grief and cold still found it easy to give up and pass into the peace of death. The task of laying a large ship alongside small boats that were in some cases overcrowded and in others not manned by proper sailors was not an easy one. Finally, getting the half-frozen survivors on board was not straightforward. But Captain Arthur Rostron of the *Carpathia* demonstrated excellent seamanship and by the end of the day had picked up 705 survivors, whom he then transported to New York. Behind, floating on the surface or dragged deep into the dark of the ocean, were some 1,500 bodies.

Among those lost were eight men from the shipyard, ranging in seniority from Thomas Andrews to three young apprentices. A fourth apprentice survived and settled in America. Also among the survivors was Bruce Ismay. By all reports, he was a devastated man. Although consulted by Captain Rostron on everything to do with the rescue and putting the survivors ashore, he was incapable of making a decision. After the disaster he retired effectually from public life. He was not allowed to return to Britain until the completion of the American inquiry into the sinking. He later bought an estate in Ireland and spent most of the rest of his life there. As for Lord Pirrie, who might well have been on board, the shock of the sinking and the loss of his nephew prolonged his already slow recuperation, and he was not fully recovered till late 1912.

Harland and Wolff came quite well out of the inquiries. Captain Smith, conveniently dead, was blamed for sailing too fast in an area where ice was known to be present. The Board of Trade was censured for its failure to upgrade its regulations to match the requirements of the new breed of large liners, particularly in the matter of watertight subdivisions of hulls and of lifeboats. Harland and Wolff, on the contrary, was praised for the quality of its workmanship and exonerated from all blame. There was a suggestion, nevertheless, that watertight bulkheads should in future be extended to the highest continuous deck.

The new chief designer at Queen's Island, who had trained under Thomas Andrews and had worked with him on the drawings of the *Titanic,* set himself the task of finding new ways to make large passenger liners safer. Over the next three years Harland and Wolff patented new designs for systems for lowering and raising lifeboats, working watertight doors and keeping bulkheads open in emergencies.

The *Olympic* was not allowed to wait for these developments. It had left New York on 13 April but was too far from the *Titanic* to help in any constructive way. It arrived in Southampton on Sunday 21 April. Although it was due to sail again on the 24th it was subjected to several inspections before it would be allowed to leave. First of all, it was fitted with twenty-four extra lifeboats. Its crew was also increased, so that there would be enough able seamen to man the extra boats.

But the capacity of the boats was only half the problem. The *Titanic's* boats had left the ship while they still had spare capacity. Lifeboat drill was needed, and several practices were undertaken by the *Olympic* before the authorities were satisfied with the speed and efficiency of the manoeuvre. Even after this the crew were unhappy about the collapsible boats, but these were shown to be, for all practical purposes, watertight. In addition, 168 new crew members were signed on. Still the original crew were unhappy. The newcomers, they said, were inexperienced and would prove a liability. White Star gave up at this point and cancelled the scheduled trip. This gave the line time to find union-approved crew and boats.

The *Olympic* left Southampton on 15 May and arrived in New York on the 22nd. As soon as it was berthed the chairman of the American inquiry into the sinking of the *Titanic* came on board. He was shown the ship's safety features and investigated the capacity of its lifeboats. He seemed to be satisfied, and the *Olympic* made several more round trips that year before it was recalled to Belfast for modifications in keeping with the British inquiry's recommendations.

The changes were drastic. It had an inner hull installed, so that in any future collision it would have a second line of defence. Its bulkheads were also raised, as recommended. The most obvious external change was to the number of lifeboats. The new lifeboats were stacked in such a way that the ship was now able to carry a total of sixty-eight. The extra lifeboats took up space, but this was compensated to some extent by the promenades on B deck being made into passenger cabins. The revamped *Olympic,* now thirty-one tons heavier than the *Titanic,* left Belfast for Southampton on 22 March 1913 and on 2 April began its first crossing of the Atlantic in its new role as the largest ship in the world.

Modifying the *Britannic* was less of a problem, as it was still on the slip and the changes could be incorporated in its building programme. Its keel had been laid late in 1911, and when it was duly launched, on 26 February 1914, an extended watertight double skin ran the full length of the boiler and engine rooms, rising four feet above the maximum load line. Its bulkheads were extended, as they had been in the *Olympic,* giving it seventeen watertight compartments. It was calculated that it could remain afloat if any six compartments were flooded.

Changes were made to the arrangements for lifeboats as well. The *Britannic* would carry forty-six open lifeboats, arranged in four groups on each side of the boat deck. There were even facilities for transferring some boats from one side to the other if the need arose. There was more passenger space on the boat deck as well, which meant that passengers could board the boats here rather than have to transfer to them from a lower deck, an operation that had caused difficulties and delays on the *Titanic.* The davits were motor-powered, and there was a light on the end of each.

Problems of communication were also addressed. A pneumatic tube ran from the wireless room to the bridge, so that navigational messages could be passed without delay from one place to the other.

There were improvements for passengers too. The forward end of the promenade deck was covered in to provide shelter in heavy weather, while the aft shelter deck was enclosed for the benefit of steerage passengers. New facilities were planned: a hairdressing salon for women; a children's playroom; dog kennels; a gymnasium for second-class passengers; and an extra lift—the fourth—for first-class passengers. It was hoped the *Britannic* would be in service by the spring of 1915.

Fate intervened in August 1914. After a sequence of diplomatic exchanges among their governments that had all the logic and perspicacity of an exchange by clowns in a circus, the people of Europe found themselves at war. Many greeted the calamity with enthusiasm, as something that would pass the long days of autumn and early winter and would help to shorten the winter. The British government, as sanguine as any retired major airing his chauvinist views after a round of golf, nevertheless had to make some prudent preparations. One of these was to channel the flow of raw materials to war production. This had grave implications for Harland and Wolff.

Bereft of components, the *Britannic* was left on its slip. For the *Olympic*, on the other hand, it was business as usual for the time being, except that its port of embarkation was changed to Liverpool, to minimise the threat from German submarines. It left the Mersey on 16 September, packed with Americans and Canadians anxious to leave Europe and the war behind. Liverpool was unsatisfactory as a port, as a ship of the *Olympic's* size had to anchor in the river, and so on its return, on 3 October, it berthed in Greenock. The White Star management decided to send it for one last round trip to America, with the intention of laying it up in Belfast afterwards. It left the Clyde on 9 October, steered a zigzag course across the Atlantic and was in New York by the 16th. After five days it was ready to return, sailing on the 21st. It would be an uneventful trip to Greenock, then to Belfast, until it was needed for the war effort.

But it was not to be so simple. It was not only the captain of the Olympic who was concerned about the dangers of German submarines. The Admiralty was concerned that Scapa Flow in the Orkneys, the main base of the Grand Fleet, was within easy reach of German submarine bases and decided that it would be unwise to allow the fleet to remain there until the base's anti-submarine defences were substantially improved. In the meantime the fleet was ordered to Lough Swilly in County Donegal. This remarkable sea lough is a genuine fjord, at its deepest in the centre and at its shallowest near the mouth. In this way it had its own anti-submarine defences, as it would be a brave U-boat commander who would risk his ship trying to enter the lough submerged. Shore batteries were there to deal with any German vessel that was foolhardy enough to enter the lough on the surface. The Germans, not being foolish, decided to make things difficult for the fleet in the approaches to Lough Swilly and had accordingly laid minefields.

On the morning of 27 October, while the *Olympic* was nearing Ireland, the Second Battle Squadron was conducting manoeuvres near Tory Island, ten miles off the west Donegal coast. At 8:50 the brand-new battleship *Audacious* struck a mine. Unsure whether the explosion had been caused by mine or torpedo, and aware that a squadron of battleships milling around would provide a tempting target for any passing U-boat, Admiral John Jellicoe ordered the light cruiser *Liverpool*, together with some smaller craft, to stand by the *Audacious* while he led the remainder of the squadron to safer waters. (It is interesting to note that Jellicoe's fear of torpedo attack would later allow the German High Seas Fleet to escape from his grasp at the Battle of Jutland.)

At about 10:30 a.m. the captain of the *Liverpool* saw a huge liner appear over the horizon. Having identified the newcomer as the *Olympic*, he signalled that he wanted the liner's assistance in evacuating the crew of the crippled battleship. Two hundred and fifty sailors were left on board the *Audacious* as a skeleton crew, and it was decided to try to tow it to safety, using the *Olympic* as a tug. The tides in this area flow very strongly westwards during the ebb and eastwards in the flood. The tide may have helped the rescue effort in its early hours, but when the *Olympic* turned on a southerly course to approach Lough Swilly the situation got out of hand. By this time the steering gear on the *Audacious* had failed and its huge bulk became unmanageable, and the towing cable parted. The *Olympic* stood by while several attempts were made by naval ships to come to the aid of the battleship, but all failed. It was obvious that the ship was sinking, and by 6:30 p.m. the remainder of the crew were taken off. At 8:55 the evening was lit by a huge explosion in the forward magazine of the battleship, and within moments it capsized and sank. Not a single member of its crew was lost, and the men were later transferred to a new battleship, the *Queen Elizabeth*.

This was not the end of the affair as far as the *Olympic* was concerned. First of all it had to disembark the survivors of the *Audacious* in Lough Swilly. As many of its passengers, although American citizens, were of German origin, they were not allowed to catch a glimpse of the Grand Fleet. They had seen the sinking of the battleship, but the British authorities, in an effort to delay the spreading of the news by having extended interviews with German-American passengers on disembarkation, arranged for it to berth not at Greenock, as planned, but at Belfast on 3 November. Captain Haddock was given command of the Special Service Squadron—a number of merchant ships that were being redesigned to look like battleships in an effort to confuse the enemy. The *Olympic* itself was to remain in Belfast for ten months.

Nearby was the *Britannic*. As the war had begun to spread about much of the world, the British government realised that it would have need of large, fast ships capable of transporting large numbers of soldiers to distant theatres of conflict. In the light of this, shipyards had been allowed to complete liners that were under construction but were required to modify them so that they were more suitable for use as troopships.

In the early months of 1915 the main focus was on the Turkish peninsula of Gallipoli, where it was hoped that a concentrated effort would knock Germany's ally out of the war. By May the *Britannic* had completed its moored engine trials and was prepared for entry into emergency service in as little as four weeks. As the year progressed, the fighting grew in ferocity and the need for moving troops increased. In September 1915 the *Olympic* was requisitioned for service as a troopship. It was moved to Liverpool, where it was rapidly painted—as it had been moored in the dirty water of Belfast Harbour for ten months—and on the 24th left Liverpool for Moúdros, on the Greek island of Lémnos, under the command of Captain Bertram Hayes.

The *Olympic's* war continued to be eventful. On this first trip it rescued passengers from the French liner *Provincia,* which had been sunk by a German submarine. The gesture was much appreciated by the French government but earned a rebuke for the *Olympic's* captain from the Royal Navy, as the fully loaded ship, carrying six thousand soldiers, would have made a tempting target for any passing enemy submarine. It was more than nine days in Moúdros, as that was how long it took to disembark the soldiers.

Now came the *Britannic's* turn. In November 1915 it was requisitioned as a hospital ship. The brutal nature of the fighting at Gallipoli meant that there were huge numbers of wounded to be treated and evacuated. The ship's civilian fittings were put in storage and its public rooms and upper decks were converted into wards for the wounded, as was the partially covered first-class promenade. The first-class dining room and reception rooms became operating theatres and main wards. Medical personnel were accommodated on B deck, while medical orderlies and the more lightly wounded would occupy the lower decks. It would be able to carry well over three thousand casualties.

There was a problem with the number of lifeboats, and fourteen extra davits had to be fitted, each capable of handling two lifeboats. This gave it a total of fifty-eight lifeboats. Modifications also had to be made to its hull. It was to wear the internationally recognised livery of a hospital ship: it was painted white, with a green bank from stem to stern, broken in three places by large red crosses. Two more large red crosses were placed on the boat deck, and these were illuminated at night. There was also a line of green electric bulbs running the length of the promenade deck. To ensure that there would be no misunderstanding, the Admiralty, through unofficial channels, let the Germans know of the *Britannic's* new status in early December 1915. The ship completed its sea trials on 8 December and left for Liverpool on the 11th, where the *Olympic* was also berthed. Here its medical equipment was fitted and its new captain, James Bartlett, took command. Finally, on 23 December, it left for the eastern Mediterranean.

Its first stop was Naples. The *Britannic*, like its sister-ship *Olympic*, had been designed for the relatively short North Atlantic route and did not carry enough coal in its bunkers to sail to Greece and back without refuelling. As it needed to get its wounded to hospital in England as quickly as possible, it made more sense to top up its bunkers on the outward rather than the return journey. Troopships took on coal on the way home.

The journey was busy in other ways. The hospital areas of the ship had to be disinfected and 3,309 beds got ready for patients. The *Britannic* arrived in Moúdros on New Year's Eve and immediately began embarking its complement of sick, transferred from smaller hospital ships that had brought them from Turkey. The transfer took a few days, but the *Britannic* was soon at sea again, making for Southampton. As it passed Gibraltar, Captain Bartlett signalled the number of walking wounded he had on board, as well as the numbers of those with notifiable diseases, such as dysentery and cholera. This was done so that arrangements could be made at Southampton to transfer patients to the appropriate hospitals with minimum delay.

The *Britannic* completed two more round trips to the eastern Mediterranean before, in the spring of 1916, the Gallipoli campaign was wound down and the surviving soldiers withdrawn from the peninsula. As there was no longer any need for large hospital ships, the Admiralty paid it off, releasing it from war service, as well as the *Mauretania* and *Aquitania*. The *Britannic* returned to Belfast on 6 June, and Harland and Wolff began to convert it to passenger work.

The generals had other ideas, however, and began an offensive in Salonica in the summer. The casualties began to mount once more, and first the *Aquitania* and then the *Britannic* were recalled for service. Harland and Wolff, having read the signs, had already begun the re-conversion.

The *Britannic* had another two successful trips to Lémnos and began another, its sixth, on 12 November. It stopped at Naples for coal and was held up by bad weather for a couple of days, but Captain Bartlett took advantage of a break in the weather and was at sea again on Sunday 19 November. By early on Tuesday morning the *Britannic* was travelling at full speed into the channel between Cape Soúnion, on the Greek main-land, and the island of Kéa. At 8:12 a.m., while the nurses on board were having breakfast, there was a loud explosion. The force of the blast was so great that it allowed the sea into the four watertight compartments at the front of the ship. That should not have been a problem. Unfortunately, the firemen's tunnel, designed to keep the stokers away from the genteel sight of first-class passengers, had also been damaged, and water was now filling watertight compartment 6. Still not a problem, except for the fact that the watertight doors between compartments 5 and 6 would not close properly, and soon compartment 5 was also filling. This was beginning to be a problem: though the ship was designed to float with six compartments flooded, it would not be able to propel itself.

This was when something was noticed that almost turned the scene on board into farce. To ensure that the air within the ship would be as pure and fresh as possible, the nurses had opened nearly all the portholes in the lower decks. Now, fifteen minutes after the explosion, as the ship settled lower, water began to come in through the portholes. The ship was doomed. It was time to prepare the lifeboats.

Captain Bartlett saw only one hope. Kéa was only about three miles away, and if he could keep his ship afloat long enough he would be able to beach it there. It was going to be a difficult feat of seamanship, as the *Britannic* was down by the bow and also listing to starboard. The rudder, while not jammed, was not responding properly, and he had to manoeuvre by balancing the thrust of the port and starboard engines. Slowly the ship began to turn right, towards the island.

Meanwhile a scene was taking place on the boat deck that was worthy of the worst moments on the *Titanic*. Most of the seamen behaved well enough, but some of the stewards panicked and, when they saw the boats ready for lowering, commandeered one. The order came from the bridge that no boats were to be lowered, as the captain was trying to beach the ship. This did not prevent some boats' crews from lowering themselves, using the automatic release mechanism, and soon several boats were in the water, as were several men who had simply jumped. They had gone, however, from the frying pan into the mincing machine. The propellers were still turning. Onlookers watched in horror as two of the boats were sucked into their grasp and the boats and their occupants disappeared in a foam of white and red. Those who could manage it clung to the ropes hanging from the davits; those who could not were dragged inexorably to their fate.

By this time Captain Bartlett was aware of what was happening. He was also receiving reports that the water was rising more quickly, and estimated that it would be unlikely that he could reach shallow water in time. He ordered the engines stopped—much to the relief of a group from the Royal Army Medical Corps, whose lifeboat was just about to come under the propellers.

At 8:35 the order was given to abandon ship. The list to starboard was becoming so great that it soon became impossible to use the davits. Collapsible rafts and deckchairs were thrown over the side. One small lifeboat was even manhandled over the side. At 9 o'clock Bartlett sounded the whistle a last time to warn any remaining engineers to leave their posts. That done, he stepped into the water, which was already up to the level of the bridge. The engineers escaped through a ladder that took them to a door in funnel 4 and from there they dropped into the water. Most of those in the water were soon picked up. Shortly afterwards, the *Britannic* rolled over on its starboard side in a roar of water and falling deck machinery. Then, as the bow sank, its stern reached high into the sky once more and it began its final plunge. As the water closed over its stem the time was 9:07—less than an hour after the explosion. At 48,158 tons, it was the largest war loss the British merchant service ever suffered, and, in spite of all the additional safety features that had been incorporated in its building, it had sunk three times as quickly as its more famous sister, *Titanic*.

The rescue effort began when some Greek fishermen from Kéa arrived and began to pick up survivors and transfer them to the island. Here doctors and nurses immediately opened an improvised dressing station to treat the wounded. Royal Navy ships began arriving after 10 o'clock and began picking up more survivors. In total, 1,036 were saved. Thirty died, although only five bodies were recovered. Another twenty-four were injured. Had there been casualties on board, and in view of the rapidity with which the *Britannic* sank, it is likely that the number of deaths would have been higher even than that of the *Titanic*.

There was an investigation, of course. It concluded that the explosion had probably been caused by a mine, though it would have suited British propaganda if it had been possible to prove that an enemy submarine had torpedoed a hospital ship. An expedition to the site of the wreck in 2003 found a number of mine anchors, supporting the investigation's conclusions.

It may well be considered that the Olympic-class ships were an ill-fated trio, but the oldest sister at least would live into solid middle age and earn for itself the nickname 'Old Reliable'. For the time being the *Olympic* had plied its trade to the eastern Mediterranean until the end of the Gallipoli campaign. After that there was some debate within the Transport Division about how it could best be used. At first the idea of using it to take troops to and from India was considered, but its size and limited range made this a logistic nightmare. While coaling at Cape Town it would be three-quarters of a mile from the harbour mouth, while at Bombay it would have to anchor three miles offshore. The idea was quietly dropped.

Just at this time the Canadian government asked for extra help in moving troops from Halifax to England. The *Olympic* was chartered accordingly and arrived in Halifax on 28 March 1916, ready to take on the waiting soldiers. There was a moment of crisis when Captain Bertram Hayes realised that the Canadians were expecting him to travel as part of a protected convoy that would be moving at 10 knots (12 miles per hour). He pointed out that this would provide German submarines with an almost unmissable target, and that the *Olympic's* best defence was its speed. The Canadians eventually agreed, and it set sail for Liverpool on 5 April. In its continuing series of close encounters with smaller vessels the

Olympic collided with the boat coming to take off the pilot. There were no casualties, but the Canadian boat's mast carried off two lifeboats, damaging one of the davits while doing so.

By the end of the year the *Olympic* had completed ten round trips between Liverpool and Halifax. Soon after arriving in Liverpool at the end of its ninth trip the crew learnt of the loss of the *Britannic*. This meant that, of the three great liners planned by Ismay and Pirrie, only the *Olympic* had ever made it to New York. The war was going on, however, and the *Olympic* made its last trip of the year to the unromantic destination of Halifax. By the time it got back to Liverpool it was long overdue for a refit. It was sent to Belfast, where it arrived on 12 January 1917. It took three months for Harland and Wolff to refit the ship, and it was not till 4 April that the White Ensign was raised on His Majesty's Transport *Olympic*.

Although America joined the war on the Allied side just two days later, on 6 April, for the rest of the year the *Olympic* continued in its Liverpool–Halifax–Liverpool routine, and it was not until December that it was ordered to New York to pick up American troops. It arrived on Christmas Day, the first time it had been to its old berth in three years. The weather was so cold, and the River Hudson so frozen, that it was not until 11 January 1918 that it was ready for its return journey. The American authorities wanted to put two thousand more soldiers on board than it was designed to carry, but Captain Hayes, horrified at the prospect, persuaded them that it would be putting too many eggs in one basket.

By May 1916 the *Olympic* was on its twenty-second trooping voyage. It had left New York on 6 May, and on the very early morning of the 12th it was heading up the English Channel at full speed. By the first light of dawn a lookout spotted a German submarine, travelling on the surface. Captain Hayes ordered the fo'c'sle gun fired, but it could not be depressed sufficiently, and the shot went high. The gunfire alerted the submarine's captain, who suddenly became aware of the fact that there was a huge ship bearing down on him. He tried to dodge to one side, but Hayes altered course at the perfect moment and struck the submarine, damaging it fatally. One of the *Olympic's* escorting destroyers, the USS *Davies*, remained behind to pick up the thirty-one survivors, while the liner made its way to Southampton, arriving there later the same morning. It had received some damage in the incident, but the integrity of its hull was unimpaired.

The rest of the *Olympic's* war was less exciting. The overwhelming capacity of the United States to fight a war, together with a ruthless blockade of Germany by the Royal Navy—a blockade that some people claim killed more German civilians than the Allied bombing of the Second World War—brought Germany to its knees, and the German government sued for peace in November 1918.

In its first peacetime trip in more than four years, the *Olympic* left New York with almost no passengers on board. For the next three months it began to return soldiers from the European theatre of war to their North American homeland. It had a brief refit in February, when it was noticed that it had a dent and a crack below the waterline, which had allowed part of the double skin to flood but had done no serious damage. Given the position of the crack, Captain Hayes believed it had been caused by a torpedo that had failed to explode.

Although the *Olympic* was decommissioned in February and began to sail again under the Red Ensign of the merchant service, it was still employed in taking troops back to America. It made one trip to New York with soldiers it had embarked at Brest. As they approached Manhattan they all moved to one side of the ship, giving it such a list that docking had to be suspended until some of them could be persuaded to move to the other side. After that it made five more trips to Halifax, returning to Liverpool from the last of these in July. Its patriotic duty done, it was sent back to Belfast to be completely refitted, arriving at Harland and Wolff's yard on 16 August 1919. There it was effectually gutted as the process of transforming it into a modern, post-war liner began.

The main change was to its propulsion system, which was converted from coal to oil-burning, so the old bunkers had to be taken out and replaced with new storage tanks. Oil at the time was more expensive than coal, but it had a number of advantages beyond being simply cleaner. It could be loaded in a much shorter time than coal—hours rather than days—so an oil-fired ship did not need to spend as much time in harbour, costing a fortune in harbour fees and earning nothing for its owners. Another advantage was that an oil-fired ship needed a much smaller crew in its engine rooms. The complement for the *Olympic* was reduced from 350 to a mere 60. The cumulative saving in wages, together with the greater number of days that the ship could be earning money, must have produced a net gain for the company.

The *Olympic* was ready for sea in June and left Belfast for Southampton on the 17th. On the short voyage a banquet was held, at which the great and the good could celebrate the return to service of the last of the three giants—'Our one ewe lamb,' as Harold Sanderson called it. But while the merriment was going on in first class, things began to go wrong in a boiler room. It must be remembered that the engineers were new to this system and were not altogether conversant with the idiosyncrasies of the new machinery. When an attendant in the forward stokehold was opening the supply of oil into one of the furnaces, the handle came off in his hand. A pressurised jet of superheated oil came into the compartment just as another attendant was lighting the burn. The resulting fire was so hot that the valve handle could not be replaced, and oil continued to pour in until it was turned off in the next stokehold. It took fifteen minutes to get the fire under control. For the six days after the *Olympic* arrived in Southampton men cleaned up the forward stokehold while others modified the valve handles so that the same accident could not happen again. It was not till midday on 26 June that the *Olympic* pulled away on what turned out to be an uneventful trip to New York.

This was to form the pattern of its existence for the rest of its time on the North Atlantic run. There were occasional excitements, as when Charlie Chaplin travelled to London and agreed to appear in the ship's concert. Other events were less cheerful. In December 1921 the *Olympic* sailed into a strong gale as it made its way towards Cherbourg. It was forced to reduce speed, and to reduce speed again when mountainous seas broke a number of portholes. The seas got worse, and at about 2:05 in the afternoon the ship was thrown about so violently that some of the clasps securing the watertight doors failed. One man had his foot trapped, requiring amputation below the knee; another had his back broken and was killed instantaneously. When the *Olympic* limped into Southampton on 17 December it took the all-out efforts of Harland and Wolff's local workers to have it ready for its scheduled sailing on 22 December. At the end of this trip Captain Hayes left to become captain of the *Majestic,* a 56,000-ton German liner that had been taken by the British as reparation at the end of the war. The *Majestic* was now to become flagship of the White Star fleet.

The nature of the North Atlantic run was changing. Apart from the glamour, one of the main reasons for building giant ships was that they could move large numbers of steerage passengers to America. These, the humblest passengers on board, were the bread and butter of the shipping lines. Their modest fares paid the bills; the contribution of first class was a rather substantial bonus. Now, in May 1921, the American government had begun to restrict immigration. In future it would allow only 360,000 immigrants per year; in July 1924 this number was reduced again to 160,000. Before the war roughly a million Europeans per year had emigrated to America.

There were continuing incidents. As the *Olympic* backed out of its berth in New York on 22 March it collided with the smaller liner *Fort St George.* The smaller ship had serious damage done to its superstructure, but the *Olympic* suffered only a broken sternpost. This it had completely replaced, the first time such a repair had been done. In June it transported the body of Lord Pirrie back to Ireland. He had died on the *Ebro* while on a business trip to South America. For the first time since the war, and so for the first time since Irish independence, the *Olympic* called into Queenstown Harbour, to land the body for transport to Belfast.

In April 1925 a new class was introduced: tourist third cabin. On the *Olympic* the least-favoured second-class cabins were combined with the best of steerage class to accommodate this new category. By 1928 second class and third class had been done away with completely and replaced by tourist class.

The changes in operational procedures confirmed in the International Mercantile Marine group the desire to sell off the White Star Line. In late 1926 Lord Kylsant of the Royal Mail Steam Packet Company agreed on a price, and on 1 January 1927 the *Olympic* became a British ship in every sense of the word, not simply a British-registered one. For all the changes, however, the future did not look bright. At the end of the decade passenger traffic on the North Atlantic was continuing to dwindle, and signs of deterioration were beginning to show in the *Olympic's* hull and super-structure. Subsequent refits showed that the problems were continuing to get worse, and the engines were beginning to show their age. Kylsant borrowed heavily but was unable to come up with the £60,000 necessary for completing the *Oceanic*, which had been ordered from Harland and Wolff to replace the *Olympic*. Work on the *Oceanic* was sus-pended in 1929.

The Royal Mail Group finally collapsed in 1931, when Kylsant was imprisoned for publishing a false prospectus. Worse, the Australian government refused to extend payments due on the Commonwealth Line, another member of the group. The Commonwealth Line ships were sold at a huge loss.

The Cunard Line was also having difficulties, and the British govern-ment agreed to help, but only if Cunard and White Star would merge. White Star brought ten ships to the new fleet, but the *Adriatic*, *Albertic* and *Calgaric* had all been sold for scrap by the end of 1934, and it was obvious that the *Olympic* would soon be going the same way. By this time it had had another spectacular collision, the fifth and most costly of its twenty-four year career.

On the foggy morning of 15 May 1934 the *Olympic* was approaching Nantucket Lightship, off the coast of Massachusetts. Its speed was down to 10 knots (12 miles per hour), but a navigational error caused it to be much closer to the lightship than the officers realised. The red hull of the light-ship suddenly appeared directly in front. The captain ordered full astern on the engines, but the ship was still travelling at 3 to 4 knots when the collision occurred. The momentum of 46,439 tons even at that speed is frightening, and the lightship was reduced to matchwood. Boats were lowered, but the fog made the search difficult. In the end four survivors and three bodies were picked up. Four men were missing.

At the subsequent inquiry, Cunard White Star accepted liability for the accident, although it disputed the $500,000 being claimed from the company. Even without these damages the *Olympic* was no longer economically viable: there had only been two hundred passengers on board when it hit the lightship. It arrived in Southampton for the last time on 12 April 1935. Here it remained berthed until October, when it was sold to ship-breakers in Jarrow, on the Tyne. It tied up at Palmer's Yard, and at 5 p.m. on 13 October its captain rang down to the engine room for the last time, 'Finished with engines.'

The last of the three Graces had given up her spirit. The dream was over.

Chapter 6 ❧

THE THIRD HOME
RULE CRISIS

Gladstone worked hard to eliminate the worst iniquities that absentee landlords and an alien administration had visited upon Ireland. As far back as 1868, in the aftermath of the failed Fenian rising, he declared that he saw his mission as the pacification of Ireland. He was as good as his word, and by 1881 most of the worst features of the Irish land system had been addressed.

This did not satisfy Gladstone, however, as he claimed that while he was on holiday in recently independent Norway, in 1885, he had come to realise that the only long-term solution for Ireland was to grant it a measure of self-government. The date is significant, because it was not until the following year that his government became dependent on the support of the Irish Party (the general name for the home rule and nationalist MPs elected under different names between 1882 and 1918). This allowed him to claim that his belief in home rule was not a conversion of convenience.

Once in power, Gladstone began work on the Government of Ireland Bill (commonly called the First Home Rule Bill). He was at the head of a divided Liberal Party, and it is usually assumed that the divisions arose because of the home rule issue. This is only partially true. There are many complaints in the early twenty-first century of prime ministers having a 'kitchen cabinet'—an inner circle where the real decisions are made. Gladstone went further than that: he made the decisions himself and was always secretive about what he thought and planned. Many party members felt excluded, and it was the way he went about implementing home rule, as much as the issues themselves, that caused the rebellion in the Liberal ranks. Against this simmering background, the Government of Ireland Bill was introduced on 8 April 1886.

There were members of Her Majesty's Loyal Opposition who saw this as a glorious opportunity to bring down the government. Randolph Spencer Churchill, like his son, was a many-sided individual. He found it difficult to fit comfortably within the Conservative Party and indeed had his own breakaway group. He had spent much of his young adulthood in

Dublin, and those who knew him there would have expected him to sympathise with home rule. Churchill, however, was an astute politician and saw politics as a game that combined skill and luck. Luck had delivered the ace of trumps to the Conservative Party, and because he had had the skill to anticipate this Churchill was ready to play the 'Orange card'. He travelled to Belfast and spoke to a packed meeting in the Ulster Hall. During his talk he quoted a poem popular with schoolmasters of the time:

The combat deepens. On, ye Brave
Who rush to glory, or the grave!
Wave, Munich, all thy banners wave,
And charge with all thy chivalry!

The Belfast Conservative establishment might not trust Churchill, seeing him—correctly—as someone who was using a convenient stick with which to beat Gladstone. It was different with the Unionists of Belfast. Churchill went on: 'Ulster at the proper moment will resort to the supreme arbitrament of force; Ulster will fight, and Ulster will be right.' The cheers were deafening.

In the event, the Orange card was not needed: fatal divisions within the Liberal parliamentary party saw to that. When the Government of Ireland Bill was voted on in the House of Commons a substantial number of Liberals voted against the measure, and it failed. The government fell.

Gladstone did not give up entirely. He tried once more in 1892 and this time enforced a great deal more discipline on his party. The bill was passed by the House of Commons but was rejected by the House of Lords. By this time the 'Grand Old Man' of Victorian politics was too old to withstand the blow. He retired from politics, exhausted and broken. The Conservative Party entered more than a decade of uninterrupted rule.

The Liberal comeback occurred in 1906, when the party won a landslide victory and obtained an overall majority in the House of Commons. For the moment, the Irish Party was irrelevant. This ceased to be the case in 1909 when Lloyd George, who was Chancellor of the Exchequer, introduced his 'people's budget'. This was intended to bring in a measure of social security, to be paid for by taxes on land and on income. The aristocracy saw this as an impertinent attack on their wealth and position, and the House of Lords rejected it out of hand. This time the Liberal Party decided to take on the Lords in a battle of wills. In November 1909, after the budget failed in the House of Lords, the Prime Minister, H. H. Asquith, called a general election. This resulted in another Liberal government, but with a reduced majority. When the budget was rejected yet again in 1910, Asquith called yet another general election. This time he lost his overall majority, and it was obvious that he would need the support of the Irish

Party, who by now thought of themselves as nationalists. Home rule was back on the table.

King George v, who had ascended the throne only recently, was mindful of his role as a constitutional monarch and saw his duty as the protection of all his subjects. He agreed that it was intolerable that the wishes of a government for whom the people had voted could be obstructed by an unelected body that seemed to be putting its members' welfare ahead of that of the nation. The government had introduced the Parliament Bill, which would limit the veto of the House of Lords. The King now told the Lords that he would appoint as many Liberal peers as it took to get the Parliament Bill passed. Faced with the threat of their privileges being devalued, the Lords submitted, and the Parliament Act (1911) became law from 1912. From now on, the House of Lords could reject a bill for only three sessions; after that it would automatically become law.

The political classes in Belfast were horrified. Their last bulwark against home rule had been swept away. It was time to reach for the Orange card again; and the Conservative Party was there to help them play it.

The Lord Lieutenant of Ireland in 1912 was John Hamilton-Gordon, Earl of Aberdeen. His Chief Secretary was Augustine Birrell, a man whose brilliance was to be found in wit and literature rather than political acumen and whose besetting sin was complacency. John Redmond was the leader of the Irish Party. He was no Parnell, but he was a handsome man and an adequate speaker. He had been elected leader in the aftermath of the O'Shea divorce disaster, when Parnell's love affair had split constitutional nationalism in two. It was felt at the time that Redmond could hold the two wings of the party together, and so he did. His problem was that he was dangerously out of touch with powerful resurgent belief in nation-hood, which was drawing sustenance from the visions of Ireland that were inspired by such poets as Yeats.

Redmond had some good lieutenants, though they too were remnants of the old century rather than leaders for the new. Tim Healy had a wicked sense of humour and was well liked by everybody. He survived in politics long enough to become the first Governor-General of the Irish Free State. John Dillon was another lieutenant, less well liked than Healy but feared in debate. Joseph Devlin, known to everyone as 'Wee Joe', had grown up in the cockpit of Belfast politics; he could be friendly and was well liked but could be ruthless if he thought there was political advantage to be gained.

The combination of complacency and detachment made the forces for home rule weak. It was a battle that the Conservatives and Unionists felt they could win. They had been on their guard since the House of Lords had been defeated, and they prepared their team with care. Their leader, Arthur Balfour, gave the impression of being so delicate that he earned the nickname 'Tiger Lily', and he certainly did not appear robust enough to deal with the campaign of whispering against his leadership carried out by his backbenchers, or the more open attacks in some Conservative newspapers. He resigned. The Conservative Party, already split along several fault-lines, looked as if it might rip itself to death. The main candidates were Water Long and Austen Chamberlain, who detested each other. Realising the danger of a damaging struggle, both sides compromised and elected as leader Andrew Bonar Law. Originally Canadian, he had spent a great deal of his life in Glasgow. His father was a Presbyterian minister who had retired to his native Coleraine; his brother practised medicine there, and for the last five years of his father's life Andrew visited Ulster every weekend. His heart, the Unionists might have said, was in the right place.

The Ulster Unionists did not form a separate party in the House of Commons but were a group within the Conservative and Unionist Party. From 1910 their leader was Sir Edward Carson. He claimed that his sole purpose in entering Parliament, in 1892, was to thwart the home rule movement. Born in Harcourt Street, Dublin, he was the son of a Scottish architect of Italian extraction whose family name had been Carsoni. His father wanted him to be a barrister, so he studied law at Trinity College, Dublin. He was never a hearty and avoided physical games, with the exception of a little rowing and, ironically, hurling. Mildly radical as a young man, he identified more with the establishment as he grew older. He even became Solicitor-General under the Conservatives. He made his name in a few famous cases. The first was when he defended a Royal Navy cadet from the charge of stealing a postal order, an incident that became celebrated enough for Terence Rattigan to write a play about it, *The Winslow Boy*. Other cases were less pleasant. Carson was prosecutor in the Oscar Wilde libel case and destroyed the playwright (who was a near-contemporary in Dublin) in the witness box. He had the ability to see what was at the core of a case as well as an uncanny knack of seeing a witness's weakness and by the use of aggressive and unremitting questioning to get the result he wanted.

This single-minded focus was Carson's strength in the courthouse but was a weakness in the wider field of politics. Used to prosecuting, he was unable to see opponents other than as criminals. He saw the home rule movement as a criminal conspiracy to do down the Ulster Protestant. The Catholic home-rulers whom he opposed had gained their power with a combination of Land-Leaguing and minor atrocity. Against the posthumous advice of another Trinity graduate who was an infinitely greater politician, Edmund Burke, he was trying to indict a nation, trying to say that the wishes of the vast majority of the people of Ireland were treasonable.

Carson was a good lawyer all the same, and when Balfour was sent to Ireland to keep agitators in order, a man of Carson's nature and ability was just what was needed. Before then he had been an outstanding defender of tenants' rights. After Balfour arrived in Ireland in 1886, and Carson was appointed Crown Counsel, he changed sides. Now he prosecuted men who had been driven to desperation by rack-rents and evictions, men who had tried to gain strength by becoming part of a national movement. Controlling these unfortunates, Carson and his like believed, were the Irish Party and their turncoat leader, Charles Stewart Parnell. Even when attempts to implicate Parnell in agrarian atrocity failed, all who opposed unionism were lumped into the criminal category. Carson knew Healy, and Redmond, and as an intelligent man must have known that they were not criminals. That did not stop him from standing on political platforms and accusing them, as well as a respectable majority in the Liberal Party, of being co-conspirators in a plot to deprive Irish Protestants of their ancient, and dominant, liberties.

Anyone who has seen the statue of Carson in front of Stormont, his body twisted by emotion, his face in a scowl of determination, his hand raised as if to stop the South, which he faces, from attempting any further encroachment on Protestant hegemony, will realise what a fine figurehead he made. However, if we may carry the maritime image a little further, it is not the figurehead that causes a ship to arrive safely at its destination: rather it is a complex organisation combining skill and brawn that masters the vessel and brings it to the security of its anchorage. Carson would have got nowhere if it were not for the hard work and organisational skills of a number of Ulster's home-grown Unionists, which allowed the campaign against home rule to be so successful.

Foremost among these was Captain James Craig. Born in Sydenham, Kent, he entered his father's whiskey business as a clerk and left it as a millionaire. Dissatisfied with his life, he joined the army and fought in the Second Anglo-Boer War. He distinguished himself in the fighting, though he and his men were forced to surrender. The shame of this haunted him, although it was through no fault of his own. He had hidden, refusing to be transported in ox carts with the other officers, and then marched into captivity with his men. An injured ear-drum was giving him great pain, and the Boers allowed him to cross the border into Mozambique, where he was able to take ship in Delagoa Bay and return to Britain. He became member of Parliament for East Down in 1906.

Craig's appearance and demeanour stood him in good stead with his fellow Ulster Protestants. He was a tall man, big-boned and with a red face. He acted the bluff soldier but was as adept as any of the Irish Party at wasting the time of the House of Commons with questions that others found tiresome but his followers considered prudent. Courteous and imperturbable, he made use of his external resemblance to an absent-minded squire to take his political opponents off guard. As far as the campaign against home rule was concerned, he played an essential part in explaining the attitudes of Belfast Protestants to Carson.

It was difficult for people outside north-east Ulster to believe that the battles of the Reformation were still being fought in that small corner of Ireland. Belfast Protestants saw the Pope as a secular force, with an attitude to world domination such as was later ascribed to communism. They were told by their clergy of dungeons and plotting Jesuits, as anxious to bring down the English monarchy as had been their predecessors in the time of Queen Elizabeth. English politicians of the time never really came to terms with it. The Belfast Protestant would not be surprised to hear that the Pope was plotting to take over the shipyards.

George Bernard Shaw, a Dublin Protestant, tried to explain in his book *The Matter with Ireland*. 'The Ulsterman . . . is inured to violence. He has thrown stones and been hit by them.' Even in a colony that was three hundred years old, they felt as if they lived on the frontier, as if, should they let their guard down, the Irish kerns would rise out of the woods to slit the throat of every Protestant in the province. The same fear exists in some parts of rural Ulster to this day, and at crossroads in Unionist areas flags are still nailed to poles or trees, flapping in tattered defiance until they are replaced each July.

Better-informed Protestants feared that home rule and an independent Irish government would give precedence to the Catholic hierarchy and that they would have to live in a society dominated by Catholic moral teaching, where their freedom to live and worship would be under threat and where the priest would interfere in the marriage bed. It has to be said that they had a point. Only a couple of years previously, in 1908, the Catholic decree of 'Ne Temere' was promulgated. This taught that in a marriage between a Catholic and a Protestant the marriage was valid only if the wedding ceremony was carried out according to the rites of the Catholic Church. Further, both partners had to sign an agreement under-taking to raise any children of the marriage as Catholics. (Previously, boys had tended to follow the religion of the father, while girls followed the mother.) Many Protestants saw this decree as an attempt to breed them out of existence. There had already been a distressing case in Belfast when a Catholic husband, Alexander McCann, had left his Protestant wife and taken the children with him. Although, like Carson, Craig had little time for religious intolerance, he was content that the declaration 'Home rule is Rome rule' helped to concentrate the minds of his followers. Religion has its own dynamic in Ulster, no matter what else happens.

The Unionists had started their campaign in good time. When they saw that the House of Lords was going to lose its veto on bills passed by the House of Commons, the political classes in Belfast and its hinterland acted. There were three ideas they wanted to get across: that there was solidarity in the unionist population of Ulster; that their opposition to home rule was steadfast; and that there were no limits to what they were prepared to do in defence of their ideals.

The first major demonstration took place on 23 September 1911, when fifty thousand men marched to the City Hall from all over Belfast. Carson declared that they would govern the 'Protestant province of Ulster' themselves if home rule was passed. With that in mind, a 'Commission of Five' had been set up to frame a constitution for the provisional government that Ulster would need in the circumstances. A few days later Carson went to Portrush and said that Protestants had to be given government over 'those places we control' or the 'Ulster People would become violent.' This was the first example of the particular double-speak that Carson and the other Unionist leaders used—using the same word to mean different things at different times, so that its meaning became blurred at the edges. What did he mean when he spoke of Protestant Ulster?

Ulster was one of five ancient provinces in Ireland. One of these was the Kingdom of Meath, ruled by the High King. This has been absorbed into Leinster, while Ulster, Munster and Connacht have had roughly the same boundaries since the Iron Age. When Ireland was divided into shires in Elizabethan times, Ulster had nine counties, including Cavan, which was transferred from Connacht. Of these nine only four—Antrim, Down, Armagh and Derry—had a Protestant majority in the early 1900s. A further two—Tyrone and Fermanagh—had roughly equal populations of Protestant and Catholic, while Donegal, Monaghan and Cavan had very definite Catholic majorities. The balance is emphasised when the representation of Ulster in the House of Commons is examined: the Unionists had one more seat than the Nationalists. This situation was actually reversed in the middle of the campaign, when the Nationalists gained the Derry City constituency. By claiming Ulster for Protestants, Carson was implying that there was a much larger opposition to home rule than existed in fact. When he referred to 'areas we control' he was being more realistic about the extent of the territory that was to become known as Northern Ireland.

All these meetings had taken place before the government had made any formal announcement of its intentions concerning the Home Rule Bill. Ironically, it was Winston Churchill, son of the man who had played the Orange card a generation before, who made the announcement, telling a meeting in Dundee in October that the bill would be introduced during the next parliamentary session.

A meeting of the Ulster Liberal Association was scheduled to be held in the Ulster Hall for 8 February, with Lord Pirrie in the chair. The *Times* correspondent made unkind remarks about Pirrie changing horses when the Liberals came to power, but that was to ignore facts. Pirrie and his wife had supported home rule and had joined the Liberal Party before 1902. He had wanted to become a member of Parliament for Belfast, but the Conservative Association had nominated Charles Dunbar Smith in the election of 1902. Smith was not a popular candidate, and he was opposed by the leader of the Belfast Protestant Association, Thomas Sloan.

Sloan worked at Harland and Wolff, where he held evangelical meetings in the platers' shed at lunchtime. At these he denounced Catholics and also what he saw as the excessive ritual of the Church of Ireland. The Conservatives were convinced that Pirrie had financed Sloan in a fit of pique. When Sloan won, it led to a split in the Orange movement. When the 1906 elections came around, Pirrie financed several Liberal candidates in Ulster. In recognition of this he was made Viscount Pirrie in that year's birthday honours.

At about the same time Pirrie was able to buy out Wolff's shareholding. It was said at the time that he would not promote either of his relations, Carlisle or Andrews, to the post of manager, as they were convinced Unionists. Instead he appointed J. W. Kempster, an agreeable yes-man. In 1911 he claimed that the Harbour Commissioners were withholding land that Harland and Wolff needed because he was a supporter of home rule. His wife apparently encouraged him to be more open in his support of the cause, and that is how he was invited to take the chair at the February meeting.

Churchill was invited to be the guest speaker. The Unionist Standing Committee were outraged, as the Ulster Hall was dedicated to the cause of unionism, sanctified to the cause in 1886 at the meeting addressed by Churchill's own father. The committee saw the use of the hall as an insult to Ulster and was determined that such a desecration would not take place. They announced that they had hired the hall for the previous day and would not vacate it till the threat was over. The Liberals blinked first, and cancelled the booking. They now found that no other hall in Belfast was prepared to host the meeting. With Churchill's permission, they had to make arrangements for a huge marquee to be brought to Celtic Park.

By 6 February more than 3,500 soldiers had arrived in Belfast. Interestingly, it was the Unionists who had called for such a large number to be made available. The leaders wanted their own supporters to be intimidated, because they believed that the government would allow serious violence to take place so they could blame it on the Protestants. In the event, some level of violence was almost inevitable. When Churchill landed in Larne on the morning of the meeting he found the quays lined by crowds singing 'God Save the King'. He went by train to the Midland Station in Belfast and then by car to the city centre, where he was to have lunch. Both sides of York Street were lined by hostile crowds. When, after lunch, Churchill and his wife got into their car it was attacked by a gang of shipyard workers, who attempted to overturn it.

The welcome in the Catholic area of west Belfast was a complete contrast; but the meeting in Celtic Park was not a success. The weather was not as welcoming as the Nationalists, and heavy rain deterred many people from attending. The marquee was only two-thirds full. Pirrie attacked the Unionists for being loyal only to 'inherited phrases' and seeing any change or development as being an insult to their ancestors. After the meeting Churchill was driven by a circuitous route through Catholic areas back to the Midland Station. As he sat in his special train to Larne he may have been comforted to think of the crowds of protesters standing in the rain outside his hotel, getting drenched in vain.

Churchill got away lightly compared with Lord Pirrie. When Pirrie arrived in Larne to catch the ferry on 12 February he was pelted with rotten eggs, flour and herrings and was accused of being a turncoat and a traitor.

When the new session of Parliament opened a few days later, the Government of Ireland Bill was, as promised, in the King's Speech. Pressure of other business, however, meant that the bill was not introduced until after Easter. Once again the Unionists were able to get their protests in first. On Easter Tuesday they held a monster rally in the Agricultural Society's grounds at Balmoral. Seventy trains brought demonstrators to Belfast from all over Ulster and beyond. Seventy British members of Parliament had come to join their Unionist friends. The tram service in the city was suspended for the day. The meeting opened with prayers from the Protestant Primate of Ireland, the Archbishop of Armagh, and from the Moderator of the Presbyterian Church. From a 90-foot flagstaff flew a Union Jack, 48 feet by 25 feet—the biggest yet made, it was claimed. The crowd heard speaker after speaker comment on the sanctity of their cause. Bonar Law claimed they were preserving the British Empire.

Bonar Law was becoming more and more caught up in the issue, and after the Government of Ireland Bill had been published and it was obvious how limited the scale of self-rule to be granted was, he still spoke against it in language that seemed more suitable for Armageddon than Westminster. Although John Redmond welcomed the bill, its terms were not universally popular among Catholics. Cardinal Logue called it 'a skeleton on which to hang restrictions.' Arthur Griffith commented: 'If this is liberty, the lexicographers have deceived us.' Yet at a rally in Blenheim Palace in Oxfordshire—ironically, Winston Churchill's birthplace—Bonar Law described the Liberal government as a 'revolutionary committee' that had seized power by fraud. He claimed he would support Ulster no matter how far they went. He was speaking in terms that were not only

Clarendon Dock, 1917: Sailing ships needed a steam tug to enter and leave Belfast Harbour. (*Ulster Museum*)

Unloading coal at the gasworks: Water was the cheapest way to move bulk cargoes such as coal. (*Ulster Folk and Transport Museum*)

Young woman at damask loom and woman at Belfast sink: Young and old, women had to work to supplement the family income. The washerwoman (*opposite*) is lucky: the two taps show that she has hot water. (*Ulster Museum*)

Shops in Cromac Street: Magee's kitchenware and McNulty's fruit are displayed on the pavement. McKay's drapery has a sunshade to stop the clothes on display from fading. (*Ulster Museum*)

Poorer shoppers had more chance of a bargain in Smithfield Market. The owner of the 'Cheapest House in the City' is not concerned about sunlight fading these working-men's suits. (*Ulster Museum*)

A view of the Newtownards Road and Strandtown: Although most of the shipyard workers came from this area of East Belfast, many also came from across the River Lagan, on the other side of the city. (*Ulster Museum*)

The South Yard at Harland and Wolff: This shot gives some idea of the hazardous environment in which the yardmen worked. The wooden staging looks none too steady. (*Ulster Museum*)

Many other industries developed in support of the shipyards, before taking on a life of their own. This picture shows the range of products exported from Belfast's ropeworks all over the world. (*Ulster Museum*)

The *Olympic* and *Titanic* in the stocks: While the *Olympic* had a long and successful career, it is the *Titanic* that is forever associated with Belfast. (*Ulster Museum*)

The turbine casing of the *Britannic*: This gives some idea of the size of the engines needed to drive each of the White Star Sisters. (*Ulster Museum*)

Shipyard workers leaving the yard: For more than a century the evening rush from the shipyard was a regular part of the Belfast day. (*Ulster Museum*)

The 150-ton floating crane: Everything about the shipyard was on a grand scale. (*Ulster Museum*)

Sailing into an uncertain future: The *Titanic* is manoeuvred into the channel with the help of tugs. (*Ulster Folk and Transport Museum*)

The eve of Ulster Day: Anxious that everything will go well, Edward Carson makes final arrangements for the great covenant. (*Ulster Museum*)

3rd Battalion, Belfast UVF: They felt that they were ready for anything, but they could not have expected the carnage on the Somme. (*Ulster Museum*)

As the threat of confrontation intensifies, the Technical College is converted into a bakery to supply the UVF. (*Ulster Museum*)

The 36th (Ulster) Division in review, passing the City Hall. It is poignant to wonder how many of them lived to see the City Hall in 1918. (*Ulster Museum*)

A recruiting drive in Great Victoria Street at the beginning of the Second World War. (*Ulster Museum*)

Young women in the munitions industry: Most people welcomed regular employment and the chance to earn overtime. (*Ulster Folk and Transport Museum*)

Donegall Square in wartime: The air-raid shelter offers pitiful protection against the prospect of German attack. (*Ulster Folk and Transport Museum*)

The Auxiliary Fire Service: There was no attempt to include these units in disaster planning, and they were left to make the best of what they could find. (*Ulster Folk and Transport Museum*)

Launch of the *Beaverbank*: Built for Bank Line Shipping, this ship operated all over the globe until the 1970s. (*Linen Hall Library*)

The *Southern Cross*: The innovation of moving the machinery to the stern of the ship gave increased room for passenger accommodation. (*Ulster Folk and Transport Museum*)

The *Sea Quest*: In the effort to diversify, Belfast shipyards were prepared to take on any challenge, however unusual. (*Bill Kirk*)

unparliamentary but could be considered treasonable. Whether he was using this language because he believed what he said or merely because he wanted to increase the hysteria surrounding the issue of home rule it is difficult to tell at this distance.

Meanwhile the Unionists in the House of Commons had come up against another dilemma, and once again had turned it to their advantage. At the committee stage an English Liberal member had moved an amendment to exclude the four north-eastern counties from the provisions of the bill, saying, 'I have never heard that orange bitters will mix with Irish whiskey.' If Carson supported the amendment he would be accused of abandoning unionists in the rest of Ireland to their fate; if he opposed the amendment he would be accused of refusing what was achievable for the sake of a hopeless ideal. Calculating that the amendment would fail anyway, as Liberals and Nationalists would vote against it, he instructed Unionists to vote for it. This allowed him, when the inevitable defeat of the motion came, to claim that Asquith's attitude to the amendment was nothing less than a declaration of war on the Protestants of Ulster.

A limited war was taking place in Ulster already. On Saturday 29 June, Whitehouse Sunday School had their annual outing. They went by train to Castledawson, where they had a pleasant day. In they early afternoon they returned to the station, led by a band and by several Union Jacks. By an unpleasant coincidence, they met a Hibernian band, out for an evening practice. The Nationalists attacked the flags, taking no care of the children in their path. Naturally, the children were terrified and ran away. Some were completely traumatised, hiding in ditches as far as two miles from the scene of the attack. The next day their minister asked his congregation to keep silent about the incident, because he did not want ill-feeling with their Catholic neighbours. It was a vain hope. The story was reported fully in Monday's papers.

On Tuesday, Catholics were ordered out of the shipyards. All of them were forced to leave, but even those who went uncomplainingly were liable to be assaulted or to be hit by a weapon that was trivialised by the name 'Belfast confetti', consisting of the steel discs punched out of plates by riveters. These could be hidden in pockets and thrown from a distance. Each disc was heavy enough and its uneven edges were sharp enough to cause nasty gashes if it hit a person's unprotected skin. The police recorded twenty-five assaults inside the yards, and a further fifty-five outside. The expulsions were all the worse because they deprived people of their wages until they felt confident enough to return to work. When tensions were high this was sometimes a matter of weeks or even months.

There was a relative calm in Belfast until August. At a football match between Belfast Celtic and neighbouring Linfield, played at Celtic Park, a riot broke out. The police forced the rioters out of the ground, where the

Protestants were reinforced by men from the nearby Village area of the Donegall Road. Nevertheless the Catholics, on home ground, were able to drive the Protestants back into the Village. Some idea of the scale of the fighting can be got from the fact that more than sixty casualties were treated in the Royal Victoria Hospital.

Riots like these may have been exhilarating for those taking part, but Craig and Carson knew that if they continued they would rapidly lose sympathy in England for the Unionist cause. They were trying to present a picture of Unionists as disciplined and quietly determined in the face of a political development that threatened their very existence; a newspaper account presenting Protestants as the aggressors was the last thing they wanted. They sought a way of instilling this discipline by imitating the Scottish Covenant of 1580. An oath, called 'Ulster's Solemn League and Covenant', was rewritten by Thomas Sinclair and then submitted to the Protestant churches for approval. The Presbyterians were the only ones to suggest changes: they felt that the oath should be framed so that it included only the present crisis, lest it be used as a catch-all to coerce support in future developments. It was announced to the press that the Ulster Covenant would be signed on Saturday 28 September, and that the day would be known as Ulster Day.

The time remaining before Ulster Day, about a month, was used to ensure as full a participation by the Protestant population of Ulster as possible. This precaution was needed in the south and west of the province in particular, as enthusiasm for confronting the government declined the further away from Belfast a traveller went. Meetings were organised particularly in Counties Tyrone and Fermanagh, where Unionists had to exaggerate their strength in order to overshadow the claims of Nationalists.

On 19 September, in Craig's house, Carson announced the details of the text. A signatory pledged himself to two things: he would use all means to defend against the present 'conspiracy' for home rule, and he would refuse to recognise the authority of a home rule government if it came about. To emphasise the solemnity of the occasion, the evening finished with a torchlight procession, with many of the marchers carrying wooden rifles. At a rally in the Ulster Hall on the eve of Ulster Day, Colonel R. H. Wallace presented Carson with a faded yellow banner that had been carried, it was said, before William at the Battle of the Boyne.

On Ulster Day itself the plan was for everyone, employer and artisan, to march together, all wearing their best suits. The opening event of the day was at the Ulster Hall. Craig spoke first, reminding the gathering that this was a religious service and that there should be no applause. The opening hymn was sung: 'O God Our Help in Ages Past'. Then Dr William McKean preached. He took as his text 'Keep that which is committed to thy trust.' He made four main points. The people gathering that day in Belfast and all over Ulster loved peace and industry. The so-called Irish question was in actuality a war against Protestantism: it was an attempt to establish a Roman Catholic ascendancy in Ireland. Finally, if Dublin were to secure a second parliament in Dublin it would lead to the disintegration of the British Empire.

When the service was over the party moved to the City Hall. There was a guard of honour of ex-soldiers, wearing medals and sashes and armed with staves. Carson was the first to sign, with a pen specially presented to him for the occasion. Although each signatory was required to prove his Ulster birth, by his labours Carson had proved himself a true Ulsterman, and the condition was waived in his case. After that the general signing began. The organisation was so good that 550 people could sign at a time. In all, 471,414 people signed that day, more of them women than men.

At half past eight that evening a brass band played outside the Ulster Club in Castle Place. When Carson appeared at the door of the club the tune was 'See the Conquering Hero Comes'. His car was manhandled to the nearby docks, where he boarded the aptly named *Patriotic*. Amid cheers and revolver shots, the ship pulled away from the quay. As it moved out into the lough the passengers could see bonfires, not only in Belfast but on the hills around the city, from Cave Hill to Craigogantlet.

Not everyone who witnessed the demonstrations was impressed. The reporter from the *Manchester Guardian* wrote: 'Contrast the anarchic hectoring of the ascendancy party and the loyal, patient reliance of the Ulster Nationalist upon English justice and firmness.' The following months and years would show just how much Ulster nationalists could rely upon the government in London.

On 11 November 1912 Asquith announced that a parliamentary guillotine would be used to force through the Government of Ireland Bill. Two days later the Conservatives and Unionists forced a snap vote, in which the government was defeated by 228 votes to 206. Asquith refused to be bound by the result, maintaining that it was a cheap trick rather than the considered opinion of the House of Commons. Sir William Bull called him a traitor, and refused to withdraw the insult; he was then forced to leave the chamber. Ronald McNeill, a native of Ulster but member for East Kent, threw the bound copy of standing orders and hit Churchill, who had to be restrained by his colleagues from retaliating. O'Neill apologised the following day, and his apology was accepted by Churchill.

The bill eventually passed the House of Commons early in the new year but, as expected, was rejected by the House of Lords. On the positive side, as far as Nationalists were concerned, a Catholic was elected in a by-election caused by the death of the Duke of Abercorn. The majority of Ulster's members of Parliament were now Nationalists.

Along with the struggle in Parliament and the demonstrations on the streets, a potentially more dangerous project had been started. By law, men could carry arms and carry out drill and other military operations if two justices of the peace agreed that their action was done to maintain the constitution 'as now established'. Colonel Wallace had been the first to test this, in January 1912. Seeing his success, others followed. Now, in January 1913 the Ulster Unionist Council established the Ulster Volunteer Force. Carson wanted to raise 100,000 men who had signed the Covenant. Belfast was to raise four regiments. Most of the drilling would be done in Orange halls, but the fact that landowners were prominent in the force's leadership meant that there were numerous opportunities for field days and other exercises. By the end of the summer some sections of the UVF were capable of drilling in extended order. In July a 66-year-old Devon man, General Sir George Richardson, who had served the Empire in Afghanistan, China and India, came to Belfast to take command of the Volunteers.

Carson was feeling the stress of holding everything together at the same time as carrying on his legal work, and when, in June, his wife died, he suffered a complete nervous collapse. He managed to hold himself together until the July parades were over. The improvement in discipline pleased him, and he went on holiday to Germany with as good a heart as could be expected in the circumstances. By September he was back in London, continuing the fight against home rule while trying to read his opponents' strategy. For example, when Lord Loreburn suggested that Ulster be treated differently from the rest of Ireland, was it a genuine suggestion? Taking the whole of Ulster would mean taking control of a territory that had a Catholic and nationalist majority. Redmond was horrified at the suggestion, but so was Carson, for he was less certain about its implications than he had been about the previous amendment.

In September also, five hundred delegates of the Ulster Unionist Council approved the setting up of a Provisional Government if home rule became law. Carson was to be chairman of the Central Authority. Military and other committees were also established. Carson's actions were approved at a meeting of Belfast businessmen, who undertook to withhold all taxes over which they had control should the crisis ever arrive. As this amounted to about £90,000, it was little more than a gesture.

English politicians were by now beginning to support the exclusion of some part of Ulster from the terms of the bill. Carson had done his sums by now and demanded as a minimum the six plantation counties. Interestingly, for a man intending to maintain the traditional governance of Ireland, he did not know that the 'home counties' of Antrim and Down had never been planted. Counties Donegal and Cavan, on the other hand, both of which he was prepared to abandon, had been planted by English and Scottish settlers in the seventeenth century. That is by the way, because the significance of his choice was that this was the largest chunk of Ulster over which Protestants could maintain a comfortable majority. If any of the other three Ulster counties—Donegal, Cavan or Monaghan—were included, the majority would become much more tenuous.

In addition, what might be called the Southern Unionists refused to get involved in what the Ulster Unionists were threatening to do. The former accepted that, if Ulster or part of it was excluded from home rule, the bill should not be opposed for their sake. Even Churchill, perhaps chastened by his experiences in Belfast, felt that the Ulster case for exclusion should be met. Redmond and Asquith rejected his advice. Much later, in January 1914, Asquith was to offer Carson an opportunity to opt out of home rule for six years. Carson would reject the offer, demanding total exclusion. 'I go to my people,' he would say, closing the interview.

Back in Belfast, UVF staff had taken over the Old Town Hall. Here much work was being done on logistics, transport and communications. The primary task was to arm the force. Some local leaders imported guns on their own initiative. Lord Leitrim used his own small ship to bring weapons into County Donegal. In this task, however, the efforts of one man stood above the rest. Frederick Hugh Crawford had been a premium apprentice in Harland and Wolff. In December 1881 he had helped to rescue men who had been thrown into the waters of the dock when a gangway had collapsed. Later, he had sailed as an engineer with the White Star Line. He took charge of establishing the armoury.

He looked to Germany for arms. The first order he made, for a thousand rifles, was reported to the British government by the German firm. He tried again, through an intermediary. This time the rifles arrived in Belfast in crates marked 'zinc plate'. The true contents were discovered by Customs officers and the consignment confiscated, because it was addressed to a fictitious company. Crawford got in touch with the German agent, Bruno Spiro, and the latter contacted His Majesty's Customs, claiming that it was a genuine mistake and asking that the goods be returned to him. When another consignment was confiscated, the Customs officials refused to release them, as they did not carry British proof-marks. Anyone claiming the guns would have to pay £2 per barrel. Although some guns were getting through, often carried on a ship owned by the Antrim Iron Ore Steamship Company, most of them were being seized in Belfast or before they even arrived. Crawford was exhausted and asked that someone else take over.

The man who took up the challenge was George Clark, a director of the Workman Clark Shipyard. He worked through a committee and made a point of recruiting gun dealers and gunsmiths to the cause. As these men were known to the arms industry there would be fewer eyebrows raised when orders for guns came from them. Even so, only a few hundred rifles got through, most of them disguised as material for the Workman Clark yard. Sometimes Catholic dockers discovered consignments and interfered with the smooth transfer of the guns. For all the threatening postures of Carson, there was still no adequate supply of arms for the UVF.

It is interesting to speculate what the guns were to be used for. Crawford, who had fought in the Anglo-Boer War, was a realist and knew that the UVF had no chance against the regular army. Even when, by a spectacular piece of bluff, he managed to buy four Maxim machine-guns from Vickers, he knew that Ulstermen would be outgunned. Ammunition would run out, so he insisted that all rifles come with bayonets. Without firepower to back them up, however, bayonets would have been useless against disciplined troops. It seems likely that they would be more useful in maintaining internal order, in other words against dissident nationalists. One other hypothesis sometimes put forward is that these guns would be used to coerce the nationalists of Counties Tyrone and Fermanagh into the north-eastern statelet.

It was finally decided by UVF staff that only a major coup would bring in the needed weapons. The decision to go ahead was taken by Carson on 21 January. Clark felt that Crawford was the only man who could carry out the operation, so he once again took the fore. Crawford claims in his diaries that he met both Walter Long and Andrew Bonar Law before he set off. These meetings were arranged by Craig and took place in March. Crawford even brought a letter for Bonar Law from the 'Chief', Carson. This time the episode went almost without a hitch. Bruno Spiro supplied almost 25,000 rifles, together with 3 million rounds of ammunition. These were loaded on the steamship *Fanny,* which left the Baltic in late March. By late April it was off the south coast of Ireland, and on the night of 19 April it met the *Clyde Valley* near Tuskar Rock, off County Wexford. In complete darkness, the two ships transferred cargo.

While this was happening, a strange coincidence took place. As part of the plans to deal with a potential Unionist uprising in Ulster, Churchill had ordered a naval task force to be based around Ulster with a view to enforcing a blockade if necessary. Now, in the darkness of the early morning, a battleship swept past, on its way from Spain to the Clyde. It was travelling so fast that its wash nearly swamped the two small steamers. Churchill's arrangements came near to enforcing an embargo as effectively as might be wished for.

Meanwhile, in Belfast, arrangements were made for all the transport to which the UVF had access to meet at Larne at 1 a.m. on Saturday 25 April. Arrangements were made to interfere with official communications and to monitor troop movements. The planning was immaculate. Guns were landed at Larne and further down the coast at Bangor and Donaghadee.

Guns had been brought into Irish politics for the first time since the Fenian rising, and they had been brought in by Unionists.

This was to prove a grave embarrassment to Asquith, but it was not the only one he was suffering at the time. The other arose from a misunderstanding that occurred in the south of Ireland, in the green lands of County Kildare. Much has been made of the significance of this incident, with some calling it the Curragh Mutiny, and so it is worth examining in a little detail what happened.

It was obvious to the British government that the UVF desperately needed weapons. The only substantial source of guns within Ulster was official army stores. The commander in chief in Ireland, General Sir Arthur Paget, was instructed on 14 March to reinforce the arms depots in Armagh, Carrickfergus, Enniskillen and Omagh. Paget was in London a few days later and was given a more detailed briefing of the operation. He was concerned that there might be fighting, and that some of his officers, who were Ulster-born, might be put in the morally repugnant position of having to fire on family and friends. When he mentioned this to the War Minister, J. E. B. Seely, the latter agreed that anyone with family connections in the north might be excused from the mission.

This was not quite the message that Paget passed on to his officers at the Curragh Camp, County Kildare, on the morning of 20 March. He told them that the army was about to initiate a military engagement with Ulster Unionists, and painted a picture of apocalyptic civil conflict. Stunned by this analysis, sixty of his officers announced that they would rather face dismissal than initiate (and the wording is important) 'active military operations against Ulster.' It must be remembered that they were not being asked, and never were asked, to act against the Ulster Unionists, although some Unionist historians have taken Paget's statement at face value. They had voted, as it were, against something that was not going to happen anyway.

In an uncanny foretaste of their role as 'donkeys leading lions', those in ultimate command contrived to make matters worse. Seely and the chief of the imperial general staff, Sir John French, gave a written undertaking that the army would not be used to crush political opposition to home rule. French went further, assuring officers at the Curragh that their troops would not be used to enforce home rule on Ulster.

Although annoyed by what had happened, Asquith did not panic. He repudiated the document signed by Seely and French. Beyond that, there was little he could do, as the core of his problems seemed to lie with his senior commanders rather than with the officer class in general.

Preparations for the improved defence of the northern arms depots had also been made in Aldershot Barracks, Hampshire, in the Royal Navy and in Ulster itself, where the Royal Irish Constabulary had been mobilised. None of these operations gave any cause for concern. Nevertheless there now had to be a doubt about the reliability of the army, particularly of those units stationed in Ireland.

Plans were being drawn up in Dublin Castle to define what parts of Ulster might be excluded, temporarily or permanently. The Government of Ireland Bill was modified in late May to offer counties the option of exclusion for a period of six years. This had already been rejected by Unionists in March. The House of Lords altered the legislation to allow the nine-county province of Ulster to have permanent exclusion. It also included measures to appoint a minister for the excluded counties.

The issue of the time limit seemed to be getting nowhere, so Asquith decided to negotiate on the size of the excluded portion. He began by offering the four 'home counties', with the exception of the Catholic areas of south Armagh and south Down. To compensate for this, the excluded area might include parishes in Counties Donegal, Cavan and Monaghan. As these areas would be isolated from the main excluded area, however, it is unlikely that this offer would have come to anything.

In early July there was a hint that Unionists would accept a plebiscite of the six north-eastern counties and the city of Derry and concede south Armagh, south Fermanagh and 'the Catholic parts of County Down,' although no attempt was made to define the last area. Asquith, with Redmond in mind, responded by asking the Unionists to concede some of County Tyrone as well, and offered government funds for transferring Protestants and Catholics to their preferred area.

Asquith described his strategy as wait and see. It may seem pointless from the distance of almost a century, and Asquith himself was not a man to explain his reasoning, but there were contemporaries who felt he was doing exactly what was required. Alfred Milner, for example, who was a supporter of Ulster and one who was involved with Craig and Carson in making contingency plans, felt that Asquith was finding a way to avoid forcing the Unionists into any decisive action until the late summer, when Parliament would be in recess. If at that point they set up their Provisional Government of Ulster, Asquith would do nothing, nor would there be a Parliament to force the issue. The English public would get used to the rebellion and come to ignore it, while Ulster would stew in its own juices and watch the erosion of the business community and Unionist unity.

Republicans in the south had watched carefully what was happening and drew their own conclusions. They had kept their counsel as the Government of Ireland Bill had made its way slowly through the parliamentary process but had recently begun to understand that not only was home rule under threat but the very integrity of Ireland as a nation as well. Tom Clarke and others had reactivated the Irish Republican Brotherhood in 1907. They had no contact with Redmond, whose intention it was to achieve home rule without violence. This meant that he had no big stick with which to counter Carson's militarism. Independent of Redmond, Professor Eoin MacNeill had published an article calling for the formation of a volunteer movement in imitation of the Ulster Volunteers, and the Irish Volunteers were formed after a meeting in Dublin in November 1913, at which Mac Neill was elected chairman. The political shenanigans of early 1914 encouraged more people to join the movement, including up to forty thousand army reservists. At the same time its leadership was quietly infiltrated by the IRB.

Redmond's concessions in February damaged his credibility in Ireland, and he belatedly realised that the Irish Party too needed a military wing. He saw a ready-made one in the Irish Volunteers, and he threatened MacNeill that he would start his own volunteer movement if he were not allowed to nominate twenty-five members of the Provisional Committee of the Irish Volunteers. It was a stupid thing to do, and it came too late. By aligning himself with the Volunteers he damaged his reputation in England as a parliamentarian, seeming to abandon values that he had claimed to cherish, while he gained nothing in Ireland, as the young militants saw him and his twenty-five nominees as tired and irrelevant.

Interestingly, it was an Ulster Protestant who financed the arming of the Irish Volunteers, and an English Protestant who brought the guns to Ireland. Sir Roger Casement, whose home was near Ballycastle, County Antrim, raised £1,500, enough for 1,500 Mauser rifles and 45,000 rounds of ammunition to be bought from a dealer in Antwerp. Erskine Childers, who had written a famous novel warning England of the dangers of Germany's navy, landed the guns at the harbour of Howth, on the north arm of Dublin Bay, on 26 July.

It is interesting to compare this piece of gun-running with that of the UVF. The differences in scale were huge, but the Howth episode reflected the sort of numbers brought in by the UVF in some of their earlier attempts at smuggling. Equally, the differences in planning seem to be clear, as the UVF had shown a great deal of ingenuity in making sure that their landing was not interfered with by the authorities. But Bulmer Hobson, an IRB leader who had planned the operation, had different priorities and wanted a different reaction. He knew that such a small number of rifles would make little difference to the Irish Volunteers. Their value was in provoking the authorities. In this he was totally successful.

The Volunteers collected the rifles and marched off with sloped arms. The Assistant Commissioner of Police, David Harell, called for police reinforcements and arranged for two companies of the King's Own Scottish Borderers to be in support. The soldiers blocked the route back to Dublin. They were able to seize about twenty rifles before the Volunteers opened fire in the scuffle, and two soldiers were wounded in the leg. In the confusion, the soldiers were not able to prevent the irregulars getting away with the rest of the rifles.

On their way back to barracks that evening the soldiers fired on a hostile crowd in Bachelor's Walk, in Dublin city centre, killing three people and wounding more than thirty. The officer in charge, Major Haig, gave evidence that the crowd had being stoning the soldiers, and he was adamant that he did not give the order to fire. But English and southern Irish observers noted the difference in treatment of the people of Belfast and Dublin. The hostile nationalists had been shot, while the hostile unionists were being placated. The finances of the Volunteers were almost guaranteed; a hostile crowd would make contributions that meant, when the time came, that the southern militants would be fully armed.

In Belfast, Carson and Craig continued to make preparations for the crisis. Ulster was ready to deal with blockade, casualties and evacuations. Alfred Milner, concerned about Asquith's strategy, wanted the Provisional Government declared straight away. But the world outside was beginning to bulk large on the horizon, and now was not the time to advertise dissension within the United Kingdom. Bonar Law and Carson approached Asquith and suggested that the second reading of the Government of Ireland Bill be postponed until the international crisis had worked itself out. On 30 July, Asquith agreed.

The crisis was one that sneaked up on Europe when it wasn't looking. It started in a small city in a part of the continent few Belfast people had even heard of, but millions of people died as a result, including many thousands of the UVF. Although the incident occurred so far away, it is illuminating to examine the momentum behind it, as the ensuing conflict consumed the flower of Europe's youth.

For almost a thousand years the Balkans formed the frontier between the Islamic Ottoman Empire of Turkey and the Catholic and Christian Holy Roman Empire, which had shrunk to the Austro-Hungarian Empire. By the beginning of the twentieth century both empires were losing their grip. Neither had the energy to hold together the mix of nationalities contained within their boundaries. Later the Arabs would rise against their Turkish masters, but already peoples in the Balkans were trying to throw off the shackles of one empire without being consumed by the other. One of the most aggressive of these newly independent states was Serbia, which was determined to rid itself of the final strings of Austrian power. To attain this, Austrians and Serbs had fought a war in 1910. Diplomatic pressure from other countries had ended it, but there was a feeling on both sides that the issue would have to be resolved, that there was unfinished business to be attended to.

Russia was taking an interest, concerned that any expansion of the Austrian Empire would threaten the safety of the Russian Empire. Since

1910 it had financed a shadowy secret society in Serbia, the 'Black Hand', whose object was to ensure that Serbia and Austria maintained a state of enmity, if not a state of war.

The central character in the drama was an ageing Crown Prince of the Austro-Hungarian Empire, Archduke Franz Ferdinand. He was not a popular figure in Austria. He was too autocratic to be popular with the people, and had made himself positively unpopular with the royal family and the aristocracy by marrying Sophie Chotek, who was not of royal blood. It was a morganatic marriage: that is, Sophie derived no rights or honours from her husband. If he succeeded to the throne, she would not be empress; any children of the marriage would have no right of succession.

This unfortunate couple were to pay a formal visit to Sarajevo on the last Sunday in June 1914. Both being very religious, they began the day by attending mass in the private chapel of their hotel in the city of Ilidža, near Sarajevo. Afterwards they took the train to Sarajevo, only thirty minutes away. At the station a motorcade of at least four cars was waiting to take them to the Town Hall. The cars moved off some time before 10 o'clock. In the leading car were the mayor and the chief of police. Following them in the second car were Franz Ferdinand and Sophie, together with the military governor, sitting together in the rear seat. In the front the car's owner, Count von Harrach, sat beside the driver. The authorities were sensitive to the tensions surrounding an Austrian royal visitor to the Balkans. They provided a guard of honour of 120 men, and there were 22,000 soldiers stationed in the immediate vicinity.

The authorities were right to be concerned. A group of Black Hand members, under the leadership of a Serbian student, Gavrilo Princip, planned to attack the Archduke. Princip stationed men at three places along the embankment, where bridges crossed the river. He appointed his friend Danilo Ilić to act in a co-ordinating role. As the royal cavalcade approached the first bridge one conspirator asked a policeman which was the archduke's car. He then knocked off the cap of his bomb against a lamppost and threw it. The bomb bounced off the hood of Franz Ferdinand's car and blew up against the wheel of the following car. The flying detonator grazed Sophie as it flew past. A colonel was wounded. The conspirator now jumped down to the shallow river and tried to escape. The police caught up with him and he swallowed his poison pill. Unfortunately for him, it was old and did not work.

A second conspirator later claimed that the crowd was so jammed together that he could not get the bomb out of his pocket. A third felt he was being watched by a policeman and decided that it was not a good time to make any sudden moves. A fourth felt sorry for Sophie and did nothing, while a fifth conspirator kept his hands in his pockets and went home.

Only Princip was left, and he began to wander aimlessly along the embankment, near the Latin Bridge.

Meanwhile Franz Ferdinand entered the Town Hall. A man used to the rigours of court, he acted as if nothing had happened, and the normal speeches were made and refreshments taken. After eating, perhaps concerned about Sophie, though her wound was slight, he decided to cancel the rest of the day's engagements and return to their hotel. Before he left, however, he wanted to enquire after the welfare of the Austrian officer who had been wounded in the explosion and decided to visit the hospital. The couple and their escorts returned to the cars and made off, as they thought, for the hospital. Unfortunately, nobody had troubled to tell the drivers of the change of plan. Accordingly, the first car turned into the street leading to the museum that was the first item on the original itinerary. The governor ordered the car to stop, but those following turned as well, and soon the junction was a tangle of vehicles. In a coincidence that was to cost millions of lives, this was exactly where Princip was standing. He reached into the car and fired two shots. One cut Franz Ferdinand's jugular vein; the other hit Sophie in the abdomen. The archduke called to his wife: 'Sophie, dear, don't die. Live for the children.' They were taken to the governor's house, where they died within fifteen minutes of one another.

Princip didn't even try to escape. His efforts to turn the gun on himself were frustrated by the crowd. He did succeed in swallowing his poison pill, only to vomit it up again. By now the crowd were beating him to the ground. Deciding, perhaps, that being murdered was less dignified than committing suicide, he tried to defend himself with the butt of his pistol. The police eventually forced their way through the mob and arrested him.

What happened subsequently is often portrayed as an inevitable fall to war. This was not so. There are elements of the spaghetti western in the story so far, and the comparison holds for what was to follow.

The move to war was powered by a mixture of pride and fear and good intentions. Austria feared the growing nationalism of Serbia. Russia feared any expansion of the Austrian Empire. Germany feared the growth of an effective army as Russia modernised. France feared a repeat of the Franco-Prussian War and allied itself with Russia, so that Germany would have to fight a war on two fronts. Britain resented the growth of the German Imperial Navy, and was already allied to France. Each country sought to maintain its self-esteem. Each country was prepared to buy that self-esteem in the lives of its young men.

The guns of August roared, and the lights of what was, in retrospect, a Golden Age went out all over Europe.

Chapter 7 ～

| THE GREAT WAR

The United Kingdom may have entered the war against Germany and Austria almost by accident, but a small British Expeditionary Force was despatched to France within a few days. There was a certain euphoria in the air, and the uninformed considered that it would be a short war, over by Christmas. Lord Kitchener, however, the Secretary of State for War (no prissy 'Ministry of Defence' in those days), had enough foresight to realise that the struggle was going to be much more prolonged than that. He calculated that the regular army would not be sufficient to deal with the threat, and he asked Parliament for permission to raise an army of volunteers numbering half a million. His caution was reinforced by the news from France, where the BEF was suffering heavily and was forced to retreat in front of a steamrolling German army.

In England, large groups from the same locality or factory joined together in what came to be known as 'pals' battalions'. In Ireland there already existed a cadre of such battalions. The sectarian tensions that had surrounded the issue of home rule had led to the formation of two paramilitary organisations. The Ulster Volunteer Force purported to represent the interests of the unionists in Ulster, while the Irish Volunteers claimed to guard the interests of nationalists in the entire island of Ireland. At the outbreak of war the political leaders of both declared a truce and offered the services of their volunteers in the defence of what many still thought of as the motherland.

In the event, the two organisations were treated in different ways. There were prolonged discussions during August between Edward Carson and the General Staff in London. By the end of the month agreement had been reached that the UVF would form the core of a new Ulster Division. Carson was offered, and accepted, a place in the War Cabinet.

It was different with the Irish Volunteers. Only half were prepared to follow Redmond's call and join the British army, although, as it was a much bigger organisation than the UVF, there were still very many stepping forward. There were enough to form another division, which became the 16th Division. Unfortunately, the General Staff did not have the generosity of spirit to allow it to be called an Irish division until much too late in the war. To be fair, Redmond too was offered a place in the Cabinet, but refused. His son was turned down for an officer's commission.

All this negotiation was too slow for some hardy spirits, who were afraid of missing the adventure if they waited too long. Adventurers from both sides of the religious and political divide volunteered together and together were posted to the 10th (Irish) Division, which was already being formed. Newspapers made much of this new tolerance in adversity. One Friday night in Omagh the Ulster Volunteers, Irish Volunteers and Royal Inniskilling Fusiliers paraded together. Later the different Volunteers met one another as they marched to their various districts and saluted each other most respectfully.

The others had not much time to wait. The formation of the 36th (Ulster) Division under the command of Major-General Herbert Powell was announced. There would be three infantry brigades, each consisting of four battalions. In addition there would be the usual divisional troops: pioneers, engineers, signallers and a unit of the Royal Army Medical Corps. One brigade, the 107th, was to be made up from Belfast. The 108th Brigade would be made up of volunteers from Counties Antrim, Armagh, Down, Cavan and Monaghan. The 109th Brigade would have volunteers from Counties Donegal, Fermanagh, Derry and Tyrone. As there were not quite enough of these to form a brigade, it also had a Belfast battalion, which saw itself as an elite, the Young Citizen Volunteers. The specialist divisional troops were also recruited from the ranks of the UVF and were also a form of pals' units. Pioneers were recruited from men in the Lurgan area, while the engineers and signallers were recruited mainly from the shipyards.

In all, some six thousand men left the shipyards in the first months of the war. The vast majority joined the armed forces, and the majority of these joined the battalions of the 107th Brigade. By 7 September the first to sign up were already in Ballykinler, County Down, doing their basic training.

The rush to enlist caused a certain embarrassment to the authorities. There were already two Irish divisions, the 10th and 16th. Practically all barrack accommodation in Ireland was required for them, so matters had to be improvised for the 36th (Ulster) Division. Camps existed at Ballykinler and at Finner, County Donegal, and these were allocated to the 107th and 109th Brigades, respectively. The 108th Brigade had to make do with a temporary tented camp in the grounds of the Clandeboye estate at Bangor. The conditions here were very poor and there was a great deal of illness; there were even cases of meningitis. The men had to be billeted in neighbouring towns until huts were provided. Even then the estate was unsatisfactory, and the brigade was moved to Newtownards.

Major-General Powell stressed the importance of fitness, and all units went on regular route marches. As they did not yet have their full equipment, soldiers carried rucksacks full of stones. Interspersed among marching, drill and PT were more interesting activities, such as bayonet work and throwing Mills bombs (hand grenades). Shooting practice was limited. They had only been issued with drill rifles and had to borrow German Mausers from the UVF to conduct live practice. There was a formal syllabus that they were supposed to follow, covering everything from basic training, drill, discipline and hygiene up to battalion, brigade and divisional exercises. The 36th Division never had time to complete it.

When the division was deemed ready, arrangements were made for a parade through the streets of Belfast on 8 May 1915. Friends and relatives of the men travelled by train from all parts of Ulster to say farewell. It was a serious occasion, made sombre by the fact that the *Lusitania* had been sunk the day before. The 17,000 men of the division took an hour and a half to pass the City Hall. The men stayed in Ireland long enough to read the glowing reports in the newspapers, but everyone knew it was time to go. In June orders came for them to move to Seaford, in Sussex. They travelled by train to Dublin and from there by ferry to Holyhead. Another train took them at a leisurely pace through Wales and England to their new base.

Most of them enjoyed their time at Seaford. It was pleasant summer weather and they were near enough to Brighton to visit the town when they got a chance. Some even went to London, which was an interesting experience for men who had thought Belfast was a big city. But the war was always around them. Aeroplanes flew over them as they trained, and on calm evenings, when the breeze came from the south, there was the quiet rumble of guns in France.

On 27 July 1915 Kitchener inspected the division. He did not stay long but was pleased by what he saw. One thing he became aware of was the problem caused by shortages of weapons and ammunition. There had been too little training in the firing of rifles and machine-guns. At the beginning of September the division was moved to the Aldershot district in Hampshire, where they had intensive training. Some wondered whether the training was too little, too late.

The Boys from the Shankill—now the 9th Battalion of the Royal Irish Rifles—started off badly. On the trip over some of their number stole alcohol from the ship's bar. Their commanding officer, Lieutenant-Colonel Frank Percy Crozier, signed for the stolen drink, then lined the men up along the quay and informed them that the money would be deducted from their pay. The reprimand over, they marched to the station, where they entrained for Amiens. If their experience was like that of the Young Citizen Volunteers—now the 14th Battalion of the Royal Irish

Rifles—the journey was a slow one, for the men were able to sit with their feet swinging over the edge and talk of picking flowers as they went. One of the officers with the 15th (North Belfast) Battalion noticed that the men were being transported in horse boxes: eight horses or forty men, the notice said. The officers had a first-class carriage to themselves.

From Amiens the Ulster battalions marched to the villages in which they were to be billeted. The North Belfast men went to Vignacourt, a dirty, primitive village where conditions were little changed from the Middle Ages. The officers had maps but no instructions where to go. The resulting confusion caused an unpleasantness that marred relations with the villagers for some time to come. The Ulstermen were not impressed by what they saw. Most Frenchmen were at the front, and in their absence the yards were swimming in dirty water, and manure heaps were piled in front of the houses. Nor did the Ulstermen endear themselves to the French by helping themselves to any fruit or vegetables they fancied.

Worry about the front line had its effect on the Shankill boys. When Crozier paraded the battalion for its first march to the trenches, several of the warrant officers, who were expected to be the backbone of any unit, were absent, drunk. They were court-martialled, reduced to the ranks and sentenced to a period of hard labour.

At the front the Young Citizen Volunteers discovered that nights would be disturbed by the sounds of rats squeaking in the dugouts. None of the food was safe, even when hung by a cord from the rafters. It could be beautiful at night in the trenches, and the men were fascinated by star-shells colouring the skies.

All through the winter the Ulster Division took its turn in the front line. Each battalion would have two companies in the first line of trenches; the third company would be in the support line, while the fourth was held in reserve. Spells in the front lasted from four to eight days. Before dawn they would stand to, ready to repel an attack by the enemy. The mornings would normally start with an exchange of gunfire, called by the soldiers the 'morning hate'. Most days were quiet, as neither side wanted to expose itself in broad daylight. In the evening there might be a repeat bombardment, and after dark the routine work began. The next day's rations had to be fetched from the rear, while any damage to the trenches or barbed wire caused by the day's bombardment had to be repaired. To cover this work, the number of sentries would be increased and patrols sent out into no-man's-land. Sentry duty at night was particularly difficult, as it required continuous concentration from a man who was on his own for between two and three hours. A sentry's greatest sin was to fall asleep; this was a crime for which he could be shot.

The secret of survival was to make yourself as comfortable as the circumstances allowed. The dugouts sheltered the men from the rain but were scarcely welcoming. Ventilation was poor, and the smell that built up over a period in them must have been more of the latrine than the dormitory. Men smoked to cover the stink, but non-smokers found this to be almost as bad. One soldier reckoned that the most important thing he learnt was how to open a tin of bully beef with a bayonet without blunting the bayonet or getting any of the oil from the weapon on the beef.

Even in the rear areas there was little rest. The soldiers were kept busy building huts or carrying out exercises, leaving them as wet and exhausted as they had been in the trenches.

For some time during that first winter the 107th (Belfast) Brigade was transferred to the 4th Division, where it was to practise its trench warfare among some more experienced units. Although the brigade was to benefit from the experience, the transfer was done as a punishment. The divisional commander, Major-General Oliver Nugent, was dissatisfied with the brigade's reputation for indiscipline and in particular for looting. The final straw came when some NCOs were absent from parade and were found, drunk on brandy, in a local drinking den. The men concerned were reduced to the ranks and imprisoned. Nugent spoke to the officers of the brigade, expressing his displeasure very forcefully, before banishing the Belfast men to the 4th Division.

Whatever the intention, the 107th (Belfast) Brigade learnt how to use the weapons of trench warfare. Its new Lee Enfield .303 rifles had to be kept clean and free from rust. Although the men had bayonets, their preferred weapon was the Mills bomb, a hand grenade that could do devastating damage. The men were intrigued by the German version, which had a handle that allowed it to be thrown further. Grenades were the weapons of choice when patrols had to go out to no-man's-land to repair or replace the barbed-wire defences or, worse, to reach enemy trenches and bring back objects that could be used by brigade headquarters for intelligence purposes, to identify which German troops they were facing. The men had to be prepared to freeze if they were caught in the open under the light of a flare, and had to develop a sense of direction that took them not only back towards their own lines but to the gap in the wire that was their gateway to safety.

The ordinary soldiers hated nothing worse than a patrol sent out without real purpose. To die on one of these seemed completely pointless. In spite of this, some individuals developed the necessary skills to such an extent that they were assigned almost permanently to patrols. Tommy Ervine, a shipyard worker who had collected his tools from the yard as he walked to the depot to enlist, was one of these. His skill with the bayonet and his way with Mills bombs made him a valuable member of any patrol.

Gas was a weapon that everyone hated. The masks were primitive and uncomfortable, and at 'gas school' the men were forced to march while wearing them, making them breathless in less than a mile. Worse, they were inefficient and did little to protect the wearer. Medical Corps soldiers and stretcher-bearers were taught how to deal with gas casualties; for example, they had to be sitting upright, rather than laid out like more conventional casualties. It was not just the rank and file who dreaded a gas attack, and the merest hint of chlorine in the air was enough to get soldiers rushing for their gas helmets.

As the winter drew on, the situation became worse. The Germans introduced phosgene, a much more powerful gas, which was invisible as well as odourless. Death from phosgene was slow torture, with the victim racked with coughing fits and vomiting, bringing up gallons of a vile yellow mucus before dying up to two days later.

The first man of the division to be killed in action was Samuel Hill of the Mid-Antrim Volunteers. He came from Whitehouse, just outside Belfast, and he died on 22 October 1915, less than a month after arriving in France, of shrapnel wounds to the head. Although the Ulstermen were occupying a reasonably quiet sector, death was a regular visitor that winter. Tommy Ervine had a friend who was shot dead by a sniper. Jim Maultsaid, an American citizen who had been a member of the Young Citizen Volunteers, was horrified when a friend was blown to pieces before his eyes.

As their time in the trenches went on, each soldier's survival skills improved. Most developed a sense that they could take all the precautions possible yet be annihilated by a stray shell in their part of the trenches. Ironically, this fatalism made life in the trenches more endurable. Some never achieved this and sought refuge in alcohol. This was easier for officers, and Crozier wrote later of one officer who sat in his dugout drinking, refusing to go outside to supervise his men, only to be killed by a shell that penetrated his refuge. Others, for whom alcohol was not so readily available, were unable to await a German bullet and did the job themselves, shooting themselves with their own rifles. One of the saddest stories is that of a young lad who abandoned his position and tried to make his way home. The court-martial decided that the death sentence was justified, even necessary, so that no other soldiers would be tempted to desert. He was allowed to write his last letters before being encouraged to get very drunk. He was then taken to the back garden of a villa, where he was tied to a post and shot in front of the entire battalion. Although the boy's family was told that he had died in action, the truth filtered back to Belfast and caused great offence to many in the city. For them it confirmed the reputation that Crozier was gaining as a callous officer, willing to sacrifice anything in the name of efficiency.

If a man was wounded or incapacitated by illness he would be taken to the regimental aid post, near the front line. Medical facilities there were very basic. If a wound was serious the man would be sent back to the advanced dressing station, where injuries could be dealt with properly and morphine could be administered to help control the pain. If there were any complications he would be passed on to the main dressing station, where surgical operations could be performed. Assuming that the man survived, he would then be moved to a base hospital to recover. To ensure that medical attention would be available as quickly as possible, doctors would be on hand if a situation developed where casualties would be expected, such as during a period of shelling or if a large patrol was going out.

The people the soldiers really admired were the men of the Royal Army Medical Corps, particularly the stretcher-bearers who made their way into no-man's-land with no more to protect them than their stretchers and the field dressings they carried. Medical orderlies were the first to deal with casualties, usually treating them as they lay on their stretchers. Often it was the first aid administered at the aid post that enabled a soldier to survive long enough to reach the hospital. In real emergencies the orderly might have to carry out procedures that would normally have been done only by a doctor. The conditions were cramped and hygiene non-existent near the front line, so there was always the danger of clinical shock, or tetanus, or gangrene for those whose open wounds became infected.

Medical orderlies were less popular at quiet times in the trenches. It was their job to see that water was properly chlorinated and to administer the debilitating immunisation against typhoid. It was also their job to make an initial diagnosis, which put pressure on them. If they allowed a sick soldier to go back to base for treatment, word would get round and there would be a queue of men with the same symptoms. The temptation was to assume that they were skiving; but what if one of them really had typhoid? To miss a case of this disease would mean that an entire battalion might have to be withdrawn from the trenches for six months. The responsibility for all this drove some orderlies to use alcohol to help them get through. This particular stress was not seen by the infantrymen, who watched in envy as they marched to some destination while the orderlies rode in the comfort of their motor ambulances, snug and out of the rain.

Although there were many hideous ways to die on the Western Front, it was the persistence of discomfort that was the hardest burden to bear. A combination of persistent rain and heavy soil meant that, for weeks at a time, men had to stand and move about in trenches that were knee-deep in water. Cloying mud was everywhere, and one officer wrote about feeling like a fly in treacle any time he moved off the duckboards. Cold could freeze a man's boots to the firing step, or make a finger stick to the trigger. Snow was worse, because it could prevent rations or even fresh drinking water from getting to the front line. In the worst of these conditions the side of a trench might cave in and have to be repaired. Rural Ulstermen used to repairing ditches had no problem with this, but the city tradesmen of the Belfast battalions found it more difficult.

When they got back to their billets their first task would be to try to rid themselves of the accumulated muck of the trenches. Then they would try to unburden themselves of their cargo of parasites, the most obvious of which were the lice and fleas. There were also rats, whose curiosity might lead them to test the edibility of any exposed bit of flesh. Such a bite might lead to blood poisoning, as dangerous in those days before antibiotics as 'superbugs' are in modern hospitals.

Even without such unpleasant incidents, health was not good in the Belfast Brigade. Many men suffered bouts of shivering, accompanied by fever. Only the worst cases were removed to hospital; others had to wait in the dugout for a day to see if a 'bitter powder' would clear up their symptoms as effectively as it dried up their mouths. If there was an outbreak of stomach trouble the sergeant might insist on dosing his entire platoon. Unfortunately, he would usually use the same spoon for every-body, thereby ensuring that everybody caught the bug.

Even as simple a thing as living outdoors most of the time had its cost for men who had had indoor jobs before the war; their hands and feet tended to swell and their joints grew stiff. Trench foot was an occupational hazard for all, brought on by boots and socks being permanently wet. Bits of skin simply peeled off, exposing sores that would not heal until a combination of ointment and dry socks became available. The problem was exacerbated when they had to make a route march. On one of these each man carried a minimum of 60 pounds of personal equipment. This equipment was inspected regularly to make sure that nothing was lost or left behind. Each soldier had to pay for any equipment lost.

Even the worst of winters passes, and the weather began to improve in early March. At about the same time it was judged that the 36th Division was capable of taking its full part in the trenches, and their front was extended to include the whole of Thiepval Wood, with the Hamel section to the north. The River Ancre flowed through their positions. After an initial raid on 10 March 1916, when, after a heavy bombardment, the Germans penetrated the lines of the Derry Volunteers and inflicted casualties, the front went quiet for the rest of the month, allowing the Ulstermen to settle in and celebrate St Patrick's Day and enjoy the warm sunshine of a Picardy spring.

The shelling resumed in April, and the Young Citizen Volunteers suffered casualties on the 6th when their position took some direct hits. As Easter passed, the two sections that made up the division's front took on very different characters. Thiepval Wood had grown its foliage and was full of birdsong, but it was dangerous, as it was regularly shelled by the Germans. The Hamel section, on the other hand, was relatively peaceful in those first weeks of spring, and some of the men even managed to shoot some ducks in the swampy ground along the Ancre.

For those who kept their eyes open there were signs that the peace was not going to last. In April work began on two causeways across the Ancre, designed to allow the free movement of troops up to and along the front line. Although the work was supervised by the Royal Engineers, much of the labour was carried out by infantrymen, carrying forward sandbags filled with chalk. This work was done from dusk to dawn, but the Germans could see what was going on and shelled the construction sites and the approach roads regularly, inflicting many casualties. Trenches had to be dug for the forward observers of the artillery. A tramway was also made to enable the wounded to be evacuated quickly, and all defensive positions were strengthened. In particular, dugouts were reinforced and their doors and ceilings strengthened in anticipation of a heavy German bombardment. Raids were carried out on the German lines, sometimes in parties of up to ninety. Ominously, on quiet nights noises could be heard from the trenches opposite as the enemy in turn reinforced their positions.

In the rear areas the priority was now on training for the 'big push'. There were regular attacks on dummy trenches, where the emphasis was on rapid fire, use of the bayonet and consolidating ground that had been captured. There were shooting and bombing competitions. Towards the end of May each battalion spent some time at Clairfaye Trenches, where the German defences opposite the 36th Division's sector had been replicated. Huge dumps of food and medical supplies were set up in central clearing areas. The blankets that had been issued to the men during the winter were taken back. From now on they slept in their great-coats; but this was no real hardship, as the weather remained mild.

The plan for the coming attack was straightforward. Put at its simplest, the British artillery would smash the German defences in a sustained bombardment, killing or incapacitating the German defenders. When the bombardment had done its job the British soldiers would simply walk forward and occupy the now defenceless enemy positions. To make assurance doubly sure, a British barrage would keep in front of the advancing troops, ensuring that any surviving Germans would keep their heads down. Because it was felt important that the infantry should advance in a disciplined manner, maintaining their alignment, they were ordered to go no faster than a brisk walk. Kitchener's army was about to have its first real test, on a battlefield that would become a killing zone if anything went wrong.

The main objective of the Ulster Division was a maze of interlocking trenches, tunnels and gun emplacements known as the Schwaben Redoubt. Possibly the strongest position on the German line, it sat astride a low hill opposite to, and dominating, the Ulstermen's Thiepval section. Its guns also guarded the approaches to the villages of Thiepval and

Beaumont-Hamel. The men of the 108th Brigade would start from the Hamel section and attack Beaucourt station, to the north of the Ancre. This would necessitate crossing a ravine, capturing the German trenches at Beaucourt and capturing a mill on the bank of the river. This task was assigned to the Armagh Volunteers and the Mid-Antrim Volunteers. South of the river the 1st Battalion of the Down Volunteers and South Antrim Volunteers would attack Saint-Pierre Divion, where there were German machine-gun posts. When the machine-guns were put out of commission they would turn and attack the Schwaben Redoubt from the north, with the North Belfast Volunteers in support.

The direct assault on the Schwaben Redoubt was the responsibility of the 109th Brigade. The Derry Volunteers and Tyrone Volunteers would lead the way, taking the first three German trench lines, and would be supported by the Donegal and Fermanagh battalion and the Young Citizen Volunteers. The supporting battalions would consolidate these three lines, while the East Belfast, West Belfast and South Belfast Battalions would pass through them and continue the attack until they reached and occupied the German fifth line, beyond the redoubt. It would be as simple as a cross-country stroll on a summer morning.

In the early part of June the river valley bloomed. The weather was much better, and health and morale improved in the warm sun. The 107th (Belfast) Brigade remained in the trenches, while the 108th and 109th practised their attacks on the dummy trench system in the rear.

It wasn't all waiting in the sun. On Monday 5 June the Mid-Antrim Volunteers came back to the front and conducted a major raid on the German trenches along the railway line that would be their primary objective when the day came. There had been a pre-raid shelling, and one of the raid's objectives was to find how much damage had been inflicted by the guns. The trenches seemed suitably smashed about, so the assumption was made that the huge bombardment planned to precede the battle would devastate the entire German front line. The retaliatory raid by the Germans on the North Belfast Volunteers, carried out the following Saturday night, seemed a small price to pay for success.

The good weather was interrupted by two days of rain in mid-month; but even the bad weather did not interrupt the preparations for battle. Gun-pits had to be dug for the divisional artillery, and huge amounts of ammunition had to be brought to the front. Assembly trenches were dug at Thiepval Wood. As the Germans continued to shell this area, there were many casualties among the workers. There were moments of rest too, particularly during the day, when logistical operations had to be interrupted. The river itself provided welcome relief from the heat and was used by all ranks as a swimming pool.

In the third week of June, preliminary attack orders reached the battalion commanders. These had to be translated into orders for each company in the battalion, and all the officers had to understand exactly what was expected of them. Lieutenant-Colonel Crozier of the West Belfast Battalion had a huge map mounted in a barn and lectured his officers for hours before he was satisfied that they were ready.

The pace of work increased, and the work was made unpleasant by the fact that the rain returned. Tools and stores were placed in the assembly trenches. On the night before the bombardment was to begin the Young Citizen Volunteers stretched in a wet, glistening line 600 men long, from the ammunition dump to the front line, carrying ammunition and working from dusk to dawn without a break for food. As the hours before the bombardment slowly passed, units took up their positions. The Tyrone and South Antrim men occupied the Thiepval Wood section. The Armagh Volunteers were in the Hamel trenches. All of them knew that, once the British bombardment began, the Germans would concentrate their guns on these positions and that they would have to experience hell before even going over the top.

The noise of the guns when they opened fire on Saturday was so loud that it could be heard far away in the London night. Closer to hand, the experience was one of shock and awe. For those in a position to see, it seemed that nothing could live in the German lines. Tommy Jordan from Ballynafeigh complained of the pain in his ears. Later they began to bleed. On Sunday, church services were held in spite of the diabolical raging of the guns. Afterwards, commanding officers passed on their final orders to their officers. In the 107th (Belfast) Brigade the two rear platoons in each company were to carry iron stakes and barbed wire to consolidate their hold on the German third line. On the third day, the Monday, the 36th Division planned to use gas for the first time, in support of a raid going out from Thiepval Wood. By coincidence, some German shells landed just as the gas was being released, and the Down Volunteers suffered casualties. They suffered more casualties on the way back from the raid, when six men were killed by machine-gun fire.

The rain continued, and the decision was taken that the Somme offensive, which was supposed to begin on Thursday 29 June, should be postponed until the weather improved. This meant that the men holding the front had to be relieved, exposing themselves to shell-fire as they moved forward or back. This realignment in turn meant adjustments to the divisional plan of attack; it also meant that even more shells had to be brought forward in miserable conditions on wet, slippery ground. And if damage was being done to the enemy defences, the German counter-bombardment on Thiepval Wood, against which they seemed to have a particular antipathy, meant that the trenches were in a dreadful state and that the Ulstermen were suffering a steady stream of casualties.

The postponement was brief, however. Friday dawned a fine day; a bright sun shone, and the ground steamed as it dried. The decision was taken to attack the next day, Saturday 1 July. All the men in the division now learnt what their role would be in the big push. Many senior officers toured the front, to wish the soldiers luck and to glean the last little bits of intelligence that would be useful on the following day. Fresh drinking water was distributed. Last-minute letters and postcards were collected for posting. Medical orderlies checked their supplies. Specialist units, such as trench mortar batteries, fused their bombs. There were religious services for some. Some Catholics in the division—and there were Catholics in the Ulster Division—found English soldiers attending mass at a field altar and were able to join in.

In the early evening the men behind the lines were given a hot meal, and were encouraged to eat as much as possible. Afterwards most of them checked their personal weapons, on which their lives might depend the next day, and tried to get a final bit of rest.

All too soon, the move forward began. As usual, the Germans carried out nuisance firing, though there were few casualties. When the units reached the assembly trenches, equipment was distributed and the men tried to settle down for the remainder of the night. They were surrounded by flame and din and confusion. The smell of high explosive was in the air, and the noise was so great that friend could not speak to friend. The organisation that had been formed to defy the British Empire was about to confront the might of the German Empire. The men had come a long way from the Shankill and the Newtownards Road. How far they would go the next day was an imponderable that kept many of them awake long into the night.

Crozier could not sleep and heard the birds begin to sing at about four o'clock. The cooks were getting good breakfasts ready for the Shankill men: tea, bacon, fried bread and jam. Into their water containers many men put cold lemon tea. Some wondered why zero hour was so late—not till 7:30— though dawn came long before that. Officers moved to occupy their command posts. These would be sandbagged, with little ventilation. Light would be from paraffin lamps, adding to the heat and the fug. There would be a bank of telephones, by means of which the commander hoped to control his troops. Some officers had tried to maintain an air of normality by shaving carefully and by putting on clean socks. Others, as the German fire concentrated even more on the Ulster positions, simply waited.

By six o'clock, shells were falling on the positions of the Young Citizen Volunteers, and soldiers were being killed. Hugh Stewart from Lisburn survived a shell that killed the other member of the machine-gun team. As the gun itself was also destroyed, Stewart was given a rifle—a poor substitute for a Lewis gun.

The British bombardment opened up at its usual time, 6:25. Each morning there had been an intensive bombardment beginning at this time, continuing until 7:45. On this day it would stop at 7:30, hopefully catching the Germans off guard. The shells passing over the Young Citizen Volunteers made a mighty rushing sound in the sky, and as they exploded they reminded one volunteer of the hollow noise of a great door closing. The intensity of emotion meant that there was always the danger of error. One group of Ulster Volunteers was unlucky. They were sharing out grenades when the box fell from its shelf, and two of the bombs fell to the ground, shaking out their pins on impact. Billy McFadzean threw himself on top of them, being killed instantly but protecting the rest of the men in the dugout from probable death. For this action McFadzean was awarded a posthumous Victoria Cross, the first of the Battle of the Somme. Although he had been born in Lurgan, his family had moved to Cregagh in east Belfast, where, after school, the young Billy had entered the linen trade. His father was to be given a third-class railway ticket so that he could receive the medal on Billy's behalf.

There was an issue of rum at about 7 o'clock. Quite a few men in the division did not drink alcohol, so they shared it with their friends. Others had got hold of some of the local spirits, such as Calvados—rough stuff made on local farms. Yet others, from the west of the province or from the Glens of Antrim, had a bottle of poitín carefully stored against the day it would be needed. For some, as a result, the final minutes before zero hour passed in an alcoholic daze.

As the bombardment still roared overhead, groups of wire-cutters went forward to clear a path. Steps had been cut in the forward sides of the trenches to make it easier to climb up into no-man's-land. Major-General Nugent, commander of the 36th Division, realised that the men would be at their most vulnerable as they climbed out of the trenches, especially if the Germans were firing back. He ordered the first wave of the attack to move out while the bombardment was continuing, judging that the Germans would be keeping their heads down and wouldn't notice. The Armagh Volunteers, north of the river, moved gingerly forward at 7:10. South of the river the Derry, Tyrone, Down and South Antrim battalions moved out five minutes later.

As soon as the first wave had left the trenches, the second wave took up their vacated positions. This ploy enabled the 36th Division to get further forward than their neighbouring divisions to the north and south. Now, in the last five minutes before the attack was to begin, the guns increased their rate of fire. For some soldiers, lying in the open, it must have felt as if the final trumpet was sounding. Where were the quiet fields of mid-Ulster now?

At 7:30 the guns ceased. The silence was almost as shocking as the shelling had been, but it was soon broken by the officers' whistles, and the men rose to their feet, unsteady under the weight of their equipment and careful as they stepped on the broken ground. In a long line, the men spaced about fifteen feet apart, they began their long walk forward.

At first it seemed that the guns had done their job. The leading ranks broke into a charge as they reached the German front line and dropped into the enemy trenches. At that moment, however, it became obvious that British hopes had been too sanguine. Machine-guns opened fire on the Ulstermen, not simply from the Schwaben Redoubt but from Thiepval and from the higher ground to the north of the Ancre. The deep dugouts that the Germans had had time to perfect had survived the bombardment and were now pouring very accurate fire at the advancing soldiers. The German artillery shortened its range and began to scour no-man's-land with high explosive and shrapnel. Men were falling so quickly in front of him that Albert Bruce from Lambeg took shelter in the sunken road that crossed in front of his objective. One rural volunteer said that the bodies lay like sheaves of corn. They were terrified of the barbed wire. If you got stuck on that you were a sitting target once you were spotted by the Germans.

The wonder is that the attack kept moving forward; but the third line of German trenches was reached by 7:50, and hand-to-hand fighting began. They had been clearing the dugouts by throwing two or three grenades down the steps and shutting the door. This was not as effective as they thought, however, as the Germans often built their access to dugouts in a spiral, so that many of the grenades did not even reach the floor but exploded harmlessly on the steps. Under pressure of time to keep moving forward, the men were leaving enemy soldiers behind them who could counter-attack from the rear.

Meanwhile the second wave had started from the trenches, ten minutes after the first. Again they were caught in the crossfire from Beaumont-Hamel and Thiepval. As the Young Citizen Volunteers moved forward, men saw friends whom they had known since schooldays scythed to the ground or, worse, dismembered by shell or grenade. Some men died slowly, calling quietly for friends; others screamed screams that would be remembered by survivors for the rest of their lives. Increased firing from the Germans made it difficult to move forward at all, with groups pinned down in shell holes, waiting for a pause in the shelling before advancing a few more yards. Those soldiers at the front, waiting to be reinforced, were impatient of what they saw as excuses. Machine-gun fire was being concentrated on the line of the British trenches, and some soldiers got no further than the parapet. Instead of climbing out they began to roll over the edge. Stretcher-bearers did not even have to leave the trenches to collect their first casualties.

The most dangerous ranks to be in during the Great War were those of the junior officers. They were easily identified by their different uniform and by the fact that they carried a revolver rather than a rifle. Officers took a much more prominent role in the British army than in the German. They led from the front, a role that the German army left to warrant officers and senior NCOs. To kill an officer was to leave men, at least temporarily, leaderless, and could remove the initiative from a unit. This was where good NCOs mattered, because it was up to them to keep a unit together and keep them on the move. This was what was happening in front of the Schwaben Redoubt. Sergeants kept pressing the men forward until, they hoped, they could join up with another officer. They took few prisoners. They had seen their friends killed and were in no mood to show mercy to Germans, even if they tried to surrender. Besides, they could not afford to detail men for guard duty. Every man was needed to push forward.

By 9 o'clock the German fourth line was in Ulster hands and the redoubt had, effectually, been stormed. The forward troops consolidated their positions while small groups of soldiers cleared the trenches on each side of the advance. The 107th (Belfast) Brigade was to move forward through no-man's-land, ready to advance on the German fifth line at about 10 o'clock. There was a problem, however. The divisions to the north and south of the Ulstermen were static, with the first waves failing to gain any of their objectives. If the 36th were to advance, it might be stretching out its neck and inviting the Germans on each side to chop it off. At about 8:30 Major-General Nugent had asked his superior at corps headquarters if the final assault could be postponed till there was proper support on both flanks. He was ordered to go ahead with the attack. Later, corps headquarters changed its mind and the Belfast Brigade was ordered to hold its position until the situation on the flanks had improved—at least that would have been the order if the message had got through. Unfortunately, the only way of communicating along the front was by field telephones. These depended on lines laid between command posts, and by this time most of them had been destroyed by shell-fire. The order to hold back did not arrive, and the attack went ahead on schedule.

The Belfast men knew what they were getting into. They could see what was happening as the 32nd Division attacked the village of Thiepval to their right and could see unit after unit being annihilated under German fire. The South Belfast Battalion was beginning to suffer casualties as shells stripped away the cover of Thiepval Wood.

The shelling eased slightly at about 8:30, and Crozier moved his West Belfast men forward to the shelter of the sunken road. The South Belfast Battalion was to follow, but its commanding officer, Barnard, was fatally wounded. His battalion wavered and might well have retreated if Crozier had not seen what was happening. He took command and ordered the South Belfast men forward to the sunken road, threatening to shoot any who held back. Before returning to battalion headquarters he looked around at the wounded men lying in no-man's-land, waiting to be reached by stretcher-bearers. Even headquarters was full of dead and wounded.

The East Belfast Battalion left the British lines last. Tommy Ervine was following a friend of his from the Beersbridge Road. The friend fell back into the trench on top of Ervine. The man's tunic was soaked with blood; there was a slit across his forehead where he had been hit by shrapnel. Ervine laid the man to one side and then went over the top himself. As he rushed forwards he felt a stinging sensation in his shoulder. It was only later that he discovered he had been struck by a piece of shrapnel. When he got to the German lines he found that the enemy were counter-attacking, coming along the trenches from Hamel and Thiepval. In the melee he was badly enough injured to become a stretcher case.

Back at the Ulster Division's own front-line trenches the confusion caused by the lack of information led to some tragic errors. Crozier witnessed some of his men firing a Lewis gun at an approaching group of Germans, even though the Germans had surrendered and were being escorted by wounded Ulstermen. The men ignored his call to cease fire. 'They're only Germans,' some youngster told him.

The British barrage was concentrating on the German fifth line, the division's final objective. One thing that the Belfast Brigade was determined would not happen was that the enemy defenders would have time to take up firing positions when the barrage lifted. They wanted to be as close as possible to the defences when the shelling stopped. With that in mind, parties of them began to make their way forward. Many of them were joined by soldiers from other battalions. British shells sometimes fell short, and many were killed. Finally the shelling lifted and they charged.

They had lost so many men that only a small length of trench was taken, perhaps about one hundred yards. The men tried to consolidate it, even rewiring it to defend it against a counter-attack. But they were too few, and in a very vulnerable position. German shell-fire stopped reinforcements getting through, while German reinforcements were coming up the trenches from the northern flank, which remained open. Around mid-day the surviving Belfast men fell back on the German fourth line and reconsidered their position.

It was not a happy one. The Germans had held their positions to the north and south, doing it so effectively that the Allied divisions had scarcely left their own front line. The fifth line, in front of them, had been freshly reinforced. Enemy artillery was dominating no-man's-land. They were effectually besieged. Now they were defending the Schwaben Redoubt, or at least part of it. The survivors, by now a mixed bunch of all the battalions engaged, tried to consolidate on the German third line. Extra officers arrived from the British lines, but parties of Germans were coming up their old front-line trench and were starting to engage the makeshift units from the rear.

The men were exhausted and, on that warm July day, dehydrated. All had been fighting for hours. Their faces were yellow from the explosions around them. A thick pallor of dust covered everything and was even getting into the mechanism of their rifles, jamming the action in many of them.

The dead and dying lay on the open ground and in the shell holes of no-man's-land. As early as 8:30 there were reports of three to four hundred casualties in no-man's-land. There were only six stretcher parties to cover this, and the stretcher-bearers were under such pressure that they concentrated on those casualties who seemed to have a chance of living. If the others were lucky they might have a companion in their last hours or minutes. Most waited to meet their maker in an agony of pain and thirst and fear.

North of the river, things had also begun well. The first wave refused to be bound by the order to proceed at a brisk walk and charged across the dangerous open ground to the German first line. The guns had done their job here: there were large gaps in the wire and the few defenders were disoriented. Their momentum took the Ulstermen right through to the third line, from where a group began its attack on Beaucourt Station. The second wave was not so lucky. By the time it was moving the German defenders had taken up their firing positions. Once again the energy of the Volunteers had taken them so far forward that they had an open flank. Beaumont-Hamel was to their left and above, and well-directed machine-gun fire cut down men as they tried to go forward. It became obvious that the gaps in the wire might be big but there were few of them. By concentrating their fire on these points the Germans were able to deal with the ever smaller groups of Ulstermen trying to push forward. Once again Germans filtered in from the flanks and retook their own first line, effectually trapping yet another portion of the division. The men, mostly Armagh Volunteers reinforced by men from Mid-Antrim, began to fall back, singly or in small groups, before the net should tighten. They collected wounded as they went, hurrying to leave their own Armageddon. Of six hundred men of the Armagh Volunteers who went over the top at zero hour, fewer than seventy returned unscathed or only slightly wounded. The battalion had ceased to exist.

As the sun passed mid-day, the Belfast Brigade was still in trouble. Observers could see trainloads of German reinforcements being delivered to Grandcourt. The West Belfast men who were holding the German third line became aware of enemy soldiers infiltrating towards them along the communication trenches from the fourth line. Some of the men were tempted to run but were prevented by their officers. They waited. At 3:45 p.m. a skirmish began around a trench on the south side of the redoubt.

After an hour of fierce fighting the Germans prevailed. Cut off from supplies as they were, the Belfast men had to ration their ammunition. Even the machine-guns could fire only in short bursts.

Just as things seemed hopeless, a message came through that they would be reinforced in little over an hour's time. This was not to be: the troops earmarked to reinforce the redoubt had already been used elsewhere. By the time a fresh battle group had been assembled it was too late. Even eight companies of the 146th (Yorkshire) Brigade could not stem the flood of valiant counter-attacks that the Germans were making. In the long daylight hours of mid-summer the British troops were an easy target for machine-guns in Thiepval. As the carnage continued, men who had been fighting continuously for twelve hours reached the end of their tether, too exhausted for even morale to hold them, and small groups began to slip back to what seemed the safety of their own lines. Even shots fired into the retreating groups by their own officers were not enough to hold them, and by dusk all those who could make it were back in the British trenches. Some of the officers looked back across no-man's land. The Germans were filling in the trenches that the Belfast Brigade had tried to hold. The entire division was back at its starting point. It seemed that all that long day's dying and suffering had been for nothing.

Not all the men had got back. The badly wounded could not, nor those caught too far behind the enemy lines. They lay in their pain and loneliness and waited for death or capture. Some survivors remembered little of their ordeal: being given a drink of schnapps, perhaps, or a cigarette in the safety of the German trenches. For them the war was over, but they were further from home than ever. There were more men in no-man's-land, trapped in shell holes until darkness gave them the opportunity to escape. They made their way back, freezing any time the Germans sent over a flare.

Even getting back to the British lines was no guarantee of safety. The Germans were still shelling Thiepval Wood quite heavily, and some soldiers got as far as here only to be killed.

One ghastly job that had to be done was sorting out the corpses. Their identity tags were taken and the bodies stored in dugouts for burial later. The wounded were being treated by doctors who were working flat out, ignoring their exhaustion, trying to staunch the bleeding of wounds so large that a fist could be put in them, or carrying out amputations, with basic anaesthetics and the flame of a candle for sterility. Those who had waited all day in command posts were in despair as they realised the extent of the destruction and tried to get information about their own units.

At 11:30 p.m. a message arrived stating that the 146th Brigade would be put at the disposal of the 36th Division in a renewed attack on the Schwaben Redoubt. It was decided that it would not be practical to launch an attack by night over ground that was strange to the men. Equally, an attack by daylight would be suicidal unless the machine-guns in Thiepval were neutralised. Common sense for once prevailed, and the operation was cancelled.

The next day dawned mistily but with the promise of sun. By 7 o'clock the mist had gone and watchers realised that there were still groups of British troops in the German trenches. Major-General Nugent decided that an attempt should be made to support them by sending ammunition and water as well as more machine-guns. Hurriedly, the Pioneer Battalion began bringing ammunition to the front. It was not an easy undertaking for a man to carry a box of grenades on his back and to stumble through shattered trenches towards the front line, knowing that a pin could slip from one of the grenades and the entire box would explode.

Major Woods of the West Belfast Volunteers was given charge of a group of four hundred men that would leave the front line at 2 p.m. These men were to be taken from the reserve units that had been holding the Ulster line, reinforced by men from the 148th Brigade. With them would go two machine-guns.

When John Kennedy Hope of the Young Citizen Volunteers heard that another attempt was going to be made on the redoubt, he was overcome by fear. He had been feeling comfortable. He had lit a fire and had eaten a tin of pilchards, washed down by hot, sweet tea. Now he did not know if his courage would be strong enough to take him back up the hill. Luckily, he was not required. The surviving Young Citizen Volunteers were ordered back from the front, marching in single file across the causeway that had been built with such official optimism earlier in the spring. There were 120 of them, and only two of the officers that had gone over the top the previous day.

They had gone by the time Major Woods led his men in the scramble across no-man's-land to the British outposts. The supplies they carried were as important as the men were, and if a man fell those around him would add as much of his load as they could carry to their own; some men were carrying double the weight they started out with by the time they got to the German trenches. They had suffered terrible casualties, however, and only two men out of every three reached the objective.

The reinforcements and resupply made it possible to hold out. The 49th Division was to take over the line from the Ulstermen later that night. It would be just in time for men who had been fighting for a day and a half with little water and less rest. The handover took place in darkness, and survivors of the 36th Division made their way back to the wood. A perfunctory effort was made to sort them into battalions before they made their way back to Martinsart, where the continuing bombardment did not prevent them from falling asleep as soon as they lay down. The casualties of the first day's battle were still being recovered, some of them still alive.

On the Monday morning the men themselves began to count the cost. In the West Belfast Battalion only seventy of those who had gone over the top were available for duty. In each battalion men watched anxiously for those who were still making their way back. Their emotions were heightened; the sense of satisfaction from having performed so well was counterbalanced by the guilt they felt because they had survived when so many had not. Men wept openly at roll call when so many names went unanswered. Field postcards were handed out, as it was realised that the people at home would be anxious to know the fate of their fathers and husbands and sons. When this had been done some groups went out to look for friends among the casualties. Incredibly, on Tuesday a party from the Young Citizen Volunteers found twelve men still alive in the sunken road.

The infantry battalions were moved to the rear a few days later and out of Picardy completely by 11 July. On the 12th the Orangemen marched— some even found orange flowers to wear; but they were marching towards a new battlefield in Flanders.

After two years of war the people of Belfast knew about casualties. Many of their sons had served in the regular army, and many had fought at Gallipoli. That battle had been a great killer of men, and newspapers throughout the province carried sad biographies of fallen heroes throughout 1915. During the winter of 1915/16 the steady run of casualties in the Ulster Division, though it was usually small, never quite dried up. In mansions and in terraced houses, in city streets and on farms, everyone knew the significance of the small buff envelope, and neighbours would gather around and try to show solidarity with the bereaved family.

The difference in July 1916 was one of scale. By the time the battle was reported in the Northern newspapers, the Ulster Division had already suffered its agony. Over the next few weeks it was the turn of the families back home to endure. A postman in the Shankill realised that he had two letters for the one family. Unable to face the task of letting a mother know that she had lost two sons, he held one letter back till the next day. Sometimes the local clergyman was called on to deliver the news, particularly if a list of wounded men came through. Newspapers carried lists of dead, wounded and missing. Most newsagents posted a copy in their window, because not everybody could afford a newspaper every day. As the week and the month progressed, the newspaper lists grew longer and there were those who found from these lists that their loved ones had died, before the buff envelope had arrived at the door. As well as this, many inserted death notices in the papers, giving a brief account of a soldier's death. By the end of the month, Ulster was awash with grief.

Politicians made much of it, of the heroic sacrifice the sons of Ulster had made as they marched into battle, of the fact that their loyalty to the

Crown had been demonstrated in such a heroic manner. Memorial services and commemorations echoed the theme. The 36th Division had somehow offered a holocaust to the Lord, and the Lord would ensure that the link with Great Britain would be maintained. Many of those who had been through the battle found such sentiment offensive, high on the nobility of war and very light on the carnage. With the smell of blood and torn flesh in their nostrils, they knew the untruth of what was being said, knew that it was a blasphemy.

A truer judgement was made on 12 July. Instead of parades there was a five-minute silence at noon, observed throughout the North. Traffic stopped in the streets and trains stopped on their tracks. Public courts were adjourned and blinds were drawn. In streets where nearly every house had been touched by tragedy there was a shared anger as well as distress. Carson sent a message to the Ulster people regretting the loss of so many 'personal friends and comrades'; but it was Carson who had offered the Volunteers to the War Office. It was the people who lived in Lurgan and Cookstown and Cregagh who were paying the price in grief.

It went beyond religion. Most Catholics, even nationalists, had Protestant friends and neighbours, and grieved with them. And Catholics too had died, some with the 36th Division, others in famous Irish regiments or in regiments recruited in England, such as the Manchester Irish. Death was no bigot; death dealt with communities indiscriminately.

But the Orange Order was particularly stricken. The best of its young and not so young members had gone. After one battle it had suffered more than five thousand casualties, about two thousand of them dead. Of the survivors, many had such injuries that they would never work again. Local lodges came together for joint remembrance services. At one meeting more than 150 names of the dead were read out before the women made tea and sandwiches. It can only be hoped that the solidarity shown by the order and by their neighbours helped to assuage some of the grief felt by the bereaved.

It was the beginning of the end for the Ulster Division, at least in the form of its Ulster Volunteer roots. After the first surge of patriotic enthusiasm in 1914, recruitment for the army had dried up, both in Great Britain and in Ireland. The reality of war, the suffering and savagery of it, had become apparent to all during the long months in the Western Front and the cauldron of Gallipoli. It did not seem such an adventure now, and men made judgements before committing themselves to it. In Ulster, after Easter 1916, there was also the sense that the Union might still have to be defended and that young men were needed at home as well as in France. Even before the Battle of the Somme there were rumours that the division was to be broken up because of lack of reserves.

East of the Irish Sea the recruitment shortage was overcome by the introduction of conscription. This solution was politically unsustainable in Ireland, and the threat of its imposition united nationalist and unionist in hostility to the move.

The numbers in the 36th Division were made up immediately after the Somme by replacements from the reserve battalions, but that was it. The well was dry. At the core of the Ulster Division would always be the surviving volunteers from the early years, but as they fell their places would be taken by recruits from the Home Countries—even by Irish Catholics.

After a winter during which the Ulster Division trained hard to integrate the new recruits in the depleted ranks of the experienced soldiers, it was prepared to play its part in the battles of 1917. The Ulstermen were now stationed in Flanders, near Ypres. This was a strategically important city that had been in the front line since August and September 1914. It was held by the British, and to the east was the Ypres Salient, a thin thumb of territory sticking into the German lines. The problem was that the salient was dominated on three sides by German trenches on higher ground. One vital area was a low ridge, about five miles long, from which the Germans dominated the southern sector. If the army was to break out from Ypres, this ridge had to be taken. The ridge took its name from the town of Messines, at its southern end; but the objective of the 36th Division was the heavily fortified village of Wytschaete. On the division's left was the 16th (Irish) Division.

The Ulster Division was now in IX Corps, part of the Second Army, under General Hubert Plumer. He had a reputation for husbanding the lives of the men under his command and for thorough preparation before battle. He proved it in his planning for 7 June 1917. Every officer saw that every group of soldiers, down to corporals' sections, knew the movements they would have to make and knew how these fitted in with the general plan. But Plumer had started long before. He had used ex-miners to dig shafts in an area of relatively strong clay between 80 and 120 feet underground. They worked at it for nearly two years. The Germans could tell that they were digging but did not know how deep. They assumed the mines would be relatively shallow and that the explosions, when they came, would be limited. Plumer expected that large explosions, detonated so far down, would devastate the German defences and demoralise the German soldiers. In the meantime, enthusiastic counter-battery bombardments had vastly reduced the number of guns available to the defenders. The British had one gun to every seven yards of front. The German commander, Field-Marshal Rupprecht Wittelsbach, Crown Prince of Bavaria—otherwise Prince Rupert—knew he was in trouble even before the attack began.

Just after midnight on 7 June there was a sharp thunderstorm. The soldiers of the 36th Division made their way forward through the communications trenches and on to the front, where white tapes had been laid out on the ground to show their jumping-off points. The men were uncomfortable. The ground was wet and sticky. Worse, they had to wear gas masks, because the Germans had tried to disrupt their preparations with a sustained bombardment of gas shells. The warmth of the night made it even worse. When the rain cleared they could see the ground rising above them in the light of the moon and could see the flashes as British shells pounded the German position. At 2:40 a.m. the British guns stopped. In the silence birds could be heard singing, and the first light of dawn began to streak the sky above the ridge. There were signs of German panic, flares and some machine-gun fire. The men waited on their lines.

Just before zero hour some British guns began firing again. An instant later, at 3:10 a.m., nineteen gigantic mines, made up of 600 tons of high explosive, were detonated under the German lines. Seven of these were more or less directly in front of the 36th Division. The waiting soldiers felt the earth shake below them. As they stood up to advance, the ridge seemed to lift into the sky, driven by pillars of flame that united to form mushrooms of fire. The noise, when it hit them, stunned the British soldiers. It carried on through the Belgian countryside, across the channel, over the fields and orchards of Kent, and was heard by Lloyd George, waiting nervously in Downing Street.

The British artillery laid down a barrage, as had been attempted at the Somme, ahead of the advancing troops. Most of the German survivors could not fight. They surrendered *en masse*, weeping in their trauma. Thousands of them had disappeared, vaporised in the explosions or buried beneath hundreds of tons of earth. The entire ridge was in British hands by mid-afternoon. Wytschaete had held out for some time before being overwhelmed, jointly, by the Ulster and Irish Divisions. The British began to dig in near the crest of the ridge.

As always, German defences tightened as they got over their first shock. Machine-guns took their normal toll of the most advanced troops and of those moving up in support. Small pockets of Germans who were spared by some fluke of geology also joined in and fought with their usual ferocity. Tragically, many British soldiers were killed by fire from their own guns as the shock troops from the assault were relieved and were making their way to the rear. Time and again, as they came out of the fog of war along the ridge, they were mistakenly identified by artillery observers as German counter-attackers. Many hundreds were killed and wounded at a time when they were entitled to think that they had survived the battle.

In the end it could be said that the battle was won before the men moved forward. It was costly, nevertheless. The Germans suffered about 27,000 casualties, the British 24,000. However, a vital piece of preparation had been completed for the future battle to escape from the Ypres Salient. The Germans were grateful that it was not worse; they felt that if the

British had pressed home their advantage they might have won the break-out that been sought at the Somme almost a year before.

Once more the 36th Division was taken out of the lines, brought up to strength, and rested. It was obvious that another 'big push' was coming; the Battle of Messines was only the preliminary to this. There were several aims in the coming fight, which became known officially as the Third Battle of Ypres but was more commonly called Passchendaele, after one of the ridges that the British were attacking.

The aim paramount to Lloyd George was to allow the capture of the Belgian Channel ports and to deny their use to German submarines. Without these being neutralised there was some doubt whether Britain could sustain the war till the Americans arrived in force. A secondary concern for Lloyd George was the collapse of the French army as a fighting force: the pressure had to be kept off them until they had time to regain their morale. The aim of Field-Marshal Douglas Haig, commander in chief of the British Expeditionary Force, was much more straightforward. He wanted to beat the Germans before the Americans arrived, and he thought the best way to do this was by attrition. He meant by this that the British should not worry about the number of casualties they were suffering, as long as the Germans suffered more. Although such a casual approach to the death of his own men is abhorrent to modern minds, the irony is that Haig's approach probably worked, sucking in and pulverising almost every major unit in the German army, leaving it few options in the battles of 1918. Haig's army reached the village of Passchendaele, barely six miles from the start line, after four-and-a-half months of effort and at a cost of 300,000 casualties.

The battle, which was entrusted to General Hubert Gough's Fifth Army, began with a bombardment of 3,091 guns on 22 July. By the time the infantry moved forward on 31 July, 4¼ million shells had been fired. The advance began at 3:50 a.m. as elements of twelve divisions moved forward on a front eleven miles wide. They plodded in driving rain, on heavy wet clay that stuck to boots and clung to feet, making each step an effort. The attack was halted almost before it began, after only three or four hundred yards, and the men slithered into cover. Tanks were assigned to support the infantry, but few of them got beyond the front line. The rain continued day after day, and the army lay open to the elements and to the counter-bombardment of the Germans.

It became obvious that Gough's staff work was not of the quality of Plumer's. The Germans were using carefully sited pill-boxes, many more than the British had realised, and were able to use the guns in them to stymie the slaloming tanks. As early as 9:30 on the morning of the first day the Germans were beginning to press determined counter-attacks.

Casualties again were horrendous. Some of the assault brigades had lost 70 per cent of their fighting strength by mid-morning. Towards the end of the day some units were under such pressure that they were falling back towards their start lines. Haig described the scene in a despatch to the government. The heavy clay soil had become a maze of shell-holes that were partly filled with water. Rivers and streams had been blocked by the bombardment, and their waters were spreading along the low valleys, turning them into bogs. There were some tracks through these; to leave the track, for man or beast, was to run a real risk of drowning. Yet the Germans had the tracks in their gun-sights and shelled them continually. It was impossible to move more than a few men at a time.

Gough cancelled the attack he had intended for 2 August. Instead he concentrated on removing those of his divisions that were most badly mauled and getting them replaced by fresh men. This brought forward both the 36th Division and the 16th Division, the victors at Wytschaete. The transfer of the 36th was a miracle, given the conditions, completed on the night of 2/3 August.

The men's quarters were not very welcoming. For the next fortnight they lived in trenches that were shallow scrapes in the mud, protected by sandbags filled with more mud. The rain was unceasing. Supplies were brought forward only with the greatest difficulty. Ironically, clean water was in short supply, and hot food non-existent. It was an early autumn, and there was no way of keeping warm. Yet it was from these conditions, unpromising to say the least, that the 36th Division had to launch an attack on the village of Langemarck. It did so at 4:45 a.m. on 16 August, moving forward behind a creeping barrage that kept German heads down while it lasted. German fire actually fell behind the advancing troops, so it did little to worry them. The German front line, however, was a series of small forts and pill-boxes, linked by well-prepared trenches. These laid down a crisscross of machine-gun and sniper fire that did great damage; but the village of Langemarck was taken.

There was a series of intense counter-attacks from the Germans, pressed home with ferocity, which forced some of the battalions of the 16th (Irish) Division, on the Ulster Division's right, to fall back on their original positions, having sustained 60 per cent casualties. Even against the 36th Division, most of the counter-attacks were successful.

It was portrayed as a small victory, albeit temporary and costly—the only advance since the opening day. Newspaper reports made the most of it, but a lot of men paid with their bodies for gains that were in reality illusory. Even before it began the attack, while it was defending defenceless positions, the Ulster Division had lost nearly two thousand men. In the attack it lost another two thousand, including more than a hundred officers. Both Irish divisions were shattered. There was almost a mutiny among their senior officers, who complained that they had been sent into the attack after sustaining heavy shelling for almost two full weeks.

Worse came later, because they received no care after the battle. At a time when more motorised transport was available to the British army than ever in its history, the survivors were left to tramp back to the rear areas, exhausted and disoriented. The 16th Division was the worst treated. Its surviving remnant, without time for rest or even for baths, was sent back into the line further south. The contrast for the ordinary soldier between fighting under General Gough and fighting under General Plumer was never more apparent. Even Haig was appalled and, towards the end of the month, replaced Gough with Plumer. The battle dragged on till early November, when Passchendaele was captured and held against German counter-attacks, when it was officially ended.

The next major battle in which the Ulster Division was involved was probably the most significant of the year, if not of the war. It would prove that the British had a weapon that, if properly used, could swing the balance away from the Germans.

This weapon was the tank. The Tank Corps in fact had existed for nearly two years, and tanks had been used already in battle. The results had been disappointing, but the fault—protagonists of armoured warfare insisted— was in the piecemeal way in which they were used. To be fully effective, tanks should be concentrated, they thought, and used on the proper terrain. They would now be given the opportunity.

On the misty morning of 20 November, 381 tanks made their slow advance on the Hindenburg Line near the town of Cambrai, and cracked it like an egg. The Germans were caught completely by surprise, as there had been no preliminary bombardment. On that day the British gained an average of four miles, took 10,000 prisoners, and captured two hundred guns, all at the cost of only 1,500 British casualties. The Ulster Division had been on the extreme left of the line, the only division not to be supported by tanks that day, yet it was able to push forward along the Canal du Nord as far as the road from Cambrai to Bapaume. It could go no further till Bourlon Wood, on its right flank, was taken.

The results were spectacular; yet the British could have achieved a great deal more. Because of the casualties suffered in the battles of late summer they had no reserves with which to exploit the gaps they had made in the German line. This was compounded by the fact that army headquarters was twenty miles behind the lines, and was not inclined to believe the reports of early success. This gave the Germans time—time, for example, to discover that their shells did not have to pierce the armour of a tank to put it out of action but only to blow off one of its tracks. By nightfall it was too late. The Germans used the long, dark night to bring forward rein-forcements, and a supply of armour-piercing shells. By morning, when a new attack began, there were three fresh divisions in the German line and six more on the way. The attack soon stalled.

The original idea behind the attack was of a raid in strength. Haig had given the attacking forces forty-eight hours to achieve their objectives. Now he had to decide whether to break off and withdraw to a defensible line or to continue the attack. Desperate to deliver a major victory, he ordered his commanders to press ahead. His decision was to involve the Ulster Division in another attack.

The key to victory was the ridge and the wood of Bourlon. The Ulster Division would attack on the left, through the village of Mœuvres. There would be more than ninety tanks in support. The attack began through early mist on the morning of 23 November. Although some progress was made in the centre, the Ulstermen and the 51st Division, on the left and right flanks, were held up by stiff and increasing resistance. As the Germans reacted, the forward troops were gradually annihilated over the next few days. The British soldiers were exhausted, having fought in a series of battles over most of the year. After gaining some ground from the starting position, Haig closed the battle down.

This did not fit in with German plans. The Germans realised that the British had shot their bolt by 23 November and began to concentrate forces for launching a counter-attack. Twenty divisions were moved into the area, of which three were to attack from the north through the Bourlon area. In preparation, German artillery began to lob a steady stream of mustard-gas shells on the Bourlon positions. This was to be a decoy, however, and the main attack was planned for further south.

After a short preliminary bombardment the southern attack began in dense fog at 7 a.m. on 30 November. The Germans used new tactics, sending forward storm-troopers and flamethrowers to infiltrate British trenches. By 8:30 they were well behind the British lines. Their rapid advance, however, had reduced their cohesion, and they had to be halted and regrouped before pushing on. This was a vital delay from the point of view of the Ulster Division and the others in IV Corps. The Germans had hoped that the storm-troopers would move on to take the Bourlon positions in the rear. Because they were unable to do so, the Ulster Division was able to concentrate on holding its line to the left of Bourlon Ridge. Although the British front had been destabilised by the German attack, this steady defence of the left flank allowed General Julian Byng to push forward the Guards Division, the 62nd Division and the Cavalry Corps (without their horses and fighting as infantry). This was enough to stem the tide, particularly as sixty-three tanks were available to support them. As with the British a few days before, the German attack had run its course.

In the spring of 1918 the German army was ready to undertake a bold stroke aimed at ending the war before the Americans could get fully established in Europe. Since late 1914, and with the exception of Verdun, the German army had stood on the defensive along the Western

Front, inviting France and England to do their worst and limiting itself to counter-attacks to regain ground it considered strategically important. Now, however, it was in a hurry, and it had available considerable reinforcements, released when Russia had sued for peace on the Eastern Front. It had also adopted new tactics, concentrating its bombardment not on infantry trenches but on artillery batteries or on transport and communication hubs. Its new aim was to disrupt British command and control.

On 20 March 1918, a damp morning with thick fog, the shell-fire of four thousand German guns hit the front of three different British armies, the Fifth, Third and First. After about three hours of bombardment German infantry began their attack in stages, between 7 and 9:40 a.m., probing forward, looking for gaps. The storm-troopers left surviving British units to be surrounded and mopped up by following troops. This meant that any enemy behind them was effectually neutralised.

The main weight of the thrust was just to the south of Saint-Quentin. Manning the front here was the Ulster Division. From 22 February the division had maintained a three-brigade front, with the 108th on the right, the 107th in the centre and the 109th on the left. Each brigade kept a battalion in the forward zone and a battalion in support in what was still the battle zone, about six thousand yards behind the front. The third battalion was kept in reserve. On 20 March the Mid-Antrim Battalion of the 108th Brigade held the forward zone, the 1st Battalion of the Royal Irish Fusiliers in the battle trenches. For the 107th (Belfast) Brigade the North Belfast Battalion was forward, with the 1st Battalion of the Royal Irish Rifles in reserve. The 109th Brigade had the 2nd Battalion of the Royal Inniskilling Fusiliers, which had been transferred to the 36th Division a month earlier, backed up by the 1st Battalion of the same regiment.

The division was overwhelmed by the weight of the German push and was driven back faster than was believed possible. The push was gaining momentum, moving so fast that the British artillery could not shorten its range quickly enough, and much of its fire fell behind the German troops. Around noon there was a breakthrough to the right of the Ulster Division's lines, on the front held by the 14th Division. In a short time the right flank of the 108th Brigade was under threat. The 1st Battalion of the Royal Irish Fusiliers turned to face the danger, and the 9th Battalion was brought forward to extend the exposed flank.

But by 2:30 p.m. the Germans were already beyond that. The entire forward zone had been taken, although one group at Le Pontchu and two others near Grugies continued fighting. The former held out till after 3 p.m., while the others lasted till 6 p.m. Gough knew that the situation was critical, yet he had difficulty persuading his superiors of the danger.

The 12th (Mid-Antrim) Battalion held on longer than anyone could have expected, despite being in the middle of the storm. The Germans assaulted their trenches several times during the morning, supported by flamethrowers. After fierce hand-to-hand fighting the enemy was thrown back. By noon, when the fog began to lift, the Mid-Antrim men could see Germans up to a mile behind them.

Attacks were now coming in from both flanks. It was impossible to retreat, because there was nowhere to retreat to. By 4 p.m. there were only a hundred men still fighting, and most of them were wounded. The survivors destroyed their rifles and gave themselves up. Their plight had gone unnoticed by those in the higher echelons, though their part in delaying the German advance was probably crucial.

Meanwhile there was still the problem of the flanking move on the Ulster Division's right, and the 108th Brigade was ordered to defend against this. The front remained steady for a while, but early darkness meant that the Germans could bring forward reinforcements, ready to resume the assault. During this build-up the fighting continued elsewhere. By 5:30 p.m. the remnants of both the 15th Battalion of the Royal Irish Rifles and the 2nd Battalion of the Royal Inniskilling Fusiliers were forced to surrender.

The division's losses were catastrophic. The three battalions in the forward zone had ceased to exist. The three battalions in the battle zone were down to roughly 250 men each, though the three reserve battalions were still at reasonable strength. The division's total strength was down to less than 3,000 fighting men. It is some comfort that 2,392 of the losses were prisoners, who would return to Ireland after the war.

There was no let-up the following day. The Germans were able to bring heavy artillery up under cover of the spring mist, and the weight of shell-fire forced the 109th Brigade to fall back to link up with the 108th. It was decided to make a further withdrawal to the Canal de Saint-Quentin, which offered the possibility of a defensible line. This decision meant a fighting retreat over a distance of nine miles, in contact with the enemy all the way and inevitably suffering yet more casualties and giving a tactical advantage to the Germans.

Now the 107th Brigade took up position on the right of the Ulster Division's new positions. The 109th Brigade took position in support, while what remained of the 108th Brigade took position on the left flank, on the canal bank. There were also remnants of other divisions that had attached themselves to the Ulster Division. Together they held a section of the line about five miles long. Here they were joined by the divisional artillery. The move was completed by 11 p.m.

There was no time for rest. Early next morning the Germans broke through further along the line, in the area of the 14th Division. The leak could not be plugged, and by 11:15 the British army was in retreat again. There were no more fixed defences, and the day's bitter fighting was over open country. The 16th Battalion of the Royal Irish Rifles was put under the command of the 9th Battalion of the Royal Irish Fusiliers and spent the entire day fighting. Town after town was lost to the enemy, but that night the survivors found shelter and a relatively quiet night in a farmhouse near the town of Villeselve.

The 109th Brigade had planned a counter-attack for the morning, but German reinforcements were discovered in a town to the north-west. Brigade headquarters wisely cancelled the attack, and the division remained in a defensive posture. The German pressure was relentless, and by 11 a.m. the Ulstermen had to retire once again. Because this was being done while they were in contact with the enemy, it had to be staggered, with some units retreating while others kept fighting. This inevitably left gaps in the line, which the Germans were quick to exploit, and the line lost its cohesion. The line held by the Ulster Division collapsed. It retreated into Villeselve; but the German artillery began a heavy bombardment of the town at noon. The British attempted to hold the line, supported by French troops. The French were ordered to retreat, however, and the British had no choice but to go with them. The German barrage followed them.

At 11 p.m. the remnants of the Ulster Division were placed under the command of the French 62nd Division and ordered to retreat, filtering back through the French lines. The trauma was not over yet for the 9th Battalion of the Royal Irish Fusiliers, as it was left as rearguard on the ridge joining Berlancourt and Guiscard, where two of its remaining officers became casualties. The rest of the Ulster Division was to be withdrawn fifteen miles from the immediate front line to rest and reorganise, although it still had to be available as support for the French troops. About midday, unfortunately, while it was having a few hours of rest, it was ordered to form part of a new front line. The Germans were advancing even faster, as soldiers and civilians tried to escape along the roads ahead of them. In what seemed no time, the enemy was once again in front of the French lines.

The Ulster Division was in place by 2 a.m. on 26 March. Unbelievably, it was able to get six hours' sleep, the longest continuous rest it had had since the attack began. There was no rest for the 9th Battalion of the Royal Irish Fusiliers, which, having completed its harrowing spell as rearguard, now had to make a thirty-mile forced march, much of it by night, through the confusion of the retreat, to reach its designated position on the new front line. It arrived, exhausted, at 11 a.m. on the 26th. The main German force was only three miles behind it, and advance units had already established contact. The Ulstermen were arranged in brigade order, with the 107th, 108th and 109th spread from left to right. With the support of a company of field guns, the Lewis guns of the well-rested Ulster Division succeeded in driving back wave after wave of German assault. Gradually, however, the Germans reached the line in greater strength, and by 1 p.m. a full-scale battle was in progress.

The exhausted 9th Battalion of the Royal Irish Fusiliers no longer had internal organisation. The front line was held by an ad-hoc group of soldiers under Major Brew, while a few were kept in reserve under the command of Captain Despard. The division continued to fight off direct attacks, but it was not long before the Germans realised that the Ulstermen had no artillery of their own. The German artillery could safely be brought close to the front, and at dusk the bombardment of the Ulster lines began. It was followed quickly by a concentrated infantry attack, and by 8 p.m. the attackers had severed the Ulster Division's lines.

The serious situation was made worse by an incident that contained an element of farce. The commanding officers of the 1st and 9th Battalions of the Royal Irish Fusiliers met a member of the divisional staff to obtain permission to retreat. The car in which they were travelling ran into a German patrol, and they were captured. A German fired a shot into the engine, immobilising the vehicle, before the officers could retreat. The Indians were running out of chiefs.

Unable to withdraw without orders, the men spent the night under heavy shell-fire. No water, food or ammunition was reaching the front. The Germans attacked at dawn, and this time the French on the right of the division retreated. To avoid being trapped, the 109th Brigade retreated with them, but that left the 108th Brigade hanging out to dry, with no support on its right flank. Those fighting in Erches got no order to withdraw, so they fought on till 11 a.m., when they were finally overrun. Reports of the time say that only one officer and nineteen other ranks remained alive.

The surviving brigades were forced back, though the 15th (North Belfast) Battalion of the Royal Irish Rifles held out till near noon, when it withdrew and joined up with the 1st and 2nd Battalions of the Royal Irish Rifles on the way. The survivors of the three battalions numbered no more than half a company: three officers and sixty men. They remained on the line till they were relieved by the French on the morning of 28 March. They were the last of the 36th Division to be withdrawn from what was called the Battle of Saint-Quentin.

The total casualties of the 36th (Ulster) Division came to 7,252, the heaviest of any division in the battle. Missing were 5,844, including 185 officers. Among the officers alone, 127 were killed or wounded. The next in number of casualties was the 16th (Irish) Division, which suffered 7,149. The worst that any English division suffered were the 7,023 casualties of the 2nd (East Lancashire) Division. All three divisions had been destroyed and had to be withdrawn from the order of battle to be rebuilt.

What they had done was to save the war for the Allies. Although the Germans had penetrated so far—up to forty miles in places—the delaying action of the 36th (Ulster) Division and others on the line meant that the Germans were unable to reach the Channel ports before the British and some newly arrived American divisions were in position to stop them. What the Ulstermen had done on the first day of the Battle of the Somme had been glorious. What they did in the ten days of the Battle of Saint-Quentin helped to save the Allied cause, and it should be remembered.

Chapter 8 ∾

THE WAR AT HOME AND THE WAR AT SEA

Interestingly, the first effect of the declaration of war in August 1914 was a slump in shipbuilding in Belfast. For a start, the government diverted all shipbuilding materials to yards that were producing ships for the Royal Navy. In most yards the shortage of materials led to a slowing of production and the laying off of men. As a result, many men enlisted, presuming that there would be little need for their skills until the war was over.

To begin with, Pirrie was of a like mind and wanted the yard to go on half-time working. His managers persuaded him that such an approach could lead to the yard losing some of its most important men. Instead night shifts were discontinued and severe restrictions were put on capital expenditure, while work would continue on all thirty-two ships on order. This decision was taken at a time when there was no prospect of getting the material needed to have the orders completed. It could have led to disaster, but it succeeded in retaining the bulk of the work force. Most of Harland and Wolff's competitors lost half their men, while the Belfast yard lost 6,000 out of 24,000. To maintain the loyalty of those who had joined the forces, Pirrie ordered that their wages be made up to what they earned in civilian life.

This state of affairs continued for the first three months of the war. The Admiralty was content to concentrate on those yards where contracts had already been placed. Winston Churchill, that bane of Unionist Belfast, was now First Lord of the Admiralty, and it was unlikely that such a mundane approach would last for long. Always keen on the idea of deceiving the enemy, he came up with the idea of converting ten cargo liners into imitation battleships. Each conversion would be based on a specific ship in the Grand Fleet. Pirrie was happy to use his fertile imagination to show how it could be done. Wood and canvas were used to construct naval super-structures, false gun turrets were fitted, and small hearths were installed in false funnels to produce realistic smoke. The construction of false bows and sterns needed a more skilled approach, as they would have to be robust enough to cope with heavy seas. Finally, as merchant ships are much higher relative to their length than warships, roughly 3,500 tons of ballast was loaded on each ship to give it the proper silhouette.

Even as this work was going on, Harland and Wolff received the first of its battle casualties. Ironically, this was its own ship *Olympic,* damaged in a dramatic attempt to rescue the battleship *Audacious.* Churchill announced that it was the battleship that had arrived at Queen's Island, and to maintain the deception the *Mountcalm* became the new *Audacious.*

The first of the dummy ships were ready by the first week in December and were to be formed into the Special Service Squadron, commanded by Captain Herbert Haddock, late of the *Olympic.*

Another casualty of the war was the First Sea Lord, Prince Louis of Battenberg. Even changing his name to Mountbatten was not enough to assuage the anti-German feeling of the British public. He felt it best to resign, and he was replaced by Lord Fisher. Fisher met an American shipbuilder called Charles Schwab, who wanted to help the British cause. As well as undertaking to build twenty submarines for the Royal Navy, he offered four twin 14-inch gun turrets that had been prepared for a ship being built in Germany. Fisher, by nature a 'big gun' man, was delighted at the prospect and began to work out how best to use them. He had been considering the potential of a ship that would have a shallow draught yet would carry big guns. Much of the North Sea coast of Germany was very shallow for a long way out, and if it ever became necessary to make an invasion of this area a ship such as he was considering would be able to go close inshore and bombard enemy defences. He roughed out some drawings and spoke to Pirrie, who agreed to have three of the new craft, named 'monitors', ready for delivery within five months. All this work, including the repair work, required an increased work force, and the payroll was back up to twenty thousand by the end of the year.

The novel idea produced by Fisher set Churchill's mind spinning. Always looking for a way to engage the enemy to its disadvantage, Churchill had the idea of attacking Turkey, the weakest, he thought, of Germany's allies. The ships that Fisher had envisaged could be used for shore bombardment there, as a landing on the German coast was unlikely (and indeed never happened). In a flurry of activity it was decided to build a further eight monitors, slightly smaller this time, with 12-inch guns. Five of them would be built in Belfast, and all five keels had been laid by 1 February 1915.

At the same time a contract was signed for yet another new type of ship. Fisher had been largely responsible for the building of the dreadnoughts and super-dreadnoughts that were the backbone of the Royal Navy's battle squadrons. He had also introduced the battle-cruiser, a ship with the same size and firepower as a battleship but without the battleship's armour. The resulting vessel was very fast, and the idea was that its speed would enable it to escape from any ship that had guns big enough to sink it. The government had decided that no more capital ships (as battleships and battle-cruisers were called) should be built. Churchill and Fisher thought they could get around this prohibition by inventing the 'light battle-cruiser'. In reality this was a large cruiser with much larger guns than would normally be carried: 15-inch guns in the case of the new ship, to be called the *Glorious*. It was to weigh 22,354 tons, only slightly more than half the weight of HMS *Hood,* which was to be the largest of the battle-cruisers.

The pressure continued to build up. Pirrie agreed that Harland and Wolff would service the entire Irish Coast Patrol Squadron. The company was ordered to complete the *Titanic's* sister-ship, the *Britannic.* At the same time the first four dummy battleships returned to Belfast, their crews well and truly thankful that they had not been spotted by any German warships. The ships were to be converted back into troop transports, ready for use in the invasion of Gallipoli.

The pressure resulted in longer working hours for the men, and by April some men were working eighty-five hours a week. Even then, Harland and Wolff got a reputation for poaching workers from other employers, including Workman Clark. Control over workers became more draconian after the setting up of the Ministry of Munitions to oversee war production. A recalcitrant workman could now be sent to the front. Not only were the workers under the microscope, but the new ministry could even tax what it considered excess profits. Wage rates were now fixed to nationally agreed scales.

The money was good. The Admiralty paid in advance (cost plus a percentage of profit), and the firm was able to clear its overdrafts. And the work just kept coming. The yard began building destroyers, and converted the *Britannic* as a hospital ship.

One continuing problem was that the Ministry of Munitions was jealous of the number of skilled workers on Queen's Island. It wanted to bring in more semi-skilled and unskilled workers, while sending some of the skilled ones to other, less fortunate yards. The work force itself continued to grow, and it is a tribute to the management that industrial relations remained harmonious, in contrast to many other yards and to some of the clashes of the previous decade or so.

Belfast as a whole made a great contribution to the war effort. Unlike cities on the east coast of Britain, it was safe from naval bombardment and was well out of range of the German Zeppelins. It was not only the ship-building industry that was working flat out: the mills and engineering plants of Belfast also strove to maximise their contribution to the war effort. Linen was in great demand to provide the outer skins of aircraft. Exports were valued at £20 million in 1916. Ireland was providing essential food to Britain, and much of it passed through the port of Belfast. In 1916, 192,958 head of cattle, 33,367 tons of grain, 121,700 tons of potatoes and fruit, 9,107 tons of aerated water, 17,546 tons of wine and spirits and 4,544 tons of tobacco passed through the harbour. In addition there were 13,177 tons of rope and cord, 95,533 tons of linen and cotton, 41,454 tons of ores and 173,777 tons of general cargo. There was little unemployment, but war was pushing up prices and it was necessary to work long hours to earn more than survival wages.

For the Admiralty, Workman Clark concentrated on building small warships and auxiliaries: thirty-two boom defence vessels, sloops, patrol boats and a stern-wheel hospital ship for use in the rivers of Mesopotamia. It also built two monitors, subcontracted from Harland and Wolff. As well as this, 1,319 ships were repaired or overhauled. The first work of this type was the conversion of four old cruisers into coastal bombardment vessels to reinforce Flanders. A merchant ship was converted into a destroyer depot ship, with a workshop capable of carrying out most repairs for its charges. Like Harland and Wolff, Workman Clark converted many liners into troop transports or hospital ships, while others were converted into armed merchant cruisers.

Harland and Wolff built the conventional cruiser *Cavendish* and the light battle-cruiser *Glorious*. The latter was laid down in early 1915 and completed in December 1916. The yard's impressive achievement is in no way diminished by the fact that the light battle-cruiser was one of the worst variations of one of the worst-thought-out types of warship ever built. The *Cavendish* was eventually completed as a seaplane carrier.

By the middle of 1916 Pirrie realised that more was needed than a concentration on building warships. Much has been made of the 'great naval race' between Britain and Germany in the years leading up to the Great War, but it was a race Germany never expected to win. The German navy knew it could never achieve even parity with the Royal Navy. The original intention of Admiral Tirpitz had been to create a fleet of ships big and powerful enough to inflict such damage on the enemy, even if it did not win a sea battle, that the enemy would hesitate to engage in battle. In a way, it was to be the nuclear deterrent of its time. Even this aim became impracticable, and senior officers recognised that in a straight fight between the British Grand Fleet and the German High Seas Fleet the latter would probably be destroyed. They knew that the British would try to blockade the German coast. They would allow their own battleships to leave harbour only where they had a local superiority over the blockading forces. To take the fight to the British, the Germans decided to rely on their relatively new and untested submarines, the u-boats.

Only two days after Britain declared war on Germany in 1914, the first submarine war patrol in history took place. Ten u-boats left their base on the German island of Heligoland; their orders were to engage and sink ships of the Royal Navy. They were not immediately successful. They were small and slow and had a very short endurance. Nevertheless, on 5 September Lieutenant Otto Hersing launched the torpedoes that sank HMS *Pathfinder,* a light cruiser. The unfortunate warship was low on coal and could not maintain full speed, which made it an easy target for the submarine. It sank in four minutes, and 259 men died with it. It had the unenviable distinction of being the first warship ever sunk by submarine. It was another six weeks before the first British merchant ship, the *Glitra,* was sunk by U-17.

After this shaky start the effectiveness of the U-boat menace increased exponentially. To begin with, the German commanders assiduously followed what were called cruiser rules. When they came across a merchant ship they surfaced and called on it to stop. The ship's papers would be examined to see if it was a legitimate target. If the submarine captain concluded that he had a right to sink the ship he would give the crew time to abandon it before sinking the vessel, usually by gunfire.

The British countered the offensive by introducing the Q ship. This was an apparently inoffensive merchant ship. If intercepted by a U-boat, however, it would drop its disguise and reveal its teeth. It was armed with heavy guns and depth charges and could outfight any submarine on the surface. The effectiveness of the Q ships forced the Germans to change their rules of engagement. They defined an exclusion zone around Britain and Ireland, effectually a blockade, and claimed the right to sink without warning any merchant ships crossing those waters.

Immediately the number of sinkings rose again. The German move was a tactical success but a strategic disaster, as it brought upon Germany the disgust of the western world, and in particular the United States. This reached a climax in 1915, when on 7 May the German navy sank the Cunard liner *Lusitania* off the southern coast of Ireland, with the loss of almost two thousand lives. Among the dead were more than a hundred Americans, including some of the most influential people in the country. America was outraged, and so was the world. The weight of world opinion was so great that, later in the year, Germany stopped the policy of firing on merchant ships without warning.

In 1916, therefore, the hopes of the German navy rested on its surface fleet. The German naval authorities realised that they could not face the Grand Fleet in a straight fight. They conceived the idea of tempting some of the British battleships out into a submarine ambush by offering some German battle-cruisers as bait. Because of a series of unpredictable problems, the U-boats were not in position. Instead, on 31 May both the German High Seas Fleet and the British Grand Fleet put to sea in their entirety. The two sides' battle-cruiser squadrons stumbled on one another.

The German squadron turned south, following the German plan B, to lure the British towards the guns of their main battle fleet. The British, under the dashing Rear-Admiral David Beatty, followed. When the British realised they were sailing into a trap they swung north again, though by this time they had lost two battle-cruisers. As the Germans surged north in pursuit they did not realise that they in turn were heading into a trap. Luckily for them, the fleet encounter did not take place till late in the evening. Rear-Admiral Reinhard Scheer sacrificed his battle-cruisers so that the battleships could escape.

Admiral Jellicoe was later criticised for not taking the battle to the enemy; but, as Winston Churchill was to say, Jellicoe was the only man who could have lost the war in a single afternoon. The fight went on as ships clashed through the night, but the Germans escaped back to their base. By a combination of better shooting and safer management of explosives, the Germans sank fourteen ships while losing eleven of their own. There were many more casualties on the British side, so the Germans could claim victory. But it was only a tactical victory.

The Imperial Navy decided that the only hope it had of beating the British was a return to unrestricted submarine warfare. The German battle fleet never put to sea again, until it was to sail to Scapa Flow to surrender. It was neutralised as a threat, and the British blockade of Germany grew that bit tighter. The German navy could only resort to submarine warfare to impose a blockade of its own. Although this was partially successful, it was not enough. Germany raised the stakes again in February 1917 when it announced the return to unrestricted use of the u-boat. This was too much for President Wilson and was the factor that brought the Americans into the war in April 1917. The Germans had shot themselves in their watery foot.

Even before this, in early 1916, Pirrie had realised that there was a need for new merchant ships. Even forgetting the ones that had been sunk, many ships had been requisitioned by the Admiralty, and those remaining had been worked so hard that their active life would be severely shortened. As the building of merchant ships had been virtually halted at the start of the war, Pirrie calculated that there would be a shortfall in the merchant fleet by late 1917, even if the war ended in 1916. He also saw great advantages in the use of diesel engines, even for passenger ships. In the middle of 1916 he contracted to build fifteen diesel-engined ships for the Royal Mail Group. This was the first of many contracts he made that year. He was taking a chance, because there was little possibility of fulfilling all his obligations unless the yards at Belfast and at Govan on the Clyde were extended. As so often happened, luck was on his side.

The Admiralty was appalled at the loss of so many capital ships in the Battle of Jutland. To ensure that they could be replaced it offered to make machines and material available to any yards that expanded their facilities.

By September, Pirrie was planning extensions for all the company's yards, extending his holdings in Scotland by buying the Greenock yard of Caird and Company and trying to buy the steel company that provided Harland and Wolff with most of its steel plates.

The fact that merchant shipping was once again the main target for German submarines was reflected in the increasing tonnage sunk. For the early part of the year the average sinking had been 80,000 tons a month; by the end of the year it was 175,000 tons. Even the government began to get worried, and a Ministry of Shipping was formed in December 1916. A Shipping Controller, Sir Joseph MacLay, was appointed, and he put in hand a scheme to build massive numbers of standardised ships. These would have interchangeable parts and could be built very quickly. All other orders for shipping, other than tankers and refrigerated meat ships, were cancelled, although some hulls had to be completed to clear slips for the new standard classes.

Harland and Wolff took orders for seven of the new type, four on the Clyde and three in Belfast. Some of the managing directors were concerned that the extension would be a white elephant after the war. Pirrie reassured them by getting further orders, to be completed when hostilities ceased, from several shipping lines, including a new subsidiary of the Royal Mail Group.

Meanwhile, the war still had to be won. In April 1917 shipping losses totalled 555,056 gross tons, while new ships launched were a mere 69,711 gross tons. (Gross tonnage is based on the internal volume of a ship and is an indication of how much cargo it can carry.) It was beginning to look as if Britain might be starved into submission before Germany surrendered.

The Ministry of Shipping asked all yards how big an extension they could cope with if they did not have to worry about men and material. Pirrie estimated that output could be raised by half, although the works committee in Belfast cut this to 40 per cent. Both may have been a little sanguine, as there were quite a few obstacles to overcome. While Belfast did not actually have strikes, as was the case on the Clyde, arbitrators had to be called in on a number of occasions to sort out demarcation and pay disputes. Shipwrights would allow unskilled or semi-skilled labour only when they had a guarantee that no 'real' shipwright would be laid off till twelve months after the others had returned to their original jobs or left the firm. In spite of all this the *War Shamrock*, the first standard ship to be built in the United Kingdom, was launched on 21 June. It was delivered to the operating company, Thomas Dixon and Sons of Belfast, on 20 August. Four standard ships were to be delivered by the end of the year.

Most of the problems were solved by common sense and a little give on the part of the management. They lost this leeway in the late summer, because the government set up yet another bureaucracy, the Shipyard

Labour Department. There was a short strike by the plumbers in September, but the management remained firm and prevailed.

HMS *Glorious* was commissioned in January 1917. It had been built as a light cruiser but with enormous guns. It was assigned to the First Cruiser Squadron, under Admiral Sir Charles Napier. It did not get an opportunity to use its main guns till that November. German minesweepers clearing a path through a British minefield were intercepted by two British cruisers. The German ships fled south, where two German battleships, the *Kaiser* and *Kaiserin,* were waiting to protect them. The British cruisers promptly engaged the Germans, with the intention of keeping them in play till their own reinforcements, the First Battle-Cruiser Squadron, should arrive. The German ships and their escorts were engaged, and the *Glorious* fired its main armament, scoring direct hits on a German cruiser.

A new headache for the Harland and Wolff management came when Pirrie discovered that he was required to recruit the extra men needed for the merchant shipping programme. He had been given to believe that the extra men would be assigned to the yard by the Admiralty. More problems were caused when the Admiralty ordered HMS *Cavendish* to be converted into a seaplane carrier. This was a sign of the increasing importance of aircraft in the war. Undaunted by the labour problems he already had to deal with, Pirrie volunteered to set up an aeroplane works in Belfast. Within a few days the model office had become an aircraft drawing office, the ships' electric store was cleared and ready to start assembling fuselages, and the joiners' shop had begun work on six de Havilland machines. The workers were recruited with the co-operation of the Furniture Trades Union. Then the Admiralty applied more pressure. It needed facilities for reconditioning submarines that had been damaged in carrying the war right to the enemy coastline. By the end of October, eight submarines had arrived for repairs.

Now the Controller of Auxiliary Shipping told Pirrie that unless Harland and Wolff undertook massive extensions the government would build its own shipyard in Ulster. Pirrie approached the Harbour Commissioners and leased forty-one acres on the east side of the Musgrave Channel, and plans were prepared for a six-berth East Yard, at a cost of £600,000. A new fitting-out quay was to be built to the north-east of the Thompson Dock.

The Air Board wanted Belfast to build a new heavy bomber that would be able to reach Berlin, the Handley Page V1500. A new joiners' shop the length of two football pitches was started, to be ready in March 1918. Further orders came, and Pirrie bought land for an aerodrome at Aldergrove, a 170-acre farm north of Belfast.

Ship deliveries in the same month allowed the yard to concentrate on standard ships, although building was often interrupted to cope with the steady stream of Admiralty repairs. Lloyd George invited Pirrie to become the first Controller-General of Merchant Shipping. When he was asked what staff he would need he replied that his present secretary would be sufficient. Just to be sure, he was given an aide-de-camp, Captain A. T. Marshall, who had experience of shipping in civilian life. He also delegated some of his work load in Belfast, choosing the engine works manager, George Cuming, as his deputy. Deputy or not, Cuming was never given access to the private ledger.

Pirrie tried to increase efficiency by involving the unions in the monitoring of shipyard productivity, and he established joint committees of unions and management. He set himself the daunting task, at the age of seventy, of inspecting four or five shipyards each week. What he saw persuaded him that the only way to deal with the shortage of skilled men was to introduce labour-saving machinery. One item that particularly drew his attention was the pneumatic riveter. To ensure that firms adopted devices such as this he had capital grants discontinued. In future, firms would receive subsidy only when they were installing machinery that would increase productivity. Pirrie managed 260 berths, and for each he demanded better statistics and financial information. He was able to use this information to streamline the allocation of contracts and had each yard concentrate on a single standard ship design. He held back steel and other materials and released them only as required. He also insisted that the building of hull and engine be synchronised so that there was no delay in fitting out. One of his men from Belfast, Charles Payne, was appointed head of the new National Shipyards, with the job of bringing them into production quickly. His commitment was such that he was able to increase shipbuilding by 50 per cent in the last eight months of the war.

Harland and Wolff produced more standard ships than any other shipbuilder: ten from Belfast and six from Govan before the end of the year. The other Belfast yard, Workman Clark, set an incredible record for speed of fitting out: one of its standard ships was launched on the morning of Tuesday 10 September and was ready for sea by the evening of Saturday the 14th.

When the armistice was declared on 11 November 1918 the workers at Queen's Island downed tools and took a week's holiday. By 18 November, Pirrie was organising the construction of the twenty-one merchant ships that had been stopped by the Ministry of Shipping's embargo. A week before, the damaged hospital ship *Asturias* was towed to Harland and Wolff to be converted into the cruise ship *Arcadian*. In January 1919 shipowners were told they could place orders for new ships. For a while, it looked as if everything was back to normal.

Chapter 9 ~

BIRTH PAINS OF A
NEW STATE

In the last years of the war, much had been done to improve the conditions of the unskilled worker. Differentials between the wages of skilled and unskilled had shrunk during the emergency. Before the war, a shipyard labourer had earned slightly more than half the wages of a top tradesman, such as a plater or fitter; in 1918 he was earning two-thirds of the top rates.

Those who saw themselves as the aristocracy of the shipyard workers were not content with the erosion of differentials and, as soon as hostilities were suspended, wanted the pay rates of the leading trades increased accordingly. They felt it was a good time to make their demand. Every berth in the Harland and Wolff Group was occupied by a standard ship. Pirrie was pressing ahead with this programme, making only a few modifications to suit peacetime conditions. It looked as if shipbuilding prosperity would last for some time.

Another grievance in the yard was the long working week—54 hours while the war continued. This had been legally enforced by the Ministry of Munitions during the war years, and, as soon as he could, George Cuming, the deputy chairman, offered to return to the 47-hour week. The trade unions were not satisfied, as the men had voted unanimously for a 44-hour week, and the entire work force went on strike in January 1919.

These were heady times for the working man. There had been revolution in Russia, and Germany and Italy were in the throes of socialist agitation. There was a general strike in Glasgow. Now, following the example of the shipyard workers, other unions joined in. In particular, gas yard workers and electricity station workers went on strike. This had the effect of closing down the city, as trams could not run and cinemas could not operate, while those industries not directly affected by the strike had to lay off men because their machinery could not operate. There were unpleasant scenes as workers smashed the windows of shops still using gas or electricity. Although the linen mills continued to operate, it was at a reduced level. Even newspapers were affected. The *News Letter* was much reduced in size, while the *Irish News* was not able to publish at all. Supplies of food and fuel were threatened.

At the head office of Harland and Wolff at Queen's Road, the firm was in a state of siege. Pickets were in such numbers that it was possible to gain access only by the use of armoured cars. The management wisely decamped to the offices of the Belfast and County Down Railway in Station Street. Cuming was leading the negotiations for the management, but he was suddenly struck down with pneumonia and died on 1 February, at the early age of forty-four. Pirrie travelled from London for the funeral. On the ferry, some members of the strike committee came to speak to him; some of them were becoming uncomfortable with the socialist rhetoric of the more militant strikers. Pirrie was unbending. Public services had to be restored, and the working week would be 47 hours.

Pirrie and many of the other leading employers demanded military intervention. This was resisted by Unionist politicians, who were afraid of alienating their working-class voters. The acting police commissioner for Belfast was also reluctant to intervene. Many of the strikers were men he had helped organise into the UVF before the war.

It required the intervention of Dublin Castle and the arrival of the commander in chief of the army in Ireland before anything was done. Soldiers occupied the gasworks and the electricity station early on the morning of 14 February, and by the following day, trains were running again. That day—a Sunday—there was a mass meeting in Custom House Square, and the strikers voted to continue. Only men from the yards and the engineering works actually stayed away from work on Monday, and by the Thursday of that week the strike had collapsed. The workers had been defeated; but they were not reconciled to the result.

The resentment of the workers did not concern Pirrie. Orders were pouring in, and he had to take advantage of them. He bought new machinery that would counterbalance the loss in productivity brought about by the shorter working week. Much of his time was spent developing facilities on the Clyde, in particular enlarging the engine works at Finnieston, which he hoped would provide enough diesel engines for eighteen ships per year. In Belfast work was resumed on a 40,000-ton White Star Liner to replace the *Britannic,* to be named *Homeric.* (Its original name, *Germanic,* no longer seemed suitable.) Shortly after its keel was laid, the *Olympic* arrived to be refitted and reconditioned for peacetime duties.

The order books were full, and priority was given to ensuring that no shortages of materials would hinder production. Pirrie spent much of his time ensuring that there would be supplies of oil for the new diesel-engined ships. He also obtained shares in the Scottish steel firm of Colville and Sons, which ensured a continuous supply of steel plating for the shipyards. The new East Yard in Queen's Island was brought into commission in November 1919, and the new berths would eventually treble the capacity for building large ships.

The berths themselves were full of innovations. They were fitted with portable coffer dams to keep out the sea during construction. Concrete causeways housed pumps, pipes and cables, and on top of the causeways were electrically operated tower cranes. A new platers' shed was built behind the slips, designed for the efficient handling of materials and in particular of prefabricated parts. The Harbour Commissioners did their part by building two fitting-out wharves in the Musgrave Channel near the yard.

Prosperity on Queen's Island was in contrast to the rest of Belfast. As early as December 1919 thousands of unemployed gathered outside the City Hall, asking the Lord Mayor to implement the 1914 act that required councils to provide free school meals for the children of the very poor. They were given short shrift by the Mayor, who complained that reports of poverty and unemployment in Belfast were greatly exaggerated. In fact there were fourteen thousand out of work in the city at the time.

In these years just after the war Pirrie gave a lot of thought to the political situation in Ireland. Tension had increased steadily since the Rising in Dublin in April 1916, a few short months before the Battle of the Somme. Sinn Féin was now going beyond the demands of the old Irish Party and was demanding nothing less than a republic. Although the IRA campaign that began in 1919 was supposed to be aimed at the British forces, in practice much of it was directed against the unionist community, particularly in the South. The British government made matters worse by enlisting ex-soldiers into two paramilitary organisations, the RIC Reserve Force (commonly called the Black-and-Tans) and the Auxiliary Division of the RIC (commonly called the Auxiliaries), which adopted a policy of counterterrorism—terrorising the terrorist. This resulted in a wave of revulsion among even non-militant nationalists, and even more recruits joined the IRA. Feeling in the north-eastern counties was running high.

The Workman Clark shipyard was a particular focus of discontent, as its management had been involved in smuggling arms for the UVF and its workers were more openly loyalist in consequence. But Harland and Wolff was not far behind; and although the management had tried over the years, with varying amounts of energy, to discourage sectarian discrimination in the work-place, the yard's situation in the Protestant district of east Belfast and the methods of recruiting practised in the yard meant that the work force was overwhelmingly Protestant. The fact that the business had been established at a time when there was no technical education for Catholics in Belfast meant that the skilled trades were exclusively Protestant. Many of the new recruits to the yard came from Scotland, and many of these brought their prejudices with them. If things did not work out well, Pirrie was making contingency plans to move the entire enterprise to Great Britain.

Unfortunately, this was not the light of a new, non-sectarian dawn over Belfast. Loyalty to labour did not interfere with loyalty to traditional unionism and the Orange Order. In the rest of the country Sinn Féin won an increased mandate from the people, increasing unionist fears. In parts of the country there was outright war, with full-time IRA volunteers operating in flying columns, ambushing Crown forces before disappearing in the shelter of the hills and a friendly population. Already military operations were taking place in rural Ulster. More worryingly, from a unionist point of view, was the fact that the system of proportional representation had resulted in a Catholic being returned as Mayor of Derry. When republican prisoners were being moved into the city's jail in late April a riot began. This was followed in May by further riots, in which there was IRA and UVF involvement. A small Catholic enclave in the Protestant Waterside area was attacked, followed by reprisal attacks on Protestants in the Bogside and Brandywell. In two months of rioting forty people were killed, and the military had to be called in to stabilise the situation. Derry was considered one of the shrines of the Protestant and unionist cause in Ireland. If Catholics were flexing their muscles there, what might happen in the rest of the country?

The Orange parades to be held on 12 July were awaited with concern. In Derry there was a voluntary agreement not to hold them. The *Times* claimed that they were a challenge to Catholics and a threat to peace and should be suspended that year. The Orange Order refused to cancel the celebrations but, in Belfast at least, made sure that the parade was marshalled with military vigour and would pass off peacefully. In the waving of banners and the beating of drums, wrote the *Times*, the seventeenth century was reborn for a few hours.

Into this anachronism strode Sir Edward Carson, icon of unionism, who had kept in touch with Orange sentiment even while being absent from Ireland. He was concerned not only about rising republican violence but, like Pirrie, was concerned about the future of the shipyards. He also wanted to use what he called the 'cream' of the UVF to establish an auxiliary police force. In a phrase reminiscent of his pre-war challenge to Asquith, he reminded Lloyd George that unionists had an alternative to political action. He had noted that working-class Protestants and Catholics had united in the strike of 1919 and was concerned that class politics would tempt working-class Protestants away from unionism, so he reminded them that the real battlefield in Ireland was the Union.

His diatribe—for that is what it was—did not go down well with the British press. The *Manchester Guardian*, which had always supported Irish unity, thought his speech barren, bitter and provocative and implied that he preferred rhetoric to real remedies. Even papers that had given Carson support during the Home Rule Crisis, such as the *Times,* stated that the British public would not support 'counter-provocation' from the Ulster Volunteers. Loyalism, it said, had no prerogative that entitled it to defy the law. The unionist papers in Belfast were more welcoming, concentrating on those parts of Carson's speech that spoke of Sinn Féin's threat to Ulster and the contrast between the peaceful North and the revolution in the rest of Ireland.

In the meantime the United Kingdom government introduced a new system of voting for local government elections in Ireland. The Local Government (Ireland) Act (1919), which passed into law on 3 June, changed the voting system for local councils to proportional representation. Boroughs would be divided into wards, and each ward would elect a number of councillors—at least six. It was felt that the system would allow minorities to be elected that might occupy a middle ground between the irreconcilable forces of Sinn Féin and extreme Unionists.

There was a local election in January 1920, at which the turnout was 66 per cent. Lack of familiarity with the new system meant that it took three days to count the vote. When the results were announced, it seemed that the old Unionist monolith had been shattered. Nationalists won five seats and Sinn Féin another five. But the workers had remembered how the political and business classes had treated them in 1919. Belfast Labour Party won ten seats, Independent Labour three and Labour Unionists six. The Unionist share of the seats dropped from 52 to 29. In 1901 only five members of the Belfast Council had not been upper middle-class. Now nineteen were working class, and of those ten were trade unionists.

Within Catholic Belfast there was a sense of dread at the sound of the Lambeg drums, coming and going on the summer breeze. The nationalist *Irish News* took a defiant position, lampooning the Orange leaders as a Punch and Judy display, mocking the Orange marchers in a satirical cartoon and stating that the future lay with nationalist Ireland. Catholic fears were increased, however, when news broke of the killing of an Ulster-born police officer, Colonel Gerald Smyth, in Cork. He was almost certainly assassinated because of his part in the death of Tomás Mac Curtáin in the city in March, but in Belfast it was seen as an attack on a Northern unionist. The insult was compounded when the southern rail crew assigned to return the body to Banbridge refused to do so. In Banbridge and in nearby Dromore there were attacks on the small Catholic communities on the day of the funeral, 21 July.

There are differences of opinion about whether what happened next was a spontaneous reaction to Sinn Féin violence or a carefully orchestrated plan to eliminate the Catholic population of Belfast. Many Protestants who had returned from the war had expected a better tomorrow and were disgruntled to find themselves on the dole. They felt that they had a moral right to regain their jobs, which had been taken, as far as they were concerned, by disloyal Catholics who had refused to fight for the United Kingdom. In this they were supported by politicians, and not simply Unionists. An Independent Labour councillor, Alexander Boyd, was to claim in August that workers in the shipyards during the war had come from the south and west of Ireland, 'to replace our brave boys in the trenches.' Belfast employers, he went on, had not acted fairly towards those ex-soldiers they had formerly employed.

In May an economic slump had begun, and the unskilled worker in particular was concerned about his future. Suffice it to say that the timing of events, on the first morning of the return to work after the July holidays, and the scale of the action, suggest that there was at least some premeditation; but the result, for Belfast Catholics, was just the same.

On the morning of 21 July, the day of Colonel Smyth's funeral, groups of men belonging to the Belfast Protestant Association posted notices on the gates of both shipyards on Queen's Island calling for a meeting of 'all Unionist and Protestant' workers outside Workman Clark at lunch-time. About five thousand attended and called for the expulsion of all 'non-loyal' workers. The mob then made their way to the premises of Harland and Wolff, used sledge hammers to break their way in, and then searched for their victims. Some Catholic workers had guessed the way the wind was blowing and left after the morning's work. Others were lucky enough to be only verbally assaulted before getting away. The rest had no such luck. The decision of the management to lock the gates meant they were trapped inside. Some even chose to try to swim to safety, but while they were in the water they were pelted with iron nuts and bolts, rivets and 'Belfast confetti', the sharp circle of steel punched out of a ship's plates in preparation for riveting.

Where there was doubt about a man's religion his clothes would be torn open to see if he was wearing any Catholic emblems; anyone carrying these was severely beaten. Included among those driven out were several who had fought in Irish regiments during the war. Known socialists were also attacked; and the yard was 'ethnically cleansed', if an anachronism may be used, by mid-afternoon. Twenty victims required hospital treatment, and as the rest made their bloodied way home to the safety of Catholic districts their friends and neighbours met them with a mixture of horror at what had happened and determination that it would not go unavenged.

That evening, trams carrying shipyard workers past the Catholic Short Strand in east Belfast were attacked, as were trams in the equally Catholic Markets area. Workers were pulled out onto the street and beaten up. When a group from Donegall Pass made their way to Cromac Street a riot broke out. Police were sent to the area and had to make repeated baton charges, and fire blank ammunition, before they could separate the crowds.

As darkness fell the sound of live firing could be heard in the streets. Many of the shipyard workers lived in the Shankill district and had to endure the attacks near the Short Strand and Cromac Street on the way home. In the early evening many of them gathered along the Shankill's long border with the Falls Road. Catholics were ready to meet them, and tension soon boiled over. The military were called upon, and two Catholics, one of them a twenty-year-old ex-serviceman returning from the dog racing at Celtic Park, were shot by army bullets.

The Short Strand was also in trouble. Surrounded as it was by the staunchly Protestant district of Ballymacarret, it was inevitable that it should be attacked by people from the nearby Newtownards Road. St Matthew's Church and the Cross and Passion Convent were attacked. When an attempt was made to set fire to the convent, soldiers from the Norfolk Regiment opened fire on the crowd. This state of affairs continued for three days and left seven Catholics and six Protestants dead. It appears that most were shot, deliberately or not, by the police or military. This robust reaction on the part of the authorities to civil unrest contrasts sadly with the inertia shown in later months.

The tram system seemed almost designed to cause problems in Belfast. The varying tracks from the outer edges of the town funnelled their way into the city before crossing the river and spreading out on the other side. The social geography of Belfast, a product of the city's history, meant that tram lines were bound to pass through ancient religious enclaves, both Catholic and Protestant, just outside the city centre, and that passers-by could make a reasonable deduction about the religion of a tram-load of workers if they knew where the tram had started from. The economic geography of the city meant that you could make an educated guess at what industry employed those workers from the direction in which the tram was travelling. It was a simple matter, therefore, to set up an ambush and kill or hurt the people you wanted to. You could take your time, for even if they could get off the vehicle there was nowhere for your victims to go. Time and again that year and the next, trams delivered their passengers into killing zones.

The following morning, 22 July, a crowd of Catholics were waiting on the Springfield Road when tram-loads of Protestant workers arrived at Mackies' foundry, where Catholic workers had already been expelled. The police arrived and baton-charged the protesters. A Catholic priest, anticipating Ghandi's tactics by a number of years, stood in the road confronting the police and demanded that they withdraw to their barracks. The order came and the police left, and there was peace for a while. It did not last long. Towards dark there were reports of Catholics in Bombay Street and Kashmir Road being forced from their homes. Shots were fired. The military said that they came under fire from snipers in the Clonard area, and that some came from the tower in the monastery there. Although there was no substantial IRA presence in Belfast at the time, it is quite likely that there was some republican involvement. There certainly were loyalist gunmen about, and one killed a Mackies' worker on his way home. Most deaths, however, were caused by the soldiers. There were six Catholic deaths and four Protestant. The most controversial of these was when soldiers fired into Clonard monastery itself, killing a young Redemptorist brother. The firing was so intense that priests wishing to give the last rites were not able to reach the dying brother.

Unusually, the Crown accepted responsibility at the inquest a few weeks later, agreeing that the deed had not been provoked by anyone in the monastery.

One sad echo of nineteenth-century violence was the systematic assault by Protestants on pubs and spirit grocers. Most publicans were still Catholics, as were most owners of spirit groceries. The latter were particularly vulnerable, and sixty of them, as well as twelve public houses, were damaged in the first forty-eight hours. Fourteen of them were set on fire.

The possibility of defending your faith while drinking your fill was too great a temptation to resist, so the stock of spirit grocers was normally raided before the premises were destroyed. In McGurk's spirit grocery in Bankmore Street, inconveniently situated between the Catholic Markets and the Protestant Donegall Pass, the taps on the beer barrels were allowed to run till the barrels themselves were empty. Men, women and children helped themselves. Even the unionist press was appalled at the extent of the destruction. The *Northern Whig* lamented, in an image that would be echoed by Catholics later, that parts of Belfast looked like Picardy following the German attacks of 1914, as if it the districts had been 'bombarded or sacked.' Catholic owners of licensed premises in Protestant areas took their resentment with them as they sought refuge in the Short Strand or the Falls Road. This was fuelled by what they saw as police indifference to the attacks and later by the lack of understanding or sympathy shown to them by magistrates as they sought compensation for their losses.

In the short term, the only person who seemed to be working for peace in east Belfast was the Rev. John Redmond of the Church of Ireland, rector of St Patrick's Church. Although a unionist, and no lover of Sinn Féin, he realised that something had to be done to defuse the tension. There were perhaps ten thousand people on the Newtownards Road each of these summer days. Most of them were motivated by mere curiosity, but their very numbers were a handicap to the soldiers, in that, concealed among them, were the minority rabble. He called for a meeting of ex-servicemen in Albertbridge Orange Hall; he felt that they would be in a position to help the authorities simply by being there. The volunteers were asked to form a line between the mob and any building that was being threatened. Their moral authority would be enough to stop the mob. He believed, while others hoped.

The systematic intimidation of Catholics did not end with that first day, nor did it end with the shipyards. Similar tactics were used the next day in engineering works, linen mills and foundries in different places around Belfast until almost every industrial establishment had been visited by the enforcers of the Belfast Protestant Association. Although Catholics had to escape from the Sirocco works by climbing the perimeter fence, the extravagant violence of the shipyard expulsions was not repeated.

In the past, Catholics had been able to drift back to work as soon as the worst of the Protestant hysteria had subsided. This time was different. Although in some of the smaller establishments Catholics were able to continue working as long as they kept their heads low, in Queen's Island and elsewhere the Protestant Association policed the work force to ensure that the expelled dis-loyalists did not slip back to work unannounced. It has been estimated that ten thousand were driven from their place of work, including several hundred women who worked in the linen mills.

Some of those expelled were 'rotten Prods'—socialists whose anti-unionist views were seen as treacherous and who refused to sign an oath of loyalty. It has been claimed that these formed as much as a quarter of those ejected. Some leading Labour Party members felt it necessary to flee to Glasgow or London, and the north Belfast hall of the Irish Labour Party was burned down. Even such a senior Unionist as Sir James Craig claimed that Sinn Féin was working in conjunction with Bolshevik forces towards the destruction of the British Empire.

The expulsion of these socialists might be taken to indicate that the violence had been political rather than sectarian in origin, but that is naïve. Socialism was condemned because it had worked with Catholics during the Belfast Strike, and because Carson had condemned it. The basic sectarian nature of the violence is shown by the fact that two brothers, who were neither socialist nor Catholic, were expelled from the shipyard; their sin was that their widowed father had married a Catholic.

It has to be said that it was not only Catholics who were victims. There were some jobs traditionally done by Catholics, such as on the docks or in the brewing industry and in the licensed trade. Here there were no dramatic expulsions, but many Protestants were edged out of their jobs; others were assaulted or even shot on their way to or from work. Managers of factories in Catholic areas where Catholics had been expelled were put under great pressure to close down. There were threats that factories would be burned down.

At that time there was no official relief for the expelled workers, and they were dependent on charity, but that did not stop them organising themselves. Two thousand of them met to appoint a committee that would look into the circumstances of each expulsion, with a view to reporting to both the employers and the unions. These groups, who should have been protecting their employees and members, had done little in their defence. At the beginning of August, when it was obvious that the crisis was going to last, a register of victimised workers was opened, based on the various trades. An advertisement in the nationalist press outlining the needs of the workers and their families brought in many donations from such groups as the Ancient Order of Hibernians, which organised fund-raising events. An alliance of Joe Devlin, the Nationalist politician, and Bishop MacRory spread the net during the autumn through the rest of Ireland, as well as in Britain, France, the United States and Australia. A man, they said, had a right to live by his wages; that right was denied to the Catholics of Belfast. What was being done to them was similar to what had been done to the people of Belgium in 1914, but this time it was not done by the Hun.

Because of the efforts of the Rev. John Redmond and others, some of the tension began to ease as the month progressed. Representatives of workers from Harland and Wolff met in Dee Street Hall. They stated that they wanted to show the hand of friendship to their Catholic fellow-workers, particularly those ex-servicemen who had fought for King and Country in France. It was necessary, however, to distinguish between 'decent' Catholics and 'rebels', and to this end Catholics who would carry signed 'loyalty cards' would be allowed to return to work. Whether the representatives really believed that Catholics would be prepared to allow political discrimination to be substituted for religious discrimination, or whether they were making a cynical offer that they knew would be refused, was never put to the test.

On Sunday 22 August Detective-Inspector Oswald Swanzy, who had been involved with Colonel Smyth in the death of Tomás Mac Curtáin, was assassinated by the IRA in Lisburn. He was leaving Christ Church Cathedral at the time, having just attended morning service. The IRA murder gang escaped in a taxi. They were from Belfast but dispersed outside the city, though their driver was arrested and eventually charged with murder. In Lisburn itself the houses of at least eight Catholic families were burned down. Taking the hint, many Catholics left the town. Most probably went south, looking for safety in the Dundalk area, but others made the shorter journey over the mountain into the Catholic areas of Belfast.

On the afternoon of 25 August riots once more engulfed east Belfast, over a much wider area than before. Two young Protestants were shot near Dee Street; but this did little to deter the violence. The Fire Brigade was stretched almost to breaking point by the number of arson attacks. St Matthew's Church was attacked by a large mob, but the intervention of soldiers prevented serious damage. There were incidents all round the city, and the violence continued for some days. On Saturday 28 June a Catholic received a fatal wound to the leg. On Monday the 30th a Protestant shipwright was shot dead as he rode in a tram to his work on Queen's Island.

It was estimated that 150 Catholic families from the Newtownards Road and Woodstock Road were in need of shelter. The Catholic authorities were able to give some of them temporary accommodation in schools. Even papers that had been supportive of the Unionist cause were appalled. The *Daily Mail* suggested that Belfast was suffering because of an attempt to deprive Catholics of work and drive Catholic families from their homes. The *Times* agreed and worried that recruiting the UVF as an auxiliary police force could only result in civil war. On 30 August the military established sand-bagged strongpoints around Belfast.

Fighting still occurred in parts of Belfast. On Sunday the Marrowbone, a small Catholic enclave off the Oldpark Road, had come under sustained attack by Loyalists and soldiers. All but one of the six Catholic dead were shot by the army. Two more Catholics were shot dead in Townsend Street by the army. One, Patrick Gilmore, was a soldier home on leave. One Protestant was shot while crossing the nationalist Millfield area.

On Monday, Protestants travelling to work along Great George's Street and York Street were attacked by Catholic gunmen. In addition to the shipwright killed on the tram, a driller who worked at the Workman Clark yard was shot dead in this area, and there were four more fatalities, including an eleven-year-old boy. In Sandy Row four people were shot, two of them fatally, when soldiers fired into a crowd attempting to wreck a Catholic-owned public house.

The following day there were incidents spread around the city, resulting in six more deaths. Danger had come to the city centre when shots were fired in Castle Street, causing panic among the fashionable shoppers of Castle Junction and Donegall Place. That day a curfew was introduced, which was to last till 1924. Trams stopped running and places of entertainment closed at 9:30 p.m. Civilians had to remain indoors from 10:30 p.m. till 5 a.m. Despite the curfew, a soldier and a civilian were shot dead that night, though it is believed that the soldier died as the result of an accidental discharge.

Even on Wednesday the firing continued, this time with shots being fired at loyalist workers in Peter's Hill. Later in the day four Protestants were killed in the Oldpark area, three of them probably by IRA snipers, near the Marrowbone. One of these was an eighteen-year-old shipyard worker. One ex-soldier was leading a group of Protestants in pursuit of a Catholic; it is believed that he was shot by a soldier. At around lunchtime a large mob from the Shankill, some of its members armed, surged through the connecting streets to the Falls Road. Two Catholics were shot dead, one at his front door, the other standing at the corner of his street.

The weight of the military presence, which included armed escorts for people going to work and strongpoints equipped with machine-guns at important junctions, gradually damped down the violence. It was only a temporary respite, however. In late September a group of IRA gunmen stopped a two-man RIC patrol on the Falls Road and demanded that they raise their hands. When the police refused the gunmen shot one constable dead and wounded the other. Early the next morning, 25 September, a gang of four armed men with blackened faces shot three republican activists in their homes on the Falls Road and Springfield Road. Official statements claimed that two were shot by persons unknown and that the third was shot while resisting arrest; but local people had seen an armoured car in the area, the murderers had been wearing uniform, and all three killings were close together in place and time. The official denials persuaded most Catholics that the government was covering up for rogue elements within the police.

On 27 September workers returning home were attacked from the Marrowbone. Two shipyard workers, one a UVF drill instructor, the other prominent in the Orange Order, were killed by rifle fire. A Catholic mother whose infant had just died discovered that her house was caught in the crossfire. She had to leave, helped by a neighbour, who carried the dead child. On 29 September four Catholics were shot dead on the Falls Road after street disturbances. The inquest later found that the army had been justified in firing into the crowd.

It was also in September 1920 that Lloyd George introduced the idea that home rule should be granted not only to the rest of Ireland but also, separately, to the six so-called plantation counties in the north-east. These would have their own parliament, with devolved powers, and the resulting unit would be known as Northern Ireland. The jurisdiction would still send thirteen members to the British Parliament in London.

There was little else that the Prime Minister could do. His coalition government was dominated by Conservatives and Unionists. Even Sir James Craig was a junior minister. As a gesture towards eventual unity, a Council of Ireland was to be set up to look at the possibility of forming a single parliament for Ireland in the future. Ironically, as Sinn Féin refused to accept the Government of Ireland Act, Northern Ireland was the first Irish region to achieve home rule. Craig saw the advantage. Having a parliament of their own meant that Unionists would be able to resist British pressure to join the South.

The chorus of violence continued in Belfast. The underlying pressure came to the surface in October. On Saturday the 16th a Catholic who had been intimidated from his home in a loyalist district of north Belfast was being escorted by police away from the scene when he was attacked by a mob. When they heard of this, a large group of Catholics came to the area, seeking redress. Some were thought to be armed. They turned back when a military vehicle appeared. Later in the afternoon a group of Protestant supporters of Cliftonville Football Club, returning from a match, was fired on from the nationalist crowd. More soldiers arrived, and there was an exchange of fire between the military and Catholics gunmen. Bizarrely, it was three Protestants who were killed, one of them knocked down and crushed by an armoured car. All three worked in the shipyards.

The following week, after the announcement that Terence MacSwiney, Lord Mayor of Cork, had died on hunger strike in London, there were exchanges in the Foundry Street area and a 22-year-old Protestant died of gunshot wounds to the head. It was not the last death of the year, although the city remained for the most part quiet. In the earlier riots a spirit grocery in the Beersbridge Road area had been wrecked; on 9 November the structure collapsed, killing a young boy and injuring three others. The remainder of the year passed in reasonable tranquillity. Catholics were licking their wounds.

A review of 1920 made sad reading for a Belfast Catholic. Four months after the expulsions there was still no official move to have the victims restored to their places of work. British politicians, Pilate-like, washed their hands of the problem, saying that interfering in economic matters was no business of a government, and that you could not force a man to work with someone to whom he had an antipathy. Bishop MacRory estimated that these platitudes meant that ten thousand Catholics were still without jobs or any allowances, and their forty thousand dependants were being left by the government to starve.

In the meantime, Catholic Belfast was trying to help its own. The Society of St Vincent de Paul organised a Christmas dinner and film show in St Mary's Hall, attended by ten thousand children. Money collected in Belfast and outside it could do little, however, and the poverty of the dis-employed in the face of wintry weather brought to mind scenes from the middle of the nineteenth century. One witness spoke of seeing into a burnt-out house in Cupar Street. There was a simple tallow light. A fire burned in a pot that was hanging from the roof, and about a dozen men and women were standing around it. In the shadows close to the wall children slept on straw. The only charity the inhabitants of the ruin had received was the wood for the fire.

Protestant and Unionist were more concerned with the battles that were being carried out in the South and in Dublin. By castigating the violence of Sinn Féin and by emphasising the Catholic and nationalist nature of the Sinn Féin cause, Unionists were able to blame Belfast's minority for being authors of their own misfortunes. To ratchet up this sense of threat from the Catholic community, a UVF businessman distributed revolvers to his workers for their own protection and stated that he carried an automatic any time he had to go through a Catholic district.

In December, Northern Ireland received from the British government the Christmas present of its own parliament—a Protestant parliament for a Protestant people, as would soon become apparent. For many ordinary Protestants there was an ambiguity about this development. On the one hand, they would no longer live under the threat of being coerced into a unitary Irish state; on the other hand, there was the sense that now they had to face down Sinn Féin and the IRA by themselves, and that they would have to be more careful than ever about the enemy within, a Catholic population scarred by violence and resentful that the promises made in 1914 had finally been broken.

Concerns like this did not stop them from having an excellent Christmas. Those who had money were prepared to take advantage of the trouble-free streets to buy presents. Big shops offered discounts of up to 25 per cent on a range of products. Royal Avenue and Donegall Place filled with happy pedestrians hoping they would find a bargain that would suit their loved ones. There was Father Christmas in Robinson and Cleaver's and school choristers outside the City Hall.

In the back-to-back houses of the Short Strand and the Falls Road, the men and women without work stood around fires suspended from the ceilings in cooking-pots and listened to the whimpers of their children sleeping on the straw. There was little to look forward to in 1921.

In the days after Christmas the streets were quieter, often empty even before the curfew began. In the darkness, New Year was welcomed by the chimes of the Albert Clock, and the ships' sirens from the harbour echoed along the deserted streets of small houses around the docks and York Street, across Short Strand and Ballymacarret. Some citizens showed their worries about the coming year by attending an all-night prayer vigil in the Salvation Army citadel. Normal Watch Night services were impossible, because of the curfew, so it was only those with stamina who went out to pray. The service had to last all the way from evening curfew till curfew was lifted the next morning. Some people considered that the consumption of alcohol was an enjoyable way to spend the long curfew hours, and on New Year's Day a happy crowd made its way down York Street singing republican songs. An unappreciative police patrol dispersed them.

Early in the year the IRA set out to prove that there was still a need to be vigilant in Belfast. Three members of the RIC Reserve had been sent to Belfast, where one of them was to give evidence at the trial of an IRA man accused of murder. They were staying in the Central Railway Hotel, not far from Musgrave Street, site of the Belfast police headquarters. On the night of 26 January they went to bed early. Five men had been watching them, and at 10 p.m. these men made their way to the top floor. They already knew which rooms were occupied by the constables; they forced the doors open and shot their victims. Two of the policemen died, but the murder witness, Constable Gilmartin, survived and was rushed to the military hospital in Victoria Barracks. Unionist papers, in their reports of the atrocity, gave strong hints that employees at the hotel must have noted the movements of the visiting policemen and passed the information on to the IRA.

Only a few hours after the hotel murders, three men forced their way into a Protestant-owned boarding-house off the Crumlin Road and shot dead a young Catholic as he lay on his bed. There was a widespread belief that the 'retaliation' had been planned in advance and that it was triggered by the Railway Hotel murders. The report of the Protestant landlady, Mrs Morgan, that the three assassins had left the house in a leisurely manner and had taken time to talk to another group of men before escaping in a car led many Catholics to assume that the murder had been carried out by members of the police. Already the names of County Inspector Richard Harrison and District Inspector John Nixon were being linked to attacks on Catholics.

On 10 March three RIC Auxiliaries arrived in Belfast from their depot in Gormanston, County Meath. Two were English and one Scottish. Their job was to collect some military vehicles and drive them back. The next evening they were on foot patrol in Victoria Square. As they talked to a woman outside the Empire Music Hall five gunmen appeared and shot them. Two were killed instantly and the other died in hospital. A man and a woman were also wounded; the man also died of his injuries. In contrast with the January shooting, there were no immediate reprisals, perhaps because most unionists regarded the Auxiliaries as mercenaries.

There were further disturbances, and on 19 March two men were wounded, one of them fatally, during an exchange of fire in Great George's Street. The shooting dead of two Protestants in Roslea three days later provoked more street disturbances. On this occasion a Catholic woman was killed while shopping, apparently by a shot from a loyalist area. A man who went to her aid was also shot, but survived. On 24 March the IRA fired a fusillade of shots into North Queen Street, but no-one was injured.

Bad weather promised a peaceful Easter, but republicans were still active, firing shots at sentries and trying to bomb Springfield Road Barracks. To finance their operations the IRA mounted a series of robberies. Unrest around the Short Strand was chronic, but it was not until the end of April that another attempt was made on the lives of Auxiliaries, this time in Donegall Place. It happened at 9 o'clock on a Saturday evening, when the town was packed with people having a good time before the curfew. Two English-born Auxiliaries were on foot patrol when they were shot dead by two gunmen. As the IRA couple made their escape a police detective fired shots at them, which they returned. In the exchange a man and a woman were wounded.

This time retaliation was swift. About midnight in the Falls area a gang of four men wearing trench coats, probably part of Inspector Nixon's gang of rogue policemen, attacked Patrick and Daniel Duffin. The two men had republican connections, and Daniel was in the IRA. They were the only members of the family not in bed, and they were shot dead as they opened the door.

Some clue to who had carried out the killings was found the next morning when the police removed a dog from the house, recognised by neighbours as belonging to Sergeant Clarke, a Catholic member of the RIC. Whatever conclusion this led them to, the Protestants of Belfast noted the number of Catholic clergy that accompanied the bodies of the Duffin brothers to the graveside, and the fact that it was the Bishop of Down and Connor who gave the graveside oration. It seemed to many of them that the Catholic Church was endorsing republican violence.

Belfast became a capital city on 3 May 1921, when Northern Ireland officially came into existence. It was not the most auspicious of times. The Anglo-Irish War was at its height. Business in the city was going through a deep depression. Sectarian killings were going on at an average of four per month. Even unionism was going through a crisis. Carson looked on the establishment of Northern Ireland as a failure, and anyway felt too ill to remain leader of the Ulster Unionists. He took time to warn the Ulster Unionist Council that it must ensure that Catholics had nothing to fear from the Protestant majority. Unionists had to win over their political opponents and to give equal rights to the Catholic Church. His lieutenant, Sir James Craig, seemed to be on the verge of an exalted career in British politics. It was not until February that he had accepted the leadership of the Unionist Party and resigned from the coalition government. He too warned about a triumphalist approach to the new state, saying that the rights of the minority had to be 'sacred' to the majority.

Quite a few of his listeners were anything but triumphant. They shared Carson's sense that the fight against home rule had been lost. It took all Craig's powers of persuasion, supported by his popularity among the grass roots of unionism, to persuade them that they had the opportunity to create a state in their own image.

Elections were to be held on 24 May, Empire Day. Craig made sure that the constitutional issue was central to the contest. He told his listeners that they had simply to rally round him and the Union Jack would sweep the polls. The working class became caught up in the fever of the election. The only potential split in the Protestant vote, other than a perceived apathy by the middle classes, was the labour issue. There were three Labour candidates standing in Belfast. They had been effectually sidelined by the emphasis on the constitution, but to make assurance doubly sure, workers from both shipyards occupied and barricaded the Ulster Hall on 17 May, effectually cancelling a rally that the Labour candidates intended to have that day. There were Unionist parades along the Shankill. The Unionist press did its best to keep the political temperature high. Even Carson made an appearance, warning Protestants that failing to vote was tantamount to signing up for a united Ireland.

Since the riots of the late nineteenth century, workers in the shipyards seem to have considered themselves a sort of Praetorian Guard of Protestantism. There was no equivalent in the Catholic community, although Bishop MacRory echoed Carson's words about the dangers of apathy. Sinn Féin and the Irish Party (in Northern Ireland now called the Nationalist Party) had as great an antipathy for each other as they had for the Unionists, as street fighting in the Short Strand showed. The Sinn Féin leader, Éamon de Valera, met Joe Devlin to work out a compromise pact. The result was that, in Northern Ireland as a whole, six Nationalist and six Sinn Féin members were elected. This did not compare favourably with the forty Unionist members returned. Only one non-Unionist, Joe Devlin, was elected in Belfast, compared with fifteen Unionists. Worse, from a Catholic point of view, was that the Nationalists were now bound by Sinn Féin's policy of abstention. The Unionists were to be given free rein.

The disparity between Unionists and non-Unionists elected is remarkable, especially in Belfast, where Catholics formed a substantial minority. Catholic newspapers looked for reasons in the way the elections had been conducted. Personation on both sides probably cancelled itself out, but there were reports of widespread intimidation of Catholic voters. Shipyard workers had spent the day loitering around the polling stations in east Belfast. On the Woodstock Road a Nationalist agent was hit on the head with an iron bar. On the Newtownards Road, Catholics were kicked and threatened with knives, while taxis carrying Catholics to the polling station were stoned. The *Irish News* said that it was a mockery of a free election.

There had been a backdrop of violence to the election that had persisted for the whole of May, and a number of incidents during the month involved both loyalists and republicans. On 7 May the IRA shot dead Detective-Inspector Ferris as he left a meeting with Father Convery of St Paul's Parish. On the 9th it turned its attention to the Harbour Police, and Constable Alfred Craig was shot at the entrance to York Docks. There was an arms raid by the IRA on the 10th and a bomb attack by twelve of its members on a police lorry in the Springfield Road on the 17th.

Loyalist gunmen claimed their share. On 16 May a teenage Catholic, Mary Ann Carroll, was shot in North Queen Street. The next day another

Catholic teenager, Philomena Burns, was shot as she stood at her front door. She lingered till 6 June, when she died in hospital. On 18 May an IRA sniper shot a Protestant teenager, George Walker, as he took part in an Orange parade. He did not die till late July. The parade had been on its way to a meeting at the Oval football ground in Ballymacarret. When the meeting was over the organisers asked people to return to the city centre via the Albert Bridge Road. Some chose not to, and there were clashes at the interface between the Newtownards Road and Short Strand. A Catholic ex-serviceman was shot and died shortly afterwards. Later, four people in the Short Strand suffered gunshot wounds, and one, a thirteen-year-old girl, died of her injuries.

It is often thought that the Ulster Special Constabulary was a creation of the new Northern state. Strictly speaking, this is not true. As early as September 1920 Sir James Craig had become convinced of the need for a volunteer constabulary as a short-term measure to take some of the pressure off the regular police and military. He wanted an armed force of two thousand men to work within the six counties only, and he suggested that, as the UVF already had an organisation, it should be used for the purpose. Although there was sympathy among the members of the Cabinet for the formation of the force, and for Craig's other suggestion that a senior civil servant be appointed to oversee Northern Ireland affairs, the reference to the UVF was studiously ignored. There already existed legislation, dating from as far back as 1832 and as recently as 1914, under which a Special Constabulary could be raised. The order to do so was issued from Dublin Castle on 22 October and announced to the public on 1 November.

The new force was to be based on the Northern Ireland counties. Within each county there would be three sections, all of which would be armed. The A Specials would constitute what was later called the full-time reserve, of about two thousand men. It was intended that most of them would be ex-soldiers, who would be armed, equipped and paid the same as the regular police. Supporting them would be a part-time reserve, the B Specials. These would carry out duties in their own localities, usually one night per week, leaving the regular police to deal with nationalist districts. They were to be issued with rifle, bayonet and (after 1922) uniform and to receive £5 every six months for 'wear and tear'. It was considered that they could undertake such duties as foot patrols, manning road blocks and providing night-time guards for important buildings. They were to be much more numerous than the A Specials, with four thousand to be recruited in Belfast alone. On armed patrol they were to be under the command of a regular member of the RIC, and they were always to be subject to orders from the RIC. A final category of C Specials was to constitute an emergency reserve. They were not paid, other than expenses, and had no uniform. They were issued with firearms certificates. Interestingly, many Catholics in rural areas who enjoyed shooting as a pastime joined the C Specials so that they could retain their shotguns.

Select committees were formed to choose 'only men of unquestionable fidelity and efficiency' for the Special Constabulary. The oath they had to take swore loyalty to the King, rather than to Parliament; this combination of phrases was as good as a nod and a wink to the UVF, who were expected to volunteer in the same sort of numbers as they had in 1914.

Perhaps it was the memory of what 1914 had got them into that caused the UVF to hesitate. After a fortnight only 750 had joined the B Specials in Belfast, and by May 1921 it was still only 1,480. Leading Orangemen were as worried as the leaders of the UVF, particularly at the danger of the unfilled places being taken by Catholics, some of the Unionist press warning that even where Protestants were in a majority they were still liable to attack from Sinn Féin. There seems to be more than apathy behind this reluctance to volunteer. When the RUC came to be formed, its recruitment rates were equally poor. It seems likely that, in a potentially dangerous situation, people were more concerned with keeping themselves and their families safe than with sticking their necks out for others.

The authorities in London and in Dublin were less sanguine about recruiting UVF men than were the Unionists of Belfast. As early as September 1920, on the very day that Craig was arguing that the North needed a special constabulary, the Under-Secretary at Dublin Castle wrote to Bonar Law stating that an attempt to use an unarmed special constabulary in Belfast had not been a success, as three special constables had been arrested for looting on the first night. He also made the point that you cannot solve a faction fight by arming one of the parties. The most senior police officer in Northern Ireland, on the other hand, believed that the best elements of the UVF should be recruited and could eventually form regular military units within the Specials. Other Unionists claimed that it was better to have the UVF under police discipline than have them acting as rogue elements beyond control.

The reaction of nationalists was predictable, but understandable. Speaking in the British House of Commons, Joe Devlin prophesied that the Chief Secretary for Ireland was going to 'arm pogromists to murder Catholics.' The *Irish News* said that it was a force of Janissaries (referring to the emasculated Christian soldiers who fought for the Sultan of Istanbul). Once again, even the right-wing press in Britain worried about the wisdom of equipping 'private armies' in Ireland. The *Westminster Gazette* said that the entry qualifications for the new force were a job description for 'all the eager spirits who have driven Nationalist workers from the docks and demonstrated their loyalty by looting Catholic shops.' The government's move was 'inhuman expediency.'

The *Belfast Telegraph* wrote that the B Specials would 'perform a valuable adjunct to the regular forces of the Crown' and would be 'an additional safeguard for the protection of lives and property of the citizens.'

While all this controversy was taking place, the first A Special patrol took place before Christmas 1920, while the first B Specials patrolled Belfast's streets in the first week of February. For the first part of the year their operations were very low-key. They would actually be disbanded when the Anglo-Irish Truce was signed in July 1921 but recalled to the colours when continued violence in the city resulted in the ominous threat from IRA Headquarters in Dublin that they would protect the Catholics of Ulster.

Some of these Specials lined the royal route when King George V came to open the new Northern Ireland Parliament on Tuesday 7 June. Arriving by royal yacht, as had his grandmother, Victoria, more than seventy years earlier, he looked out on a grander Belfast. He saw himself as a protector of his people, and the violence in Ireland grieved him deeply. He had already rebuked Lloyd George for the officially condoned reprisals carried out by the Auxiliaries and the Black-and-Tans in the rest of Ireland in response to IRA attack. Later, during the general strike, he would allow no-one to condemn the miners who had not tried to live on a miner's wage. Undoubtedly he was aware of the tensions that were already forming a tumour in the body politic of Northern Ireland.

The Bishop of Down and Connor, Bishop MacRory, felt that the King had been badly advised and that his visit would put the seal of approval on an institution that was opposed by four-fifths of the Irish people. The King had a different view. He wanted to use the occasion to ask for reconciliation between the warring factions in Ireland. He said as much in his address to the audience in the City Hall. 'I speak from a full heart,' he said, 'when I pray that my coming to Ireland today may prove to be the first step towards the end of strife among her people, whatever their race or creed.' He did not stay long but told Craig that he was glad he had come.

The emotion of the occasion led to fulsome declarations in the Unionist press that the government of Northern Ireland must deal even-handed justice to its citizens, whatever their religion or politics. Catholics were less impressed. They agreed with their bishop. The King's visit had given both an *imprimatur* and a *nihil obstat* to a Protestant parliament.

The strict security operation surrounding the royal couple while they were in Belfast meant that the IRA had to take a break from its lethal attacks on the police. This was a relief to both communities in Belfast, who had seen in a three-day spell a week earlier fourteen people killed and more than seventy requiring hospital treatment. Once again there were allegations of police collusion in the reprisal killing of Catholics; and the widow of one young victim identified Inspector Nixon as the leader of the murder gang. The recently formed Specials were implicated in the killing of two other Catholics, after one of their own was killed in Dock Street.

Although the city remained quiet for the remainder of the month, the IRA struck elsewhere. Reasoning that soldiers returning to barracks after the King's visit would be feeling relaxed, a team under Frank Aiken ambushed a train containing 120 soldiers and 100 horses near Bessbrook, close to the new border. Four soldiers, two civilians and eighty horses were killed. The magnanimity of King George's speech had been met with hate, and the familiar emotions of fear and suspicion returned to dominate Belfast.

In the seesaw of the Anglo-Irish War, something now happened that caught the Unionists completely by surprise. On Saturday 9 July the commander of British forces in Ireland, General Nevil Macready, agreed to a truce with the IRA. On the surface, this was good news for the North, as the IRA undertook to cease its activities throughout Ireland. As the Northern Ireland government did not yet have control of security or of policing, it had no say in when recruitment of both police and Specials was frozen. Unionists were horrified when the IRA showed how seriously it viewed its undertaking to cease hostilities by attacking a police patrol in west Belfast the very day the truce had been signed. Late that evening an armoured tender was lured into an ambush in Raglan Street, just off the Falls Road. Fourteen armed men were waiting for it to arrive. The gun battle lasted ten minutes; at the end of it one policeman was dead and two others wounded.

Belfast had its own Bloody Sunday the next day. Shooting began between the Shankill and the Falls in the afternoon. When bullets struck a tram, the service was suspended. The streets filled; it is an inexplicable fact that, when shooting started in Belfast, people poured onto the streets as if they were anxious to offer themselves to the opposing snipers as targets. There had been an Orange church parade to the Ulster Hall, and shots were fired at the crowd watching them return. Shortly afterwards a soldier was wounded in Upper Library Street and IRA gunmen fired at police from around Upper North Street. There were reports of machine-guns and hand grenades being used when a loyalist crowd, allegedly several thousand strong, invaded the small streets around the Falls, some of its number carrying petrol, paraffin, rags and even bundles of wood. Eleven Catholics died in this attack, four of them ex-servicemen. Five Protestants also died, while 161 houses were burned, leaving about a thousand people homeless.

The *Belfast Telegraph* claimed that the trouble had been deliberately planned by Sinn Féin. Republican gunfire had been so widespread that rumours abounded that the IRA was going to redeploy its forces to concentrate on Northern Ireland. In spite of all the Catholic deaths, the IRA was confident enough to shoot two Protestants on Monday. A Special shot a thirteen-year-old girl from the safety of a caged lorry as she crossed the road with her mother.

Those who knew Lloyd George wondered to what lengths he would go to achieve peace. Many believed he would be quite happy to hand Northern Ireland to the republicans as a luck-penny, as long as he could end a war that was rapidly becoming more unpopular with the voters of Britain. The Unionist press stressed that Northern Ireland, and in particular the Protestant community, was in need of defence. They were all the more horrified when, later that summer, some of the British papers accused unionists of being the aggressors.

The timing of the truce between Crown forces and the IRA was unfortunate. Although there had been no major incidents within Belfast since the King's visit, there was no sense that it was at peace with itself. Worse, the treaty was agreed on the first day of the annual holidays, meaning that there would be many on the streets. In particular, the government was concerned that the emotion surrounding the Orange parades would mean that there were likely to be incidents involving youths of 'the most irresponsible age,' which would certainly lead in turn to retaliation by the IRA. Moreover, leaders of the Northern IRA were concerned about the difficulty of controlling nationalist hotheads during the period of the truce. Both sides were right to be worried. There were minor incidents leading up to the celebrations, with an attack on an Orange parade in York Street and reports of gunfire in the Short Strand; but the day itself passed almost peacefully. From the following day, however, Belfast was caught up in a crescendo of violence, which, for a time, seemed as if it would never reach a climax.

To catalogue every incident for the remainder of that summer would be to produce a doleful list of slaughter, where killing differed from killing only in the amount of cruelty involved. It began with shots being fired at two policemen on the morning of Wednesday the 13th and went on from there, building up a momentum and an intensity that seemed unstoppable and uncontrollable. By evening, 26-year-old Maggie McKinney, a Catholic mill worker, was dead. The following day most of the trouble was in north and east Belfast, with shooting in North Queen Street and the Short Strand area. The score for that day was two dead. There were no more deaths till 5 August, when an IRA gunman, Freddie Fox, was accidentally shot dead by his accomplice while trying to escape after an attack on police in Ballymacarret. The same day a Protestant tradesman was shot dead during a robbery at his business.

There was a gunfight at Queen's Quay the following week, and bombs began to be used. On 21 August a hand grenade was thrown into a group near Clifton Street, with two children among the six injured. A house in Nelson Street was bombed by a loyalist mob on the 27th. The IRA shot two

Protestants, including a shipwright who died later, in the North Queen Street area. Overnight, firing could still be heard. The next day four Protestants, including a five-year-old girl, were killed by gunfire in the area, as well as three Catholics. Two other Protestants were shot in other areas, one in York Street, the other on the Donegall Road. Shipyard workers were attacked on their way from work, and shots were fired into crowds in Donegall Street and Royal Avenue. The terrible month ended the following day, Wednesday the 31st. There was no slacking of the terror. By that evening seven were dead, four of them Catholics.

The army and police flooded Belfast and limited the casualties over the next fortnight, although there is something distasteful in saying that 'only' one person was killed, a Protestant teenager. It could not last, however, and trouble broke out again on the 15th. It began with rioting in the area around North Queen Street and York Street, where two people were shot. On the 17th three more people were shot in the same district. This was a Saturday, and more shooting began at about 10 o'clock that night, while bombs were thrown just before curfew.

Sunday looked as if it was going to pass peacefully, but there was a particularly revolting shooting in the early evening. A single bullet fired by an IRA sniper passed through the head of Maggie Ardis before striking her friend, Evelyn Blair. Both girls were twenty-two, and both died. In an effort to remove targets, the curfew in the area was implemented at 8:30 that evening.

On the following Friday rioting began in east Belfast, where Loyalist gangs attacked thirty Catholic workmen who were re-laying tramlines on the Newtownards Road. The rioting developed into shooting and bomb-throwing around the Short Strand. A Protestant was killed by a military vehicle. On the Saturday there was sporadic shooting, but the trouble did not become serious till the middle of Sunday afternoon. Street fighting began after an attack on a Special. A well-known IRA member was attacked by a mob as he left St Matthew's Church and was shot dead. When an ambulance came to take away the body it in its turn was attacked savagely. A Catholic woman was shot dead by a stray police bullet as she sat by her fireside, while a Protestant was fatally injured when a bomb was thrown through the fanlight above his door. A bomb went off on the tramlines, and two Protestant teenagers were killed and twenty other people injured. Firing around St Matthew's Church had been continuous, and several bullets hit the front door. After the explosion everything was quiet. At the funeral the following Wednesday of one of the Protestant bomb victims, IRA gunfire was directed at the mourners. One man died, while three others were wounded.

All that summer people continued to be intimidated from their work. This was no longer done in any organised way and tended to happen immediately after some particularly vile atrocity. Catholic tramline workers were forced to leave their jobs after the cemetery shooting, and Catholic workers in a timber yard on Donegall Road were also forced out. Protestants working at the brickworks on the Springfield Road and others at a mill in Flax Street were harassed as they went to and from work but did not have to give up their jobs.

Even beyond the danger to life and limb, it was an unpleasant time to live in the Catholic districts of Belfast, even in the Falls, much the biggest of them. The streets and houses were overcrowded as people fled from more dangerous accommodation. Money was short, because so many breadwinners did not dare report for work. Strangers automatically came under suspicion. Most of the utilities workers were Protestants, and their courage in entering such hostile territory has to be admired, even though they usually had a police escort.

The RIC were distrusted, but the Specials were detested. There are stories of people in bed during the curfew, watching the lights of an approaching police tender reflected on the ceiling and wondering where it would stop. Not unnaturally, fear of the police mutated to support for the IRA. A warning system using banging dustbins and coloured torches gave notice of patrols approaching. Most positive help was given by those who left doors ajar, hid weapons, or lent their houses for meetings. In daytime, on the Falls Road itself, there was a veneer of normality, with shops open and trams clanking along their tracks. Yet there was always the knowledge that the little side streets that sparkled in the light of day were a jungle, and could become deadly at night, when the predators were out.

Substantive negotiations between Sinn Féin and the British government began on 11 October. The Northern Ireland government was excluded, on the reasonable grounds that, as Ireland was already partitioned, what happened beyond the border was no concern of theirs. Although Craig made several trips to London, he found that Lloyd George always tried to force him to make concessions, probably tempting him with inclusion in the talks if he agreed.

Violence in Belfast settled down to a steady ache, like a toothache that nags during the day and is not quite severe enough to prevent you sleeping at night. Senior Unionist politicians condemned Dublin Castle for not doing more to stem the violence. Fred Crawford complained that his 'tiger'—the UVF—was getting hard to control and would become unmanageable unless Britain delegated responsibility for security to Northern Ireland. Great efforts were being made by both sides to control their wild ones, but there were signs that tensions were increasing within communities. Catholics faced another winter without wages. Protestants wondered whether their new-born state would survive infancy. The magma was working its way back towards the surface; and towards the end of November the volcano erupted.

With impeccable timing, the decision was taken on 8 November to relax the curfew, allowing it to begin an hour later, at 11:30. Less than a fortnight later there was serious rioting both in east Belfast and around York Street. On the 21st shipyard workers were attacked on their way to work, with bullets spraying the area for some time. A painter at Harland and Wolff who had survived the Battle of the Somme was killed by a shot to the head. Another Protestant was killed on the Beersbridge Road. Yet another, again a shipyard worker, was shot on the Newtownards Road, though he did not die till six months later. At tea-time a Catholic barman was shot in the head and died shortly afterwards.

Tit-for-tat killings continued for another three days, until 24 had died and 91 had been wounded.

Right in the middle of this, on Monday the 22nd, the British government transferred responsibility for security to the Northern Ireland government. It is tempting to think that Lloyd George was glad to leave Unionists to accrue blame for any future security failings. Things were still too hectic for anyone to consider all the implications. As workers on the Oldpark tram went home that evening along Corporation Street a bomb blew up in front of them, and the passengers were raked with gunfire. The floor fell out, and shards of glass from the windows flew among the shocked passengers. Amazingly, only three people were killed, two of them workers from Workman Clark.

On Wednesday there was another attack. This time the bomb was thrown into a Shankill tram. It was so crowded that the damage was limited to those immediately beside the device. Four people were killed, two of them workers at Harland and Wolff. A serious tightening of security meant that the city centre was too dangerous for undertaking spectacular operations, so the IRA turned to a soft target. It shot a harbour policeman six times, leaving his body in the Milewater Road after stealing his revolver. There were soft targets among Catholics too. A Catholic shopkeeper was killed outside his premises in Little Patrick Street. A few days later someone threw a bomb into Keegan Street, killing a Catholic woman. The IRA felt the need for reprisals and shot dead a shipyard worker as he waited outside a tobacconist's shop on the Ormeau Road.

The Anglo-Irish Treaty was signed on 6 December. A copy was rushed by train and destroyer to Belfast; when Craig read the details he was aghast. Ironically, concessions to the Irish Free State that were too little for de Valera were too much for Craig. Ireland was to be treated on the same terms as the dominions of Canada and Australia. Worse, there was to be a Boundary Commission, which would adjudicate a new frontier between the two Irish states, the frontier to be determined by consultation with the people who lived along it. Once more the infant Northern Ireland was threatened, this time by amputation. As the majority in the area of the

Mourne Mountains and south County Down were Catholic and nationalist, this district might be transferred to the Free State. Belfast would lose its supply of water. Worse, huge chunks of Counties Tyrone and Fermanagh might also be lost, reducing the state to a rump that stood little chance of surviving. Catholic Belfast rubbed salt in the wounds by lighting bonfires and flying the Tricolour flag of the Free State.

A personal meeting with Lloyd George gave Craig no crumb of comfort. When he got back to Belfast he disinterred the language of the old, defiant UVF. He threatened to turn to the Orange Order for arms and money, to seize government departments and, like Ian Smith in Rhodesia fifty years later, to make a unilateral declaration of independence. When Catholics reconsidered their position in the cold light of the Ulster day they realised that they had been abandoned, that their exclusion from the Free State was permanent. Catholics and Protestants considered what they had lost, and determined to lose no more in 1922. The gunmen among them resumed firing on their usual targets.

Catholics were attacked in their districts or coming from mass. Protestants were attacked as they went to work or at their work. Since Catholic maintenance workers for the trams had been forced out, gangs working on tramlines became a convenient target for republican gunmen. By the end of the year the death toll for twelve months was 109.

There was one change in security policy. The secretary of the Ulster Unionist Council, Richard Dawson Bates, had become Minister of Home Affairs. He set about recruiting more Specials as a priority. A new factor was in play that perhaps made service in the Specials slightly more attractive. Until the responsibility for security had been transferred to the Northern Ireland government, the regulation that required all Special patrols to be accompanied, and in effect commanded, by a regular RIC constable meant that they were under the command of Dublin Castle, an establishment that Northern Ireland Protestants simply did not trust. Bates hoped that recruitment would increase now that the Specials would be controlled by their own people.

There was another encouraging sign for unionists. It soon became obvious that there were deep divisions within the republican movement concerning the Treaty. De Valera claimed that he objected to it on the grounds that it did not address those problems that had led to centuries of conflict between Ireland and Britain, namely the subservience of one to the other. The other political heavyweight in the South, Michael Collins, stated that it was the best deal that they would get; it probably was. He also pointed out that the delegation that had been sent to London had been plenipotentiaries, with full powers to agree to a treaty on behalf of the Provisional Government. In those circumstances he believed that the only honourable thing for Dáil Éireann to do was to ratify the treaty.

In spite of the esteem in which Collins was held by the republican movement, the motion to adopt the treaty was passed by a slim majority. Many of those opposed, including de Valera, walked out and refused to recognise the validity of the vote. It is worth noting that the main bone of contention at the time was not the exclusion of the six north-eastern counties but the oath of allegiance to the British Crown that members of the Dáil would be required to take.

If the Belfast government thought that republicans would be so tied up in their own problems that they would leave Northern Ireland alone, they were to be sadly disappointed. At first things looked promising. An agreement was signed in London on 21 January between Michael Collins and Sir James Craig that would end the long-standing Southern boycott of Northern goods in exchange for the restoration of expelled Catholics to their jobs and the removal of political or religious tests for Belfast workers. The agreement also contained proposals concerning political prisoners and the future of the railway network. But these were promises that neither side could deliver, as was demonstrated by the lack of progress in the weeks following the agreement.

The year had started badly. Two Catholic children were killed in the York Street area by a Protestant sniper on the evening of New Year's Day. The bullet passed through the head of a fourteen-year-old boy before lodging in the abdomen of a 21-month-old infant. The following day gunfire again claimed the lives of four people in the same area, while there was trouble around St Matthew's Church in east Belfast. Another man was killed in crossfire in the Carrick Hill area of west Belfast. On 3 January soldiers shot dead a Protestant teenager on the Newtownards Road.

The possibility of being killed in crossfire was increased by the large crowds that came out to witness the exchanges of gunfire, cheering or groaning at the success or otherwise of what they saw as their defenders. Few murders were obscene enough to repel both sides. When a Protestant married couple living in the mainly nationalist Hooker Street were shot dead at their doorstep, the unionist press condemned the atrocity, making much of the five little ones left behind.

Frustration was growing at the apparently pusillanimous reaction of the authorities to the increasing violence. The three main Protestant church leaders issued a joint statement urging Protestants to stop criminal acts. Although they claimed that Protestants had not been the original aggressors, Protestants were now being involved in the outbreaks of violence. There was also frustration that the perpetrators of violence, when brought to justice, were being given very lenient custodial sentences. There was approval in the Unionist press, on the other hand, for Major-General Cameron, the military commander, when he threatened to evict all people from any building from which firing had taken place, to close and destroy the premises and to arrest the owner or occupier. It was against this background that the meetings between Craig and Collins took place and that the pact was signed. There was a distinct reduction in violence for a while, as people waited to see what would happen.

The return to serious violence in the city was triggered, as so often before, by events that happened far beyond Belfast. Along the Tyrone and Fermanagh border the IRA kidnapped forty-two loyalists, one of whom was the son of an MP. Many of the others were Specials. The republicans claimed it was in response to the detention of the Monaghan football team by the Northern police on their way to Derry. In their comments, the unionist press did little to ease the tensions of the situation. The *News Letter* called it an act of war and, in a curious phrase, 'an act which, if perpetuated [*sic*] by an alien people, would be visited with retaliatory violence.' Matters got worse a few days later. The Specials along the border had been mobilised, and were being reinforced. A patrol of sixteen A Specials was being sent from the barracks at Newtownards to Enniskillen. Because of the meandering nature of the border along the route, the railway line went through Clones, in County Monaghan. Here the Specials had a thirty-minute wait for the connecting train. Somebody told the IRA of their presence. The local IRA commander boarded the train and demanded their surrender. He was shot dead for his pains, and a gun battle began. There were four trains in the station at the time, and passengers threw themselves on the carriage floors to avoid the bullets. Four Specials were killed and nine wounded. The *Irish Independent* rubbed salt in the wounds by blaming the Northern police for detaining the Monaghan football team.

It did not matter that the Specials had fired first and were probably technically guilty of murdering a member of the Irish police while resisting arrest. It is, after all, quite usual for armed men, even members of the police or military, to be arrested if they stray into the wrong jurisdiction.

A powder keg had been lit in Clones; but the explosion took place a hundred miles away. Over the next five days thirty people died in Belfast. The shooting began in the flash-point around York Street on Saturday 11 February. The first to die was a Catholic shopkeeper, who was shot by a youthful gunman as she tidied up her shop before closing. Shooting began again the following evening, and several churches cancelled their evening services. Three people died, two of them probably shot by B Specials in the Millfield area. Early on Monday morning the shooting of a Catholic barman in the markets area introduced the bloodiest day of the winter. As it ended, on a beautiful moonlit night that bore promise of spring to come, four Protestants were dead, as well as twelve Catholics. Six of the latter had been killed when a large bomb was thrown into a Catholic street off the Protestant Shore Road. Children had been skipping as their parents watched.

Winston Churchill was so horrified that he sent a telegram to Michael Collins condemning the incident as the worst thing to happen in Ireland in the previous three years. British public opinion was revolted. Fear multiplied in Catholic Belfast, and the bishop begged Lloyd George to send military reinforcements. Perhaps the greatest damage was done to children, who were traumatised, at a time before the concept was in general use, by the mayhem that was going on around them. The greatest damage done to the future of Northern Ireland was that the IRA, rather than the police or military, from now on would claim to be the defenders of the Catholic people. It was a precursor of the Provisional IRA in the 1960s and 70s.

When the violence of the Anglo-Irish War had overflowed into Northern Ireland from 1920 onwards, most Catholics had supported Joe Devlin and constitutional nationalism. Even Séamus Woods, later to become commanding officer of what was rather grandly called the 3rd Northern Division, admitted that Sinn Féin and the IRA had the support, to begin with, of 10 per cent of Belfast Catholics at most. Somewhere between five hundred and a thousand volunteers formed the Belfast Brigade. They suffered from poor liaison with Dublin, and although they were derided by many as the AOH with rifles, there were not, in fact, very many rifles. When the Anglo-Irish Truce came about, Michael Collins himself ensured that Belfast was properly armed, and by mid-1922 the Belfast Brigade would have six hundred rifles and five machine-guns. A liaison officer, Eoin O'Duffy, was appointed in mid-July 1921, and he made his headquarters in St Mary's Hall, near the city centre. He ordered that IRA sniping should take place only in self-defence. During the period immediately after the truce there had been a rush to enrol in the IRA. Many of the volunteers took it upon themselves to attack workers' transport, showing that it was in the nature of the Belfast Brigade to attack Protestant workers as well as their nominated target, the police and military.

When Collins sent arms to the Northern IRA he was not being sentimental about Ireland's 'lost green field'. He knew he would soon have a civil war on his hands, and he wanted republicans in the North to know what hand was feeding them, lest they should bite it later. The more commitment he showed to supporting the besieged Catholics in the North, the less likely they were to side with the anti-Treaty forces of Liam Lynch. This is significant, as it was the only real assertion of the goal of Irish unity on either side of the Free State's republican divide. Collins's immediate reaction to the wholesale slaughter of February was to set up a special group, called the Belfast Guards. This was a full-time unit of eighty-one men, paid £3 per week. The existence of the group was kept secret, as Collins was aware of the danger of jealousy and division in the ranks of the Belfast Brigade.

These manoeuvrings had little influence in Belfast to begin with. The slaughter of mid-February continued. After the bomb atrocity there were the usual reprisals and re-reprisals. On Tuesday the 14th four Protestants and five Catholics died and on Wednesday three Protestants and four Catholics. One of the Protestants was a B Special whose full-time job was as a plater in the shipyard, while one of the Catholics was a five-year-old boy. Violence continued for the month. It did not reach the same orgiastic proportions as the 'Clones' weekend, but it spread to parts of the city that had been quiet up till then, such as the Ormeau Road. It was as if the city suffered from some dreadful psoriasis, always there but flaring up every few weeks and gradually spreading until it seemed that the whole body would be covered.

Up to March 1922 there were definite areas that were dangerous to be in or to pass through. The ghettoes around the city centre, Protestant and Catholic, and the city centre itself, opened the possibility not only of being deliberately attacked but of being caught in crossfire. People working in the 'other side's' district were in constant danger. But the violence had, in the main, touched the poor and the working class and not those members of the middle or upper middle classes, who, if they made it safely home, could feel safe till the next day.

Kinnaird Terrace, just off the Antrim Road, quite close to the Waterworks, is a row of three-storey red-brick houses that still look very prosperous. Owen McMahon lived at number 3. One of five brothers from County Down, all of whom were in the licensed trade, he owned a bar in Ann Street in the city. He was a close friend of Joe Devlin, was one of the richest businessmen in Belfast and was a former chairman of the Northern Vintners' Association. A sportsman himself in his youth, he still sponsored a range of sports and was on the board of Glentoran Football Club, which was supported in the main by the Protestants of east Belfast. In his home lived his wife, his six sons and one daughter, a niece, and the manager of his public house, Edward McKinney. Tucked away on the top floor were the domestic servants who were indispensable in such a home.

Thursday 23 March was wet and cold—a good night to be indoors. As midnight passed and the night became Friday, a watchman guarding a site at Carlisle Circus heard only the rain on his hut and the spatter as drops fell on the red-hot coke of his brazier. At about 1 a.m. two men in police uniform approached him. They needed a sledge hammer, they told him. It is unlikely, given the time and the place, that he demurred. The two men then made their way up the Crumlin Road, then turned right into Clifton Park Avenue. At that time a house stood in a large demesne here, known as Bruce's Farm. Here they met three more men and, by crossing the demesne, came by a quiet way to Kinnaird Terrace. They knew exactly the house they wanted.

At about 1:15 a.m. Mrs McMahon was wakened by a crash of glass. Thinking that someone had thrown a bomb into the house, she wakened her husband. Both of them ran down a flight of stairs and collided with a man in police uniform on the landing. He ordered her back to bed, but she could see others using Webley revolvers to herd the males of the family downstairs. Her husband tried to reassure her, saying it was probably 'just a raid.' The menfolk were all in the living-room downstairs, while the women gathered in the drawing-room on the first floor. No sooner were they all in the living-room than they were told, 'You boys say your prayers.' The intruders opened fire in volleys almost straight away, before their victims could react. One son was killed as he sat on a chair. Seven were hit, five of them fatally. The youngest son, twelve-year-old Michael, dropped to the floor and groaned, pretending to be hit. The man who fired at him wore a dustcoat. As bullets embedded themselves in the wall he slipped behind the sofa, where he was found by rescuers. Only he and one other would survive.

Mrs McMahon opened the window of the drawing-room and screamed, 'Murder, murder!' She could see figures retreating across the demesne. The cries awoke staff at the Kinnaird Nursing Home next door, and the matron telephoned for the police and an ambulance. Neighbours on the other side were also wakened by the noise, and a Mr Hamill, rather bravely, set out to get help. He met an RIC patrol coming along Thorndale Avenue. Even these men, and the ambulance men who followed, were revolted by what they found. The gas in the living-room burned brightly. A young man sat on a chair gasping his life out. In the room men lay dead and dying in bunches. Owen McMahon had been shot in the stomach and was writhing in agony. The smell of fresh blood was everywhere.

For those who reflected on the atrocity the next day it was not simply the number of men killed that was horrifying: it was the cold-blooded way in which these people had planned to eliminate the male line of the McMahon family. Killing the bar manager was simply a bonus.

Many people hoped that this event was so horrifying that it would purge the Northern Ireland consciousness of its violence. Others were less hopeful. One American journalist predicted that any police investigation would fail. Others said that it was worse than any atrocity committed by the Black-and-Tans. The *Nation* asserted that it was time for Craig to realise that the IRA was not the only enemy of Northern Ireland.

The day of the McMahon funeral, 27 March, was a beautiful one, in contrast to the night of the murders, and carried promise of spring. Estimates put the crowd following the four hearses at ten thousand. Among them were representatives of Belfast's business community, many of them Protestant. On the route to the funeral and at Milltown Cemetery there were soldiers and armoured cars. The commanding officer of the British forces in Belfast feared that there would be an attack on the cortege. Outsiders were beginning to believe that loyalists were capable of anything.

Michael Collins contacted Lloyd George and Winston Churchill, demanding that they put pressure on Craig to improve protection for Northern Catholics. Churchill wanted to put a large part of the city under martial law, as Catholics would feel safer with the British army than with what they saw as a loyalist police force. The doubters in England were not made any more confident when, within a fortnight of the slaughter in Kinnaird Terrace, the Royal Ulster Constabulary was established, and control of the Specials was passed to the Belfast government. Two days later the Civil Authorities (Special Powers) Act (Northern Ireland) (1922) was passed, proving to the English sceptics what they had always feared: the partisan nature of the Unionist leadership. They could only hope that the draconian powers incorporated in the act would be applied impartially.

Craig was anxious to disprove the charge that what was happening in Belfast was a pogrom. He insisted that the fight was not against Catholics but against murdering rebels and Bolshevism, that they were against the enemies not simply of Ulster but of the Empire. Nevertheless, in a meeting with Collins only four days after the killing Craig agreed to a pact that was almost conciliatory. Two of the ideas included to reconcile the Catholic minority to the police were a 'mixed' Special Constabulary and the establishment of a Police Advisory Committee.

Catholics in Belfast ignored what Craig said and concluded that they were suffering a pogrom, that they were no longer safe in their own homes, that men wearing the uniform of law officers did not represent safety. They faced a dilemma. Without weapons to defend themselves they were easy targets; if they obtained weapons to defend themselves they were likely to be sentenced to be flogged or even sentenced to death under the new legislation. Although most Catholics would agree that the RIC as an institution was not sectarian, they were convinced that there was a rogue element within it whose actions were being ignored by senior officers.

County Inspector Richard Harrison, widely believed to be the authority behind the killings, was in charge of the city's detective unit. The actual attacks were believed to be led by District Inspector John Nixon and to be carried out from Brown Square Barracks on the Shankill Road. It was widely believed that the gang even attacked Catholic members of the RIC, though at least one member of the gang was a Catholic, and is buried in Milltown Cemetery. Politicians as senior as Craig and Bates were aware of the rumours, and moves were made to stop the two inspectors from transferring to the RUC. These moves failed.

And the murders continued. Many people were shot at work or as they made their way to or from work, often because their work took them into areas dominated by the other community, which made them an easy target. A Catholic train-driver who had just brought the Magherafelt train into the Midland Station in York Street was shot dead by a gang who had discovered his religion. To show that they were not simply sectarian hoods, they robbed the station cleaners of their wages before making their getaway. No-one was safe. A pregnant woman was shot because she wouldn't leave her house in a Protestant area. A blind man was killed in crossfire on Carrick Hill. A thirteen-year-old girl was shot as she was swinging around a lamp-post.

The IRA made a point of attempting to kill policemen that were rumoured to be members of the Nixon gang. The next atrocity happened when George Turner, an RIC man accompanied by a member of the B Specials, was shot in the head as he patrolled Peter's Hill at about 11 p.m. on 1 April. The bullet came from behind and passed through his mouth. The Special ran to nearby Brown Square Barracks. There was an understandably angry reaction among the police there. One of Nixon's gang, Constable Gordon, lifted a sledge hammer—which may have been the one used in the McMahon killings—and asked for volunteers to avenge the attack. Nationalists claim that Nixon's men, together with some Specials, manned lorries and a Lancia armoured car. They drove first to Stanhope Street, part of a complex of small streets and cul-de-sacs just off Carrick Hill. The Lancia opened machine-gun fire on windows as it passed. When the lorries arrived the men jumped off and began breaking down doors. As they ran along the street, witnesses heard them shout, 'Cut the guts out of them for the murder of Turner.' In number 15 Stanhope Street they shot Joseph McCrory, aged forty. In number 26 Park Street (now demolished) they shot 42-year-old Bernard McKenna, the father of seven children, who had just returned from sea; they chased him upstairs to his bedroom and fired eight bullets into his body. In number 16 Arnon Street they shot seventy-year-old William Spallin, whose wife had been buried that day. Spallin's twelve-year-old grandson was spared, although the gunman, who was in plain clothes and whose face was familiar to the boy, took the £20 Spallin had for paying the funeral expenses. At number 12 Arnon Street they brushed passed Mrs Walsh, who had opened the door, and ran up the stairs to the bedrooms. In one they dragged Joseph Walsh from his bed, threw him on the floor and, in front of his children, smashed his head with a sledge hammer. They then shot the screaming children. Two-year-old Brigid survived, but seven-year-old Michael died the next day. Fourteen-year-old Frank was shot and beaten in the kitchen, but survived.

The killing was not over. Three men called at the house of a sixty-year-old Catholic, John Mallon, in Skegoniel Avenue in the north of the city. They asked for his son, but as he was not at home they shot the father instead.

Nixon had already shown how his gang could target a family; now he demonstrated what could be done to a vulnerable community. The families of Stanhope Street took the message to heart. Each evening women and children, and some of the men, left the district and looked for shelter in safer Catholic areas. The men remained behind to make sure the empty houses were not left open to invasion from the surrounding Protestant areas.

That Easter it was the Marrowbone area that was targeted. After two days when there was constant shooting into the area, three streets— Antigua Street, Rothesay Street and Saunderson Street—were burned. They suffered complete destruction, and there was widespread looting. There was more than one way to get Catholics to leave an area. The Unionist press blamed the Free State government, claiming that a halt to IRA violence would lead to a return of peace in Belfast (ignoring the fact that the current round of sectarian murder in Belfast had predated the Free State government by eighteen months or more); further, the Catholic community was culpable for its own destruction because it sheltered IRA gunmen. Several English newspapers distinguished between the border campaign of the IRA and the murders in Belfast. They accepted that the IRA was usually the aggressor in rural areas, but it was loyalists who initiated the attacks on Catholics within Belfast. Catholic and nationalist papers condemned the Unionist leadership for unleashing forces over which it had no control.

Nixon had campaigned against Catholics being allowed to join the new force. While he was doing this, Craig was campaigning against Nixon and Harrison joining the RUC. Belfast's City Commissioner under the old RIC consulted Major-General Flood, who was to become the RUC's Inspector-General, and they agreed that all those associated with the murder gangs would have to go. Harrison and Nixon faced down their superiors, stating that they would shoot certain members of the government and implying that they would have the full backing of the RUC and the Specials. Nixon is said to have had a notebook in which he had the name of every policeman who had committed a sectarian murder, together with the names of the officers who had given the order. He claimed he had the names of government members who had helped set up the murder squads. He felt he was untouchable, and that was what he became: an untouchable. While Harrison became City Commissioner and went on to be Inspector-General, Nixon got an MBE and no more. He was the unacceptable face of the death squads, not for what he did but for the fact that he had threatened to reveal all.

He masterminded his own ejection from the RUC in 1925 by making a political speech at an Orange Order meeting condemning the policies of the Northern Ireland government and predicting that they would end in failure. For this breach of regulations he was suspended. His superiors no longer worried about his black book. The other members of the murder squad would not support him in his allegations. They had all received promotions, and had too much to lose.

It was touch and go all the same. There was a poster campaign in the Shankill area in support of Nixon, because of, rather than in spite of, his reputation. On the night before the court of inquiry was to be held a parade of ten thousand people, many of them said to be members of the RUC and Specials, marched from the Shankill Road to the City Hall to hear speeches in support of Nixon. Under parliamentary privilege, speeches were made in his support, claiming that with a force with a few hundred more officers like him there would be little to worry about concerning the IRA.

The case against Nixon was based on articles written by three reporters who had attended the Orange hall on the night in question. As testifying against Nixon in the political climate of Belfast might be seen as a grave impediment to collecting one's pension, all three refused to give evidence, and the charges were dropped. Nixon returned to duty; but any satisfaction was short-lived. A few days later he was called to the Inspector-General's office. Here he was met by the Inspector-General and the City Commissioner. He was told that, on orders from the Northern Ireland government, he was to answer Yes or No to the questions put to him. The questions have not yet been made public, but when they were finished he stormed out of the room. He was dismissed from the RUC, on full pension. John Nixon went on to have a long life in politics, becoming and remaining a member of the Northern Ireland Parliament until his death in 1948 at the age of seventy-one.

Back in the Belfast of 1922, the horror of the Arnon Street massacre and the arson at Easter in the Marrowbone were only chancres that were raised above a current of violent death. From 1 March to 30 April a hundred people died violently in Belfast. There was no longer even a pause for reflection after the most horrific murders: the assassins simply developed their field skills. Loyalists watched as people passed Catholic churches; if individuals reacted instinctively by blessing themselves, they were marked down as Catholics and a potential target. Loyalists also adopted a technique of travelling on trams, waiting to identify a suitable victim. When they did so they would wait till the tram had reached a 'safe' area, then drag their victim off and kill him.

Remarkably, they were often able to identify Catholics simply by asking. Women, far from being protected by their sex, were often deliberately targeted. This was especially the case with Catholic shop assistants working in or near Protestant areas. Even being a child offered no safety. As three-year-old Brigid Skillen made her way to the corner shop to spend a penny that she had been given she was shot dead by a sniper.

It is obvious to anyone who examines the figures that the war of attrition was being won by loyalist gunmen and snipers. The IRA concentrated on attacking members of the police, with some success, during these months, apparently leaving the Catholics to survive as best they could and pick up the pieces. They also bombed trams taking workers to the shipyards and shot at easy targets when they could get them; but it was plain to see that the minority community was losing many more dead than the majority. If it was a war to the end then there could only be one winner.

As if to confirm this, some of the murders became almost obscene in their casualness. Jack O'Hare was a native of Newry who lived in the Short Strand. He worked in the centre of the city as a store-room porter in the Imperial Hotel in Donegall Street. On 24 May he left work for home, not knowing that tension was building in east Belfast. He took a tram to the Albert Bridge, alighting there to walk the rest of the way. A gang that had been hanging about on the bridge saw the direction in which he was walking, surrounded him, and assaulted him with kicks and punches. They left him then but returned when they heard him call out for water. Showing what can only be described as the sickest idea of humour, they tossed him over the bridge into the Lagan. A police patrol appeared just then, so they moved on. They sent back two girls to check the river and cheered when they heard that O'Hare's body had disappeared. It was not found for five days, and those searching—family and police—had to endure sniping attacks all the while.

Pleased with this achievement, the same gang less than a fortnight later beat up two Catholic girls and were only prevented from throwing them in the water by a patrol of Specials that arrived on the scene.

A greater cruelty was also developing in the attacks. A Catholic house-keeper working for a doctor in the loyalist Donegall Pass was pushed to the ground by a gang that arrived at the doctor's door. One man poured petrol over her while another set a match to her dress. She ran out into the street screaming, where she was helped by neighbours before being taken to hospital.

Although the majority of killings at this time were of Catholics, loyalists had no monopoly of depravity. An IRA gang singled out the Protestant workers in a cooperage in Little Patrick Street, shot four of them dead and wounded another. It did not seem to worry them that reprisal was inevitable, and sure enough, three Catholic carters were shot dead soon afterwards.

It had already been shown by the attacks on St Matthew's that churches provided no sanctuary. On 5 June the Mater Hospital was hit by repeated gunfire from the police that lasted for forty minutes. The standard official comment that they were merely returning fire was rejected by the mother superior of the hospital, who wrote to the International Red Cross in

Geneva to complain. She said that the Catholic community 'desired to be protected' by the military.

Although the IRA in the main concentrated its efforts on attacking the police and 'protecting' Catholics by killing Protestants, a new tactic began to emerge in May or June 1922. Reasoning that the real power behind the murder gangs was the Ulster unionist establishment of grandees and businessmen, republicans decided to target them. They chose arson as their weapon and, in the early summer, attacked between eighty and ninety commercial premises as well as 'big houses' throughout the North. In Belfast there was a concentrated campaign during a weekend in mid-May. There were seven fires on the 19th, including a serious conflagration at Donegall Quay. There was worse the next day, when eleven premises were attacked. The work of the Fire Brigade was made more difficult by the fact that several hoax alarms were also raised. Over the next few days Ferguson's motor works was attacked, as it did work for the police. Inexplicably, the Carnegie Library in the Falls Road was also burned down. A further swarm of arson attacks occurred on the 26th, when thirteen fires were started, mostly in the Falls and Divis Street areas. Although the focus of attack was mainly business premises, the Model School was also destroyed. The fire attacks continued into June, even though there was a lull in shootings.

The IRA seemed prepared to raise the stakes in whom they shot as well. William Twaddell was one of the foot-soldiers as far as the Unionist Party was concerned. In the Northern Ireland Parliament he represented Woodstock, the staunchly loyalist area at the northern end of the Shankill Road, while on Belfast City Council he represented the Shankill Road. He owned a large drapery shop in North Street. On the morning of 22 May he was followed by a group of gunmen as he walked through the city streets towards his premises. He was fired on in Garfield Street and was hit and fatally wounded by seven bullets. A woman passer-by was also hit. Both were rushed to hospital. The gang seem to have split up, some running along Royal Avenue, the rest escaping down North Street. Craig called for retribution, later modifying this to a call for calm among the Protestant community while the police brought the guilty to retribution.

In June a Unionist MP, Sir Henry Wilson, was shot dead outside his home in London. He had been appointed military adviser to the Northern government and had recommended an uncompromising approach in dealing with the IRA. His part in the 'Curragh mutiny' in 1914 had stymied Asquith's plan to neutralise the Ulster insurrection. The killers, Reginald Dunne and Joseph O'Sullivan, both aged twenty-four, had been born and raised in London. Both had served in the war, and O'Sullivan had lost a leg. Both were members of the IRA and both were close to Collins, and it seems that this assassination had been ordered by Dublin rather than by the Northern IRA. Certainly Collins called them 'two of our own' and attempted to organise a rescue.

There was a momentous repercussion of the killing. Winston Churchill assumed that it had been carried out by the anti-Treaty elements of the IRA, in particular the group in possession of the Four Courts in Dublin under Rory O'Connor. He threatened that the British army would intervene if Collins did not do something about it. Collins was happy to oblige. He borrowed field artillery from the British army and attacked the IRA garrison, thereby setting off the Civil War, in which he himself would become the most famous casualty, while Republican preoccupation with the Civil War removed any real threat to the borders of Northern Ireland.

It is a characteristic of newspapers in a divided society that they waste valuable space castigating the 'other' community, which does not read these fine words, however, but reads in its own newspapers fine words that castigate the opposition. It is this lack of objectivity in newspapers, their refusal to make a Confiteor on behalf of their own people, that makes them so dangerous in a time of civil conflict. They become the voice of the people, rather than their conscience. Nationalist papers claimed that the troubles arose out of the shipyard expulsions; Unionist papers said they arose out of IRA killings, to which they were an understandable emotional response. Sir Ernest Clark, who had been appointed to investigate the expulsions, agreed with the Unionists. What they needed, he thought, was a Special Constabulary to reassure them. A confident unionist population would not be tempted to industrial expulsion.

Later, when it became obvious that the Craig-Collins pact of March 1922 was breaking down, and that politics was failing and communal violence was thriving, Sir Stephen Tallents was sent by the British government to investigate. He said it was impossible to deal with minor issues, such as sectarian murder, while major issues, such as the IRA and the Boundary Commission and the failure of the Northern Catholics to acknowledge the Craig regime, went unresolved. He felt that a judicial inquiry would only give propaganda value to things that were best forgotten. Clearly, neither distinguished gentleman had read the *Irish News* during his time in Belfast.

Two failures did not stop Lloyd George from trying, as he at least was aware that no links had been established with the Catholic minority in Northern Ireland. He encouraged Craig to establish links with the Catholic business community. This was hard to do, as few Catholics were prepared to stand up against the flow of Catholic opinion. The murder of Catholic businessmen did little to encourage them to change their minds.

Craig was under pressure from within his own party, and from the general Protestant population. His leadership was never threatened, however, and there is a suspicion that he used what threat there was in justifying his political inertia during these years. The reaction of the

Unionist Party to the violence of Northern Ireland's first years was the same as the RUC and Specials: partisan, reactive and piecemeal. When internment without trial under the Special Powers Act was introduced in May 1922, the first batch of internees was exclusively Catholic. The *Irish News* claimed that internment was equivalent to imposing martial law without having to hand over control of the situation to the army. The claims of the *Belfast Telegraph* that nationalists who opposed internment were guilty of double standards were answered by the fact that it was some time before the first few loyalist prisoners were interned.

It was internment that beat the IRA in 1922. Its very success at that time tempted successive governments to use it again and again as the century progressed. But internment put a lid on the problem: it did not solve it. Catholic boys who witnessed the killings of the 1920s were the influential backbone of Catholic Belfast when the same streets that had been attacked in 1920 were attacked again in 1969.

This has been the longest chapter in this book, because what happened over the three years discussed in it set the tone for Northern Ireland for the rest of the twentieth century. It is central to the history of Northern Ireland, and the actions of the shipyard workers are central to it. It is dangerous to attach motivation to others, especially men who lived so long ago; it is right that we should accept at face value the explanation that the expulsions were an emotional reaction to the killing of Catholics in the rest of Ireland. What we can say is that the expulsions brought violence into Belfast once more, on a scale that had not been seen in the worst of the nineteenth-century riots. It led to the growth of prejudices and barriers that are only now breaking down. Perhaps it even influenced the eventual fall of the shipyards themselves.

Chapter 10 ⌒

THE SLIDE INTO
DEPRESSION

Lord Pirrie had become a senator in the new Northern Ireland. His politics had changed from the heady days of the Home Rule Crisis. He was a Conservative now; he never had any sympathy with the Sinn Féin position, and he distrusted those Liberals who thought it was a government's duty to interfere in the management of industry or even to nationalise vital enterprises. He delighted in the theatre of public service, wearing whenever possible military uniform or court dress, made all the more impressive when he was made a viscount for his work during the war.

Although he undoubtedly retained an affection for Belfast, the fact that Harland and Wolff was now a transnational organisation, with facilities from the Clyde to the Solent, meant that London was a more suitable place for him to live, near the centre of things, with a status he never could have imagined in his youth. He was getting too old to live among the stresses of the first few years of the Craig government. Whatever his underlying feelings were about the Irish question, he was a pragmatic Unionist.

This is not to say that he shared the attitudes of his Protestant work force towards Catholics. He and his managers used the settlement to try to engineer the return of Catholics to the yard. The Harbour Police, which had jurisdiction in the shipyards, was strengthened by the Harbour Commissioners with a view to eliminating the sectarian violence that had soured the summer of 1920. With poor grace, and with several false starts, the trades consented to reinstate Catholics. Only the Joiners' Union held out. It was a year before all the exiles were allowed to return, and not all did. More than a hundred Catholic apprentices never completed their time at the yard.

Sceptics might say that the various managements had no motivation to work for an earlier return for Catholics, because a slump in orders meant that their absence did not interfere with production. Even in 1922 there were fewer jobs for them to return to. The Great War had changed more than the map of Europe. While British shipping firms had been embroiled in the conflict, such areas as the Pacific, the South China Sea and the Indian Ocean had been left open to the attentions of Japanese and American firms, which were glad of the business. By the time British enterprises had bought replacement ships they found their old monopolies in Asian waters gone. Too late they realised how rash they had been in buying new ships in such a hurry, and at prices that had been inflated by war. In 1920 there had been a widespread collapse in freight rates that made most owners examine their commitments carefully. For most British shipping lines it would be a while before they bought any more ships. In many cases, contracts were cancelled for ships that were already on the slips, or builders were told to delay the completion date.

Harland and Wolff, with its investment in so many shipyards, stood to lose more than most. But in spite of the difficulties, and in spite of the civil strife that seemed to be pulling Belfast apart, ships continued to be delivered from Queen's Island. Among these was the *Arundel Castle,* the last of the four-funnelled liners to be built in Belfast. Another project that harked back to the glory days before the war was the completion of the German liners *Columbus* and *Bismarck,* which had been seized as war reparations by the Ministry of Shipping. Unfortunately, these were being built in Danzig (Gdańsk) and may have caused more difficulties than they were worth.

Workman Clark seemed to be in a much stronger position than its neighbours on Queen's Island. Its parent company, Northumberland Shipping, took out a loan in Workman Clark's name. It was supposed to be used to develop the yard, but Northumberland Shipping used it to pay its own debts. In 1927 its directors were prosecuted for issuing a false prospectus, and in January 1928 Workman Clark itself was declared bankrupt. A fresh start following a management buy-out was frustrated by the Wall Street Crash. The final straw came when, in 1931, the liner *Bermuda,* in the yard for repair, caught fire. Workman Clark was forced to buy the ship from its owners to avoid expensive litigation. There were no orders for new ships coming in, and although it struggled on for a few more years the end came in 1935. British Shipbuilders Ltd existed to reduce the number of slips in the United Kingdom, with a view to getting rid of spare capacity. It bought Workman Clark's yard and closed it down.

Meanwhile the government in London was concerned about the danger of recession. The last major war Britain had fought was the Napoleonic War, and that had been followed by a long depression. To try to prevent the same thing happening again, Lloyd George introduced a range of measures that would bring life back to the economy and reduce unemployment, particularly in the important areas of engineering and shipbuilding. The most important of these were the Trade Facilities and Loans Guarantee Act (1922) and, in Northern Ireland, the Loans Guarantee Act (Northern Ireland) (1922). These guaranteed that any loan approved by the government

THE SLIDE INTO DEPRESSION

would be paid back by the government if the borrower defaulted. It meant that the clearing banks were prepared to advance money to those schemes that the government identified as priorities. As the Northern Ireland scheme was administered by the Northern Ireland government, Pirrie could look forward to generous treatment from that quarter. After all, two of his relatives sat in the Northern Ireland cabinet.

Even with loans, Pirrie insisted that capital work should be strictly controlled, and that only expenditure under the guarantee scheme should continue. He closed two of the yards on the Clyde as well as the South Yard at Belfast, where he dismissed the work force. His financial strategy had always been dependent on low profits but a fast turnover. In 1922 only seventeen ships had been delivered by all the yards the firm owned. At his company's annual general meeting Pirrie admitted the difficulty and claimed a profit of more than £300,000. He may not have been lying, but he was being creative in his accountancy. He had ignored depreciation of £266,000 and had put capital expenditure of £369,129 in the following year's books.

In modern parlance, Pirrie would be known as a control freak. His main concern at the end of 1922 seems to have been that the poor order book would weaken his authority over his widespread empire. Edward Wilding, the managing director responsible for ship design, was ordered to remain in Belfast. Pirrie visited potential customers, accompanied by one of Wilding's assistants. He visited each yard regularly and was assiduous in his inspections, checking such details as whether there were expansion joints on water pipes. Everywhere he went, three despatch boxes went with him. One was for charities that his wife supported, one for business of the Northern Ireland Senate, while the third, unmarked, was for Harland and Wolff business. His personal approach to customers paid off that December when he obtained contracts from four sources: Nippon Yusen Kaisha in Japan, P&O, Elder Dempster and Andrew Weir and Company.

In a change from Pirrie's usual arrangements, all these were at a fixed price, rather than on commission. This caused problems for the managing directors. Although there were very sophisticated procedures for recording the costs of building a ship, there was no system that allowed them to predict costs with any accuracy.

Pirrie's main problem was finding work for Belfast. Overheads on the Lagan were much higher than on the Clyde. This was brought into sharp focus in 1923, when the bill for converting the *Belgic* from a troopship to a liner was presented to the International Navigation Company. This had been a cost-plus-commission contract. The company challenged the bill, on the grounds that the sum involved had not been put to it for its approval. Pirrie blamed his managing directors for this, claiming that they did not keep control of the work force and did not put enough effort into estimating costs or completion dates. He even blamed the chief accountant for not completing the final accounts quickly enough.

It has not been recorded whether Pirrie played poker. If he did, he held his cards very close to his chest. After he moved to London he kept strict personal control of the firm's accounts and contracts. He drew rough drawings of each vessel, which were then sent to the drawing office, where they were completed. Until the vessel was under construction the managing director in charge of design was forbidden to contact the owners directly: it had to be done through Pirrie.

After the war Pirrie centralised the drawing office in Belfast. The managing directors of other yards complained that this system was slow and inefficient and that it held up production. Wilding, in charge at the Belfast design office, thought that his increased authority gave him the right to directly consult the owners. This led to his downfall. While working on the order from Andrew Weir he agreed to extras that the owners requested. He assumed he was working on a standard contract of cost plus commission: he had not been told that Pirrie had accepted a fixed price that just about covered the cost of building the ships. With the extras Wilding had agreed, each ship would be built at a loss.

When Pirrie found out what had happened he sent for Wilding and berated him. The unfortunate managing director was removed from his post and was suspended for twelve months. He was refused permission to return to the Queen's Island works, and Pirrie gave orders that his desk was to be forced open. Luckily for Wilding, he must have had some premonition that he would be sacked and had cleared out his papers before going to London to meet Pirrie. Nevertheless, Pirrie made sure that his control over design was even tighter than before, and meetings with his managing directors were more dictatorial than ever. At such a meeting in February he spoke confidently but vaguely of a programme of new building, though he did not mention where the orders were coming from. He announced that these orders would be completed by March.

They were not; not even by 21 March, when Pirrie and his wife left on a visit to South America. On the eve of his departure he signed his will. He had been unwell all winter, and prostate cancer, which had been in remission since 1911, had flared up again. On the voyage he was accompanied by his private secretary and his personal doctor. The sea travel seemed to perk him up, and after completing his business in Buenos Aires he decided to return the long way home, sailing round Cape Horn, calling at Valparaíso and Antofagasta before going on to Panama. On one of his trips ashore he caught a chill, but he was convalescing by the time his ship entered the Panama Canal. Autocratic to the last, he ignored his doctor's strictures and was brought on deck. He suffered a relapse and died on 7 June on board ship.

Pirrie had kept his cards close to the end, and now he had taken them to the grave. No-one knew how serious the situation was for Harland and Wolff. When the firm had been hungry before, Pirrie had always managed to pull a rabbit out of the hat. There were hungry times ahead, and there seemed to be nobody capable of taking on Pirrie's role.

It was not only the problems of the shipyards that were causing problems in Belfast. When the fighting stopped in 1922, 23 per cent of the working population of the city were unemployed, and that figure was to remain steady throughout the twenties. The trouble resulted from the fact that there was a world surplus in the products that Belfast was trying to sell. The government in London was set against tariff protection other than for the motor and chemical industries. As a result, the country was flooded with cheap goods. There was a slight recovery in the linen industry in 1923 and 24, but the decision to return the British pound to the gold standard, made by Winston Churchill in 1925, nipped this in the bud. The pound was overvalued by about 10 per cent, and the fact that British products were overpriced abroad meant that Belfast lost its export market. To make matters worse, world linen prices fell to 40 per cent of their pre-war value. In one year, unemployment in the linen industry rose from 9½ to 32 per cent. No new industries, on which the worldwide boom of the late 1920s was founded, came to Belfast. Industrialists were hesitant to invest in an area where political loyalties were so extreme and civil violence so near the surface. The city was the centre of the most deprived industrial area in the United Kingdom.

The most important meeting of the week for one in five of Belfast's working men and women was when they came to sign on at the unemployment bureau, known without any degree of affection as the b'roo. Always alert for malingerers, the authorities would stop the allowance of anyone not 'genuinely seeking work.' Every six weeks the applicant had to provide evidence that they were trying to get a job. To do this they had to do the rounds of offices, shops, factories, warehouses and building sites asking for notes to confirm that they had applied for work but that there were no vacancies. They were at the mercy not only of the officials in the b'roo but of busy people who had to take time off to write these certificates.

In the Northern Ireland Parliament, meanwhile, moves went ahead to consolidate Unionist control. The first step was to minimise the opposition by abolishing proportional representation. Even the Unionist MP for East Belfast, Thompson Donald, feared that it was a dangerous move, and there were those in London who thought it contravened the Government of Ireland Act. These were difficult times for Lloyd George's coalition, however, and the measure was allowed to go through in September. The move killed political life in Belfast more effectively even than elaborate gerrymandering did in Derry. In Belfast the Labour Party was almost wiped out, and the corporation (city council) was a straight division between Unionists and Nationalists. The Unionists in Belfast Corporation, most of them businessmen or professionals, developed into a self-sufficient elite, despised by many working-class Protestants as 'the fur coat brigade'.

There were some improvements for the ordinary Belfast citizen. A new electricity generating station was built near the harbour and supplied not only the city but Lisburn, Holywood and Bangor. Electricity and gas prices were low, yet the Gas Department made enough profit to subsidise the rates. There were other public works, in particular in reconstructing roads. All the main thoroughfares in the city were widened and resurfaced, and three miles of roadway were built along the lower Lagan. On the other hand, public health and public housing were neglected, and social services were non-existent.

One public service that was taken up with enthusiasm was education. Although education was supposed to be compulsory, the *Northern Whig* reported that twelve thousand children in the city did not have a place at school. Lord Londonderry introduced an Education Bill in 1923 that trans-ferred the responsibility for schools to local authorities. The new curricu-lum would exclude religious instruction. The managers of Catholic schools, all of them priests, would not co-operate and so had no part in forming policy. The government would pay teachers' salaries, but only 50 per cent of cleaning, heating and lighting costs and nothing towards building costs in Catholic schools. In 1923 there were 16,324 Catholic children attending school, while there were places for only 14,725. The Christian Brothers' School, which was independent of the local Catholic hierarchy, accepted some government control in 1926 and got an extra £10,000 per year.

The Belfast Education Committee had to overcome ninety years of neglect. It began by carrying out a detailed census, which discovered that there were 59,370 children of school age in Belfast but that 64,064 children were actually attending school! When the figures were examined further it was found that 9,000 of those attending were above or below the statutory age for school. When the subtraction was done it was obvious that about 4,000 children were not at any school.

A survey of the 195 elementary schools found that only 6 were in a satisfactory condition, while another 12 had the potential to be made satisfactory. Of the remaining 177, it was felt that 40 constituted a hazard to the health and physical development of the pupils. It was obvious that new buildings had to be erected and the dilapidated schools closed down. Children below school age were allowed to remain, as most of their mothers worked (when jobs were available) in the mills. The first schools to be completed were Euston Street, off the Castlereagh Road, and Templemore Avenue, off the Newtownards Road, serving the east Belfast area, where many shipyard workers lived. Others followed in east Belfast, which was obviously seen as a priority area, while Fane Street School was built near the Donegall Road and Mountcollyer School near York Road. The rate of building was commendable; but only fifty of the old schools had been demolished, and most children were still in substandard accommodation.

The Education Committee had the responsibility for school medical services. It began by providing free school meals for the neediest children. The food was distributed from a kitchen in Tamar Street, not far from Queen's Island, with the help of Toc H (an ex-servicemen's association), the Society of St Vincent de Paul and the Shankill Road Mission.

Less money was invested in secondary and higher education. The corporation provided thirty scholarships for boys and another twenty for girls to attend the local grammar schools. It awarded five scholarships per year for university education.

House-building had virtually stood still during the war; there were other priorities. During those years, however, many people had migrated to the city from rural areas in search of work, and the housing stock was once again becoming overcrowded. The corporation did not want to get involved but was forced to by an act of the British Parliament, passed in 1919, that required that the corporation draw up schemes to provide adequate housing for the working class. Even then the reaction of the corporation's Housing Committee was modest, and a total of sixteen houses, of various types, were built.

The Northern Ireland Parliament set out to match the social reforms taking place in Britain. A measure by Neville Chamberlain to subsidise private builders did not cause a problem. In 1924, however, a Labour government under Ramsay MacDonald came to power in London. His Minister of Housing introduced a Housing Act that required local authorities to build houses for rent and that set a maximum rent that could be charged.

The fur coat brigade were horrified. The majority of corporation members seem to have seen it as their task in public life to keep the rates as low as possible. This would be impossible under the 'socialist' provisions of the Housing Act, and the corporation used its considerable influence in the Northern Ireland Parliament to make sure it did not adopt the measure. Instead, private developers would be given a subsidy for building the houses. Houses had received a subsidy of £60 under the Chamberlain provisions; this went up to £100 in 1927, fell to £25 in 1932 and was withdrawn altogether in 1937.

Perhaps it is just as well that the Housing Committee did not begin building on its own account. It delayed putting contracts out to tender until complaints were made by the Ministry of Local Government. It accepted inferior timber, and it overpaid £5,171 for building materials on a site on the Whiterock Road. As early as 1926 a report to the government on the committee described a list of irregularities: accounts were not checked; inferior materials had been accepted; contracts had not been put out to tender. Most damning of all, the City Solicitor and several members of the committee had financial interests in the land that had been chosen for development in deals in which the suitability of land for working-class housing came second in importance to who was selling it. Almost nobody would co-operate with the inquiry, and when it became apparent that only 66,000 bricks out of a delivery of a million could be accounted for, it was obvious why.

Somehow, in spite of the mixture of corruption and fatalism, many houses were built in this first decade of the new regime, almost a thousand in total. A junior minister thought the new houses were perfect 'for families with three or four children, a clean and tidy wife and a husband who preferred to pat his children on the head and settle down to read the *Belfast Telegraph* rather than go out to the nearest public house.' The only problem was that they were very expensive for the working class: houses in Cherryvalley at up to 22 shillings per week were out of the question for a man who might be earning only 30 shillings. The Housing Committee refused to subsidise the rents, so these houses were never occupied by the people for whom they were planned.

The continuing lack of decent houses meant that Belfast kept its unenviable position of having the worst death rate in Ireland or Britain. Even after the 'artisan' houses had been built, in the early 1930s, infant mortality in Belfast was 97 in 1,000, compared with 77 in 1,000 in Northern Ireland as a whole. The proportion of mothers dying in childbirth actually increased between the First and Second World Wars, while Belfast had the worst rate of tuberculosis in Britain or Ireland. A report in 1927 made 153 recommendations, but a Northern Ireland government struggling to find the money to pay unemployment benefit was in no position to take up all the suggestions. Belfast at least had a Public Health Department, although it lacked specialist staff. Its remit included the inspection of food, milk, the abattoir and ships coming into port. The policy of its Medical Officer of Health was that 'people should keep a grip of themselves.'

Pressure for change came from the Education Committee's school medical service. Its head, Dr Fulton, tried to raise public concern about the fact that there were a thousand tubercular children on his books. He wanted compulsory medical inspections, because teachers were too lethargic to care. A great many children were suffering from malnutrition or anaemia. Chronic absenteeism meant that up to a fifth of children never received medical or dental treatment.

One advantage Belfast did have was the number of good hospitals it contained. Their quality was helped by a close association with Queen's

University Medical School. Expansion took place in the Royal Victoria Hospital in 1924. The Royal Maternity Hospital, with 100 beds, was opened in 1933, with the Royal Belfast Hospital for Sick Children opening shortly afterwards. In 1927 the Workhouse Asylum was demolished and its patients transferred to the green fields of Purdysburn. Another maternity hospital, the Jubilee, was opened in 1935, and the Dufferin and Ava Hospitals could accommodate 332 patients.

But Belfast was swimming in a sea of infection. The lough was polluted by raw sewage from Carrickfergus and Holywood. Outside Belfast, tuberculosis was not a notifiable disease. Diseased animals were regularly brought to the abattoir from the surrounding countryside.

One thing that Belfast had in abundance was clean, clear water from the Mourne Mountains. When it became obvious that worries about Mourne being granted to the Free State were unfounded, the dam in the Silent Valley was completed and doubled the daily supply of water to the city.

If the experience in Belfast was like the curate's egg, good in parts, the experience of Harland and Wolff had a serious shortage of good parts. Pirrie's death had left confusion, even to the extent that no-one knew the identity of the man he had nominated as his successor. This was the tall and stout Lord Kylsant, head of the Royal Mail Group, which by now had a controlling interest in Harland and Wolff. He had been the nearest thing Pirrie had to a close confidant, and the only person allowed to go into Pirrie's office unannounced. Lady Pirrie detested him, and she fought a rearguard action against his appointment as chairman. Pirrie's will was long and complex, but when his estate was examined it became apparent that it was almost bankrupt. Kylsant approached the boards of a number of companies and persuaded them to make annual subscriptions to a fund that would allow Lady Pirrie to continue her accustomed life-style as long as she lived.

The state of Harland and Wolff was less amenable to a quick fix. Kylsant soon realised that his affable friend had been an affable rogue who had lied regularly to the shareholders' annual meeting when he had been making his financial report. There were loans that had to be repaid, and an examination of the private ledger showed that all the ships for which the contract had been based on a fixed price were actually costing the firm money. One twelve-ship contract would lose £750,000. The management structure was as bad as the financial situation. Pirrie's autocratic rule had reduced the managing directors to ciphers. Only two of them had executive experience. Kylsant restructured the management system and brought some new blood into the firm; but even with this there was no room for manoeuvre. There had to be a tight grip on expenditure, and this would be reviewed regularly. Even the most recent contracts were costing money. One ship that did bring in a profit was the 9,000-ton liner *Apapa*, which was financed under the Loans Guarantee Act.

It wasn't only in Belfast that contracts were costing the firm money. A contract with P&O for ships being built on the Clyde would lose £311,256. An investigation in January 1925 showed that part of the problem was Pirrie's insistence on the highest standards. Ships were being constructed to a higher standard than the owners needed, or even wanted. This was particularly true in Belfast, where pre-war experience with Atlantic liners had made high overheads an accepted fact of life.

Kylsant resisted the temptation to close the Queen's Island yard, and it was decided that there should be a reduction in wages and a cut-back in the amount of stock held. When it came to keeping the shareholders happy, Kylsant proved himself as able as Pirrie. In the published balance sheet he mentioned that reserves had been used but managed to imply that they were insignificant. He also made reference to an interim dividend, while omitting to say that there would be no final dividend that year.

The satisfactory reaction to the general meeting gave Kylsant time to address the real problems. He began by streamlining the management systems. James Gray, who took control of the three ship-repairing establishments, quickly realised that too much clerical time was taken up in giving extremely detailed accounts of each job. The practice had been introduced to earn the trust of the commission club, to show that they were not being overcharged for their ships. Simpler procedures would do. He felt the commission system itself led to bad practice, and he encouraged yards within the firm to compare costings with one another and with rivals.

When it became obvious that costs at Harland and Wolff were much greater than at competing yards, they knew that the problem of overheads would have to be tackled even more rigorously. Kylsant and John Craig, one of his closest confidants, found that those of their colleagues who had learnt their trade in the days of the great liners provided considerable opposition.

For the rest of the year, increasing repair work helped to maintain the balance sheet, and the loss-making contracts were gradually completed. There was brief optimism in mid-year when White Star ordered a 60,000-ton liner; gloom returned when it became apparent that the International Mercantile Marine group, which owned White Star, could not raise the money. The year ended with another flurry of optimism when several small ships were ordered. There was even a profit of £569,655, although overdrafts amounted to more than £2 million.

Freight rates improved slightly in 1926, enough for some owners to consider investing in new ships. The Northern Ireland government guaranteed loans for the construction of nine medium-sized motor ships, which kept the work force going as the Andrew Weir contract was completed. Kylsant and Craig were still vigilant in the matter of costs. One area that held out against the improvements was the engine shed. Frederick

Rebbeck was in command here. He used the excuse of having to develop a new generation of large diesel engines to maintain a hugely expensive research and development section within his department. Strictures towards economy were ignored.

Yet, as it turned out, 1926 was a year that needed great economies. A lock-out of miners in Britain on 3 May precipitated a short-lived general strike. Although most businesses were soon back to normal working, the miners remained on strike right into the winter. Supplies of steel, coal and coke almost dried up, and it was possible to complete only four ships in the second half of the year. By the autumn, two-fifths of the work force were laid off; fourteen thousand men were paid off in a period of six months. An economy committee under Craig produced cost-cutting targets for each department. The obvious solution of closing one or more of the plants was fiercely opposed by the managing directors, as it would mean one or more of them losing his private kingdom.

On the positive side, ship-owners were still confident enough to continue ordering ships; Harland and Wolff received orders for thirty-six vessels during the year, though all of them were small. On the negative side, the IMM group cancelled its contract with Harland and Wolff for both shipbuilding and repairing. The yards at Liverpool and Southampton had been established for the convenience of the IMM's White Star Line. Worse, the ship-repairing contract had been a steady source of income in hard times. Kylsant decided to buy White Star's parent company, Oceanic Steam Navigation Company, and incorporate White Star in his Royal Mail Group. It cost him £7 million.

The first reward from Kylsant's initiative came in early 1927, when White Star ordered a 27,000-ton liner, to be built in Belfast. Four smaller liners of 14,000 tons were ordered by a subsidiary of the Royal Mail Group, three of which were also to be built on Queen's Island. This was followed by an order from the Union Castle Line for the *Winchester Castle*, a 20,000-ton motor liner. The financial help of the Northern Ireland government was making it very attractive to build in Belfast, and several other smaller ships were ordered. It was the big orders that made money, however, and these were slow in coming. Although most of the men laid off the previous year had been taken on again, there was a nervousness about the prospects.

Kylsant and Craig decided that they were getting nowhere in their battle to cut overheads, so they turned instead to construction methods to see if any slack could be found. Pirrie's insistence on perfection had set standards that were uneconomically high. They found ways of doing things more cheaply while still to a satisfactory standard. One economy was to replace highly paid fitters drilling holes with less-well-paid machine drillers. They also looked at finding a reliable and less cumbersome procedure for making estimates. When they couldn't get agreement, a new system was imposed by the chief accountant. Another economy was to look at what plant was actually required by the firm. Scotstoun, which had been seen as an alternative site if the civil unrest of 1920–22 had disrupted Queen's Island's production, was put under a care-and-maintenance regime. The assets of some plants were transferred to Belfast, while others were simply sold.

The *Laurentic* was delivered to White Star in November. A beautiful ship, it was fitted out to a standard of luxury that recalled the *Olympic* and its sister-ships. The trouble was that, like nearly all the ships delivered that year, it lost the firm money. This was true whichever yard they were built in. The causes were, as usual, faulty estimates and poor cost control. Even three years after Pirrie's death the managing directors were failing at the most basic function of any business: making a profit. Without including depreciation, the year's losses amounted to £154,152. Kylsant and Craig decided to try to bypass the directors by setting up an independent estimating department. In the hope that they might eventually listen, Kylsant himself ordered the directors to be even more vigilant about holding down costs. His immediate worry was finding the cash to repay the first of the Trade Facilities loans; £300,000 was due on 17 May. Kylsant had to instruct the shipping lines within the Royal Mail Group to advance the money to Harland and Wolff against work in progress. Indeed it was the Royal Mail Group that kept Harland and Wolff going that year, with several orders for medium to large liners, including a new 60,000-ton *Oceanic*. In an effort to control losses, these ships, all but two of which were to be built in Belfast, were built on commission.

The year had been a poor one, although there seemed to be good prospects on the horizon. Unfortunately, Kylsant's preoccupation with financial problems and Craig's with a crisis that the Scottish steel industry was going through meant that the priority of their campaign to control costs had to be downgraded. The other managing directors lost interest, and much that had been gained was lost. To make matters worse, Winston Churchill, now Chancellor of the Exchequer, cancelled the Trade Facilities provisions on which first Pirrie and then Kylsant had relied so heavily. Luckily, the Northern Ireland government was allowed to continue its version of the measure—otherwise the company might not have survived.

As it was, Kylsant had to request the Treasury to reschedule the loan repayments. When this was rejected, Kylsant borrowed £100,000 from the Midland Bank and paid back only this amount rather than the £298,669 that was due. The Midland Bank was now entitled to claim its money from the Treasury under the guarantee, but it did not force the issue. The Treasury was advised to press the company to pay the outstanding amount. By this time there was a Labour Chancellor, who wrote to the company demanding the money and threatening legal action. He got no reply. Further threats and a series of meetings followed. Craig offered on behalf of the company to pay £100,000 at the end of October and the rest in January the next year, 1930. This seems to have been an aspiration rather than a promise, because there was no indication of where the money was coming from. In the middle of all the coming and going, joiners and polishers had struck in Belfast. Running out of time, the management had to accede to the demands of these trades.

Things had become so bleak that it began to look as if the money leaking from Harland and Wolff would sink the entire Royal Mail Group. Kylsant was forced to request that the group's loan repayments also be postponed. When this request was denied, Harland and Wolff could not even pay the £100,000 due in October. A complete appraisal of the group's finances was ordered. It would be conducted by Sir William McLintock, and it would be the first time since Harland and Wolff was set up, seventy-five years before, that an outsider would get a glimpse of the company's accounts. The investigation continued into 1930. Kylsant was becoming desperate, because his control of the Royal Mail Group was under threat.

McLintock reported in March 1930. His figures showed that the Royal Mail Group's liabilities were £30 million—a staggering amount at that time. It was recommended that, for the rest of the group to survive, Harland and Wolff had to be got rid of. There had been four errors of judgement that had reduced the firm to its present position. The expansion after the war had meant that money was tied up in a way that did not produce any return on investment. The steel firm of David Colville and Sons had been bought at a time when share prices were high, and it too had shown no return on investment. The losses of £750,000 on the Bank Line contract were too high to be absorbed. Paying dividends to shareholders out of reserves that did not exist meant that the firm's overdrafts had reached unsustainable levels.

In desperation, Kylsant told the Northern Ireland government that he would close down Harland and Wolff unless the loans were extended. Although several officials felt that he was bluffing, the Ministry of Finance could not afford to take the chance. Here Walter Runciman, a distinguished ship-owner and financier who had been president of the Board of Trade during the war, came into the picture. He had been asked by Kylsant to become deputy chairman of Royal Mail Group, but the negotiations had come to nothing. He now came up with a plan under which he would accept the deputy chairmanship if certain conditions were met. Although Kylsant was forced to accept the breadth of the reforms, he was reluctant to sign on the dotted line, as he knew it would lead inevitably to his removal from office. It was not until he was tricked into attending a meeting at which all the most important financial figures had been invited that he was forced to face reality. Finding himself in a minority of one, he capitulated.

The rescue package still required a lot of work, most of it done by McLintock. On 19 June the Harland and Wolff board met and transferred voting control to the triumvirate of McLintock, the accountant, Brigadier Arthur Maxwell, the banker, and Runciman, the ship-owner. It was probably no comfort to Kylsant as he walked away from six years of struggle to keep the firm in business that Workman Clark was also in financial trouble, and was very nearly insolvent. The directors of Harland and Wolff preferred to look at the beautiful new ship *Britannic* as it sailed for Southampton on 21 June. Perhaps it was symbolising a new beginning.

For the ordinary people on the streets of Belfast the struggle for existence by the shipyards was paralleled by their own struggle to survive from day to day. In 1926 thirty thousand people in Belfast were unemployed, half the total unemployed for Northern Ireland, walking aimlessly within the city's boundaries. Frustration was bound to fester. On 14 June William Patterson addressed a meeting of the Unemployed Workers' Organisation. He wanted the unemployed to occupy the workhouse for a day, to make the Poor Law Guardians listen to their demands. Such sedition was not to be tolerated, and the RUC baton-charged the crowd and arrested Patterson, who was sentenced the following day to six months' imprisonment. On 15 June there was indeed a march to the workhouse on the Lisburn Road. Two Labour MPs, Jack Beattie and William McMullen, who were also members of the Board of Guardians, were allowed to attend the meeting that was taking place inside. When the chairman ruled that discussion of outdoor relief was out of order, the two protested and disrupted the meeting. They were ejected by the police.

As the months and years of unemployment passed, unemployment benefit began to run out for more and more people. This meant that the Poor Law was the only thing that stood between desperate people and starvation. The Board of Guardians were mostly property-owners from different wards in the city. Often they had political ambitions and were keen to toe the party line. The rates, said the fur coat brigade, had to be kept low. Relief would be given only to those paupers who found refuge within the workhouse. Benefits for others outside the workhouse, known as outdoor relief, was stubbornly resisted. The same excuse was used as in famine times: it was open to abuse. The real reason is more likely to be a possible rise in the rates. Outdoor relief had been granted for a short while after the founding of the state, and the hoops through which an applicant had to go meant that only the most shameless would have made a dishonest application. Nothing would be given till all savings had been exhausted. Relieving officers were allowed to ask personal questions and to examine houses to ensure that any 'luxuries', such as a fancy clock, had been sold to raise money. Successful applicants were given chits to be redeemed at named shops—often owned by cronies of the Poor Law Guardians. No money or help was given for clothing, coal or rent. The names of successful applicants were posted on gable walls, ensuring their public humiliation.

Even this demeaning practice was considered too generous by the Guardians, who curtailed it as soon as they reasonably could. Back-bench MPs thundered against the actions of the Guardians, but the government refused to act against the wishes of Belfast Corporation, even though they were getting frustrated themselves and were worried about alienating their own supporters. It is as if the Guardians lived in a sealed building, with no knowledge of the unemployment that was destroying so many lives in the city. Comments by their chairman show the depth of prejudice in their world view.

It is [our] duty, when faced with such sloth, fecklessness and iniquity to discourage idleness . . . I know betting shops . . . which do a roaring trade among the poor. These people would make an effort to find work if they could not get relief.

The Board of Guardians was congratulated by four Protestant clergymen who, in November 1929, supported their stand against 'the wastrel class' and called on them to stop giving grants to 'parasites'.

Up to two hundred charities were involved in distributing the relief that was not forthcoming from the Poor Law Guardians. The most energetic of these was the Society of St Vincent de Paul, which spent an average of £12,150 a year until 1932 and in 1928 helped eleven times as many people as did the Board of Guardians. Free meals were served to the destitute, second-hand clothing was distributed; a factory was even set up to produce disinfectants and bundles of wood to be sold cheaply to the poor.

Although Northern Ireland did not follow Britain in abolishing the Boards of Guardians in 1928, by this time even the corporation was losing patience, as the niggardliness of the relief was alienating even Unionist voters. A law was passed to force them to extend provision for outdoor relief; but even then they dragged their heels. Applicants had to work for chits, as they were still not trusted with cash, but were glad to do so. Most were employed in street improvements. Some of the men had lived on such poor rations for so long that they were scarcely able to carry out the manual work involved.

In October 1929 the stock market crashed, and more and more of the world joined Belfast in misery. By 1931 even England was caught up, and the Bank of England was forced to close its doors. World trade contracted and foreign governments raised import controls, resulting in disaster for a city like Belfast, which was so dependent on exports. Countries that exported raw materials and food were among the hardest hit. These included the United States, Argentina, Canada and Australia, the principal markets for Belfast linen. Linen became a luxury that was abandoned in favour of the cheaper cotton. The linen industry almost collapsed in 1930, and many of the smaller firms went to the wall. The numbers of unemployed rose relentlessly. By 1932 there were 45,000 officially unemployed in Belfast—a number larger than the population of any other town or city in Northern Ireland except Derry. The real figure was much more than this, as the official statistics did not include those who had exhausted their dole.

In 1931 a new 'National Government' (a coalition of the Conservative Party, the Liberal Party and a breakaway group from the Labour Party) was formed in London. One of its first actions was to take the British pound off the gold standard. The value of the pound fell, which made it cheaper for other countries to buy British products. There was a slight recovery in the linen business, but not enough to balance the continuing growth in male unemployment. An indication of how desperate things had become can be seen in the case of a man who broke the windows of a department store. He stole nothing but waited for the police to arrive; in court he gave as his reason that prison was the only place where he could hope to get food and shelter.

The members of the Northern Ireland Parliament had something to look forward to when the summer recess of 1932 was over. After a last meeting in Belfast City Hall, scheduled for 30 September, they were to move to the new Parliament Buildings at Stormont. The plight of the unemployed had not been sufficient for them to curtail their four-month summer holiday, and when Craig rose to speak he was proposing a motion of thanks to the Mayor and Corporation for the use of their facilities. This was too much for the member for Pottinger, Jack Beattie—the same Jack Beattie who had been evicted from the meeting of the Board of Guardians. He had tabled a motion about unemployment, which had been refused. He now grabbed the mace and shouted Craig down. Tommy Henderson, Independent Unionist member for Shankill, joined in, pouring invective over the front benches. Beattie threw the mace on the floor, demanding, 'What about the 78,000 who are starving?'

The demand for outdoor relief seemed relentless. That January 884 people were claiming it for themselves and 3,124 dependants. Large families received 24 shillings per week; a family with two children got 16 shillings, while a married couple got 8 shillings. A single man got 3 shillings and 6 pence, while a single woman got nothing.

The Belfast Presbytery—in contrast to the four clergymen mentioned earlier—were concerned about the conditions of the unemployed and campaigned for an increase in the amounts paid to those on outdoor relief. It was pointed out that Belfast rates were only slightly over half the average that was paid in seventeen large towns in Britain, while the poor rate was greatly lower.

Conditions were so bad that they brought Protestant and Catholic together in common protest. On 3 October the Belfast Trades Council organised a strike among those workers who were on outdoor relief. Six hundred men downed tools, demanding increased payments. That Monday evening a march of sixty thousand arrived at a torch-lit rally on the Custom House Steps. The band played 'Yes, we have no bananas.' Two days later there were clashes between the police and groups of Protestant and Catholic workers in different areas around the city. Another march was planned for 11 October, but the government used the Special Powers Act to ban it. Instead of the march there was a series of violent clashes between the unemployed and the police. Overnight at least one man was shot dead. When crowds on the Shankill Road heard that the police were staging a pitched battle with demonstrators on the Falls Road, they charged along Northumberland Street to relieve what they saw—for too brief a spell—as their comrades. The government imposed a curfew, but that did not prevent riots in the Newtownards Road or York Street. For a second night the rioting continued. Another man was shot dead, and a list of the wounded was published in the papers. Faced by a coalition of those with nothing to lose, the government summoned the Poor Law Guardians to Stormont and ordered them to increase relief. The announcement was made on Friday 14 October. One of the few examples of working-class solidarity the city had ever seen had produced a positive result.

It is important to remember that when one person in three was unemployed, the corollary was that two out of every three were working. It depended on what industry you worked for. The Sirocco Works continued to supply 7 per cent of the world's machinery for preparing tea. Gallaher's actually increased its exports of cigarettes. The ropeworks still employed four thousand people. The Belfast mills were kept busy with imports of wheat, while the Ormeau Bakery still produced the bread that was the staple diet of the urban working man.

Another point worth considering is that, even at its lowest ebb, linen employed more workers than any other industry in Belfast. The York Street Flax Spinning Company employed five thousand people. Wages remained low in the mills, as it was largely a female work force, and working conditions were poor right up to the 1960s. Memoirs of the mills, however, make much of the camaraderie and of the fact that you were at least earning money. Basics cost less than they had before the depression, and if you could manage to save a little there was entertainment to be had. Cinemas were so desperate for custom that two jam-pots would get you a ticket. (This practice remained in smaller cinemas till the early 1950s. The author remembers gaining admission to a cinema in Derry with two jam-pots that had been begged from a generous aunt.) In the early years of silent films, someone who could not read might have to pay for a literate friend to come along, to make sure they missed nothing of the 'dialogue'. A ticket for the Orpheus dances was a straight cash deal: one shilling and six pence. Live theatre also required cash but managed to struggle along. One new playwright was Tom Carnduff, who had worked at Workman Clark before the depression. His plays, which might lack something in technique, were nevertheless powerful examinations of the workers' dilemma.

There were many creative artists in Belfast, but few of those struggling to make ends meet had time, energy or money to investigate their works. Yet William Conor painted the life with a warm affection, and even Louis MacNeice, in his hard, chiselled verse, seemed to have sympathy for those for whom time was

Hardening the faces, veneering with a grey and speckled rime
The faces under the shawls and caps.

There were free spectacles as well. The popular Prince of Wales came to open Stormont. He had a face, according to the writer St John Ervine, unsmiling and glum, and appeared sulky. It is reported that he played a Lambeg drum in Hillsborough later and enjoyed it thoroughly.

Stormont Building itself, however, was an uncomfortable symbol for Belfast's Catholics. On a hill that seemed to overlook all of Belfast, the massive building stood four-square like a Scots-Irish Fort Knox, hoarding within it the state's gold-reserve of Protestant and Unionist power. (There were Catholics who took a smug pleasure when, during the Second World War, the building was covered in manure to make it less obvious to German bombers.) The battle lines had been drawn long before, and although there were occasional truces, such as during the outdoor relief riots, or when Joe Devlin died and the Ulster Unionist Association stood in silent tribute, the foundations were never removed; the barriers could go up at a moment's notice.

Devlin's successor as leader of the Nationalist Party was T. J. Campbell, who was not inclined to compromise with the Unionists. The Catholic hierarchy became more intransigent as well, with Cardinal MacRory declaring that the Protestant Church in Ireland was not even part of the Church of Christ. Craig, now Lord Craigavon, responded in kind. 'Stormont', he affirmed, 'is a Protestant parliament for a Protestant people.' Amid such abrasive language it was only a matter of time before sectarian violence returned. In 1935 there were celebrations among the Protestants for the jubilee of King George V. Feelings ran high and a Catholic was shot dead in his shop in Great George's Street, off York Street. In the east of the city the building of a Catholic church in Willowfield sparked riots. These disturbances persisted throughout May and June, and the Ministry of Home Affairs, fearing serious problems on 12 July, decided to ban all marches from 18 June. The pragmatic Lord Craigavon was abroad as the 12th approached, and, under intense pressure from the Orange Order, it was Dawson Bates (who was so hard-line that he had tried to purge the RUC of its Catholic members) who had to face down the strong Orange challenge to the ban. He backed down without a qualm. Worried about the potential for trouble, the Church of Ireland Bishop of Down begged the Orangemen to

> forget the things that are behind. Forget the unhappy past. Forget the stories of the old feuds, the old animosities, the old triumphs, the old humiliations.

The day began well enough; but at the gathering in Belmont the Grand Master of the Orange Order, Sir Joseph Davison, replied to the bishop by restating the myth of Protestants being a victim people in Ireland and advising his audience that it was only by remembering past dangers that the 'people of Ulster' (i.e. Protestants) could avert those of the present.

Even the march back from the Field seemed to be passing peacefully, when some at the front noticed that the trams had stopped in York Street. Trouble had found the march. As the leading marchers reached Lancaster Street they broke ranks and swung into the small side street and began breaking windows. They were unprovoked, according to the *Irish News,* or had been fired upon, according to the *News Letter* and *Belfast Telegraph.* A detailed investigation by an impartial reporter, Henry Kennedy, found that the truth lay somewhere in between. A drunken Catholic was talking to a policeman when an Orange marcher left the parade and intervened by hitting the Catholic. The policeman wished to detain the marcher, when several of the latter's friends detached themselves and went to his help. A Catholic standing not far away presumed that this was a full-scale invasion of the isolated nationalist district and fired several shots from a revolver, killing a Protestant. The Orangemen, presuming that an unprovoked attack was being made on the parade, broke ranks and charged. They were soon supported by gunmen. Protestants caught in the narrow street made easy targets for a hail of stones that came over the tops of houses from the neighbouring streets.

The rioting spread, and what followed was described as the worst night of disorder since 1921–2. Ominously, people in the suburbs heard the steady fire of machine-guns.

The police were powerless, for all that they were armed, and were swept aside by sheer numbers. Armoured cars fired machine-guns and the police fired rifles and revolvers, but the rioters, like enraged pit bull terriers, were not to be turned. Fighting continued uninterrupted from Donegall Street to the middle of York Street for two hours. The military were called in and a curfew imposed, but not before two civilians had been killed, thirty-five wounded, fourteen houses set on fire and forty-seven other buildings wrecked. Three policemen were also wounded.

The following evening Protestants marched behind a band down Nelson Street, carrying a wreath for their dead colleague. After alleging that shots had been fired at them, they crossed York Street and invaded North Ann Street, Earl Street and North Thomas Street, smashing the windows of all the houses occupied by Catholics. Two more people were killed and more than fifty injured.

The city ran out of ambulances and had to requisition taxis to help out. All efforts by the police and military to stop the violence were in vain. After a week or so there were efforts by church leaders, city fathers, including the Lord Mayor, Sir Crawford McCullagh, and trade union leaders to restore peace. It was in vain, and trouble continued almost till the end of August. By then eight Protestants and five Catholics had been killed. The number of deaths might seem to indicate that the Catholics had prevailed, but that would be a false impression and helps to hide the gross imbalance in suffering. Almost all the wounded were Catholic; and 514 Catholic families, consisting of two thousand individuals, were driven out of their homes in the Dock area near York Street, while only a handful of Protestants had to move. There was a demand in the British House of Commons for a full investigation, but the Prime Minister, Stanley Baldwin, refused, on the grounds that such a course was not possible for constitutional reasons. Craigavon also refused to hold an inquiry, probably because it would have shown the foolishness of his colleague in allowing the 12th of July march to go ahead. He did say, however, that it was incumbent on politicians to take heed of what they said, as an ill-spoken word might bring about a return of violence. Even as anodyne a comment as this was too much for the Amalgamated Protestant Associations and Leagues of Ulster, which accused Craigavon of being 'step by step with Rome.'

The Catholic refugees went partly to centres in the Falls Road but also to the Ardoyne, where they squatted in houses nearing completion. They were accepted here by the largely Protestant population, but they did not become integrated. When the Troubles began again after the summer of 1969, many isolated families were once again forced from their homes.

In January 1938 Craigavon called a general election, at least partly to show de Valera, who was now in power in the South, the strength of unionist opinion in the North. In the event there was some division in Unionist ranks, with a Progressive Unionist Party entering the fray. Craigavon dismissed its members as 'wreckers'. In the non-unionist camp there were also divisions, reflecting the Labour support for the Spanish Republic, as opposed to the Nationalist Party's support for General Franco, whose rebellion was also supported by the Catholic Church. The day of the election saw violence on the streets once again, but within communities rather than among communities. The B Specials were on alert all day. When the results came out, Unionists were triumphant almost everywhere. Even in Dock the closely fought contest between Labour and Nationalist allowed a Unionist candidate to be elected.

The election brought joy for the Unionist Party, but the result brought little hope to the people of Belfast. In January unemployment in Northern Ireland had increased by 9,314. For a people who had suffered years of violence it is ironic that their road to economic recovery should be based on the build-up to another war, more terrible and more far-reaching than the one that had swallowed up the Ulster Division twenty years before.

When we last looked at Harland and Wolff it appeared that the company had been saved from the wolves by the intervention of the new committee of trustees in 1930. These well-meaning individuals soon found that they were in a worse position than Pirrie and Kylsant had been. The others had been autocratic figures, able to cow the managing directors by force of personality. Control by committee was not the same, and now the managing directors of the constituent parts of the company felt free to steer their individual firms as they saw fit. Frederick Rebbeck, for example, wanted to reassert the greatness of the Harland and Wolff shipbuilding yards. The trustees unwittingly encouraged this thinking by implying that the difficulties of the company would be eased if it was broken into manageable portions. They did not want these portions to become too ambitious, though, as the priority was still the control of costs and overheads. Their main trouble was finding chief executives with enough experience to direct large companies. Time was not on their side.

They decided to offer the post of chief executive to Rebbeck, hoping to be able to train him on the job in the niceties of controlling the business. Sure enough, by August, after the order book had been thoroughly investigated, a report showed that the group would be better off if it got rid of twelve of its forty-two shipbuilding berths.

Apparently out of nowhere there came a proposal from Workman Clark that the two firms should amalgamate. Although this offered an opportunity to rationalise the company, Rebbeck and the old hands in the management showed no enthusiasm for such a merger. In fact they were still reluctant to engage in the cost-cutting and changes in procedures that were essential to the survival of Harland and Wolff. Rebbeck could point to the fact that the yards were busier than at any time since the collapse of the post-war boom. This apparent prosperity, however, masked the fact that many of the ships were being built at a loss. Even though 1930 ended with a profit of £105,745, the next crisis was just around the corner.

Harland and Wolff was running out of cash. Whatever deals were made with banks or ship-owners, cash was needed to pay workers and to buy materials. In September 1930 overdrafts amounted to £2,163,692. Towards the end of October the firm needed £250,000 to pay wages and pay for materials, yet there was only £45,000 available in the bank. Freight rates had dropped once again, and nobody was ordering ships, so there was no prospect of advances on orders being able to fill the hole. Worse, some of the shipping lines that were part of the Royal Mail Group were withdrawing work from Harland and Wolff facilities and offering it to different contractors.

The only hope was the government of Northern Ireland. Politicians knew that the survival of Harland and Wolff was an essential element in the survival of the Northern Ireland state. They were keen to help where they could. In co-operation with the Treasury and the banks, they put a moratorium on loan repayments for a year. Even this seemed only a temporary stay of execution, and by mid-1931 the outlook for shipbuilding was as bad as it had ever been. Even before that the company had reached the limit of its new overdraft facilities, £2.3 million. Rebbeck published a brochure outlining the company's expertise beyond simply shipbuilding. In particular he was looking for contracts to build diesel locomotives for the railways, although this was financially risky and technically difficult. Some foremen and office workers took a cut in salary. Some of the yards on the Clyde were amalgamated, while others were 'sterilised'—closed permanently. By the end of the year, wages and salaries had been cut by £132,102 per year. All the office staff had had their hours and their salary cut. Most of the work force was on piecework, and the rates for this had also been cut. The total savings were about £200,000. The question was, would this be enough when only one order was placed with the company in the second half of the year? It turned out that even the Harland and Wolff pension scheme was invested in the company, without any security. The Northern Ireland government once more helped out with loan guarantees, and the moratorium on loan repayments was extended to the end of 1934.

It is an indication of how few orders were coming in that there was not a single launch at Queen's Island between December 1931 and May 1934. The Belfast yards were put on a care-and-maintenance routine, with only foremen and apprentices actually employed directly by the firm. The technical staff used the time to collaborate with the accountant's office and secretary's office in producing an improved system of cost control.

By the end of 1932 unemployment in shipbuilding and engineering for Belfast stood at 65 per cent. In late 1933 world trade built up, and on

Queen's Island work began again on two cargo liners that had been ordered the previous year. More work came in as the months passed, the most significant being an Admiralty order for a light cruiser, HMS *Penelope*, of which we shall hear more later. By mid-1934 twenty-four vessels were on order, and there were more orders for the engine department. Although the banks were not yet convinced of the validity of the costing system, work was allowed to proceed, and the company took on some ten thousand men in Belfast. Amazingly, after all that had gone before, the banks were proved right in their concerns about the costing system. Two ships built on Queen's Island were sold for £580,000 but cost £598,000 to build. Even this was exceeded by a ship built on the Clyde, which was sold at the contract price of £34,000 but cost £114,000 to construct.

The Midland Bank, the major creditor, demanded a thorough examination of the books. What was uncovered was an idiosyncratic method of bookkeeping, whereby standing costs such as rates, office overheads and staff costs were paid out of profits. There was once again the question of tenders that were too low. Rebbeck did not seem able to understand that a rival firm could put in a tender at the same level as Harland and Wolff and still make a profit, by keeping its overheads low. For a while it began to look as if making a loss on a contract would be a theoretical problem only, as for six months no new orders were placed.

Workman Clark was faring no better. It concentrated production in its North Yard, on the County Antrim shore, and after 1931 its South Yard on Queen's Island was dismantled. It was just about surviving on repair work. The staff was sacked in February 1935 and re-employed on a day-to-day basis. The firm was wound up in June 1935, when Harland and Wolff acquired Workman Clark's South Yard, which was renamed the Victoria Yard, in exchange for surrendering some interests on the Clyde.

The press wondered whether the new arrangement might be an indication that the company was thinking of going back to the airframe business. This speculation was prompted by a white paper issued in London that recommended the siting of new aircraft factories as far north-west of London as possible. Preliminary talks between Rebbeck and the Air Ministry agreed that large seaplanes would be the product of choice, and the ministry was impressed by the Harland and Wolff facilities. There was a howl of protest from the existing airframe manufacturers, and it looked as if nothing more would be heard of the scheme for the time being. Rebbeck, undaunted, went to London to discuss with existing manufacturers the possibility of setting up a jointly owned company. His offer was made all the more tempting when the Belfast Harbour Commissioners announced that they had obtained the authority to build an airport at Sydenham, adjoining the Musgrave Shipyard.

Short Brothers of Rochester found the offer tempting. The Harbour Commissioners offered 36 acres of vacant ground for the project. The Air Ministry said that orders would be placed with Short Brothers, which could subcontract the work to its Belfast subsidiary, which in turn could subcontract it to Harland and Wolff. The main condition was that Short Brothers would have a controlling interest in the new firm, and when this was registered, Short Brothers held 60 per cent of the shares. Orders came in for 50 Bristol Bombay aircraft and 150 Handley Page Hereford bombers, and work on the new factory began at once. The first components were being produced by August 1937.

There were plans to sell the yards to, or at least to merge with, Vickers Ltd of Sheffield. The preliminary negotiations took place against the background of the 1935 riots, but the Northern Ireland government put the brakes on these, in case such a merger would result in a further loss of jobs. When Vickers realised some of the problems it would be taking on, it withdrew from the negotiations.

Amazingly, in the midst of all these problems Harland and Wolff launched 127,312 tons of shipping in 1935, the highest total in the world that year. Towards the end of the year orders were forthcoming, a trend that continued into the following year. There was even a contract for a floating police station on the Thames. HMS *Penelope* was completed in November, bringing cash into the company. Even so, the Midland Bank was unsympathetic, but Rebbeck faced it down. The profit for 1936 was only £64,047, but at least it was a profit. The pressure was there, nonetheless, and a particular target was the engine works, where the striving for the perfect engine was compromising the striving for profitability. There were few new orders, and the outlook was not encouraging.

The engine works were indeed the source of the haemorrhage, but the problems were not limited to this. The Admiralty was unhappy about the late delivery of the *Penelope*. The firm was too big, and the directors did not seem to be prepared to address the problem. Their expertise was technical rather than financial.

Rebbeck was trying to bring more Admiralty work to Belfast. He was helped in this by the remoteness of Belfast from the European continent, which meant it would be at the extreme range of any bombers sent against the shipyards. To deal with the biggest ships, including battleships, Harland and Wolff would need a crane capable of lifting up to 300 tons. The estimated cost for this was £500,000—well beyond the company's means. The Victoria Channel would also need to be deepened. After consultations with the Northern Ireland government and the Harbour Commissioners it was agreed that the project could go ahead, with Harland and Wolff contributing £75,000 towards the cost of the crane. In spite of the problems with the *Penelope,* the Admiralty had placed an order for a 28,000-ton aircraft carrier, HMS *Formidable*. It was hoped that the crane would be ready in time for its launch, in the autumn of 1938.

Rebbeck was also in negotiations with the War Office and the Air Ministry. He arranged to build an armaments works, to be operated by the company, and to co-ordinate and subcontract all munitions work carried out in Northern Ireland. The Air Ministry undertook to erect a factory in the Musgrave Shipyard for manufacturing aircraft components. This factory would be managed by Short and Harland.

Once again Harland and Wolff launched more ships than any other yard in the United Kingdom. Unfortunately, almost every ship lost money for the company, and it was only the repair work that allowed the firm to show a profit for the year. The company still had a lot of spare capacity. In early 1939 thirteen of the eighteen slips in Belfast were vacant. Prospects seemed better by mid-year, when contracts for fourteen ships were received. This gave Rebbeck confidence to reopen the Victoria Yard, which had belonged to Workman Clark. The tower cranes from the County Antrim yard were dismantled and moved across the harbour.

As the world moved towards crisis, it became obvious that the full facilities at Queen's Island would be needed, and from the end of June a steady stream of war contracts began to pour in. It looked as if Rebbeck, for all his faults, had managed to steer Harland and Wolff through the stormiest times British shipbuilding had yet experienced. In the coming war, however, the stakes would be much higher and government supervision much more intense. It remained to be seen whether Rebbeck would be up to the job.

Chapter 11 ～

| THE SECOND WORLD WAR

The last ship to be launched by Harland and Wolff before the declaration of war in September 1939 was the aircraft carrier *Formidable.* The occasion might have been a worrying omen of what was to come, because the cradle holding the bow of the ship collapsed, and it slid into the water several minutes prematurely. The ship itself was not damaged, but a flying bolt killed a spectator. In fact the ship, which was not commissioned till the following summer, had a distinguished and exciting career, surviving bombs and kamikaze attacks before being mothballed in 1947. Another of the ships that had been completed that summer, HMS *Penelope,* would take part in many of the important naval engagements of the coming years.

At an emergency session of the Northern Ireland Parliament, Lord Craigavon spoke of the need for the people of Northern Ireland to take an equal share with the rest of the United Kingdom in the coming struggle. For the people of Belfast, something more basic was at stake. They had lived for more than a decade in a country and a city that were both on the verge of bankruptcy. More than a third of the city's population was living in absolute poverty. Their view of the coming of war was that it might be the precursor of increasing employment, as had happened in 1914.

Although many young people volunteered to fight, no threat of conscription was hanging over the state. At first it looked as if the hopes for better days were unfounded. Unemployment rose every month up to February 1940, caused by shortages of raw materials and the disruption created by the changeover to wartime production, but after that the juggernaut of war was able to absorb almost anyone who wanted a job.

The various fighting ministries in London had their own plans for Belfast. The Admiralty intended to use Belfast and Larne as trawler bases, whose ships would be used to protect the Irish Sea and the North Channel. The naval officer in charge of Northern Ireland set up his headquarters in the Custom House, and the light cruiser *Caroline,* which had taken part in the Battle of Jutland, was converted into a base depot ship. Ships entering and leaving Belfast Lough were examined by a naval picket based in Bangor. Coastal Command of the RAF set up a local headquarters at

Aldergrove, near Belfast, and from there anti-submarine air patrols covered the north Irish Sea and the western approaches. Gun sites were manned at Grey Point and Kilroot.

One cause for concern was that the IRA had recently returned to the scene. There had been a campaign of bombing in England, and, nearer home, the IRA had even shot a soldier in East Bridge Street the day war was declared. The border with the South was open, there was a German embassy in Dublin, and the War Office was actually moving much-needed regular troops out of the province. The vulnerable points of shore establishments and the shipyard and docks complex had to be secured against sabotage. Territorial Army units were to take over security for the time being. By mid-May 1940 the number of soldiers stationed in the North had built up again to about the strength of a division. At that time, in addition to the threat of sabotage, there was the real possibility of the German army landing on a number of eminently suitable beaches around the coast. Movement between Northern Ireland and Great Britain was restricted to 'approved' ports, and a system of travel permits was introduced.

As far as Harland and Wolff was concerned, the war came too soon for the completion of the giant crane. There would be no battleships built on Queen's Island. This was probably a blessing in disguise, as no battleships were actually built during the war, and the crane might well have been yet another white elephant. All shipping orders now came under state control, and the Admiralty also controlled orders for merchant shipping. The only ships that were licensed for civilian lines were those that would replace ships lost to enemy action. Warships were now equipped with oil-fired or diesel engines, and tankers were therefore a priority. Four tankers were ordered from Belfast, though one of these was converted into a landing-craft carrier. Winston Churchill, who was back at the Admiralty, telephoned Frederick Rebbeck and asked him to prepare Queen's Island for building large numbers of Flower-class corvettes. The design of these small ships was based on that of whale-catchers. They could stay at sea in the worst of weather, but they were very 'tender'—that is, they rolled easily—and, because of their small size, took a lot of sea on board and got the reputation of being very wet ships. They could be built simply and quickly, they had straightforward machinery and basic anti-aircraft armament. But they had the most sophisticated anti-submarine armament available. Twenty of these corvettes were ordered and were built in batches of four. The first of these, HMS *Arabis,* was completed on 5 April 1940, only five months after its keel had been laid. After that, one was handed over on average every fortnight till the order was completed in January 1941.

Other orders came that winter, including one for a light cruiser, HMS *Black Prince.* Because of the priority given to building corvettes, it was not completed till the end of 1943.

As might be expected, ship repairs provided constant business, as did the task of fitting guns to merchant ships. Before Christmas twenty-five trawlers had been converted into inspection vessels. Seven liners were allocated to Queen's Island for conversion into armed merchant cruisers, while two more were fitted out as auxiliary anti-aircraft ships. Churchill also revived his old scheme of dummy battleships, with a dummy aircraft carrier bringing the scheme up to date. At the aircraft factory they were gearing up to build the new Stirling bomber.

It was obvious that the entire area of the Harbour Estate needed protection, and not just from the IRA. Bombers were a constant worry, and it was widely believed that they would always reach their target. The only defence was to disrupt their bombing run using searchlights and anti-aircraft guns. The trouble was that the United Kingdom had roughly half the number of these needed. All that was available for Belfast were the weapons already in Northern Ireland for training purposes. These consisted of twelve 3-inch guns that were almost obsolete, eight Bofors light anti-aircraft guns and thirty-two searchlights. The heavy guns were sited at Greencastle, on the Antrim Road, in Orangefield and at Kinnegar on the County Down coast. A Belfast Territorial Army unit was mobilised to man the guns, while the 3rd (Ulster) Searchlight Regiment was transferred from Portstewart to man the lights. This was only a temporary solution, as the War Office then transferred the 3rd (Ulster) Anti-Aircraft Brigade to Great Britain in preparation for going overseas. It was intended that a newly raised Territorial ant-aircraft regiment would eventually take over.

It was during these weeks of the 'phoney war' that civilians began to be aware of the restrictions that would be imposed on them for the duration of hostilities. The Black-out Order was the first, but it was followed by controls on the coal burned in houses, the petrol used on the roads, the paper used in schools, on the felling of trees, the building of houses and the laying out of roads, among others. A divisional coal officer was appointed to ensure that there were adequate reserves in the province. An Advisory Committee ensured that prices were not inflated by war short-ages. Rationing at first was voluntary, but the compulsory rationing of petrol had already been introduced by the end of September.

A National Registration Scheme was begun. Each householder was required to list all those people living in the home, including those temporarily absent. This was treated with suspicion in some quarters, where people thought it was a first step in getting names for conscription. Craigavon had to make a statement in Stormont assuring the people that it was simply a step towards ensuring that enough supplies of food and other essentials were allocated to the state. Identity cards were issued. These, and the basic register, had to be kept up to date, and a small staff was assigned to keep a maintenance register, based in Belfast.

The rationing of bacon, ham, butter and sugar was introduced in January 1940, with the rationing of meat following in March. At first this caused little hardship, as many people had friends or relatives who farmed, and the border with the South was a short stroll for many in Northern Ireland. As more things were rationed, and every individual was issued with a ration book, there was an indication of leaner times to come.

The first winter of the war seemed endless. One after another, pleasures were curtailed, yet the war on land seemed to have entered a coma. It was as if, paralysed by memories of the trench warfare of the Great War, generals held back from committing their forces to any attack. Only at sea were things happening to freeze or to stir the blood. The passenger ship *Athenia* was torpedoed off the west coast of Ireland only hours after the declaration of war. A German submarine managed to penetrate the defences of Scapa Flow and sank a British battleship. Three British cruisers had managed to trap a German surface raider, the pocket battleship *Graf Spee*, in the 'River Plate'—the estuary of the Río de la Plata between Argentina and Uruguay—and bluffed its captain into scuttling his ship. After the experience of 1914, nobody expected a short war, but for a while it looked as if there would be no war at all, simply a series of inconveniences.

This changed in April and May 1940. As usual, the United Kingdom was poorly prepared. Most of its small standing army was sent to France as the British Expeditionary Force, leaving the Territorial Army and the Yeomanry to guard the home countries. When Germany invaded Denmark and Norway on 9 April there was little that Britain could do to stop German successes on land. The Royal Navy took advantage of the movement of enemy ships to attack them and inflicted heavy casualties on both merchant and naval shipping. The government decided that a small land force should also be sent to Norway, and this was landed at Narvik, with another at Trondheim a few days later. The Luftwaffe maintained air supremacy, however, and was able to dominate the battlefields. Troops were unable to move and were kept pinned down, except through the short hours of darkness. British planes were needed, and as airfields in Norway were restricted and were open to German bombing, it was the navy that tried to supply the answer, by using aircraft carriers.

HMS *Glorious* had been something of a disappointment as a big-gun cruiser. It was converted into an aircraft carrier between the wars and was now on station in the Mediterranean. It was one of three aircraft carriers sent to support the Norwegian operations. The trouble was that carriers of that generation had a limited range of operations. The *Glorious* left Scapa Flow on 25 April, launched an attack on Trondheim on 25 April, and was back in Scapa Flow three days later. To give proper support would require the carriers to operate on a shuttle system, yet that would increase their own vulnerability. The Trondheim operation was beyond saving, but the force was able to withdraw without serious losses. The *Glorious* now concentrated on Narvik, where another Belfast ship, the *Penelope*, was part of the Second Cruiser Squadron, which had also been transferred from the Mediterranean. The *Penelope* had suffered the indignity of running aground, but while it was undergoing temporary repairs in the Lofoten Islands its captain acted as senior naval officer while the crew fulfilled a number of useful tasks.

The command of ground forces was given to Lieutenant-General Claude Auchinleck, born of an Ulster family; but even as he landed in Norway, events elsewhere reduced Norway to a sideshow. On 13 May, German forces invaded the Low Countries. Within days it became obvious that the Allies were in trouble, as countless *blitzkrieg* (lightning war) attacks, combining tanks and aircraft, kept them constantly off balance. By the last week in May the chiefs of staff in London felt that there was a real danger of invasion and decided that they must concentrate their scarce resources in the homeland. Orders were given to withdraw all troops from Norway. While the withdrawal was taking place, the battle for Narvik went on. It was felt necessary to keep these soldiers in harm's way so that the Germans would not become aware of the evacuation elsewhere. Among the units that fought to the last minute outside Narvik was the 1st Battalion of the Irish Guards. Many Ulstermen had enlisted in this unit since the start of the war, and it won ten decorations for distinguished service in the campaign. The last soldiers were embarked by 8 June.

On the same day the old warrior *Glorious* came to a sad end two hundred miles west of the Lofoten Islands. The circumstances were controversial, and the documents referring to the sinking will not be released till 2041. Its captain, Guy D'Oyly-Hughes, had only ten months' experience in aircraft carriers, his background being in submarines. On board were two RAF squadrons and their pilots. The captain was given permission to leave the task force he was sailing with to proceed at increased speed to Scapa Flow, with two destroyers as an escort. He did not maintain a defensive air patrol, and the group was intercepted by the German battle-cruisers *Scharnhorst* and *Gneisenau*. The two destroyers launched a desperate defence, but they were like eggshells under the fire of the German guns. In two hours all the British ships had been sunk, but damage had also been done to the Germans, and the battle-cruisers withdrew to lick their wounds in Trondheim.

It may be that this was the carrier's most glorious moment, as the removal from the scene of the German capital ships meant that the way was clear for the exhausted troops in their transports. There were only 45 survivors of the three ships: 1,519 met their end in the cold waters that day. Yet about 24,000 soldiers returned safely home, brought in two convoys.

One of these was the *Georgic,* built long ago in Belfast. The second convoy contained ships that would have been familiar in Belfast and Larne: the *Royal Ulsterman,* the *Ulster Prince* and the *Ulster Monarch.*

The shock of defeat in Norway was dispiriting, although it was mitigated by the defeat of the German destroyer force by the Royal Navy during the Battle of Narvik. What was happening in France was horrifying, because daily it brought the Germans closer to the south coast of England. Several Ulster units were assigned to the British Expeditionary Force, including the 3rd (Ulster) Anti-Aircraft Brigade, the 1st Battalion of the Royal Irish Fusiliers, the 2nd Battalion of the Royal Ulster Rifles, the 2nd Battalion of the Royal Inniskilling Fusiliers and the 5th Battalion of the Royal Inniskilling Dragoon Guards. These were all involved in the fighting retreat from Flanders to the coast, taking turns to act as rearguard, often halting attacks that the Germans pressed home with bravery and skill. Soldiers in the 3rd (Ulster) Searchlight Regiment ignored their lamps and fought as infantrymen, with rifles.

By the time the BEF was given the order to fall back to Dunkerque, most of the soldiers were weary, hungry and dazed. They moved in small groups, mostly at night. Senior officers may have known that there were Germans moving on each side, threatening to envelop them, but the men just got on with it. While some units were in full retreat, the Inniskilling Dragoons formed a screen to protect them. This was one of very few armoured units with the BEF, and it was kept busy at all times protecting the bridgehead. Eventually, however, it had to fall back on the beach, where the men spiked their guns and abandoned their tanks. Getting off the beach was not easy, as the shallow water prevented larger ships coming close inshore. An armada of small ships took their place, picking up soldiers on the beach and transferring them to ships further off. It was an amazing achievement in the direst of circumstances, a triumph of organisation in chaos. The naval beach-master had been a Belfast civil servant; there was a merchant captain from Newry; and there was an able seaman from Cushendall, decorated for twice entering the water to rescue survivors of a sinking ship.

Dunkerque was a defeat, but there was also deliverance. Thirty thousand British soldiers died, but 311,739 Allied soldiers were rescued. Things happened that were almost miracles. The Germans made no attempt to pinch the bridgehead east or west with its armoured troops. The RAF planes were flying from bases close to the scene of the action, in Kent, while German airfields had not kept up with the rapid advance of their panzer columns. Most miraculous of all, however, was the bravery of individuals, military and civilian, who put themselves in harm's way to help deliver others. Britain still had an army, though that army had no equipment.

Within three weeks of Dunkerque, French resistance collapsed, and the French government signed an armistice with the Germans. Under this agreement Germany took control of northern France, together with the Channel and Atlantic ports, while the rump of the country was governed by a neutral French administration based in Vichy. The Germans now controlled every continental European port from the North Cape to the Pyrenees. The Baltic was closed, and maritime traffic in the North Sea much impeded. Surface raiders had a much greater choice of routes to and from the high seas. In particular, these new ports effectually extended the u-boat front line many hundreds of miles further west into the Atlantic.

The south-west approaches to Britain, through the English Channel or the Bristol Channel, were now much too dangerous, and in future all shipping was directed to the north of Ireland. Northern Ireland was the obvious base for escorts for the convoy system that had been introduced for all but the fastest merchant ships. Because of its importance to the war at sea, the possibility of a German invasion had to be taken seriously. The Irish army was very weak, and had a very limited supply of heavy equipment. The Southern government had declared itself neutral, though Germany's treatment of the Low Countries and Scandinavia had shown that simple neutrality provided no security. The British army in Northern Ireland, therefore, had to be prepared to respond to an invasion in the South as well as in Northern Ireland. The army presence in the North consisted of the 53rd Division at the time of Dunkerque, together with some odds and ends, but it was quickly built up to four divisions by the end of the year. The 183rd Brigade of the 61st Division was charged with the defence of Belfast.

Over the winter of 1941/2 the RAF presence in Northern Ireland was also increased. This consisted mainly of seven squadrons of Coastal Command, whose job it was to patrol the waters to the west of Scotland and Ireland and frustrate any German activity they came across. They were followed by fighter and medium bomber squadrons. The RAF was hampered by the fact that no-one had done a survey of possible sites for airfields in Northern Ireland, while maps did not give enough detail to make it a desk exercise. Ballykelly, County Derry, would in time become the most forward air base in the Battle of the Atlantic.

After the fall of France, Northern Ireland came within the range of the main German bombing force. Before that only the giant Condor, which ranged out into the Atlantic, had posed any threat. Yet Ulster had a low priority for anti-aircraft defences, well after south-east England and the Middle East and North Africa. The 3rd (Ulster) Anti-Aircraft Brigade had been moved abroad, and the only air defences were scattered along Belfast Lough, protecting the city.

A problem of the new system of using the north-west approaches was that it concentrated shipping in an area to the north of Ireland and to the west of Scotland and made convoys easy to find. At a time when the Germans had few truly ocean-going submarines and the Allies had a grave shortage of effective escorts, this was like providing a feeding station for the enemy, and many ships were sunk within sight of shore.

German tactics at that time were very basic. When a submarine spotted a convoy, it would follow at extreme range on the surface, where powerful diesel engines made it much faster than any convoy. As night approached it would come closer, following in the wake of one of the escorts, as it was difficult to detect here. When full darkness came it would go into the middle of the convoy and attack as many ships as possible. In the darkness and confusion it would normally get away.

For a while even the Irish Sea was dangerous. Ships going to Bristol or Merseyside would assemble in Belfast Lough, anchoring off Bangor. When all the ships had arrived they would be given a close escort of trawlers that had been converted for mine-sweeping or anti-submarine duties. More than seventy of these trawlers were based in Belfast. Outgoing convoys would also shelter in the lough, then be escorted by the trawlers until they joined the destroyers and corvettes that were based on the Foyle.

The naval presence in Belfast put real pressure on the harbour facilities. Royal Navy ships aside, it was one of only three ports in the United Kingdom considered safe after Dunkerque. Even in peace-time it had been the fifth most important port in Britain and Ireland. Somehow the navy had to be accommodated without interfering with the normal working of the commercial docks. Pressure was relieved by a combination of relocation, where possible, by the navy and a vast building programme taken on by the Harbour Commissioners. The Pollack Dock was assigned exclusively for Admiralty use. Two thousand feet of deep water was added to the facilities, with twenty extra mooring dolphins for trawlers on the east side of the Herdman Channel. A vast 171,200 square yards of sheds was built. Additional trawlers were based in Larne, and the larger escort vessels operated out of the Foyle. To save these ships from travelling to Belfast for the repairs inflicted by the Atlantic or the enemy, Harland and Wolff set up a repair organisation in Derry.

The British government was particularly worried about the dangers posed to merchant shipping by surface raiders. Though it was to be the u-boats that nearly brought the country to its knees, ships like the *Graf Spee* had the potential of wiping out a convoy in a single afternoon. It was now a ruined hulk in the Río de la Plata, but there were more of its type, ready to appear suddenly out of the grey Atlantic and spit red death at its prey. The *Admiral Scheer* was a sister-ship, another pocket battleship. It left its Baltic lair on 24 October 1940 and went hunting. Its supply ship, the *Nordmark,* had left six days earlier; it was its job to feel its way along the pack-ice, then in the night to break through the narrow waters that separate Greenland and Iceland. It was breaking a trail for the *Admiral Scheer*, whose task was to disrupt the operations of the Royal Navy by catching them off balance. It was to attack a convoy sailing from Canada to Britain, then to cruise the seas of the world, looking for targets of opportunity.

The convoy that the Germans found was Convoy HX84, bound for Britain. The ships had been assembling at Halifax, Nova Scotia, a dreary outpost that merchant sailors found unwelcoming. One ship in the convoy had started from Belfast on its round trip. This was the *Kenbane Head*, owned by the Head Line of Belfast. It was twenty years old and had been built at Workman Clark. It had been built for the convenience of its owners rather than for the comfort of the crew, and many crew members who transferred from other lines complained about the lack of facilities, though most of the men had served with the Head Line for their working lives and were inured to the discomfort. Almost half the forty-two came from Belfast, with others from Counties Antrim and Down and a smattering of English and southern Irish. The assistant cook was Canadian. It had taken a load of china clay from Fowey to Three Rivers in Canada and was returning with general cargo from Montréal. On 20 October 1940 the convoy began to make its way out into the Atlantic swell.

The *Admiral Scheer* had good luck coming through the Denmark Strait on 30 October. The weather that kept the ship safe was so bad that two crew members were lost overboard. Many others were seasick. There was a fright the next day when a ship was sighted about four miles away. It was probably an armed merchant cruiser of the Northern Patrol, but it did not see them in the gloom. By 2 November, All Souls' Day, it had broken through to the broad Atlantic. Its captain knew that he was in the mid-Atlantic gap, beyond the reach of shore-based aeroplanes.

Convoy HX84 was not fast. Moving at the speed of its slowest ship, it made less than two hundred miles a day. Even that was too much for a Polish steamer, which had already fallen behind. The ships were spread out over a large section of the ocean, three-quarters of a mile from front to back, four miles from side to side, thirty-seven ships in four ranks. The southernmost ship in the last rank was the *Kenbane Head*.

The two Canadian destroyers that had escorted them from the coast had gone. Their sole protector now was the armed merchant cruiser *Jarvis Bay*. It had been taken over by the Royal Navy in 1939 and had been fitted with 6-inch guns that had been left over from the Great War. It was its duty to conduct its charges, like a Good Shepherd, to the rendezvous with their British destroyer escort in the eastern Atlantic. It was sailing in front. By 5 November it was as if the ships had become used to each other, and the convoy zigged and zagged like a well-drilled entity. Half their journey was over. There was one break in the routine that day. The fast banana boat

Mopan, sailing independently at a speed more than half as fast again as the convoy, appeared in the west and, as the day progressed, overhauled it and disappeared into the east.

The skies were not empty, however. The *Admiral Scheer* carried a float-plane, and that day its pilot scoured the waters, looking for a target. At 12:40 he appeared over the mother ship, signalling that the convoy was sailing 88 nautical miles to the south-west. It took time to get the float-plane back on board, but by 1 p.m. the *Admiral Scheer's* captain had the information he needed. He calculated that he could be up with the convoy by 4 p.m., which would give him more than an hour before darkness would begin to hide his prey. He ordered full speed and had the ship cleared for action. Then, at 2:30 p.m., he met the *Mopan.* He dismissed his first suspicion—that he had come upon an armed merchant cruiser—when he realised the other ship was too small. He ordered the *Mopan* not to transmit a contact report but to abandon ship and row to the *Admiral Scheer;* then—contrary to the stereotype of the ruthless Nazi—he waited till the merchant seamen were safely on board before sinking the unfortunate banana boat. Meanwhile, daylight passed. He had lost an hour of valuable time.

The German captain now decided that he would have time to make only one charge through the convoy, damaging as many ships as he could and finishing them off as he came through it for a second pass. But the convoy had already been alerted. A lookout on the *Rangitiki,* the largest ship in HX84, saw smoke to the north. Captain Fegan on the *Jarvis Bay* was alerted immediately. He ordered that a special watch be kept to the north. For the time being he saw no need to alert the other ships. On the *Kenbane Head* and the others the routine carried on: watches changed at 4 p.m., and cooks began their preparations for the evening meal. On the *Jarvis Bay* lookouts saw a ship to the north at 4:35. Ten minutes later it could be identified as a warship. A further ten minutes later Fegan ordered his ship to action stations and ordered full speed towards the intruder. As he went he ordered that the challenge 'A' be flashed by signal lamp. It was this lamp that helped the Germans to identify the *Jarvis Bay* as a warship: it was much too powerful to be on a merchant ship. Then the *Jarvis Bay* sent up red signal rockets. It and all the other ships began to make smoke in order to make things difficult for the German gunners.

At a range of eight miles the *Admiral Scheer's* main guns opened fire on the *Jarvis Bay.* At the other end of the convoy, on the *Kenbane Head,* it looked as if a fireworks display had been put on for Guy Fawkes' Day, and all hands came on deck to see what was happening. The captain ordered those on watch to get to their posts and turned the ship back on a reverse course, so that it was heading the way it had come. Behind him he could see the *Jarvis Bay* burning. The old passenger liner, ornamented with wood throughout its accommodation, was tinder-dry and ready to burn. In its dying moments the single gun it could still fire managed to keep the attention of the guns on the *Admiral Scheer* for twenty minutes, while its flock scattered. By the time it died, so had daylight.

It should have ended there; the sacrifice of the *Jervis Bay* should have been enough. Life does not follow romance, however, and another five ships were lost that night. The *Admiral Scheer* had been firing on the tanker *San Demetrio* with its secondary armament from the start; it was abandoned and sinking in flames. The German captain wanted the *Rangitiki* next, because he thought it was a troopship, but he lost it in the darkness. Instead he stumbled on the *Maidan,* which blew up, sinking with all hands. Another ship, the *Trewellard,* was carrying steel and pig iron. It went down in minutes. The *Beaverford* was carrying a deck cargo of timber, which kept it afloat until a German torpedo broke it in two.

On the *Kenbane Head* they watched the action astern of them in horror, imagining the screaming of shattered bodies and the cold clutch of the water. As the flames died behind them and there was only the black night ahead, they may have dared to think that they had got away. Then, at 6:15, a flare appeared overhead, picking it out as if it was the only ship on the ocean. It wasn't, of course, and the Germans fired a single salvo of its main guns. The *Kenbane Head* lay dead in the water, listing and sinking.

The crew manned the Number 2 lifeboat and lowered it to the water. To their horror it had been 'sprung' by the explosions and sank immediately. Only the fittest managed to climb back on the ship. The others, exhausted or wounded, lay in the sea, holding onto the sinking lifeboat. Those on board managed to launch a life raft and were delighted to see that the jolly boats—small, basic dinghies—had not been damaged. They tied these to the raft and then towed the raft away from the sinking ship. The ship sank about an hour after being hit.

It was severely cold, and the wind got up to almost gale force. This wind nearly brought disaster, because the burning *San Demetrio* began drifting towards them. It looked as if the tanker's bow would crash onto one of the jolly boats, so it was set loose with orders to keep in touch through the night. It was never seen again.

By the time morning came, the cold had been too much for eight of the crew. Only twenty of the forty-two who had signed on were left alive. The dead were pushed over the side with sympathy but no ceremony. There was now enough room for all the survivors in the boats, and the clumsy raft was cut adrift. All day they bobbed on the waves; they were cold and wet, hungry and, worst of all, thirsty. The first ration of water was handed round in the afternoon. The only living thing they saw that day was a fulmar. The second night was calmer, and the skies had cleared. They watched the planets circle over their heads. By dawn of that second day most of the survivors were at the end of their resources.

In the early afternoon, when hope had gone, a ship appeared almost beside them. Their rescuer was the *Gloucester City,* whose master had risked his ship by looking for survivors from the convoy. It picked up nearly a hundred and took them all the way back to Nova Scotia. But the Atlantic was still between them and home.

It was only now that families and loved ones learnt of the fate of their menfolk who had sailed from Belfast over two months earlier. Of those who died, eleven were from Belfast, two from Carrickfergus, four from County Down, two from the South, two from England, one each from Scotland and Wales, and one from Canada. In small streets near the docks families grieved for fathers and brothers and sons. They had sailed as volunteers, with no glamour and with wages that were a pittance compared with the uniformed services. Their wages had even stopped from the moment their ship had sunk. Anyone lucky enough to survive would be sailing again soon, because it was their job. By their phlegmatic approach to danger they overcame difficulties and saved Britain from starvation. Around the world, there are few memorials to the sacrifice of merchant seamen.

Death was to come even closer to the small streets of Dock and Tiger's Bay only a few months later. It would be wrong to say that people became blasé about air-raid sirens: there were too many graphic images of the blitz in London and the rest of England for that to happen. It was just that they heard the sirens in Belfast so often and yet there had not been an attack. There had been attacks on the Clyde, and on the night of 7/8 April another large stream of bombers flew up the west coast of Britain, apparently heading for Glasgow. Six bombers detached themselves from the main armada and changed course to the west, flying towards Belfast. They flew in at 7,000 feet, coming in ones and twos, with long intervals between each attack. First the plane would drop flares, then incendiaries. These would be followed by high explosive and by parachute mines. These last were particularly feared, because they produced a huge blast, which spread damage over a much greater range than conventional bombs. The last plane, flying over at 3:30 a.m., did the most strategic damage, scoring a direct hit on the fuselage factory at Harland and Wolff with a parachute oil bomb, which combined the effects of high explosive and the flames of an incendiary. It was a small consolation that one of the escaping bombers was shot down near Downpatrick.

The planes' target had been the docks and the shipyards, but several residential areas were also hit. The Newtownards Road in east Belfast and the Shore Road and Northern Road near the docks had all been showered with incendiaries. St Patrick's Church in Ballymacarret and McCue Dick's timber yard in Duncrue Street had both been set ablaze. People who had been working the night shift were trapped in Rank's flour mill. The following day two hundred people had to be moved from their homes when an unexploded bomb was found in Alexandra Park Avenue, near Tiger's Bay, only two hundred yards from the home of Mart McAughtry, who had been drowned on the *Kenbane Head.*

Although it is true to say that few cities were prepared for German bombers, it has to be added that Belfast was less prepared than most. There were no night fighters, the searchlight regiment had been sent overseas, and there were no barrage balloons and few anti-aircraft guns. These sins of omission were laid at the feet of the British government, but other sins were committed for which the culpability could not be passed on so easily. There were no shelters for the 30,000 workers engaged in vital war work, let alone the 300,000 citizens who had been promised them at the beginning of the war.

It was Belfast Corporation that was guilty of the greatest dereliction of duty towards its citizens. When those first bombers deviated from the stream of planes heading towards Glasgow, Belfast employed 230 full-time firemen, under a chief fire officer so incompetent that an official report a month before had recommended that he be retired at once. He entirely disregarded the 1,600 partly trained auxiliary firemen available to him, refusing to include them in what emergency planning he did. When the bombs fell he stayed in his office and wept. He was one example of many in the employ of Belfast Corporation, promoted far beyond his personal competence because of who he knew rather than what he could do. The mortuary service had planned for a maximum of two hundred deaths— less than a quarter of the total on the worst night. Estimates of the numbers left homeless were grossly below the reality. Preparations were made for only a tenth of those who needed food and shelter.

Unaccustomed to attack from the air, the people of Belfast found it difficult to believe that so much damage had been done by half a dozen medium bombers. Thirteen people had been killed and eighty-one injured, with varying degrees of severity. The authorities reacted by bringing in some anti-aircraft reinforcements, some searchlight units and a light anti-aircraft battery. They also wondered about reactivating plans to evacuate children. They decided to start moving the children on the Wednesday after Easter, 16 April.

On the night of Easter Monday a solitary German reconnaissance plane could be heard high over the city, flying at 22,000 feet. The following night the Germans launched a major air assault on the United Kingdom. A large air fleet split in two over the west midlands of England. One group attacked Merseyside, the other, of more than a hundred planes, pressed on towards Belfast. Three planes turned aside; one went to Derry, where its bombs killed fifteen people, another bombed Bangor, killing five people in Ashley Park in the Ballyholme district. In Belfast the sirens were sounded at 10:40 p.m. In the darkened, quiet night the ominous growl of aircraft engines could be heard approaching from the direction of Dromore in the south-west.

First there were flares, lighting the city and the lough as bright as noon. Even the moon looked dull compared with them. The flares drifted slowly on the breeze, falling gently towards Jordanstown and Whiteabbey. Their deceptive beauty was soon replaced by the twinkle of falling incendiaries and the blunt roar of high explosives.

The telephone communications centre suffered a direct hit at about 1:45 a.m. This disrupted communications between night fighters and their cross-channel controllers. Not knowing where to go, the fighters stayed away from Belfast altogether. It was up to the anti-aircraft gunners, and they were joined in their efforts by every naval ship in the harbour. For some reason the Germans missed the docks almost completely and spent their efforts on the residential areas of York Street and the Antrim Road. There is a hypothesis that they saw the glint of water in the Waterworks, along the Antrim Road, and mistook this for the docks. This could be attributed to a very successful smoke screen released over Queen's Island. While this saved strategically important facilities, they were saved at the cost of Belfast lives. The concentration of bombs around the Waterworks meant that many water mains were damaged, and water pressure was only half of what was normal, making it difficult for the fire service to control fires.

Huge conflagrations built up in York Street, the Antrim Road and the Shankill Road. A lucky hit had put the Harland and Wolff boiler shop out of operation, and Ewart's mill was gutted. A shipyard worker saw rats moving up the streets like an army, leaving the shops and engine works. The all-clear was not sounded till 5 a.m. By then 203 tons of high explosive and 800 fire-bomb canisters had fallen on the city.

When the cost in buildings was totalled the next morning it was discovered that damage had been done to thirty business premises, eleven churches, seven motor works, seven stores, two hospitals and a nurses' home, two banks, two schools, two cinemas, two tram depots, the Central Library, and eleven other buildings. Whole blocks of houses had been obliterated in some streets. Blast had brought down sixty yards of the York Street spinning mill. Houses were so disrupted that seventy thousand people had to be fed in emergency centres the next day. The planned evacuation of children had to be postponed.

The human cost extended to much more than homelessness. When the York Street Mill collapsed, more than thirty people were killed instantly, while the debris obliterated forty-two houses in Sussex Street and damaged beyond repair twenty-one houses in Vere Street. In Percy Street, between the Falls and the Shankill, sixty people were killed by blast when a bomb fell near a shelter. In Ballynure Street, off the Oldpark Road, sixteen people died in one house, nine of them from the one family. Altogether more than 700 people died and 1,500 were injured; 1,600 houses were destroyed completely.

Survivors walked through the rubble, trying to find what had become of friends or relations. Objects in burnt-out houses were still too hot to lift. Bodies were removed for identification, 150 at St George's Market and as many again in the Falls Road Baths. Many were the bodies of the homeless poor, lying in their own shabby blankets. Only London had had so many of its citizens killed in one night's air raid.

Some among the living tried to cause trouble. The Falls Road itself had not been touched, and no Catholic church in the city had been damaged. This was taken by some Catholics to show that God recognised which churches housed his true followers. Less kindly, some Protestants considered that it proved that Catholics on the Falls Road had been guiding the German planes by signalling with torches from the rooftops. The strife that these malicious rumours might have caused was countered by the action of the fire brigades of Dublin, Dún Laoghaire, Drogheda and Dundalk, which sped north through the cold spring night. The fire engines in those days were open to the weather, and the men had to sit on their hands to stop them becoming numb. Many of the drivers had never been to Northern Ireland before and had only a hazy idea of the route: some simply followed the telephone wires. To show solidarity with his Northern colleagues the Lord Mayor of Dublin, Alfie Byrne, travelled to Belfast on one of the fire engines, to offer his help and sympathy to the people of Belfast. In fact many families left Belfast and took the train to Dublin. The Dublin Red Cross was ill-prepared for this but managed to arrange for dormitories to be set up in halls around the city.

At last the authorities tried to put their house in order, building shelters and reorganising fire-watch duties. A rather sad preparation was having all the dangerous animals in the zoo destroyed, in case they escaped next time.

It was not the end of Belfast's purgatory. On Sunday 4 May the biggest raiding force of bombers that Belfast had yet seen arrived over the city in the very early hours. The moon was so bright that the two hundred bombers did not even have to waste time dropping flares. They could see their targets clearly below—the shipyard and the docks—and the bombing was much more accurate. It was pre-eminently a fire raid, though some high explosive was used to disrupt salvage efforts. Ships that were tied up in dock were hit. The aircraft carrier *Furious* blazed away with all its guns, making itself an obvious target, but did not receive a hit. The *Fair*

Head broke its back and sank at its moorings, blocking the channel in Dufferin Dock for many months. Three corvettes in the fitting-out basin were damaged. Damage to the aircraft sheds slowed up the production of Stirling bombers. Factory roofs were destroyed and there was no light to allow night shifts to work. Harland and Wolff suffered seventy-seven hits. The electrical department, the main stores office, many of the workshops and most of the records were destroyed. It was two days before any work could be done on the site, and six months before full production could be resumed.

Other facilities in the Harbour Estate were damaged. The Harbour Power Station was hit, leaving Belfast without electricity for twenty-four hours. York Street Railway Station was completely destroyed. Once again water mains were fractured, so many that within an hour water pressure had disappeared completely. Some men got their hoses into the Farset River and Connswater River, but these sources dried up when the tide began to ebb. They did not have hoses that would stretch to the bountiful Lagan, and it was not till morning and the arrival of the Southern fire engines that they were able to rectify this situation. In the meantime watchers on the hills around the city saw a circle of flame spread out from the centre. Overhead a pall of smoke and grime was as thick as fog. As morning dawned, people in the suburbs found their properties covered in thick, oily grime that contained the charred remnants of the night's destruction.

The bombers' success in attacking their industrial targets and damaging the war effort meant that fewer than half the number of people died in this raid, though twice as many planes took part. Another factor may have been that citizens were more conscious of the value of shelters, or had simply evacuated themselves after the Easter raids. Some had already made a practice of leaving the city as night fell, returning to their homes in the morning. Deaths in this raid came to 150, with a further 157 badly injured. As many as 56,000 houses had been severely damaged, and the homes of 15,000 people had been obliterated. Thousands of people left the city to live with relatives or friends or to rent accommodation in safer places; the official figure was 49,000, but that is probably too low. For most of the early summer about 10,000 people slept in fields and ditches round the city, sitting on folding stools or lying on groundsheets. Catholic and Protestant, they mingled together and bantered with one another and made their families as comfortable as they could. Luckily, it was a mild summer, and although there was a small-scale raid the following night, involving one or two bombers, and a mine crashed into a shelter in Ravenscroft Avenue near the Holywood Arches, killing fourteen people, the Germans never returned in force. Hitler had turned his fickle attention to the Balkans and North Africa, and then to Russia.

There was anger abroad in the city—anger with those whose duty had been to protect the people. Other cities in the United Kingdom had received or would receive worse raids from the Luftwaffe, but no city of comparable size would have such a high mortality rate. The protection for citizens that should have been arranged simply wasn't. There is a story that the cabinet at Stormont spent more time discussing how to protect Carson's statue than they did on identifying a strategy for building air-raid shelters. The Independent Unionist Tommy Henderson put it in words in a Stormont debate: 'They all say the same thing, that the government is no good.' There had been too few shelters built, they were too reticent to buy up-to-date equipment for the fire service and too inept to carry out the evacuation plans. Destroyed factories put people out of work, and many thought themselves back in the dark days of the 1930s. Unemployment rose by 350 per cent in one month and in the linen industry was as high as it had ever been.

At a time when the reputation of Belfast Corporation was at its lowest, a report was published showing that the city's tuberculosis sanatorium at Whiteabbey had been planned without any regard for the hideously expensive site and its unsuitability for its purpose. The government took advantage of this to focus attention away from their own failings. They suspended Belfast Corporation and installed three commissioners, reporting directly to the Minister of Home Affairs, who would carry out the necessary functions for the running of Belfast for a period of three-and-a-half years. This was not sufficient to deflect all criticism, however, and in a by-election that December in the safe Unionist constituency of Willowfield the Labour veteran Harry Midgely was elected. Members of the cabinet began to move against the Prime Minister, John Andrews, but it was 1943 before they got rid of him.

At sea, the early part of 1941 was as fraught for the Royal Navy as it was for the citizens of Belfast. Although always wary of surface raiders, most officers identified u-boats as the priority. In dealing with them the real problem was one of range. Destroyers had not been designed for spending long times at sea, often working at full speed. They could escort a convoy only as far as 400 miles west of Ireland, while u-boats, even in 1940, were able to go another 300 miles and stay there, hunting. Canadian destroyers could pick up the convoy 400 miles east of Halifax; for the space in between their only help was the armed merchant cruisers, and we have seen in the case of the *Jarvis Bay* that there is a limit to what even the highest valour can do. Corvettes could only help out. They were slow and could not keep up with, let alone catch, a German submarine on the surface, but they were easy and quick to build and their increasing numbers at least meant that u-boat captains would be careful operating near convoys. Even with these new escorts the merchant seamen were glad to sail in winter gales, when it was impossible for u-boats to operate.

Vice-Admiral Karl Dönitz, in charge of u-boats, used the winter respite to rest, regroup and retrain his men. He introduced the concept of the wolf-pack. This involved a group of u-boats stretched across the probable path of a convoy. The trick was in the timing, so that the pack was deployed only when it was established that a convoy was actually on the move, to avoid wasting time at sea. As convoys left fixed ports—Halifax or the North Channel—it was not difficult for an observer to say when one was setting out. The German naval authorities worked out the approximate course, and the u-boats deployed at right angles to this, just close enough together to ensure that the convoy could not slip through a gap unnoticed. When a submarine spotted the target it would send a contact report, giving its position and size. The captain would then shadow the convoy, while the others in the pack would use their superior surface speed to assemble around the shadowing submarine.

When all the submarines had assembled they would wait for nightfall. They then worked their way upwind of the convoy, remaining on the surface, and would attack as many ships in the convoy as possible. By staying on the surface they made it difficult for the ASDIC operator to be aware of their presence, as the sound-locating equipment was designed for picking up noises from underwater. Often the first an escort knew of the wolf-pack's presence was the flash as a torpedo crashed into a merchantman's side. Sometimes the flash allowed an alert lookout to spot a submarine, but on the surface the u-boat could move faster than any escort vessel, other than destroyers or frigates. The most the escort could hope to do was to force the enemy to submerge by attacking it with its guns. More often the submarine simply turned away and vanished, but it meant that another attack had been aborted, at least temporarily.

The wolf-pack was a devastating weapon and one that could be used night after night till there were no more ships to sink, or until the convoy had reached the safety net of a destroyer escort. For a while it seemed that the only limiting factor was the number of suitable u-boats: Dönitz had only thirty at this time. By the time he had built up the number, long-range bombers had closed the Atlantic Gap.

Sunderland flying-boats from Lough Erne and Liberators from Ballykelly made the surface a very dangerous place for u-boats. Their speed advantage, during daylight hours at least, had been neutralised. Incidentally, it was a Catalina flying-boat from Lough Erne, flying through the secret Donegal Corridor to the Atlantic permitted by the Irish government, that, two weeks after the last German air raid on Belfast, found the *Bismarck* when it had almost escaped from the pursuing British fleet. Its ultimate destruction by a combination of battleships, bombers and torpedo planes made the North Atlantic a safer place.

In Belfast, things began to get back to normal, and better than normal.

As the different industries came back on stream, unemployment fell. At Harland and Wolff the number employed gradually built up towards the 20,600 it would be at the end of the war. Projects were not limited to shipbuilding, though 500,000 tons of shipping, consisting of 150 ships, were launched in the six years of the war. The company also made 10,000 field guns and, up to November 1943, 550 tanks. After that date it would concentrate on building aircraft carriers for the Pacific. The nearby Sirocco Works made hand grenades, gun mounts and radar equipment. In the west of the city James Mackie and Sons made armour-piercing shells. Dozens of other businesses, less well known, produced a variety of munitions and components. Short Brothers, fearful of another attack, dispersed as many of its operations as it could around the city and beyond. The King's Hall in Balmoral, more accustomed to the farming industry, now housed the manufacture of fuselage and other components. In Mackies', women assembled undercarriages and other fuselage parts. A linen mill in Lambeg made tailplanes, flaps, fins and rudders. Sheet metal pressing took place in Newtownards. Aircraft wings were produced at Long Kesh and Largymore. Even garages and farm outbuildings were pressed into service as stores and temporary hangars. The bulk of Shorts' output—865 Stirling bombers—was used to inflict on German cities devastation undreamed of along the Antrim Road.

Only the linen industry was caught in a stop-go cycle. Although there were many orders from governments for fabric for uniforms, tents, flying suits, parachutes and even aeroplanes—a single Wellington bomber needed a thousand yards of linen—the industry was subject to the delays imposed by the U-boats, and there were violent swings in employment. The real problem was that the flax-growing areas of Belgium, from where most Belfast flax was imported, were in the hands of the Germans. Local farmers were encouraged to grow more flax to try to make up the gap. Military orders took priority, and what remained was used as utility garments for civilians. Some mills closed or converted to munitions work. Many employees left to work at better-paid jobs in England.

Prosperity was coming to the city all the same, and people used to earning only half the average wage of the United Kingdom were now earning three-quarters of it. Even though they knew that this relative wealth depended on the war, people were quite happy to live for the day. Between 1941 and the end of the war there were fifty-seven disputes at the shipyards, leading to a loss of 320,000 working days. Workers at the shipyard earned a particular reputation as 'fly men', ready to take advantage of any loophole. One man would submit the time cards of two or three of his friends; they would then have the day off on full pay. A Belfast man—not a shipyard worker—remembers going to the cinema on a summer afternoon. He was surprised when the usher conducted him almost to the front of the auditorium. When the lights came up at the interval he saw why: the place was full of men from Queen's Island. Absenteeism at Harland and Wolff was twice as bad as the worst British yard. At the same time, people celebrated their prosperity by painting their houses. It may have been no more than coincidence that most front doors in east Belfast were painted the same shade of battleship grey.

The aircraft manufacturers Short and Harland did not perform much better. The company had the worst strike record of any military supplier in Northern Ireland. When it was taken over by the government in 1943 it was estimated that the company was working at 65 per cent efficiency. An official claimed that 'any amount of people are drawing pay for loafing about.' In the docks, 30,000 days were lost through stoppages, and in general engineering another 52,000.

One product of Belfast that had a legitimate claim to wear battleship grey was HMS *Penelope,* the light cruiser that had been completed by Harland and Wolff in the lean days of 1936 and had already had an adventurous time in Norway during the Narvik campaign. When it had been repaired, which took until August 1941, it was ordered to Malta, to be part of Force K. Only two weeks after arriving in Malta both escort cruisers intercepted an Italian convoy sailing for Libya. In the subsequent battle all the merchant ships and one of the escorting destroyers were sunk. Further battles followed in November and December, but the *Penelope's* luck ran out on 19 December, when it struck a mine off Tripoli. It was not badly damaged, however, and was repaired in Malta and back in service in January 1942. For the next few months it escorted convoys to and from Malta. It was back in Malta on 26 March, when it was caught up in an air raid. Near misses caused so many holes from shrapnel that it was given the nickname HMS *Pepperpot.*

On 26 January 1942 two large transports anchored off Bangor. Too large to enter the Victoria Channel, they waited while a small flotilla of tenders arrived from Belfast. As these smaller boats tied up alongside, each in turn filled with troops—American troops. Although the attack on Pearl Harbor had taken place only six weeks before, America was showing its commitment to the European theatre of operations. The first strategic decision, now being implemented, was that America would take over the defence of Northern Ireland, releasing British troops to fight in North Africa and the Far East. The first four thousand were now arriving. With the Japanese attack on Pearl Harbor in December 1941, and more particularly with Hitler's rash declaration of war on the United States a few days later, it became probable that the Allies would win the war in the long run. Germany had forces committed in Russia, the Balkans, North Africa, on the high seas and, increasingly, in Germany itself, as the strategic bombing campaign of the RAF gradually took shape. Germany's allies had in the main low-quality troops, certainly when compared with the supremely professional Wehrmacht, and when these were used in the front line they offered points of weakness that the Allies could exploit. While short-term strategy might require time to consolidate the Allied position, in the medium term planning would go forward on the basis of future offensives.

Plans had already been agreed for American naval bases at Derry and Lough Erne, and bases were already established in Newfoundland and Greenland. These were necessary to ensure the safe transport of men and material to Britain in preparation for the invasion of Europe. Work on them had already begun in July 1941, with American contractors using American technicians but local labour. The American government informed the British that the Royal Navy was welcome to use these facilities as they were completed, as long as they were returned to the Americans when the United States joined the war. As it turned out, the Americans were not able to move to Derry in the strength that they intended, because new, longer-range u-boats had taken the war to the American coast and into the Caribbean. American ships were too busy defending home waters to deploy ships in the eastern Atlantic.

The build-up of ground forces was not delayed. The soldiers arriving off Bangor in January were the precursors of the us 34th Mechanised Infantry Division and 1st Armored Division. These units were earmarked for Operation Torch, the landings in North Africa that would take place in November. To make room for these incoming troops the 5th Division was moved out of Northern Ireland. By the end of May, 38,000 Americans had arrived. The armoured division had landed in Larne, and the sight of two hundred tanks caused great interest. Original plans had involved another three divisions coming to Northern Ireland, but a series of crises in the Far East had necessitated them being sent to the Pacific. In June it was decided that any new American units would be accommodated in Britain.

The Americans had at first been based in the north-west, but they were afterwards moved south, with headquarters in Omagh, Lurgan and Castlewellan. They spent much of their time in joint exercises with units of the British army. Units of the us Army Air Forces began to arrive in July. Three fighter squadrons, flying Spitfires provided by the RAF, took up residence at Eglinton, County Derry. Further squadrons arrived in the autumn. Problems with transport caused by a shortage of shipping meant that other types of aircraft did not begin arriving till the following year.

Although few Americans were stationed in Belfast, it was one of the favourite destinations for soldiers on leave. There was a huge American Red Cross Club in the city, which was the focus of rest and recreation. Americans were particularly popular with children, because they seemed to have access to unlimited supplies of chocolate and other sweets, and they were unstintingly generous in distributing them. Cinemas were packed, and the American taste for entertainment gave a new lease of life to the theatre and music hall. Their uniforms were made of much better material than those of the British army, and they were tall and well fed, fit and friendly. They were much sought after by young Irishwomen, many of whom married and followed their men to America after the war.

For the first time there were large numbers of black people in Northern Ireland. The Irish found the racial discrimination distasteful (black soldiers were given 'separate but equal' accommodation). In some areas a rota had to be established for going to pubs, in case fights developed between black and white.

The entertainment value of the American soldiers could not drive the war completely from the minds of Belfast people. There were sons in regiments fighting around the world. The 1st Battalion of the Royal Inniskilling Fusiliers was fighting a costly battle in Burma. Belfast's own Territorial unit, the 8th (Belfast) Heavy Anti-Aircraft Regiment, was in Egypt. One battery of that regiment, the 5th Light Anti-Aircraft Battery, had been sent by sea in late 1941 to support the defences of Tobruk. It had survived the famous siege that had been relieved after two months by the advance of the Eighth Army. When the Germans attacked again, in their last great advance, Tobruk was swept up, and two hundred of the men were made prisoner. When the casualty list, including a list of the missing, was published it brought back memories of the first days of the Battle of the Somme.

With a logic that defies analysis, the IRA decided to react to the American presence by launching a new campaign. It chose the wrong time. Sir Basil Brooke had taken over from John Andrews as Prime Minister of Northern Ireland, and he was made of much sterner stuff than his predecessor. In the South de Valera had been ruthless in shattering the IRA, using what methods he thought were needed: hanging, gun-fights, and internment in an army camp under much bleaker conditions than those under which German or British internees were held. Brooke used methods only slightly less draconian. He reintroduced the curfew, and armed patrols of the RUC used armoured cars and caged lorries. There were more than sixty attacks in the second half of the year. One policeman was killed, but most attacks ended in failure, usually followed by arrests. The IRA was effectually eliminated, north and south.

The Allies could look forward with some confidence to 1943. The Battle of al-Alamein, fought in the deserts of North Africa by General Bernard Montgomery, whose family still lived in Ulster, had defeated Rommel and was putting the Afrika Korps under pressure from which it would never recover. British and American forces that had been stationed in Northern Ireland had landed at various places in Morocco and Tunisia. As well as the two American divisions, the British 38th Infantry Brigade, made up of

Irish troops, and the North Irish Horse went ashore. Although they would receive a bloody nose at Kasserine (al-Qasrayn) Pass, their drive to join up with Montgomery's Eighth Army would ultimately be unstoppable.

Perhaps most significantly of all, Hitler had allowed his Sixth Army to be trapped in Stalingrad. In the first six weeks of the new year his casualties for the whole battle would come to 1½ million men killed or wounded and 91,000 captured. Of the captured, only 5,000 lived to return to Germany in 1955. The Wehrmacht also lost a fifth of its heavy equipment in the battle.

The Battle of the Atlantic had still to be won, and in the first half of 1943 it looked as if the Allies were at last beginning to squeeze the enemy. At the Allied conference in Casablanca in January 1943 it was decided that invading continental Europe would have to be postponed until the u-boat menace had been dealt with once and for all.

Admiral Max Horton was put in charge of the western approaches. He had been a submariner in the Great War and brought a new way of thinking to the task. The first thing he did was to consider the strengths and weaknesses of the forces at his disposal. He had a good supply of corvettes, but they were very slow. If they left a convoy to chase a u-boat they had the greatest difficulty in catching up with their charges. Because of this they tended not to press home their attacks on u-boats, which were able to escape and return later. He did not have enough destroyers and frigates. If he allocated these as close escorts to individual convoys they would be too thinly spread to provide an effective defence. Instead he organised these faster ships into support groups that would come to the rescue of a convoy that came under attack. In particular, they would press home any attack on a German submarine until it was destroyed. One escort group would be allocated to each convoy while it passed through that part of its journey when it would be beyond air cover. The group would work in consultation with the close escort but would be held some distance away, in reserve. u-boat commanders would be expecting counter-attacks from the close escort, not from the open sea. Surprise was further intensified by the installation of 'hedgehogs', which could fire depth charges in front of an attacking ship, rather than having to wait till the destroyer was above the submerged submarine.

It took a while for these tactics to be worked out, and for the first three months of the year it looked as if they might come too late. The rough weather of January kept casualties low, but in February 400,000 tons of shipping were lost, and another 627,000 tons in March. There were those who thought the Battle of the Atlantic had been lost. By 20 March, however, Horton had his forces in position. In the last third of the month sinkings fell by almost three-quarters. This rate was halved again in April, and fell yet again in May.

From 1 April, charge of the North Atlantic routes was placed in the hands of the Royal Navy and the Royal Canadian Navy. The Americans gave them VLR (very long-range) Liberators and even put an escort carrier under British command. The result was not simply an increase in the number of ships saved but an increase in the number of German submarines sunk. In May, three-tenths of all U-boats that put to sea were lost, a rate of attrition so great that Dönitz withdrew all his submarines from the Atlantic on 23 May. He ordered them to sea again in June. A total of 86 tried to cross the Bay of Biscay, according to German records; of these, 55 were sighted, 17 were sunk, and 6 forced to turn back. More than a quarter of them were destroyed before they were in position to look for a convoy. In July more Allied ships were built than were sunk. The Battle of the Atlantic had been won.

When Dönitz tried again in September he lost twenty-five submarines and sank only nine merchant ships, out of a total of 2,468 that sailed. The final key had been the VLR Liberators that flew from Ballykelly and were capable of closing the Atlantic air gap, and the inclusion in support groups of small escort carriers.

One of the three corvettes that had been sunk in the blitz of May 1941 was K192. When its damage was examined it was decided that it could be salvaged and rebuilt. The work took more than a year, but on 4 June 1942 it was commissioned as HMS *Bryony*. Its crew transferred *en bloc* from HMS *Arabis*, which was being transferred to the Americans. Crew and ship together went through a two-week training course at Tobermory in the Hebrides and then were allocated to Liverpool, where they spent their first two months escorting submarines between the Mersey and Scapa Flow. The ship was then converted for Arctic work and assigned close escort duty with convoy PQ18. The crew found this rather sobering, as the previous convoy, PQ17, had been almost wiped out by submarines and aircraft during the long Arctic days when it had been ordered to disperse and head for Russian ports, as it was believed that there was a German battle-cruiser in the area. The escorts abandoned the merchant ships, as they were ordered to do. Only ten out of the thirty-three merchantmen reached Russia.

This time the navy took no chances. The September departure meant there would be less daylight for enemy aircraft to use. The close escort consisted of an anti-aircraft cruiser, two destroyers, two anti-aircraft ships, four corvettes, three minesweepers, two submarines, and four trawlers. Two support groups were assigned to the operation, consisting of sixteen ships, including an aircraft carrier. The Germans met the convoy with attacks from the air and the sea. At a loss to themselves of three submarines and twenty-two aircraft, they sank thirteen merchant ships, including a tanker. The return convoy was without incident, except that the weather was so bad that two of the ships being escorted sank in a storm.

The *Bryony* was due to escort another Arctic convoy, but a collision at anchor meant that it had to return to Liverpool for repairs. It was not ready for sea again until April 1943, when it joined escort group A3, a mixed group of American, Canadian and British ships. By this time the voyage across the Atlantic was a less hazardous undertaking, and it was not long before the *Bryony* was ordered to Lough Foyle, where the new priority was escorting convoys to Gibraltar. On the second convoy it continued into the Mediterranean, where it provided cover for the Allied landings in Sicily, which began on 10 July.

The invading force consisted of the US Seventh Army and the British Eighth Army under Montgomery. Once again the 38th Infantry Brigade, which was part of the elite 78th Division, was involved, although it did not disembark until 28 July. It won new battle honours when it captured the mountain fortress of Centirupe in Sicily, which had seemed almost impregnable. This opened the way around the western flank of Mount Etna, a situation the rest of the 78th Division were able to exploit. The British and American forces met on 13 August, and Messina fell on 17 August. The next step was an attack on the Italian mainland.

This took place with barely a pause. On 3 September the 2nd Battalion of the Royal Inniskilling Fusiliers was among the first ashore. Within thirteen hours of the landing an armistice was signed with the Italian government of Pietro Badoglio, who had replaced Mussolini on 25 July. The agreement was not revealed for another five days, allowing the Allies to establish their bridgehead before the Germans could react. The British also moved small garrisons to the Greek islands of Kos, Léros and Sámos. The Germans, once they recognised the threat to their hold on the Balkans, attacked these islands and recaptured them. The 2nd Battalion of the Royal Irish Fusiliers was particularly unfortunate. It had endured three years of siege in Malta. Released from there, it was transferred to Syria. When the Italians capitulated it was moved as part of the 234th Infantry Brigade to Léros. The Germans landed on 12 November in overwhelming force, and on 16 November the garrison was forced to surrender after five days of intense casualties and with no air support.

Operations in Italy itself were going much better. On 9 September the US Fifth Army had landed in Salerno, not far south of Naples. The German commander, General Albert Kesselring, after a week of trying to dislodge the invaders accepted the inevitable and withdrew from southern Italy, shortening his defensive line to the width of the Italian peninsula. To counter this, in January 1944 the Allies launched another amphibious landing behind enemy lines, this time at Anzio. This was a much harder-fought affair, with the Germans reluctant to give an inch. The troops ashore were supported by the heavy guns of the fleet.

One of the ships taking its turn in the bombardment was HMS *Penelope*, which was getting the name of being a lucky ship, as it had been hit so many times yet had not been sunk. But it was on this campaign that its luck ran out. It was returning to Naples on 18 February when it was hit by a torpedo. This damaged its engine and slowed it down. The men were called to action stations. About a quarter of an hour later it was hit by a second torpedo, which hit the boiler room and caused such an explosion that the ship sank immediately. The captain and 415 of the crew were lost. There were 206 survivors, almost all of whom had been at action stations on the deck. Although they were less than twenty miles out of Naples, they had to swim for some time before being rescued. The water was covered by a thick layer of diesel oil, and it was almost impossible for them to avoid swallowing it. Although none of them died of the poison, some were so badly affected that they were never again able to go to sea. The *Penelope* had been travelling at 26 knots (30 miles per hour) when it was first hit, making it the fastest-moving ship to be torpedoed during the war.

At this middle stage of the war there was a change in the type of ship being ordered at Harland and Wolff. As the Battle of the Atlantic was gradually won, the Admiralty had to look at its future needs. The European war would soon reach its climax and would be fought inland, far away from the supporting fire of even the biggest ships. After that, however, there was the problem of the Japanese and the Pacific. The experience of the Americans had shown the importance of aircraft carriers in the vast waters that separated the Japanese island fortresses. Seven carriers in total were ordered at Queen's Island. They were given such a high priority that the building of tanks was phased out. Also being built were eight tank landing craft in preparation for the landing in continental Europe.

Throughout 1943 and early 1944 the people of Northern Ireland watched a renewed build-up of American forces. It was becoming obvious that the second front in Europe was soon to become a reality; when the Americans disappeared again in the spring, they knew it was imminent. In the invasion, on 6 June 1944, engineers from the 591st (Antrim) Parachute Squadron were among the first to land in France. At 3 a.m. they were dropped east of the Orne bridges to clear a landing site for gliders due to arrive half an hour later. There were poles and other obstructions to be moved. The paratroopers found that it was easier to remove the poles by brute strength than with the explosives provided. While this was happening a group of volunteers, including many from the 1st Battalion of the Royal Ulster Rifles, landed near Merville, to destroy the gun batteries there. They managed to do this just as dawn was breaking.

On the beaches the 2nd Battalion of the Royal Ulster Rifles landed about noon, just west of the town of Ouistreham. By this time the fighting had moved inland about a mile. The Ulstermen were ordered to some high ground, where they were to help in the defence of the Orne bridges. At about the same time the gliders carrying the 1st Battalion of the Royal Ulster Rifles were landing on the ground cleared by the Antrim engineers on the other side of the river; the next morning it was ordered to advance in a south-easterly direction and to take the village of Sainte-Honorine. It met with stiff opposition, however, and suffered 143 casualties. When it began another attack two days later the Germans counter-attacked. There was a furious fire-fight, but neither side could impose its will on the other. Although fighting was almost continuous, for almost two months the lines east of the Orne River were static.

West of the river the 2nd Battalion was undergoing a similar sort of experience. It was ordered to occupy the village of Cambes, which it expected to do without much trouble. The approach to the village was across open ground, however, and it found itself under fire from neighbouring woods. It was forced back on the 7th. On the 9th, supported by tanks, it tried again. It was mid-afternoon and the battalion was attcked with mortar and field artillery fire, as well as rifles and machine-guns. Although it suffered heavy casualties of 199 men it was able to capture its objectives and to hold them against a sustained counter-attack by the Germans.

Both battalions continued in the long struggle to capture the important French city of Caen. It was the 2nd Battalion that entered the city first, joining up with the Canadians inside the city on the evening of 9 July. As the soldiers rested and enjoyed the welcome of the newly liberated French, there was great delight when an old Frenchman approached and told them he had been a regular in Mooney's Bar in the Cornmarket in Belfast.

A few weeks later the two battalions met. As the 2nd Battalion was moving up to the front line it passed the 1st Battalion, stationed in Le Mesnil. Progress was halted long enough for an exchange of news and hospitality.

The end in Normandy, when it came, came very quickly. The Americans swept west and south, around the main German forces, then north again to cut them off. Seeing the danger just in time, the Germans began to retreat east through an ever-narrowing passage near Falaise. The pocket in which the German army was held was a killing zone for German soldiers. Ground attack planes strafed every movement during daylight. It was a beaten army that fled east to the Seine, leaving most of its hardware behind. It was a happy army that followed, confident that the end could not be long delayed. News of Russian successes that meant the Red Army was closing in on the borders of Germany itself; the noise of bombers that, twenty-four hours a day, delivered a devastation to German cities that was unimaginable even to the survivors of the blitz in Belfast; the burnt-out staff cars and tanks; the field guns lying at crazy angles at the side of the road; and the bodies, pitiful in death, of teenage Germans who would suffer no more for the Fatherland—all these spoke to the soldiers of a nation on its knees, at the end of its tether.

Basic strategic mistakes on the part of supreme headquarters threw away this advantage. The failure to secure adequate ports in Belgium and the Netherlands meant that, for the rest of 1944 and the early part of 1945, supplies had to be brought hundreds of miles, from ports in France, to the advancing Allied armies. The shortage was enough to limit the options open to the generals. The one they chose—to attack and capture the bridges at Eindhoven, Nijmegen and Arnhem and so secure a crossing of the Rhine—taught both British and Americans lessons about warfare. The first was that it is difficult to keep to a timetable if you have only a few roads along which to advance and those roads are higher than the surrounding countryside and that countryside is too soft to allow tanks to be moved. It took only one German with a *panzerfaust*—the German equivalent of a bazooka, but much more effective—to hold up the entire column by blowing the track off the leading tank; nothing could move until the crippled tank was pushed off the road.

The second lesson was that airborne troops cannot hold out indefinitely without support from conventional troops and their much heavier equipment. The paratroopers who landed at Arnhem fought bravely but too long; they were forced to surrender long before help could reach them.

The final lesson was how quickly the German soldiers could be regrouped and rearmed. The Allies had expected to find them still reeling from the setbacks of the summer; instead they found soldiers more determined than ever to stop the invasion of their homeland.

This lesson was reinforced in December when the Germans launched a completely unexpected armoured attack in the Ardennes area. For a few days it looked as if American defences would be brushed aside; but the reality of the situation was that the German tanks, for all their firepower, had only limited amounts of fuel, and this simply ran out. For all the fright that the attack caused at all levels of the army, it was Hitler's last throw of the dice, and it was a foolish one. He had thrown away his last resources. By the time the spring came the only limit on the Allied advance was the reluctance of amateur soldiers to get killed so near the end of hostilities. When the United States dropped two nuclear bombs on Japan in August 1945 those who had been in harm's way for up to six years may have had some sympathy with the thousands of civilians who had been incinerated in Japan; but relief at getting out of the nightmare was what really mattered.

Chapter 12 ∾

| BRAVE NEW WORLD

By 1 p.m. on 8 May 1945, Belfast was a cacophony of sound. The bells of all the churches rang out, the music of their joyful message reinforced by the raucous sounds of ships' sirens and the horns from the factories. Donegall Square filled with service personnel and civilians, celebrating Germany's capitulation.

At 3 p.m. there was a hush as Churchill's victory address was relayed by loudspeaker from the City Hall. When the speech was ended a group of servicemen, more serious, perhaps, than the run of the mill who had listened from the nearby YMCA building, rose to their feet and praised God.

Praise God, from Whom all blessings flow;
Praise Him, all creatures here below;
Praise Him above, ye heavenly host;
Praise Father, Son, and Holy Ghost.

The lord mayor told the crowd that there was much to be thankful for but reminded them that when the celebrations were over there was another war to win, against Japan. For the people of Belfast, though, this was a time to celebrate, and they did. Protestant districts adorned kerbstones and air-raid shelters in red, white and blue. Celebrations in Catholic areas were less colourful but just as heartfelt. Unlike the Great War, which had seemed to many a disastrous trial of strength between great powers, the Second World War had been a fight of good against evil, and people knew it to be so and rejoiced that a genuinely evil empire had been overcome. To keep the party going, the Belfast YMCA handed out four thousand free meals that day.

Perhaps the most poignant moment in the day came at 10:40 p.m. In a city that had had darkened streets for six years, the street lighting was switched on again. There was a tremendous cheer as the City Hall and the Albert Clock were floodlit. The bonfires that evening were not confined to Protestant areas, nor were the celebrations curtailed till the next day's dawn was in the eastern sky.

Sir Basil Brooke moved quickly to call a general election for the Northern Ireland Parliament, to be held on 15 June 1945. For most of rural Northern Ireland this was simply a re-run of all the pre-war elections, and voting would almost certainly be along traditional lines. There was some concern about Belfast. The working class had acquired a self-confidence and a solidarity during the war years that might bode well for the labour movement. In the event, one Independent Labour, one Commonwealth Labour, one Socialist Republican and two straightforward Labour candidates were elected. The Unionist Party still held 37 of the 52 seats, however, and its grip on power was as strong as ever.

This was in complete contrast to what happened in Great Britain three weeks later. In the House of Commons the Labour Party was returned to power with a majority of 180, the largest margin it ever had and a clear mandate to introduce the radical programme of social reform it had published in its manifesto. Some people saw in this result a slap in the face for Churchill, who, many thought, had almost single-handedly held the country together and prevailed. It was a view Churchill would have agreed with, as he showed in his *History of the Second World War*, written over the next few years. The reality was that many servicemen remembered their fathers returning after the Great War to an ungrateful country that was not prepared to compensate men for the limbs they lost and later, during the General Strike, was prepared to use violence and middle-class volunteers to break the spirit of the working class. They were determined to have something come out of the war that they could be proud of. The women who had taken their men's places in the factories had built up their own sense of labour solidarity. They were not voting against Churchill: they voted for a welfare state.

Elections did not end with 1945. The following year the Belfast City Commission came to an end and there was an election for a new corporation. Once again left-leaning parties made small gains, mostly at the expense of the Nationalist Party.

It is easy for the comfortably off to forget the extremely poor in the normal run of things. The extremely poor have their own districts, far from the leafy suburbs. They suffer from the lassitude of hunger and do not stray far, because they cannot afford to waste energy. The terror of the blitz had driven them from their homes, and suddenly they could be seen wandering the streets, seeking new shelter. For some, they were like woodlice when someone disturbs a log: they seemed to want to get out of the light, as if it were not their natural environment. The Moderator of the Presbyterian Church that year, J. B. Woodburn, described them as

wretched people, very undersized and underfed down-and-out-looking men and women . . . Is it creditable to us that there should be such people in a Christian country?

Farmers were horrified when such people arrived in the countryside, looking for help. A report in 1946 commented that the shock of learning what had happened to Belfast was only slightly greater than the shock of finding that such unfortunates lived in the city. These were the people who had been abandoned by the Poor Law Guardians.

Four years later, they were not forgotten. The social legislation in Stormont matched that of London, act for act. In some ways Belfast was in advance of London, as when it introduced a Housing Trust to manage the building of social housing in Northern Ireland, the first such body in the United Kingdom. The Poor Law was to be repealed at last, and the workhouses were to be converted into hospitals. The reason that all of this became possible was that the United Kingdom government was prepared to subsidise Northern Ireland so that it could provide the same level of social services as the rest of the country.

The priority for Belfast seemed to be housing. Even in 1941, before the blitz, a report had noted the age and decrepitude of a significant portion of Belfast's housing stock. The worst houses were no more than hovels, with living conditions of dirt and squalor. Others were seriously affected by damp, or had rickety stairs, or had leaking roofs. Many of the houses were built before the Great Famine. The blitz increased housing needs, as it destroyed 3,200 houses and damaged another 53,000.

A survey of the housing stock completed in 1943 was a shock to the Unionist cabinet, and it was spurred to organise a survey for the whole of Northern Ireland. By 1944 Belfast Corporation had repaired 48,000 of the houses that had been damaged in air raids. A total of 74,590 houses in the city were either fit for habitation or could be made so. There was overcrowding in 23,479 houses. This left 4,537 houses that were totally unfit for habitation yet were still lived in. Overcrowded and unfit houses made up 27 per cent of the total. The immediate need was for 23,591 new houses.

As expected, the situation was worst in the centre of the city. Almost two-thirds of the houses in Smithfield and more than half the houses in the Court Ward, off the Crumlin Road, were either overcrowded or unfit. In the poorest areas of Belfast there was an average of sixty buildings per acre, and in these buildings lived three-fifths of Belfast's population. It was too great a problem for local authorities to cope with, even one as big as Belfast's, and the Minister of Health and Local Government, William Grant, incorporated a Housing Trust in his Housing Act of 1945. The Trust could borrow money from the government in order to build houses. Repayments, with interest, would be made over sixty years. Rents had to be set by the Trust, which would allow it to build further houses without having to go back to the government for more money.

The beginning of the Housing Trust did not promise much. There were five members, and they were allocated vacant offices, unfurnished and without even a telephone, in Donegall Square, South. Two civil servants were on loan to help build up the framework of the organisation. The first houses to be completed were on an estate in the Shore Road that had been begun before the war. New estates were begun in Andersonstown, Cregagh and Finaghy.

When Lucius O'Brien, the first chairman of the Trust, did his sums he had a shock: to meet the government requirement for self-sufficiency, he discovered that the rent would have to be 14 shillings per week. This was much more than the people for whom the Housing Trust had been set up could afford. The houses were soon occupied, and that at least relieved some of the pressure in the inner city. Belfast Corporation set up a 'Hustle the Houses' Committee, which built houses on blitz sites. It also erected prefabricated bungalows, the 'prefabs' of an Ulster generation, in different clusters round the city. Even private builders were getting involved. If they built practical houses of a certain dimension, each house became eligible for a subsidy of £48 per dwelling from the Stormont government. This may not seem much, but the equivalent subsidy in England was only £10.

There were 23,000 applicants on the corporation's housing list. The progress was not sufficient to deal with current need, let alone cope with the two thousand or more marriages taking place in the city each year. In the city-centre slums there was no decrease in the overcrowding. There was a density of more than two people per room in 30 per cent of the houses in Smithfield, 20 per cent in Court, 20 per cent in Dock and 19 per cent in Falls. In Dock, 242 families had to crowd into one room, while 544 families had two rooms to spread out in. More than 17 per cent of the families consisted of five or more individuals.

Eleven thousand new houses were built, mostly on new estates on the outskirts of the city, in the ten years following the war. The suburbs spread out to Glengormly in the north, Dundonald in the east and Finaghy to the south. Spaces within the city boundary were being built over. For the first time in its history, Belfast was running out of building space.

The other great post-war priority in Northern Ireland, and in particular Belfast, was health. When children had been evacuated from Sandy Row and the Shankill, rural hosts were horrified at the level of infestation with lice. Other children were obviously wasting away from tuberculosis, which was the principal cause of death in the 15–25 age group. Infant mortality was higher than it had been in 1920, and the death rate of pregnant women was the highest in Ireland or Britain. Part of the problem within Belfast was that responsibility for health matters was split three ways: the Poor Law Guardians, the government, and the corporation. The state of affairs was so bad that remedies were needed straight away. A new Ministry of Health was set up even before the war was ended, headed by William Grant, a former shipyard worker.

As there was ample evidence that there would be changes in the health service in Great Britain as soon as the war was over, it would have been foolish to set up institutions too quickly. There was one disease, however, that needed addressing immediately. Tuberculosis was endemic in Ireland and was an extremely efficient killer of young adults. A Tuberculosis Authority had been set up in 1941 with a view to eliminating the disease completely. A few years later the Southern Minister for Health introduced similar measures, and a campaign throughout the thirty-two counties of Ireland was so successful that the authority could be dissolved in 1959, and chest hospitals throughout Northern Ireland were converted to other uses.

When the National Health Service was introduced in 1948 it produced a revolution in medical provision in Belfast. The old divided system of dispensaries and separate hospitals was replaced by the overall authority of the Northern Ireland General Health Services Board. The hospitals came under the control of the Hospitals Authority, except for one. The Mater Hospital, on the Crumlin Road, had been set up as a charitable institution by the Sisters of Mercy in 1883. The streets near it had been some of the poorest in the city. From the time the main hospital opened, in 1900, it had treated the Catholic and Protestant working class, and from 1909 it was recognised as a teaching hospital by Queen's University Medical School. The problem was that it was still resolutely administered by nuns. The Health Act in England had promised that hospitals associated with a religious group would be allowed to maintain their character after being taken over by the Health Service. This clause, for some reason, was omitted from the Northern Ireland act, and the management of the Mater felt that it could not hand over control under those conditions. At a practical level, this meant that the hospital could not claim for the outpatient services it provided. In spite of being left out in the cold, the good work of the hospital continued, and there was even a modernisation programme. An organisation called the Young Philanthropists raised money by running a Northern Ireland Football Pools competition with the slogan that older readers will remember: 'If you're not in you can't win!' It was not until 1972, after the demise of the old Stormont government, that the Mater was taken into the fold of the National Health Service, although it had been getting increased funding from 1968.

Meanwhile the workhouse was handed over to the City Hospital and its former inmates were accommodated in some of the buildings, now designated a welfare hostel. Funds were granted to Queen's University to set up chairs of mental health and dentistry. The Central Laboratory, the Radiotherapy Centre and the Blood Transfusion Service were established in the city. Outpatient clinics were increased in number and a geriatric unit, Wakefield House, was set up. Deaths in childbirth were the lowest in Ireland or Britain by the 1960s.

The blitz had destroyed eighteen schools in Belfast. After that thirty thousand children and half the city's teachers had been evacuated. Once again improvements in the schools' services to children were made before the war ended. Poorer children were given free milk from 1942, and a school meals service had been operating from 1943. At the end of the war the number of scholarships to grammar schools was raised to two hundred. There was a nursery school, a school for delicate children and a new high school.

A new school system was introduced in Great Britain under the terms of the Education Act (1944)—commonly called the Butler Act. Primary school education would finish at eleven, and children would then go on to secondary school, which would be one of three types: grammar school, intermediate school, or technical school. The response of the General Assembly of the Presbyterian Church was to applaud the changes and insist that they be introduced in Northern Ireland. That was easier said than done, and it took three years of acrimonious debate after the white paper had been published before the Education Bill was finally passed.

The problem was that every section thought it had to betray its principles. The government offered to increase grants to Catholic schools for building projects from 50 per cent to 65 per cent. It would also provide free milk and free school meals to poorer pupils, and provide all books free of charge. Far from being pleased, Catholic school managers complained that this was in reality religious discrimination. As state schools were in effect Protestant schools, they argued, and they were getting 100 per cent grants, Catholics should be treated the same way. The government could face down the Catholics, but there was just as much opposition from Protestants. They focused on the fact that the requirement of compulsory Bible instruction that had existed since 1930 was being replaced with a requirement of collective worship and religious instruction in state schools. There was even a conscience clause that allowed a teacher to opt out of religious instruction. Protestant clergy were insisting on retaining a Protestant ethos in state schools, effectually proving the Catholic objections to be true.

The Dean of Belfast preached against the move. A meeting of the Ulster Women's Unionist Council addressed by the Minister of Education became so unruly that the chairwoman, Lady Clark, felt she had to abandon the meeting and walked off. At another meeting Professor Robert Corkey was certain that the state schools were being abandoned to 'Jews, agnostics, Roman Catholics and atheists.' When members of the audience heckled him, they were ejected from the hall with the cry 'We don't want communists here,' introducing another category of infamy that Corkey had overlooked. In spite of the fact that many Unionist MPs thought the move was a betrayal of protestantism, the bill was eventually passed and became law in 1947, though in 1949 a move for the government to pay Catholic teachers' insurance and superannuation was overturned by the Prime Minister.

In a way, the more conservative unionists were right to be concerned. There were provisions in the 1947 act that would see the end of Northern Ireland as it had existed since 1921. It was not the withdrawal of compulsory Bible instruction that was the worm within the bud: it was the fact that working-class children in both communities now had access to grammar schools and, more importantly, to universities. A new examination, the Eleven Plus, was supposed to identify the most able fifth of the school population, who would be allocated free places in grammar schools. Some of the rest would go to technical colleges, but the majority would go to intermediate schools. The government might have been able to ignore Catholic complaints, and to overcome Protestant reservations, but the existing grammar schools co-operated only on their own terms. They were able to do this because the success of the act depended on them, as there were almost no state grammar schools in the province. The traditional ones successfully kept control of their own affairs and kept their identity intact.

Even when the Education Committee had its own grammar schools at Annadale, Carolan and Grosvenor, many middle-class parents still preferred to pay supplementary fees and send their children to the traditional grammar schools. This in turn meant that there was little to break down social barriers for Protestants compared with the Catholic sector, where there were only traditional grammar schools, many of which had begun as junior seminaries for the diocese in which they were situated.

The problem in finding school places was compounded by the famous bulge in birth rates that followed the war, and the only solution found was to convert unneeded elementary schools into intermediate schools. Purpose-built intermediate schools did not open till the mid-1950s; in the cash-strapped Catholic sector, which depended on the personal donations of parishioners towards a building fund, it took even longer for intermediate schools to be introduced.

The 1947 act also looked for ways to provide further education for those who had missed out on the Eleven Plus and were unlikely to go to university. The Stanhope Street Further Education Centre was opened to provide day-release classes for young people in the GPO. A Juvenile Instruction Centre in Whitehouse catered for unemployed school-leavers with low academic achievement; it later moved to the Jaffe Centre in Cliftonville Road. The College of Technology expanded its provision, and the Workers' Educational Association organised classes at different venues around the city. Developments were almost continuous, and Rupert Stanley College was opened as late as 1965.

There was one way in which the original act failed. The Minister of Education, Samuel Hall-Thompson, had removed compulsory Bible instruction from the state curriculum, and accepted all the opprobrium that Protestants had heaped on his head, for one purpose: he wanted to remove any barrier that would prevent Catholics from attending state schools. The resistance of the Catholic clergy, reinforced by the howls of anguish from their Protestant equivalents, prevented the attempt to break down sectarian boundaries in education. It was only in later life, in further or in higher education, that Catholic and Protestant students could rub shoulders.

There was a sort of momentum to the prosperity in Belfast's manufacturing industry that carried on into the early post-war years. People all over the world celebrated the end to years of austerity, as they thought, by buying consumer goods. Of course there were war debts to be paid, and the reality was that the years of austerity were to continue for some time yet. Even linen had a period of revival, but this turned to decline at an even greater rate than in pre-war years. In 1951, 31,000 people worked in the Belfast linen industry; in July 1952 it was 21,000, going down to 15,500 in the mid-1960s and 8,000 in 1971. Fortunately, this was at a time when employment was booming, and most people found alternative work.

The end of the war found Harland and Wolff with a lot of work on hand, and the possibility of getting a lot more. Two of the up-and-coming shipbuilding countries, Japan and Germany, had suffered destruction of apocalyptic proportions, and it seemed unlikely that they would be building ships for some time to come. There was once again the need to replace ships sunk by war or grown old in service, as well as to convert troopships back to their peace-time role as passenger liners. When Sir Basil Brooke suggested setting up a naval dockyard in Belfast, Sir Frederick Rebbeck had no hesitation in turning down the suggestion. There was enough work going on without committing the business to the sort of capital expenditure that, after the Great War, had nearly cost Harland and Wolff its existence.

The first concern was the Admiralty order for aircraft carriers. There were four in the yard, but one, HMS *Powerful,* the last to be ordered, was cancelled. The other three orders were to go ahead, however, and were to create work for some time. A time of rapidly changing technology, both in ships and in aircraft, meant that the Admiralty was constantly looking for modifications and that completion dates were constantly being extended. This was particularly true for HMS *Eagle,* which would be the largest ship in the Royal Navy. It was considered such a milch cow for the firm that there is a story that, when eventually the ship was launched, a board was mounted beside its berth that read:

O God our help in ages past,
Our hope for years to come,
Our shelter from the stormy blast
And our eternal home.

The year 1946 saw a flood of orders, with twenty contracts signed for ships up to 17,547 tons, though most of them were much smaller than this. The only other large ship was a whale factory ship, the second ordered from Norway. There was a sense of enterprise in the air, as people sought ways of turning other people's needs into money. At that time the lightest oils that could be produced were obtained from whales, so there was expected to be a boom in the industry. This factory ship order was frustrated, however, because the government would not grant a licence for the necessary steel, as it was classified as a tanker and all tankers had to be available to lease to British Petroleum or Shell. Another problem with steel threatened. There had been a long-standing arrangement that steel would be delivered to Queen's Island at the same price as delivery to yards in Britain. This problem was resolved by Sir John Craig, a director of Harland and Wolff and chairman of Colvilles Ltd, which provided the steel.

The following year many of the orders were for medium-sized tankers. Some of these orders came from Norwegian firms that had dealt with Workman Clark before the war. Much of the routine was still taken up with restoring troopships to their peacetime glory as liners. One such was the *Reina del Pacifico*. This required a lot of work, as the hull had suffered corrosion during the war, when there was little time for maintenance. When the work was finished the ship had speed trials in the Clyde. Everything seemed satisfactory, although one of the engines, which had been fitted in 1931, seemed to overheat slightly. When the ship was sailing back to Belfast, however, all four engines exploded. The engine room was a shambles, and nobody escaped unscathed. The explosion killed twenty-eight men, including the manager of the Victoria Works, and injured another twenty-three. It was later discovered that gases in one of the crankshafts had been ignited by the overheating; this acted as a detonator and caused the other engines to explode.

Also in 1947 Harland and Wolff made a few improvements, including lengthening some of the slips, and bought from the Admiralty some of the facilities that the navy had set up on Queen's Island during the war. The most important was a welding shop that the navy had used for pre-fabricating parts for frigates. Many new ships were being butt-welded, especially Norwegian tankers. By the following year some large liners were ordered, and Queen's Island began to look more peaceful. The glut of orders, as Rebbeck had expected, began to fall off, and in 1949 only one contract came in. German shipyards had recovered from the war much more quickly than anyone could have imagined, and other countries in Europe were starting to rebuild their industrial base. The sweet life was over for British yards.

The start of the Korean War, in 1950, was a bitter or a sweet occasion in Belfast, depending on where you were standing at the time. If your husband worked on Queen's Island, where the Admiralty had ordered the rapid completion of three aircraft carriers and employment prospects were looking good, you couldn't help but be satisfied. On the other hand, if your husband served with the 1st Battalion of the Royal Ulster Rifles he was about to be called back to the colours. Goodbye to wife and young family and comfortable home built by the Housing Trust. The 1st Battalion was moved to Korea in November and early in 1951 had its first battle, north of Seoul. Forced to withdraw, it suffered 108 casualties. Later, the brigade with which it served managed to hold up an attack by 36,000 Chinese troops. Once again there were many casualties, and many bodies were carried out to sea by the flooded river and never recovered. There were many lonely widows and fatherless children in Belfast by Christmas 1951.

Yet tragedy can strike anywhere. The whale factory ship *Juan Perón* was fitting out in the Musgrave Channel. There was always a great rush to catch the bus at the end of the working day, and so, to prevent a stampede, a manager would board a vessel just before the final horn blew, assemble the workers on deck and then allow them to leave in an orderly manner. On the afternoon of 31 January—just about the time the first casualty reports from the Royal Ulster Rifles were arriving back in Belfast—the manager supervising the *Juan Perón* was suddenly taken ill. Nobody thought to reassign another manager, so when the workers came on deck there was no-one to insist that they behave sensibly. Instead of waiting on deck they thought they would gain a few seconds by waiting on the gangway. This had never been built to carry such a load, and it collapsed, throwing men into the water and onto a fender floating between the ship and the dock. Eighteen men were killed and another fifty-nine seriously injured.

Two years later, in January 1953, something happened that seemed to affect everyone in Northern Ireland. The shortest sea passage between Scotland and Ireland was the British Rail service between Stranraer and Larne. It had been the route of choice for most Belfast people travelling to Great Britain for quite some time, and had been the route taken by Winston Churchill when he was making his way home from the disastrous home rule rally in Celtic Park. Although the ferry had only twenty miles of open water to cross, the journey at times could be very uncomfortable, as these waters could be some of the roughest around Britain and Ireland. When a north-west wind swept down the North Channel and met an ebb tide going the other way, the sea in the narrows between the Mull of Galloway and the coast of County Down could become a maelstrom.

Weather forecasting in those days before satellites, let alone weather satellites, was a less scientific process than it is now. There were weather ships, and both aircraft pilots and master mariners reported weather observations to the meteorological service, but a storm could appear out of nowhere so quickly that it caught everyone by surprise. The storm that struck on 31 January and 1 February 1953 killed people as far apart as the North Channel and the Netherlands. Even London was threatened with flood.

It was up to the captain of a ship to decide whether the sea was too rough for a crossing. He had to combine his experience and knowledge of the sea and sky with the information gleaned from the weather forecast and make a final decision. On that morning the captain of the *Princess Victoria,* due to cross to Larne, decided that his ship could weather whatever the North Channel could throw at it. He made that decision in the shelter of Loch Ryan, unfortunately, and when the ship faced into the huge waves of the open waters it was soon overwhelmed. The doors that allowed cars to be loaded were battered open, and water flooded on board. It was enough to cause the ship to develop a list. It tried to heave to, but it was not under control, and at 9:46 a.m. it requested the assistance of tugs. In the continuing mayhem the cargo shifted and the list increased, making it easier for waves to crash into the ship. The engines stopped, and the *Princess Victoria* drifted south into the Irish Sea. It now transmitted an sos. Two lifeboats were looking for it, but in foul visibility, without radar, they simply could not find it, because the wind was moving it at a much greater rate than anyone could have believed.

Things got worse, and at about 2 p.m. the order was given to abandon ship. It was then that the most tragic aspect of the disaster began. In the frigid January waters, bodies lost heat extremely quickly. It was worst for children, who would have died within minutes. Women began dying soon after that, and older men. The total number who died was 133, making this the worst British maritime disaster since the Second World War. Amazingly, forty people did survive. They were all young, fit men, many of them soldiers.

The great and the good who lost their lives, including Maynard Sinclair, Deputy Prime Minister at Stormont, and Walter Smiles, member of Parliament for North Down, had banner headlines lamenting their deaths. But the real effect was on ordinary families, because it seemed as if every town in Northern Ireland had lost somebody with the ship, and there were stories for weeks afterwards of lucky people who had not sailed that day. Suddenly Northern Ireland was a very small place, with people who shared each other's sorrows. The two communities were probably closer together than at any time since VE Day.

Later that year a more pleasurable shared experience brought the communities together once more. In June the new Queen was crowned as

Elizabeth II. It would be too much to say that Catholics joined Protestants in hanging out Union Jacks, or even in buying Dinky Toy replicas of the coronation coach, but many young Catholic mothers had watched her as she grew up in the newsreels they saw at the cinema. For many she had been a model for their own growth to womanhood. She had married her handsome prince in 1947, and they had compared her children to their own. The BBC brought television to Northern Ireland specifically for coverage of the coronation. Very few people had television sets, but interested people stood outside shop windows and watched the glamour of it all. Then, when the Queen and Prince Philip toured Northern Ireland, every step of the journey was followed with interest and comment: where she had stopped at Downhill for lunch; what she had said to the mayor on the platform at Ballymena Railway Station; how small she was, even by Northern Ireland standards. It was a small gesture, but by showing interest the Catholic women of Belfast and beyond were showing just a little solidarity with the royal enthusiasms of the Protestants.

A continuing problem for Harland and Wolff in the early 1950s was that of finance. There was no longer a system of guaranteed loans, backed by the government. Finances had to be carefully managed when a large contract, such as a liner, came along. The trouble was that tankers were now moving into the same category. A medium-sized cargo ship might cost £750,000, a small tanker about £50,000 less than this. Customers were more and more looking for large tankers—up to 30,000 tons. One of these would cost £1.7 million. This was a much harder amount to raise from the banks. Large liners such as the *Reina del Mar* cost £3.1 million, but somehow the glamour of the project attracted more interest. This move towards larger ships, with a lot of thought and specification going into each order, put new difficulties in the way of firms like Harland and Wolff, which had been paying its way, or at least trying to, by building large numbers of what were now only small and medium-sized ships. Yet another review was going to have to be done. As long as the Korean War lasted and freight rates remained high, there would always be a series of smaller contracts to keep the cash flowing in the right direction. This advantage was lost in 1953 when the war ended and freight rates dropped. By this time foreign competition had increased, and new orders had to be fought for. Without the contracts for smaller ships coming in, the firm's bank balance in April was down to £162,539. Harland and Wolff had gained orders by offering credit to the ship-owners, with between three and five years' payment free. The business was actually owed £2,149,663 but couldn't get its hands on the money.

It is probably true to say that Rebbeck's reluctance to introduce new production methods, which contrasted so much with the way he embraced the new in matters of technology, was a major cause of the shrinking profit levels of the firm. Productivity at Queen's Island was extremely low compared with foreign competitors. A prolonged dispute over a wage claim by riveters caused the delay of several launchings, which made the productivity record even worse. Rebbeck did not encourage contacts with rival shipbuilding firms and tended to reject initiatives from within the firm. The introduction of welding was half-hearted, partly because of the persisting belief on Queen's Island that a riveted ship was superior to a welded ship and partly because there was a shortage of suitable cranes. This meant that the firm was far behind developments in Germany, Japan and Sweden.

In spite of the financial crisis, by the end of the year things were looking a lot happier. Most of those ships that had been offered at a ruinous fixed price had passed through the system and done their damage. New contracts had safeguards built in, so there was a better chance of making money on a deal. When the banks could see that the old system of getting a contract no matter how little you charged would no longer hold sway, it was easier to get them to finance big orders, like the one that came in from Norway in 1954 for a tanker of 36,000 tons. There were other contracts as well, like the two ferries for the Belfast–Heysham route, the *Duke of Argyll* and *Duke of Lancaster*. That year the yard had the highest output in tonnage in Britain and Ireland. By the following year it had tankers of 47,000 tons under construction. For the car drivers of the United Kingdom, this development came just in time.

Almost all Britain's oil came from the Middle East, through the Suez Canal. The canal had been built and was managed by an Anglo-French consortium, the Suez Canal Company. For a long time, therefore, the size of tankers had been constrained by the canal. A new Egyptian president, President Nasser, who had come to power in 1952, was having a very fractious relationship with the British. He considered that they were getting themselves too mixed up in the region's politics, and it seemed unreasonable that they should be making money out of a canal that went through his country and could even maintain a military base on its banks. He decided to challenge Britain in every way he could. He entered into an arms deal with Czechoslovakia, showing that he was no longer dependent on western aid. The British tried to put pressure on him by having the Americans cancel their support for the building of a dam at Aswan, in the Nile Valley. Nasser responded by nationalising the Suez Canal.

The crisis grew in intensity until 1956, when Britain and France, in secret alliance with Israel, invaded Egypt and captured the canal, but not before it had been blocked by ships that were deliberately sunk by the Egyptians. World opinion forced the invaders to withdraw. The Russians threatened to attack Paris and London; the Americans blamed Britain for offering the Russians a camouflage over their invasion of Hungary. The

Saudis refused to supply Britain or France with oil; the Americans refused to make up for the lost amounts. The only dependable supply of oil remaining was Iraq, and that oil had to be taken all the way round the Cape of Good Hope, as there was no way through the Suez Canal. The only way to do this economically was by using very big tankers. Building ships with a huge carrying capacity became something of a speciality for Harland and Wolff.

The last really good year for orders for Harland and Wolff was 1957. The most important order was for the *Canberra*, ordered by P&O. In 1955 the liner *Southern Cross* had been launched for the Shaw, Savill and Albion Line. Its design was entirely new for a passenger liner, incorporating as it did some ideas derived from building tankers. The engine was moved aft, meaning that propeller shafts were shorter and there was much more space for passengers. The idea worked, and when P&O came to order the biggest liner built in the United Kingdom they wanted it incorporated in their new ship. Another feature was that it would have its lifeboats recessed, giving its passengers a much bigger sun deck. Its superstructure would be part aluminium, to reduce weight. At 45,270 tons and with a speed of 26½ knots (31 miles per hour), it was estimated that its cost would be £11.73 million.

One anachronism was that it still used substantial amounts of riveting—the last large vessel to do so. The reason was that there were not enough welders on Queen's Island to allow the *Canberra* to be fully welded. Another anachronism was that the deal had been negotiated between the chairmen of the two companies. Although there was an understanding—at least on Rebbeck's part—that costs over the contract price would be amicably settled, this was the way of doing business that had nearly destroyed the firm in the past.

This was also the last year in which the company was under Rebbeck's autocratic control. Two of his allies on the board died, weakening his position. The very position of shipbuilding within the United Kingdom economy also came under threat. Heavy industry, including shipbuilding, had been the foundation of Britain's wealth since the Industrial Revolution. The Conservative government of Harold Macmillan viewed shipbuilding as a declining industry and preferred to look towards light engineering as the future, much more worthy of subsidies and incentives. The increasing range and speed of jet airliners was reducing the demand for passenger liners. Coastal shipping was being challenged by improvements in the road network and in road haulage. Most importantly of all, the use of welding by foreign firms allowed them to offer vessels with lower costs and better delivery dates.

Although world output had doubled, and there was obviously a demand for ships to cope with it, Harland and Wolff was simply not able to compete. Rebbeck, at the head of the firm, should have become a vulnerable figure, yet he was able to remain till 1961. A new deputy chairman was appointed, ostensibly to support him in his work; and three others, including the chief accountant, were made directors. It was only after this that moves were made to modernise the Musgrave Yard in line with the developments taking place overseas. This would involve building a new welding shed and replacing ten of the forty-year-old cranes, each capable of handling only ten tons, with four electric travelling cranes, two of them capable of moving 60 tons and two with the capacity to lift 40 tons.

Against this background, there were problems with the *Canberra*. Shortly after it was launched, in March 1960, it was calculated that the firm was already losing £1.2 million on the deal. It was becoming obvious that Harland and Wolff could no longer build big ships at a profit. A sister-ship of the *Southern Cross*, the *Northern Star*, was built on the Tyne by Vickers-Armstrongs at a price that would not cover wages and materials in Belfast. Queen's Island had facilities for building many more small ships than were likely to be ordered. It was obvious that there were serious matters of restructuring to be considered, yet little could be done while Rebbeck remained chairman. When he did retire, in 1961, essential changes were made, but by then it was too late.

Rebbeck's retirement marked the end of the post-war glory days, but it also marked the end of the culture of shipbuilding as it had been known in Belfast. Till then, Harland and Wolff had relied on the highest standards of personal skill and judgement; now that skill would be incorporated in machines, while the judgement was removed from the individual crafts-man and placed in the hands of the manager. The story of Queen's Island from now on is one of decline, sometimes at such a slow rate that it passed unnoticed. It could be seen, however, in its effect on the social cohesion of the work force. Clubs and choirs survived for a while, but almost all, like old soldiers, faded away.

The *Canberra* lost a great deal of money for the firm, the first ship to do so since the war. By the mid-1960s Harland and Wolff lost money every year. By 1966 the loss was £4 million; by 1969 it was more than £8 million. The crisis in the firm was not at all obvious to people outside the ship-building industry, because it seemed as if there was no end to the technical achievements coming out of Queen's Island. In 1966, for example, the oil rig *Sea Quest* was launched, the first time such a structure had been launched in one piece. In 1969 the 190,000-ton tanker *Myrina* was delivered, the largest in Europe that year. In 1970 a huge shipbuilding dock was begun, capable of holding a ship of up to one million tons, which could then be floated off rather than launched. This was the time that the crane Goliath was built, immediately becoming a city landmark. To the citizen of Belfast casually observing all this activity from the Queen's Bridge it seemed that shipbuilding was going from strength to strength. Only the workers and the politicians realised that the number employed in Queen's Island had fallen from 20,000 in 1960 to 9,000 in 1969. Harland and Wolff was actually increasing its share of United Kingdom shipbuilding; the trouble was that the United Kingdom's share of world shipbuilding was declining fast.

Harland and Wolff's neighbour on Queen's Island, Short Brothers and Harland, was doing slightly better, after a shaky start. It had specialised in large seaplanes and bombers. The former went out of fashion about 1950, while the latter developed into a cut-throat industry as the Cold War developed. It survived for a time on subcontract work for other firms, building 130 Canberra bombers and, later, Bristol Britannia airliners. It had constant trade disputes through the 1950s, often caused by changes in government defence policy, which held things back, but in the 1960s it struck gold with a series of anti-aircraft missiles that sold all round the world. During the same decade the company developed the Short Skyvan. The name described it perfectly: for many years it was the Transit van of the aeronautical industry, particularly in developing countries, where proper landing strips were in short supply. Research and development was an expensive undertaking, however, and may have contributed to the financial problems that forced the firm to lay off 550 workers in 1966. Shorts got round the research costs by building parts of aircraft for other companies, such as wings for the Fokker Friendship and the pods for Rolls-Royce engines used in the Lockheed Tristar. With eight thousand workers, however, it was almost as important to the local economy as the shipyard, and it received a great deal of support from the Northern Ireland government.

Other engineering companies had varying fortunes. James Mackie and Sons built textile machinery, and kept themselves in touch with industry needs by developing products suitable for artificial fibre alongside its traditional lines. Sirocco, which built ventilation equipment, also did well. The ropeworks failed, however, and was closed by the end of the 1970s. The total number employed in manufacturing managed to remain the same because of the introduction of much more light engineering to the city. By the late 1960s such diverse products as oil-drilling equipment, computers and tape recorders were being made. Just outside Belfast a huge Michelin tyre factory had opened at Mallusk.

In education, many more teachers were employed, and there were more jobs in health, local government and the civil service. The service industries began to grow. Unemployment in Belfast in 1965 was about 3 per cent. More importantly, the city had broadened its employment base, leaving it less vulnerable to a crisis in a single industry.

As they had been throughout the history of Belfast, the Harbour Commissioners were active, anticipating change and providing the right conditions for it to happen. They continually widened and deepened channels, using the spoil to reclaim land on both sides of the river mouth. British Petroleum opened a refinery on reclaimed land beyond the shipyard. A daily ferry service to Liverpool began in 1959, followed by one to Heysham. A weekly service was begun to Preston. Within a few years there were daily passenger and cargo sailings to Liverpool, Heysham and Glasgow and container services to Heysham, Liverpool and Preston. Freight services went twice a week to Ardrossan, Bristol, Greenock and Manchester and once a week to Aberdeen, Cardiff, Dundee, London, Leith, Middlesborough, Newcastle, Stornoway and Swansea. A hundred sailings a week took five thousand containers a week to Britain and the Continent, with a yearly tonnage of 1.35 million. An increasing proportion of the imported tonnage was made up of oil, as generating stations changed from coal to oil and more people took advantage of growing prosperity to buy cars.

As freight services increased, more passengers began to go by air. Nutts Corner was replaced by Aldergrove in 1963, used by a million travellers in 1966. Other changes in public transport took place within the city. The last tram had run in 1954. The replacement trolleybuses were quiet and produced no fumes, but the way they had to operate meant that they got in the way of the increasing number of cars, and they too were replaced, gone completely by 1968. Rail transport was curtailed, and many lines were closed. A new phenomenon was the growth of the traffic jam.

Another phenomenon of the post-war years was the decline in Belfast's population. In the census of 1951 the population was 443,671, though roughly another 91,000 lived in the urban area but not inside the city boundary. In 1961 the population recorded was 415,856 and in 1971 362,082. In twenty years it had dropped by more than 80,000, reversing a trend that had lasted at least a century and a half. The government refused a request from Belfast Corporation in 1947 to extend the city's boundaries. Many houses built for Belfast people after this were built outside the boundary: in Andersonstown, Dunmurry and Lisburn to the south, in Newtownabbey in the north and in Castlereagh, Holywood and Newtownards to the east. This population on the fringe still looked to Belfast for employment, shopping and recreation. Geographers found it necessary to start speaking of the three cities of Belfast. The inner city was within the county boundary; greater Belfast included this and the immediate fringe of housing developments; regional Belfast stretched 25 miles from the city centre and was defined by the ability of its inhabitants to work in the city. Such a definition if used in the twenty-first century would mean that regional Belfast included Donegal to the west and Newry to the south.

The example of urban sprawl in England had worried Northern Ireland's planners after the war. In 1945 the Planning Commission recommended that a green belt be established around Belfast, and in 1951 it recommended that the population of inner Belfast should be limited to 300,000. It was estimated that building 22,000 houses would solve the problem. Sir Robert Matthew produced an urban area plan in 1962, the first practical step in realising these aims. He took as his basic premise that Belfast and the fringe were already too big and should not be allowed to grow beyond a 'stop line'. The corporation had no planning department of its own at the time and was at a disadvantage in the discussion. It was forced to accept the stop line.

The estimate of 22,000 new houses needed had been a very conservative one. In 1961 only Glasgow and Liverpool had higher densities of housing than Belfast of all the cities in the United Kingdom. It averaged 16,846 per square mile, with some areas much more dense than this. From 1945 the number of council houses built averaged 470 per year, yet the city surveyor estimated in 1959 that Belfast needed 2,600 a year for twenty years.

The corporation, the Housing Trust and private developers had built 11,000 houses in the ten years following the war. Many of these, however, had been built with a view to housing as many families as possible and did nothing to reduce Belfast's housing density. The houses were small, and many did not reach the Parker-Morris standards, the preferred standards for public housing. In 1956 the Housing Act gave the corporation responsibility for slum clearance and inner-city development. Unfortunately, it was discovered that much of the land, together with the ground rents from it, was owned by churches and was not subject to compulsory purchase. To do this would require amendments to the Government of Ireland Act (1920).

It was not until 1968 that Belfast City Council, as it had now become, adopted a scheme for redevelopment. The work began with the demolition of houses in the Divis Street and nearby Cullingtree Road areas. Kitchen houses were to be knocked down and replaced with flats.

Belfast people did not like flats. The inhabitants of the Turf Lodge flats on the Falls Road complained about the loss of community. Blocks of flats in the Shankill were called 'Weetabix' flats, because they resemble cereal packets. Neither development lasted more than a few years. Then the Troubles started, with mass movements of people in 1969 and even greater dislocation in 1971. Civil strife and redevelopment, combined with the destruction of property, made the housing situation even worse. There were still 29,750 houses in Belfast in 1974 that were unfit for human habitation.

It took some time for the innovations in primary and secondary education to bed in, but by the 1960s it was obvious that there was an increasing need for further education. New premises for the College of Domestic Science were opened in Garnerville in 1962, while a College of Art was opened in 1968 on a bomb site in York Street, near St Anne's Cathedral.

This replaced the cramped conditions into which the College of Art had squeezed in the Technical College. Rupert Stanley College for Further Education was opened in east Belfast in 1965, and the College of Business Studies followed in 1971. The Northern Ireland Polytechnic was opened at Jordanstown in 1968. Education consumed an ever-increasing proportion of Belfast's rates: 35 per cent in 1960, 43 per cent in 1970.

A new Education Act in 1968 introduced full entitlement to state grants for Catholic schools that would allow a third of their governors, of whom there had to be at least six, to be appointed by the education authority. Although this meant that there were in effect two parallel state-funded systems, the change did have the effect of rescuing Catholic schools from the grasp of individual priests, who often ruled the schools they managed in a very autocratic style. It also allowed Protestant nominees to see that Catholic schools were not the hotbeds of republican unrest that many unionists believed.

At the end of the war the main forms of public entertainment were the radio—most often still called the wireless—and the cinema. In cinemas there were four complete showings each day, and there were long queues for the most popular films, such as *The Greatest Show on Earth* and *Singing in the Rain*. Television was introduced in time for the Queen's coronation, but the small, dull sets, showing programmes for only a few hours each evening, were hideously expensive by the standards of Northern Ireland in the 1950s. They were a multiple of a working man's wages, rather than a fraction, as is often the case now. Retailers used all sorts of tricks to increase their trade, including public broadcasts of such events as the Cup Final and the Grand National. Increasing prosperity, together with wider use of hire purchase, meant that television ownership spread very quickly, encouraged by better reception and bigger sets as the technology improved. This stay-at-home viewing did not have an immediate effect on cinemas. It is true that some cinemas in places like the Shankill and the Shore Road became more run down, but a large new cinema was opened in Royal Avenue as late as the mid-1960s.

One feature of Belfast life that struck visitors from Britain and elsewhere was the 'Belfast Sunday'. A survey of undergraduates at Queen's University in 1959 showed that 94 per cent of Catholics attended church on Sunday, 64 per cent of Methodists, 59 per cent of Presbyterians and a rather lax 46 per cent of members of the Church of Ireland. Such a high rate of church attendance in a group that was probably at the least religious stage in its life shows just how fundamental religion was to life in Northern Ireland. One interesting insight into the Protestant churches is that, where churches were built after the war to replace those that were damaged by bombs, they were invariably built for smaller congregations.

Smaller congregations or not, Protestant clergy still had enough influence to ensure that the official attitude to Sunday reflected a sab-batarian tradition. Most Protestants in Northern Ireland, even those who were members of the Church of Ireland, were deeply evangelical and would not play or attend organised games on a Sunday. That would not have been a problem except that they thought other people should do likewise; and to discourage them from breaking the sabbath, the corporation ensured that public facilities were closed on Sundays. Catholics, who believed that Sunday had been given to people so that they could recreate themselves, felt that, as long as they also attended mass, recreation should be part of the Sunday curriculum. They deeply resented what they saw as a denial of their liberties. And they claimed that Protestants stayed in their back kitchens reading lurid scandals in the *News of the World* and contrasted this with their own 'healthy' interest in sport.

The corporation, and later the city council, ignored such complaints. During the war it was only after much acrimony that one cinema was allowed to remain open on Sundays, for the exclusive use of uniformed members of the armed forces. In 1964 the council's Education Committee committed heresy when it voted by a narrow majority that play centres and swings should be open for the use of children on Sundays. After a campaign involving the churches and the Orange Order, and largely co-ordinated by an outspoken young clergyman, Ian Paisley, the vote was reversed in the full council the following month. It was not till 1968, and after votes by local residents, that most of them were opened. An idea of how deeply feelings ran can be seen in the municipal elections of 1967. None of the three Unionists who had voted in favour of Sunday opening was reselected. In the case of the Labour Party, whose policy it had been to vote in favour of Sunday opening, not a single candidate was elected, in spite of the fact that three Labour councillors had voted against the party leadership.

There were few exciting moments in Belfast politics in the twenty years after the war. In Great Britain a Local Government Act in 1948 widened the franchise in local elections to correspond to parliamentary elections. This change was not introduced in Northern Ireland, where only those who occupied a property with an annual valuation of £10 or more had a vote in local elections. For each extra £10 in valuation, the occupier could nomi-nate another voter, up to a maximum of six. Lodgers and adult children were excluded, as were the poor, both Protestant and Catholic. Because the more valuable property tended to be owned by Protestants, the extra votes tended to discriminate in favour of the Unionist Party.

It is worth noting that voting in Stormont elections also differed from British practice. Owners of businesses got extra votes, and graduates of Queen's University elected (by proportional representation) four members of the Northern Ireland Parliament, in addition to voting in their own constituency. Constant reminders by the Prime Minister and others of the threat that the South posed made certain that the core issue of all elections, even municipal ones, was the safety of Northern Ireland and meant that voting continued to be along tribal lines, right into the 1960s.

Then there seemed to be something of a revival for left-leaning parties, reaching a maximum in 1964, when the Northern Ireland Labour Party polled well and even seemed to get some Catholic votes. It was a false dawn, however.

The party was caught in a pincer movement by the new Unionist Prime Minister, Terence O'Neill, and the Republican Labour Party, led by a former seaman called Gerry Fitt. In a way, the years of O'Neill's premiership were themselves a false dawn. He set out to change the relations between Catholics and Stormont, though he wanted this to happen without having to deal with the underlying problems. Chosen by the Unionist establishment in locked committee rooms, he seemed a safe pair of hands, coming from good, aristocratic stock, unlike his businessman rival Brian Faulkner, who, although more able and definitely more ambitious, would simply not do. O'Neill did make some brave steps to modernise the Unionist monolith. Links were established with the trade union movement. He visited Catholic schools and was photographed shaking hands with nuns. This was done during a period when many people thought the world was changing. Harold Macmillan had made his 'Winds of Change' speech about Africa. The election of John Kennedy as president of the United States seemed to make youth, equality and hope the themes of the incoming decade. Closer to home, a science graduate and leader of the Labour Party had become Prime Minister, and, although Harold Wilson was traditional enough to smoke a pipe, his trademark overcoat was made of a modern material. Even Pope John XXIII, old man though he was, had made changes that would loosen the grip of the Vatican on the Catholic Church.

Measured against these, O'Neill's initiatives were hardly world-shattering. Claims that he destroyed unionism are somewhat exaggerated. What he tried to do was ensure the survival of unionism in a changing world. For much of Northern Ireland's history a major concern of the Unionist Party was that the working man might forsake it and join Labour. This would have been more likely if the British Labour Party had been prepared to organise in Northern Ireland. Harold Wilson was by nature anti-unionist, so O'Neill felt that a stress on modern industry and improving religious toleration was a necessary safeguard in case of interference by London. He also wanted Wilson to feel that there was enough foreign investment in Northern Ireland for Stormont to be able to look after itself. Most of all, he wanted to demonstrate that he was prepared to forget ancient quarrels in the name of future prosperity.

There had been a change in leadership in the Republic as well, with the inward-looking de Valera replaced by Seán Lemass. He had fought in the Easter Rising in Dublin and had been a close colleague of de Valera all his political life, but he was depressed by the stagnation of the Republic's economy, largely caused by the necessity of being self-sufficient during the years of the Second World War, when he had been Minister for Supplies and had realised that it is impossible for a country to be prosperous and isolationist. Both North and South needed foreign investment, and the sensible thing seemed to be for the two states in Ireland to pool their resources. O'Neill invited Lemass to Stormont in 1965. It was a gamble, and both knew that their backbenchers might rebel, or that there might be a reaction outside parliament that would bring down one or both of them. Lemass need not have worried, because Southern opinion was very supportive of the meeting. O'Neill became a popular figure in the Republic and was voted Man of the Year by readers of a Dublin paper in 1969, the year in which he was forced to resign.

Unionist support for the meeting was also forthcoming. There were complaints that there had been unnecessary secrecy, and resentment that Unionists had been told of the meeting only on the day it happened, when Lemass had actually arrived in Stormont. Apart from this, the visit was a great success. One focus of opposition was the Rev. Ian Paisley, who, fresh from his victory on the question of unlocking swings on Sundays, staged a number of protests; but newspapers backed O'Neill, particularly the *Belfast Telegraph*.

One of the most striking developments to come out of the meeting concerned the Nationalist Party. Lemass persuaded its leader, Eddie McAteer, a businessman from Derry whose brother was a leading member of the IRA, that his party should become the official opposition at Stormont. O'Neill's language was inclusive, asking all sections of the community to take a new pride in the province and saying that the government was working for the good of all and not just unionists. One sign that he was getting through to Catholics was that a Catholic girl was elected Miss Young Unionist for Belfast in 1966!

There was a significant minority in his own party that was not listening. Their view of O'Neill was summed up by Ian Paisley, the master of the cutting phrase. Speaking about O'Neill's attempt to build bridges, he said, 'A traitor and a bridge are very much alike, for they both go over to the other side.' Since the inception of Northern Ireland people had been warned that Catholics were enemies of the state by their mere being; to bring Catholics into the fold was anathema. A new fault line was developing in Northern Ireland, between unionists who hoped that a deal could be done with Catholics and unionists who felt you could not trust a Catholic as far as you could throw him. New feathery fractures grew out from this, and from a monolithic Unionist Party there developed a sequence of groupings, each claiming to be more hard-line in its attitude than the other. It was a trend that would continue for more than a quarter of a century.

At its heart was the Rev. Ian Kyle Paisley. Easily the most multi-faceted Irishman of the second half of the twentieth century, he has continued to surprise observers even into the twenty-first. Born into a tradition of small evangelical churches, ordained a minister by his father and bursting with too much energy to be contained by somebody else's constraints, he founded and became moderator of his own church, the Free Presbyterian Church of Ulster. At first he was dismissed by many as an organiser of stunts, but his ability to put into words the unspoken fears of a great many Protestants brought him many supporters. In the past the broad churches of unionism and the Orange Order would have had no trouble in accommodating such fundamentalist views. Paisley's technique in the 1950s and 60s was to accuse everyone else of betraying the Protestant cause while portraying himself as its one true defender. Too fundamental for fundamentalists and too Orange for the Orange Order, he has always been his own man. When the slight easing of political and religious tensions encouraged Belfast City Council to fly the flag on the City Hall at half mast on the occasion of Pope John xxiii's death in June 1963, Paisley denounced the 'lying eulogies' being paid to the Roman anti-Christ. The following year he was the cause of the worst street violence in Belfast for thirty years when he threatened to remove a Tricolour from the window of Republican headquarters on the Falls Road. The police felt compelled to remove the offending item themselves and had to deal with two days of serious rioting as a result. Two years later he launched a weekly vehicle for his views, the *Protestant Telegraph*. Catholics often bought it for its entertainment value, without realising that some of its articles spoke direct to the heart of many Protestants, fearful for their position within an evolving society.

Also in 1966, Paisley established the Ulster Constitution Defence Committee and its offshoot, the Ulster Protestant Volunteers. These gave him the foot-soldiers he needed for his demonstrations. The largest that year was held outside the Presbyterian General Assembly while it was being attended by the Governor of Northern Ireland, Lord Erskine. Though Paisley was dismissed by the media as a crank, it soon became obvious that he was gathering support among the urban working class and much more generally in the rural parts of Northern Ireland.

It is surprising just how often the spark for violence within Northern Ireland comes from somewhere outside its borders. 1966 was the fiftieth anniversary of the Easter Rising in Dublin. Éamon de Valera, one of the leaders of the rising, was President of Ireland, and there was a week of celebration on the streets and on television. The tone of the coverage was every bit as triumphalist as an Orange march. There were still alive in Belfast large numbers of survivors of the Battle of the Somme, which had started only weeks after the events in Dublin, who believed that the rising was a betrayal of their efforts on behalf of King and Empire. Reading reports of the celebrations almost certainly raised old resentments. Gusty Spence was a shipyard worker who had been born on the Shankill in 1933. His parents had lived through the Home Rule Crisis and the birth pangs of the state, and he had a constant sense of its fragility, of its need to be defended. He believed that the all-Ireland rhetoric of the 1966 celebrations might well encourage a rising in Northern Ireland. The fact that Gerry Fitt had been elected to the British House of Commons for Republican Labour underlined the danger. In spite of the easing of community relations, Catholics and Protestants were still very separate, and Spence had no way of knowing that many young Catholics saw the celebrations as irrelevant jingoism. Convinced of the imminent danger, he and others formed a paramilitary group; to give it legitimacy, they called it the Ulster Volunteer Force. Several of its members, including Spence, were ex-soldiers and were used to weapons, and it was not long before they were on the streets, defending Ulster.

The first attack was on a Catholic-owned bar. A 77-year-old Protestant widow was killed in a fire started by a petrol bomb. Undeterred, they tried again, this time in the Falls area, shooting a man who shouted 'Up the Republic; up the rebels,' on his way home from a pub. The third victim fell into their lap. A teenage Catholic barman wandered into a public house in Malvern Street, just off the Shankill Road. He was shot as he left the bar. The series of killings, which took place over two summer months, was condemned almost universally, and it did not take the police long to round up the culprits, who were given long jail sentences. The *Belfast Telegraph* warned of the consequences if there was a repeat of such activities. Almost every unionist agreed with the condemnation of violence, but a substantial minority also agreed on the necessity of getting rid of O'Neill. In particular, the rank and file of the Orange Order was turning against him, and there were unpleasant scenes at the 12th of July celebrations of 1967. One Westminster MP was beaten unconscious when he tried to defend O'Neill. A few days after visiting a convent school in Belfast in early 1968 the Prime Minister himself was attacked and pelted with stones, flour and eggs when he attended a Unionist Party meeting in Belfast.

All this was happening while there were Catholic voices urging greater participation in the state. Free education had brought into being an enlarged Catholic middle class that was much more self-confident and assertive than ever before. They saw the Nationalist Party as outmoded and the IRA as archaic. John Hume, a teacher and pioneer of the credit union movement, argued that there were ways of developing resources that Catholics already had and of making a more positive contribution to the community. At the same time Gerry Fitt, at that time the most affable of men, was gaining friends for Northern Catholics among Labour MPs. He was also very good at encouraging journalists to write articles that suited his cause. There was a range of forces lining up against unionism that would soon shake the staid Belfast Sunday to its foundations.

Chapter 13 ∼

| A TERMINAL CONDITION?

When Tom McCluskie got out of his warm bed one cold Monday in early July and got ready for his first day working in Harland and Wolff he was following a tradition going back almost a hundred years, of boys following their fathers into the shipyard. The school he had attended stood on the slopes of Cave Hill and had given him a view across the Lagan to the cranes and gantries of Queen's Island and to the shapes of hulls as they rose in the slips. As he looked, he was aware of the traditions that in some families had led to six or even seven generations being 'yard men'. He knew of the close relationship between the shipyard and the small streets of east Belfast huddled around it that led to workers from the County Antrim side of the Lagan being called foreigners. He looked forward to earning good money when he completed his apprenticeship.

What he did not know was the reality of working in a hostile and dangerous environment. He did not know that there was a tradition that every newly qualified tradesman was made redundant within a week of qualifying, in case he developed too high a sense of his own importance, so that when he got his job back there was just enough uncertainty about the future for him to strive hard to keep it. He did not know that when work was short some foremen expected bribes before they would allocate work to anyone.

His breakfast was toast, made by his mother before she went to her own work. His father was a hard man, made hard by shipbuilding. He had begun work as an apprentice driller when he was fourteen, and the working conditions were so cold in winter that men had to chip ice from the machinery before work could start and in summer so warm among the hot steel plates that they became irritable and ready for a fight. When he questioned an instruction on one occasion his supervisor punched him in the face. There was no comeback.

He had tried to persuade Tom to look somewhere else for a job, but there are things young men have to learn for themselves. Now, breakfast finished, father and son left the house and walked to the docks, where there was a ferry that would take them across the Lagan.

The ferry took them to a landing stage at the end of the Victoria Wharf. The sudden list as the small boat came alongside and everyone tried to disembark at once caught the unwary off guard, and the force as dozens of feet pushed against the gunwale meant that there was a gap that Tom had to jump, landing on the slippery surface of the pontoon, which was bucking up and down in the short chop coming in from Belfast Lough. They got up onto the wharf itself and followed the crowd to the back entrance to Harland and Wolff. New arrivals had to report to the head timekeeper, and here Tom was given his works number and his board. The board was used like a time card: it had Tom's personnel number stamped on it and he collected it from the timekeeper each morning, returning it as he left work in the evening. It was a primitive way of keeping a record of hours worked, and it was easy to abuse. On the other hand, if anyone lost his board the yard refused to pay his wages.

As a school-leaver, Tom was only fifteen, and government regulations meant that he could not become an apprentice until his sixteenth birthday. While he was under age he was assigned to work in the drawing office as a message boy. As he delivered packages around the different departments he learnt not only the geography of the shipyard but its culture. This was based on the harsh need to survive, quite literally, where death and injury were almost routine matters. There was little sympathy for the injured from their fellow-workers, who seem to have delighted in using offensive nicknames, such as Nail-in-the-Boot or One Wing, the former applied to someone with a limp, the latter to someone who had lost a hand or an arm. The management itself was no more sympathetic. If a worker was injured there was usually some job that he could do in the yard, at least until he got himself fixed up somewhere else. If, however, the injured man sued for compensation, Harland and Wolff would fight the case every step of the way and would also pass the man's name around other firms as that of a trouble-maker, effectually getting him blacklisted.

Even when deaths resulted from an accident there would be a cover-up. When a riveter fell onto a concrete slip one frosty day because a faulty plank was used in building the staging, men were called in to scrape ice and bird droppings from all the staging, cover the staging and surrounding walkways with sand and remove and replace the faulty plank; all this was done before informing the accident investigators, who arrived to find a safe working environment exceeding government standards. The dead man's family received the minimum compensation, and the accident report would compliment Harland and Wolff for being a responsible employer.

Life in the Apprentice Training Centre was one of unsmiling discipline and constant assessment. It was a life governed by regulations that seem to have been designed to reinforce the control the firm had over the men.

Workers' use of the lavatory was limited to seven minutes per day, and there was even a lavatory attendant whose job it was to record the time of arrival and departure of each worker. Anyone whose insides would not accommodate these timekeepers found that he lost thirty minutes off his wages. Most men simply relieved themselves where they worked, with the resultant fetid atmosphere in summer.

Among the apprentices themselves there was a great deal of aggression. Aware of the importance of personal reputation in the yard, there were individuals who tried to make one as soon as possible, who wanted a perch high in the pecking order. To do this they would take part in stunts that rivalled each other in viciousness, as Tom was to find one morning. He was working at a bench when someone tapped him on the shoulder. Turning round automatically, he had a paintbrush of red lead shoved in his face. The pain in his eyes was agony, and he was temporarily blinded. He was helped to the medical centre, where he was shocked when the male nurse insisted on recording the cause as the accidental spilling of a tin of paint. Tom left Harland and Wolff two weeks later and took up work in the motor trade.

What Tom McCluskie left was a miniature of the Northern Ireland state, shackled by traditions that were quoted as regulations, where the underpinning law was, You will not let the other take advantage of you; where power is might and you make sure power is not distributed more evenly. Even to hint at the possibility of change is to show weakness. The softening of attitudes encouraged by Terence O'Neill was only that: a matter of attitudes. He would say later that if one treated a Roman Catholic like a Protestant he might come to behave like one; yet there was not one initiative in the O'Neill years that gave Catholics access to areas previously limited to Protestants.

Many of the new businesses that moved to Northern Ireland were established in or near Belfast and then often in Protestant areas. The new city that was planned was safely ensconced in a predominantly Protestant part of County Armagh. When it came to building a second university, Catholic Derry, with an existing university college, was passed over for Protestant Coleraine, where so little preliminary study was carried out that the two main buildings, supposed to be built together, were separated by a quarter of a mile. In an amazing show of unity, Catholics and Protestants from Derry, including its Unionist mayor, Albert Anderson, staged a motorcade to Stormont, complaining that the River Bann was a symbolic border within Northern Ireland and that there would be no developments west of it. (Later it was revealed that Anderson had been party to the decision in favour of Coleraine, but he was still elected to Stormont in 1968.) In 1967 three public boards were reconstituted. Of the seventy-nine members appointed, only seven were Catholics. Perhaps most critically, nothing was done to remedy the gerrymandered ward boundaries in Derry that enabled a Protestant minority to keep the Catholic majority in the city bereft of political power.

It was in response to this inertia that the Northern Ireland Civil Rights Association was formed at the beginning of 1967. Self-consciously based on the model of Martin Luther King, its members were a disparate lot, with representatives from Northern Ireland Labour, Ulster Liberals, the Communist Party of Ireland, the Irish Congress of Trade Unions and the Republican Clubs (the name temporarily adopted by Sinn Féin, which was banned). For some reason the Nationalist Party chose not to attend. The NICRA formulated a series of demands, which included one man one vote; an end to gerrymandering; the elimination of discrimination in government; the elimination of discrimination in the allocation of houses; and the disbanding of the B Specials.

Two main concerns in 1968 were employment and housing. Unemployment stood at almost 8 per cent at the start of the year. This does not give an accurate picture of the worst-hit areas, as employment opportunities were unevenly spread over the state. The issue that brought matters to a head was housing. Over the years there had been many complaints about the unfair allocation of houses in County Tyrone. An unmarried Protestant woman who happened to be the secretary of a Unionist politician was allocated a house in Caledon in preference to two Catholic families who were also on the housing list. Shortly after the woman moved in, a Catholic family squatting next door was evicted. When the local Nationalist MP, Austin Currie, found that he was unable to remedy the situation either in the local council or in Stormont, he made the gesture of symbolically squatting in the woman's house, before the RUC removed him. To the delight of reporters who wanted a final twist to what was already a good story, one of the policemen who evicted Currie was the woman's brother. (He later moved into the house himself.)

Seeing a suitable cause in which to get involved, the NICRA arranged its first protest march, from the Catholic village of Coalisland to the local town, Dungannon. Although this was taking place well to the west of the Bann, the Rev. Ian Paisley announced that he was going to hold a counter-demonstration. This was a tactic he had used at Easter, in his birthplace, Armagh, when he had managed to get the annual Easter republican commemoration march banned by saying that he was going to hold a prayer meeting on the route. With him this time he had an organisation called the Ulster Protestant Volunteers, whose motto was 'For God and Ulster'; the following year a small group of these would start a bombing campaign, in the hope that the IRA would get the blame. The police tried to keep the two sides apart, but stones were thrown and some of the civil rights marchers were injured.

The next NICRA march was to take place in Derry, where many of the Unionists' vices were to be seen at their worst. The Minister of Home Affairs was William Craig, who misread the situation in two ways. Firstly, because of the representation of Republican Clubs in the NICRA he reasoned that the association was simply a cover for IRA activity. Secondly, he did not realise that some influential members of the NICRA were hoping to provoke the authorities into confrontation. On 5 October 1968 the confrontation was seen on television. A small crowd of demonstrators was halted in a narrow street, one of their leaders was struck in the midriff by a police baton while appealing for calm, and then two lines of police attacked the marchers, who were trapped between them. The individual policemen were simply out of control, as they had been ordered by the county inspector not to attack. Perhaps the worst image was of an apparently senior officer laying about the retreating marchers with a blackthorn stick.

Among the marchers were three Labour MPs, and the incident was a propaganda disaster for O'Neill and the Stormont government. It provoked many Catholics who would never before have thought of taking to the streets, and it even annoyed many liberal Protestants into demonstrating against the government. Worst of all, it attracted the interest of the Labour government in London, which began to demand concessions.

Up till then there had been a tradition of the British government letting Stormont get on with things in Northern Ireland, so much so that the majority in O'Neill's cabinet felt that it was possible to resist London's pressure to reform. The reality was that enormous subsidies were paid to Stormont so that Northern Ireland could have the same level of social care as the rest of the United Kingdom. Now the British Prime Minister, Harold Wilson, at a meeting with O'Neill and Craig in Downing Street, threatened to cancel all the financial arrangements with Northern Ireland. The meeting ended when, in spite of all that Wilson had said, Craig asked for more subsidies for a Belfast firm. Wilson lost his temper and told them Stormont had become a soup kitchen that was no good to anybody.

The winter of 1968/9 passed in a series of concessions grudgingly offered and never seeming to be enough. When Derry Corporation was replaced by a commission, rumours passed among Catholics in the city that all Protestant employees had been given a pay rise. One change that was almost universally welcomed by Catholics—the exceptions were those who believed that more reform could only be obtained through continued confrontation— was the sacking of Craig, who seemed to them to be the epitome of Unionist bigotry. As for most Protestants Craig had been the epitome of Unionist resolve, it was obvious that tensions were going to increase between the two communities. Even some Catholics felt that the founding of a new organisation at the end of the year was unnecessary and provocative.

People's Democracy, an organisation of leftist students, argued that O'Neill's reforms were little more than window-dressing and that that core democratic issues were not being addressed. To demonstrate their concerns they planned to start the new year by walking from Belfast to Derry along a direct route that took them through some staunchly Protestant areas. Although only a small group began the march, the sight of unionist counter-demonstrators at many points along the way and what was perceived as police pettiness in the way the marchers were rerouted, rather than given protection, encouraged more and more Catholics to become involved. This was particularly true on the short, final stage from Claudy to Derry.

The group left the village in what was almost a carnival atmosphere; but as the marchers approached Burntollet Bridge they were entering a very vulnerable area. On their right was high ground, while on their left was a small area bounded by the confluence of two rivers. When the marchers were properly in the 'killing zone' the ambush was sprung. A mob of several hundred, which included off-duty members of the B Specials, started throwing stones and then charged the marchers and beat them with cudgels, driving some of them into the river. Television cameras witnessed the police escort standing by and doing nothing to protect the marchers. In propaganda terms, the loyalists had scored an own goal.

The crisis in unionism forced O'Neill to call an election in February. The campaign was messy on the Unionist side, and the result was no better. O'Neill won, but only just. His authority was weakened, as was his prestige. At the same time many ageing Nationalist members were replaced by younger, often more energetic, civil rights campaigners. Worse, from a unionist point of view, was that Bernadette Devlin, possibly one of the most radical of the student activists, was elected to the British House of Commons in the symbolically significant constituency of Mid-Ulster.

It was shortly after this that members of the Protestant Volunteers began to bomb public utilities, in the hope that the government would take this as proof of IRA activity. The mobilisation of B Specials, supported by the military, heightened tension even further, and in the end it was O'Neill who bent under pressure and resigned, the victim of his own inability to persuade unionism of the urgency of reform. Men like Craig and Paisley, who had seen a firm 'no' work in the past, were yet to be persuaded that it would not work in the future.

O'Neill's successor, James Chichester-Clark, had an army and farming background. Pushed reluctantly into the limelight as Minister of Agriculture when O'Neill had sacked Harry West (for alleged improper behaviour over land sold to St Angelo Airport at Enniskillen), Chichester-Clark looked the part, but his slow, phlegmatic manner made it easy for his opponents to wrong-foot him when they thought it necessary. He had been handed a poisoned chalice anyway, as civil cohesion, particularly in Derry, was being eroded at an ever-faster rate. The announcement of universal adult suffrage was now not enough. Chichester-Clark had hardly settled into his office when Derry exploded. Resentment had built up among the Catholic population as they looked for changes in the way their ambitions were treated by the state. They had been horrified when, during rioting in April, police had entered the house of Samuel Devenney, a taxi-driver, and batoned him.

The Orange celebrations on 12 July were met by trouble all over Northern Ireland. In Belfast, Orange marchers were attacked from Unity Flats by Tricolour-waving stone-throwers, while in Derry the police were stoned and shops looted. When, however, Samuel Devenney died on 16 July from the injuries received during the beating there was a realisation that the stakes had been raised to the next level.

The focus of unionist celebrations in Derry has always been the city's famous siege, bracketed between the burning of Lundy's effigy in December and the Relief of Derry celebrations on 12 August. Even Stormont had wondered whether the celebrations should be banned that year, given the worsening sectarian tensions. In the end, the march was allowed to take place. The marchers met on the city walls, beneath the statue of Derry's defender, the Rev. George Walker. Urban redevelopment meant that they could look down on the streets of the Catholic Bogside, and the practice had begun of exchanging insults with the residents and, taking advantage of their dominating position, of throwing 'charitable' pennies down into the area. Catholics in their turn attacked the march as it passed through Waterloo Place, and a riot that surpassed in scale any that had been seen before was soon in full swing. As well as bricks or other missiles that came to hand, rioters were using petrol bombs. The police responded to this by using tear-gas and even by throwing stones back at the rioters. Using their vehicles as battering rams, they managed to force their way through the barriers.

On previous occasions this would have been the signal for the Catholic rioters to melt away. A large group of Protestants followed the police in, however, and began smashing windows in houses. This brought out even more Catholics, intent on defending their territory. As the night was lit by the flames of burning factories, the strength of the police was gradually eroded by sheer exhaustion. Jack Lynch, head of the Southern government, ordered army field hospitals to the border, making many Protestants wonder if this was a prelude to invasion.

Trouble spread to other centres around Northern Ireland. In Belfast there was fighting in the small streets between the Falls and the Shankill Road, and between the Crumlin Road and the Ardoyne. Shots were fired from ancient rifles, some of them hidden in attics since 1922. On the third day all B Specials were ordered to report to their local police station for duty. At the same time, troops already based in Northern Ireland began to be deployed on the streets, starting with the Prince of Wales's Own Regiment in Derry. The Stormont government had lost its monopoly of power to the officer commanding Northern Ireland, soon to be Sir Ian Freeland. The police would not regain a leading role in the struggle till the late 1970s.

For many old people it must have seemed that the past was back to haunt them. Sadly, the first child victim of the Troubles had already been killed when a machine-gun bullet ripped through the walls of his bedroom and hit him in the head. As this could only have come from a police armoured car, it supported all the stories doing the rounds of police and B Specials getting involved on the side of the Protestant mobs. It was to be the end of the Specials, and destroyed any hope the RUC might have had of being seen as an unbiased organisation. People on both sides of the religious divide set about defending themselves and formed vigilante groups. A Protestant vigilante was shot dead by Catholic counterparts in Belfast in September, and another Protestant was kicked to death by a group of Catholics some weeks later.

Unionist resentment was now reinforced when it seemed that the British Home Secretary, Jim Callaghan, in a series of visits to the North, was taking the side of the Catholics who had started the trouble. The Specials were to go, to be replaced with a non-sectarian Ulster Defence Regiment, which would be an integral part of the British army, and a part-time RUC Reserve. A committee under Lord Hunt advised that the RUC be reformed and reorganised, and disarmed. A British policeman, Sir Arthur Young, was brought in to supervise the modernisation of the force. The report was published on 9 October and was answered by serious rioting in the Shankill. Two nights later the first policeman to be killed in the Troubles was shot by the UVF on the Shankill Road. That same night, two Protestants on the Shankill Road were killed by soldiers.

By the time the soldiers had been deployed and the smoke of numerous bonfires and arson attacks had cleared, it was obvious that Belfast had changed irrevocably. Districts had been barricaded off from one another, and people waited within their community fortresses to see what happened next. Eight deaths was probably a lucky escape, when 150 people had suffered gunshot wounds. Altogether there were 750 injured. About 180 houses and other buildings had to be demolished, while another 90 needed major repairs. Nearly two thousand families were forced out of their homes, more than four-fifths of them Catholic. One in twenty Catholic households had been displaced. Unwilling to trust the RUC, it seemed to them that they had been abandoned by the organisation to which they had turned in the past. 'IRA', they wrote on walls: 'I RAN AWAY.' It was following the recriminations of this period that the Provisional IRA separated itself from its mainstream origins. It intended to 'combine defence and retaliation.'

By the summer of 1970 the focus of unrest was very definitely Belfast. In riots in April, Protestants were driven out of the New Barnsley estate. On 27 June there was an exchange of gunfire between IRA snipers in St Matthew's Catholic Church and some Protestant gunmen in the Newtownards Road. Catholics alleged that loyalists were trying to invade the Short Strand area. Two Protestants and a Catholic died, while a senior IRA figure, Billy McKee, was seriously wounded. In north Belfast on the same day, during riots that spread through large areas of the city, three more Protestants were killed. In what seemed a planned operation, some gunmen came out of Hooker Street and fired on a Protestant crowd. One of the dead in this second incident was a plater from Harland and Wolff. The following day five hundred Catholics were expelled from the ship-yards, a reminder that little seemed to have changed in half a century.

If expulsions from the shipyards brought echoes of the past, these were reinforced in July when the army began searching houses in the Falls Road area for arms. A curfew was imposed in the area, and some twenty thousand people were confined to their homes. The claims of unnecessary brutality on the part of the soldiers, and the fact that the two wings of the IRA exchanged gunfire with soldiers, obscured the fact that more than a hundred weapons were found, together with home-made bombs, explosives and ammunition. Three civilians were shot dead and one crushed by an army vehicle. None had any connection with the IRA.

By this time the Conservative Party had taken power in London, and Ulster was famously driving the Home Secretary, Reginald Maudling, to drink. With so much tension in Belfast, Maudling formally requested that the July parades be cancelled. Leaders of the Orange Order claimed that this would do more harm than good, and refused. The marches, sure enough, passed off peaceably enough. A few days afterwards, however, the Provisional IRA began a bombing campaign that was aimed at destabilising Stormont, and gradually violence became commonplace on the city streets.

Changes were taking place within constitutional nationalism. The civil rights movement was sidelined and its prominent role was taken by a new grouping, the Social Democratic and Labour Party, led by Gerry Fitt. South of the border, Jack Lynch sacked two of his ministers, including Charles Haughey (whose parents came from Swatragh, County Derry), for their alleged involvement in attempting to smuggle arms into Northern Ireland. A subsequent trial turned into a fiasco when prosecution witnesses contradicted one another. Haughey was never acquitted by the unionists of Belfast and was regarded by them as an arms smuggler for the rest of his career.

In early 1971, in north Belfast, the first IRA man killed by the army and the first soldier killed by the IRA died on the same night, 6 February. Three days later two BBC engineers and three building workers were killed by a bomb that had been left near a transmitter in County Tyrone. In the same month two policemen were shot dead as they patrolled Alliance Avenue, off the Antrim Road. On 3 March three young Scottish soldiers were lured from a pub to their deaths on the outskirts of Belfast.

For the first time, but not the last, there were calls for a 'third force' and the reintroduction of internment. The first third force to emerge was the phenomenon known as the 'tartan gangs', particularly strong in east Belfast, who named themselves in memory of the murdered Scotsmen and undertook attacks on Catholic homes and property. Later they attacked the homes of policemen. When the soldiers' funerals were taking place in Scotland there were rallies in Belfast and elsewhere attended by up to thirty thousand people. The shipyard closed and four thousand workers marched to the City Hall, demanding the introduction of internment. When the Prime Minister, Edward Heath, refused permission for Chichester-Clark to introduce tougher security methods, the latter resigned, apparently glad of the excuse.

Brian Faulkner, who was thought to be a tougher man and was given the credit for defeating the IRA in the 1950s, replaced him. He tried to reunite the Unionist Party by bringing members from both wings into his cabinet. To develop some measure of cross-community co-operation he set up three parliamentary committees, with opposition politicians taking two of the chairmanships. Balancing this conciliatory gesture was an emphasis on a tougher army response to civilians carrying weapons. Soldiers would be allowed to 'shoot for effect'. Unfortunately for Faulkner's good intentions, it was this tough approach that got in the way of political progress. Two men were shot by the army in controversial circumstances on the streets of Derry. The SDLP demanded an independent inquiry; when this was not granted, they withdrew from Stormont.

As politics seemed to be getting nowhere, and there was everywhere talk of a Protestant backlash, Faulkner was given permission to introduce internment. Known as Operation Demetrius, the round-up began at 4 a.m. on 9 August 1971. Roughly 350 people were taken into custody, all but two of them Catholics and almost all of them irrelevant to the 'armed struggle'. The Special Branch of the RUC had lost touch with the rapidly changing IRA, and soldiers were sent to the wrong house, or arrested the wrong person. Although quite a few were released within forty-eight hours, that was time enough for them to be traumatised by their experience. Worse, it began to emerge that inhuman and degrading treatment was being used to extract information. An English judge made the Jesuitical decision that this was not torture because the interrogators were not gaining pleasure from the experience.

More and more people were interned, and the more sceptical in the Catholic community realised that the IRA could not lose, as every arrest would create ten Republican recruits.

On the streets of Belfast, gunfights broke out between the army and the IRA that went on for hours. Catholic enclaves barricaded themselves in. Public transport was suspended and other services were under threat. Everywhere was the smell of smoke, and the night was filled with the sounds of bin-lids being rattled, like jungle drums being sounded to warn of threats in the darkness. Listening to armoured personnel carriers and jeeps moving along their streets, the Catholics of the Falls Road or the Ardoyne contrasted the direct action of the IRA, and particularly the Provisionals, with the pointless posturing of Nationalist politicians. The fact that internment was not being used on a Protestant population was seen as proof that the state was assaulting a Catholic population whose only defenders were the Provisionals. Nationalists felt that it was open season on them as far as the army was concerned, and the twenty-nine Catholic deaths caused by soldiers in the following months seemed to support this.

Any thought that internment would reduce violence was soon discarded. In the entire year up to 9 August, 31 people had been killed. In the next three weeks, 35 were added to the total, with a further 120 from September to the end of the year. Up to 2,500 families moved home. Faulkner described Catholic complaints as 'the squeal of the increasingly cornered rat.' Catholics considered that Faulkner had introduced internment to bolster his position within his party rather than as an attempt to restore peace. In this, as in so much else, he failed. When it was obvious that internment was not working, his critics demanded even tougher security measures.

Ian Paisley relaunched the Protestant Unionist Party in September as the Democratic Unionist Party. The party had measures in its manifesto that appealed to the Protestant working man, but its main appeal was in its anti-republican rhetoric. There would be other parties in the future, each of them cracking the foundations of the monolith that had been the Unionist Party, each of them making it more unlikely that a Stormont government in the old form that would have been recognised by Craig or Brooke would ever be seen again. Already Harold Wilson, now in opposition, was trying to get the idea of a united Ireland onto the political agenda, and the British public were inclined to agree with him. Edward Heath was consulting Dublin ever more closely. Even Faulkner acknowledged that the economic situation was desperate and that Stormont was close to collapse.

The beleaguered Catholic population had more immediate concerns. On Saturday 4 December a small Catholic-owned bar in North Queen Street was car-bombed. The McGurks, who owned the bar, lived above it. Four members of the Ulster Volunteer Force were intent on blowing up the Gem Bar, further along the street, but realised they did not have time to reach it, so they abandoned the car outside McGurk's instead. The explosion caused the old building to collapse, killing fifteen people, including the owner's wife and fourteen-year-old daughter and a thirteen-year-old schoolboy. The army added insult to injury by briefing journalists that the bomb had been an 'own goal' by the IRA, and that it had been inside rather than outside the pub. Catholics took this as a cold-blooded attempt to support the Stormont position that no loyalists were dangerous enough to be interned.

This is not an attempt to diminish the violence of the IRA or in any way to excuse it. Already, by the end of 1971, its bombing attacks and other activities had led directly to the deaths of 107 people, out of a total of 180 for the year. Although most of the official casualties were soldiers, eleven members of the RUC and five UDR soldiers had also been killed, individuals whom the Protestant people saw as defending them as well as the state. IRA attacks were no more carefully directed than UVF ones, and the IRA response to the McGurk bomb was to place a device on the doorstep of a furniture showroom on the Shankill Road the following Saturday, in spite of the fact that this was one of the most popular shopping areas in Belfast, used by people from both communities. One of the two adults killed was a Catholic, the other a Protestant; both worked in the showroom. Tragically, two infants who had been sharing a pram, one aged two and the other only seventeen months, were caught by the debris and killed. The death toll was remarkably small, considering that the Shankill Road was crowded at the time and the showroom was having a closing-down sale. As in similar cases on the Catholic side, the atrocity was enough to send many young men to join the Protestant paramilitaries.

The animosity between Catholics and the army reached a new intensity towards the end of January 1972. In Derry there was not the same scope for sectarian attacks on Catholics as Belfast, and the Provisionals were not able to portray themselves as defenders of the Catholic community. Indeed the Official IRA remained strong here until it was largely replaced by the INLA. It was also a city where support for the NICRA remained strong.

The NICRA notified the authorities that it intended to hold a march on 30 January to protest against internment. The local RUC chief superintendent, Frank Lagan, spoke to the army commander in Derry, Brigadier Patrick MacLellan, and asked the army not to interfere. Lagan felt that there would be less trouble if the parade was allowed to go ahead and the organisers prosecuted later. MacLellan agreed, but a decision had been taken 'above GOC level'—probably by the British cabinet—that arrests should be made, at least among the hooligan element.

The parade itself passed off peacefully, but ritual stone-throwing began afterwards, and the 1st Battalion of the Parachute Regiment was sent in to make arrests. It was ordered not to enter the Bogside itself, and not to engage in running gunfights with the IRA. The Royal Anglian Regiment had placed snipers on the city walls, overlooking the march, to engage IRA gunmen if any were seen. The paratroopers ignored their orders and went into the heart of the Bogside, guns firing. Some later claimed they had been told by junior officers that they wanted some kills that day. They got thirteen, and a fourteenth who died some time later. The city's coroner, Major Hubert O'Neill, described the incident as murder. None of the dead had paramilitary involvement, and none had been carrying a gun. At the subsequent inquiry Lord Widgery took evidence only from trained witnesses, the army and police, and ignored hundreds of sworn statements collected by the NICRA. Derry swung behind the Provisional IRA with a vengeance.

Nationalist alienation was demonstrated in disturbances all around Ireland. The British embassy in Dublin was burned down in front of a cheering crowd. In Australia, dockers refused to unload British ships. Financial contributions to the 'armed struggle' from America at least trebled, and networks for smuggling arms to Ireland were set up. The Officials felt confident enough some weeks later to attack the barracks of the Parachute Regiment in Aldershot, killing a Catholic chaplain, a gardener and five women who were part of the domestic staff. No soldiers were hurt.

The Provisionals also seemed prepared to raise the stakes in the horror of their attacks. A bomb in the Abercorn Bar in Castle Lane in central Belfast on a crowded Saturday afternoon killed two young women and caused seventy other casualties, some of them horribly maimed. A particularly upsetting factor was the youth of so many of the victims. Two weeks later a car bomb in Donegall Street killed seven people and injured 150. There was a suspicion that the Provisionals had sent contradictory telephone warnings in order to maximise the damage done.

The British government, caught up in the crisis, was prepared to consider any remedy. It even considered repartitioning Northern Ireland, allowing Catholic areas to opt in to the Republic. Irish unity was mentioned in discussions, as was joint authority over Northern Ireland by the British and Irish governments. Faulkner thought he could still win, making the vague offer of magnanimity on the part of the majority once violence was ended. Internment, he thought, should continue. He would not have a guaranteed place for Catholics in government; neither would he hand over control of Northern Ireland's security to London. William

Craig's Vanguard movement was collecting right-wing unionists to its banner, and Faulkner did not want to seem weak. He was signing away the Unionist Party's monopoly of power in Northern Ireland, although he did not realise it. Stormont was about to have a personnel transplant.

Two days later Heath announced that the Northern Ireland Parliament was being suspended and that direct rule from London was being imposed. The British government had taken control of Northern Ireland, and would spend the next twenty-five years trying to hand it back.

At the time it must have seemed impossible that Harland and Wolff would come very close to following Stormont into suspended animation, but the hints were there, even during the O'Neill years, and from being a private company in 1966 it became a nationalised company by 1975. There have been several attempts to explain the decline in British shipbuilding after the war. A technological explanation claims that British shipyards simply failed to modernise and to improve productivity, compared with their competitors abroad. Another explanation focuses on poor industrial relations in Britain. A third explanation is that governments made a mess of it.

Why did Harland and Wolff fail at a time when there was an increased demand for the very large crude oil carriers in which the firm was beginning to specialise? Since the death of Lord Pirrie, successive regimes at Queen's Island had tried to reduce labour costs and increase productivity. This was reiterated by Dr Dennis Rebbeck, Harland and Wolff's chairman, in his 1966 statement to shareholders. Although he accepted that the firm had lost some of its traditional customers, he blamed its vulnerability to foreign competition on restrictive practices and the high number of days lost through industrial action. He asked the Stormont government for a loan that would cover losses the firm was already suffering and was likely to suffer in the future. The Northern Ireland government responded generously, lending the company £3½ million, with the sole provision that financial control be given to the government. It was expected that modernising the yard would make it profitable and that there would be no further need for government intervention. Rebbeck retired, and the financial controller chosen by Stormont, John Mallabar, was made chairman. It was the first time a complete outsider had been appointed to the post.

Mallabar was an accountant who had made his name as a 'fixer' of companies with financial difficulties. He made his presence felt by making a thousand workers redundant by the end of his first week. Hackles rose at Stormont, Protestant unemployment being a very sensitive issue. Undaunted, Mallabar made another 279 workers redundant in December. In the new year, having stemmed losses, it was now his job to plan the future development of the shipyard. At the time the yard was building the tanker *Myrina* for Shell, the biggest ship then built in Europe. From the problems it was creating, Mallabar knew that this class of ship could become a speciality of the yard only if a large building dock was constructed and Japanese-type manufacturing facilities were introduced. A study suggested that the Musgrave Channel should be drained and made into a building dock that could accommodate ships of a million tons. The estimated cost was £7½ million. This would be granted jointly by the Stormont government and the Shipyard Industries Board, although there were conditions attached. Final approval was given in January 1968.

At first things seemed to be going well. More orders were being received, worth £58 million by April 1969. If things continued as hoped, there was a possibility of Harland and Wolff becoming a large, profitable company on the Japanese model.

By the autumn of that year, however, some concerns were starting to appear. The building of the dock was behind by six months, and it would almost certainly go over budget. There were problems with the manufacture of some of the ancillary machinery. Harland and Wolff was having difficulty obtaining licences for building more modern engines than the firm could provide itself. On the other hand, there were enough orders to keep the yard busy until 1972, and Mallabar had halted, or at least seemed to have halted, the yard's decline. Labour relations were still poor, as was productivity, and the price of steel was beginning to show a worrying rise. At the end of the year there were two further negative developments. Shipbuilding contracts had lost £3.13 million that year, and the auditors could not say why. To compound the matter, a further £3 million seemed to be unaccounted for. The losses for 1969 were not agreed till 1971, when they were set at £8.33 million.

Mallabar's explanation was that prices had been set at a level that allowed no increase in cost, so that any changes to the underlying costs of the company would have serious repercussions. He had not understood that the history of shipbuilding in Belfast meant that there were few incentives and no threats that would encourage workers and staff to show any discipline in the area of productivity. The fault for the present crisis lay with men working on the construction of the ships, and particularly with steelworkers, who banned overtime for three months in 1969 in support of a wage claim. Delivery times slipped, and costs increased.

Mallabar resigned in 1970 and was replaced by Joe Edwards, whose background was in the motor industry. The appointment was supposed to be temporary, but the problems were happening now, and the search for a solution could not be put on the long finger. The problem was that, in a traditional stick-and-carrot situation, he lacked a stick. The workers knew that the British government would never allow the yard to close, with the loss of 7½ per cent of the North's industrial work force, most of them Protestant, and the further loss of the 10 per cent that indirectly depended upon Harland and Wolff. Both governments were trying to pacify a unionist population whose privileges were under threat. Union agitation within the yard, largely based on political issues, was combined with an unwillingness to change. Any attempt to modernise was almost certainly doomed before it began.

Some international ship-owners considered buying Harland and Wolff in the early 1970s, but the interest came to nothing, largely because of local opposition, which was largely racially motivated. A new chairman, Iver Hoppe, recruited from Denmark, set as his target a yard capable of handling 200,000 tons of steel a year. During 1972 productivity began to climb, so much so that a limiting factor became the number of workers employed. Hoppe introduced an adult training scheme for recruits from outside the shipyard, and productivity improved yet again. There were still problems. Work in Queen's Island was vulnerable to a dock strike, which duly took place, and was dependent on supplies from British Steel, which was having its own problems. These difficulties were compounded by stoppages when the shipyard workers took part in political marches and rallies. Altogether, twenty-five full production days were lost in 1972—the equivalent of half a 250,000-ton tanker. Hoppe recognised the fact that the yard's shop stewards were a moderating influence and that without them a lot more time would have been lost.

This was against a background of turmoil and political confusion. The tactic of using massive car bombs was one that the Provisionals used again and again. There were moments of hope, though one was kept secret at the time. The first was in May, when Catholic women in Derry marched on the headquarters of the Official IRA, horrified that the organisation had killed a young Derry soldier who was home on leave. This petticoat rebellion persuaded the Officials to renounce violence. The second occasion was in June, when two SDLP politicians, John Hume and Paddy Devlin, tried to arrange peace talks between the IRA and the British government. The IRA called a ceasefire and sent a delegation to London. It came to nothing, however, and hostilities were resumed in July, shortly after the Ulster Defence Association put up barricades that would have included several Catholic families in a loyalist 'no-go' area.

By 21 July the bombs were back. More than twenty exploded in Belfast. Eleven people were killed, some of their bodies so mutilated that they had to be collected in plastic bags, and another 130 injured. That evening a Catholic was kidnapped and taken to a social club on the Shankill Road, where he was hideously tortured and killed. He was the first victim of the gang that came to be known as the Shankill Butchers. July was the worst month of the worst year, and nearly a hundred people died. At the end of the year the killing spread to Dublin, where loyalist car bombs killed two people, and there were two bombs in the shipyard, though no-one was hurt and there was little damage done.

There was a slight decrease in violence in 1973. Almost unnoticed, the United Kingdom and the Republic of Ireland became members of the European Economic Community on 1 January. The British government now decided that institutionalised power-sharing was the only hope for the future, as well as a formal 'Irish dimension'. Unionists were unsure how to react, and there was further fragmentation of their ranks, but loyalists, under the auspices of the Loyalist Association of Workers, called a strike for 7 February. That day Belfast had a complete electricity blackout. There were widespread reports of intimidation. RUC stations at Willowfield and Donegall Pass were attacked, and a fireman tackling a blaze in Sandy Row was shot dead by a loyalist sniper. Near the Albert Bridge Road there were exchanges of fire between the army and loyalist gunmen. In all, five people died that day and twenty-seven were injured. There was widespread condemnation of the strike from Protestants, and when it became obvious that much of the money donated to the LAW had been siphoned off for private purposes, the organisation fell apart.

There were divisions within the nationalist community as well. The SDLP saw the power-sharing initiative as one that was worth exploring. The party was reviled by republicans for taking part in talks with the government while internment was still in force. The talks led to a white paper being published that proposed the election of an Assembly, which in turn would lead to a power-sharing Executive. There would be links with the Republic, although the nature of these would be decided later.

The lead-up to the elections, which were held in June, were particularly brutal. Among other victims were Gerry Fitt's election agent, who had his throat cut, and a woman travelling in the same car, who was stabbed to death. The results of the election were not encouraging for those Unionists who supported the white paper. Their leader, Brian Faulkner, led a minority of the Unionists in the Assembly, kept in power only by the support of the Nationalist members.

The infinitely patient William Whitelaw, Secretary of State for Northern Ireland, managed to put together an Executive. When the membership was announced, Unionist members were insulted, punched and kicked. A later conference, held at Sunningdale in Berkshire, agreed to the formation of a Council of Ireland. The loyalist response was to establish an Ulster Army Council to support anti-Sunningdale politicians, who had themselves formed the United Ulster Unionist Council.

Matters were no less fraught at the shipyard. Worried about inflation, Heath's government had imposed a wage freeze. The timing was unfortunate, because it meant that Harland and Wolff did not have time to grant a pay rise to its steel workers that had already been granted in the rest of the United Kingdom. Feeling that they were being victimised for their outspoken political beliefs, the steelworkers introduced an overtime ban, so that productivity fell below target. As it was government policy that any pay increase had to be financed by increased productivity, and the steel-workers would not discuss productivity until they got their pay increase, matters were at an impasse. A threat to close the yard unless the steel-workers restored normal working was ignored, as the workers knew it would not happen. Even direct orders from the executive of the union were ignored. Hoppe calculated that in five years the firm had lost an entire year's production because of the steelworkers. He sacked all two thousand of them by 4 May. The dispute was over by June, but there was still a great deal of resentment among the workers.

The Secretary of State knew the cause of the problem, but instead of trying to use his influence to get pay rates equalised he emphasised the danger of the yard not being able to fulfil its contracts and having to shed jobs. This time it was true, because losses were becoming so great that it was debatable whether the company could continue to trade legally, as it now owed more than its assets were worth. A promise by the government to invest in the company in 1975 seemed enough to overcome this problem, and work went ahead.

Much of the planning undertaken by Hoppe was based on the premise that there would be an increased market for very large tankers, as America needed to import more of its oil. In the aftermath of the 'Yom Kippur War', fought between Israel on the one hand and an alliance of Egypt and Syria on the other, Arab oil producers introduced huge increases in the price of oil. The result was a fall in consumer demand, which in turn meant a fall in the demand for supertankers. Already the preferred size for these had fallen from 500,000 to 330,000 tons, but now there was a danger of some of these orders being cancelled. Hoppe predicted that the size of carrier most in demand for the next decade would be 60,000 tons. He wanted to set up an engine factory in a Catholic area of west Belfast, though the idea was eventually dropped.

The winter of 1973/4 was a troubled one for the British economy. A prolonged miners' strike meant power cuts and a three-day working week for much of British industry. Although Harland and Wolff had no power cuts, delays in the delivery of material disrupted the production of ships and played havoc with productivity. To make matters worse, many employees began leaving the firm. A move to England or Scotland, away from the Troubles, when coupled with increased rates of pay, seemed very attractive to many, and fifty-nine draughtsmen left the firm in 1973, while only ten were recruited. In early 1974 more men left the yard, this time moving to other firms in the Belfast area. Recruitment was a problem, because there was no spare labour force in east Belfast and Catholics from west Belfast refused to join, as the shipyard was not considered a safe working environment for nationalists.

The power-sharing Executive took office on New Year's Day 1974. It was not an easy birth, as threats to its future were being announced by the Provisionals and the Ulster Defence Association. Relations within the Unionist Party became ever more acrimonious, and Faulkner felt compelled to resign, to be replaced by an old-time hardliner, Harry West.

Frustrated by the continuing miners' strike, Heath called a general election in February. The results were a disappointment to him, and Harold Wilson once again took office; and in March a new Secretary of State for Northern Ireland, Merlyn Rees, was appointed. The results were more disappointing to the Executive, however, as anti-Sunningdale candidates took eleven of Northern Ireland's twelve Westminster seats. In the wake of this there were demands for new Assembly elections. When these were not forthcoming, yet another organisation was formed on the loyalist side, the Ulster Workers' Council. It threatened a general strike if elections were not held. When in May the Assembly rejected a motion condemning Sunningdale and power-sharing, the UWC announced that the strike would go ahead.

The strike received almost universal Protestant support, which was not dented when loyalist bombs killed thirty-three people in Dublin and Monaghan. For almost six years Protestants had seen a succession of events that, to them, were no more than political defeats. The civil rights movement and the outbreak of violence, the role of Nationalist leaders in bringing down Stormont, the hostility of the Irish government and the half-hearted support of the British government all combined to make Protestants feel like a people under siege. Many were ambiguous about power-sharing, reluctant to give power to people who had brought down the old system. All were opposed to the Council of Ireland. Unionist members of the Executive resigned on 28 May, and the experiment was effectually over. Two days later the Assembly was prorogued.

Merlyn Rees promised elections to a Constitutional Convention. Protestants saw this as their first victory, and rejoiced. Catholics remembered the way the army had refused to confront strikers in the early days of the action, and drew their own conclusions. They also felt that the strike simply emphasised the fact that important jobs had been given to Protestants at the expense of Catholics.

The most serious long-term casualty was trust between the SDLP and the British government. Those nationalists who had been prepared to join the Assembly had been vilified as traitors by the Provisionals. To many in the Catholic community it seemed that, at the very least, they had been fools. The Provisionals decided that the only way to force concessions from the British was to attack them at home. Bombs in Birmingham, which killed more than twenty people and injured nearly two hundred, led to the introduction of new anti-terror legislation that even its sponsor, the Home Secretary, Roy Jenkins, described as draconian.

The uwc strike also brought problems to Harland and Wolff. The work force was itself involved in the action, with some yard workers taking prominent positions. It seems to have been in response to this that Wilson announced that there would be no government finance while the strike lasted. His statement, however, also contained a 'get out of jail free' card for the workers: the government would not allow the firm to go under. It was putting a moratorium of twelve months on new orders to allow time for a reappraisal of the company's activities.

How the company was to continue trading at all without breaking the law was the immediate problem, because its negative equity had crept up to £32 million. In mid-July the directors came within an hour of winding up the company. During that hour a letter came from the government outlining the support it would be prepared to give the company. That support was dependent on the government getting a majority shareholding, and a director being appointed to manage industrial relations. These terms were accepted.

The government's first move was to sack Hoppe. His management style had been autocratic, and he had made a habit of installing Scandinavians in important positions without referring to the board, creating ill will. In his years in Belfast he never lost his Danish accent, and people claimed to have difficulty in understanding what he was saying. The abrupt manner of his dismissal was unfortunate, however, and he never seems to have recovered from it.

There was little time to worry about this, as the priority was minimising the damage done to the company. A number of ships were going to miss their scheduled completion date, causing further losses, and it was necessary to cancel some contracts to prevent financial free-fall. Three bulk carriers for Maritime Fruit Carriers were taken off the order book, as it was a condition of the contract that they could be rejected for late delivery anyway. The prospect of realistic wage negotiations improved industrial relations, and the amount of time lost by internal industrial disputes fell dramatically. In early 1975 the government announced that it was going to nationalise the yard, on the grounds that it was necessary to ensure the survival of shipbuilding in Belfast. Another Ulster icon had passed out of Ulster control.

The year had started with an IRA ceasefire, declared for the holiday period and then extended till 17 January, followed by a further extension into February. What it meant in practice was that the Provisionals did not shoot soldiers, though both they and loyalists kept up a high rate of sectarian assassination. There was another blow to SDLP credibility when Rees set up incident centres jointly staffed by civil servants and Sinn Féin. It looked as if Rees was bypassing the democratic process to engage with terrorists. Constitutional nationalists began to wonder if they were going to be sidelined altogether.

Another potential for conflict between the government and para-militaries on both sides was the ending of political status for republican and loyalist prisoners. The huge numbers arrested during internment meant that adequate accommodation was not available within the prison service. They had been housed instead in old military camps, and, because nobody had any better idea, they were allowed to manage most of their own affairs. They looked like prisoner-of-war camps but were actually universities of terrorism, where the tactics and strategy that would plague Northern Ireland for more than twenty years were worked out by young theorists who had complete freedom of association within their 'cage'. The regime that allowed these concessions was called political status. It was decided that in future those convicted of terrorist offences would serve their sentences as common criminals. It was not until December that internment was ended. One important aspect of the year was the deadly feuding within the republican movement.

After a short caretaker leadership by Lord Rochdale, Sir Brian Morton took control of Harland and Wolff in October. Morton's background was in real estate, and the sceptical comment among the workers was that he had been chosen to get the best possible price for the land on which the shipyard stood. However, he had already proved himself by being chairman of Londonderry Development Commission for four years. His experience in dealing with a wide range of industrial and social interests was seen as a particularly valuable qualification in his new role. Certainly things seemed to be going well. Large tankers were being built for holding companies, which then leased them to oil companies. North Sea oil was being developed at the time, and the demand for steel for this government priority meant that there were occasional delays at Queen's Island.

The fact remained that there was a fall in demand, and that the consequence would inevitably be a lessening of the level of activity at the shipyard. Morton took it as his priority that any rundown of activity would be managed in an orderly fashion. The offer of workers' participation at the management level, introduced as part of the nationalisation package, meant that the work force was not suspicious of decisions being taken behind closed doors, though union representatives seemed reluctant to take up the positions offered. The medium to long-term prospects seemed reasonable as long as the firm could survive the prolonged downturn. The yard could produce a million tons of tankers or bulk carriers in a year, while it was estimated that British yards would receive orders for only a quarter of that each year. European rules, as interpreted by the government, meant that only 70 per cent credit could be extended to potential buyers and the rest had to be paid in advance. Interest on credit was set at 7½ per cent. Other countries seemed to be able to offer better terms, and for 1975 and 76 there were no orders for new ships. A serious attempt was made to find other uses for the workers, some of which were quite fanciful. Work for the engine section seemed to be holding steady.

For the first time since Morton took over, a certain amount of complacency was induced among the workers when three Shell tankers, weighing among them almost a million tons and the largest yet built in the United Kingdom, were floated out during 1976. The engine works had turned out sixteen sets of machinery. The public face of the company was certainly smiling. It was hard to persuade workers that they needed to increase productivity even more if the firm was to survive the depression. Political problems continued to haunt it, as when a renewed UWC strike in 1977 cost fourteen days' work in finishing a Shell tanker and a bulk carrier. To make matters worse, an industrial dispute in British Oxygen Corporation meant the yard had to lay off 3,500 men at the end of October. These two problems, over which it had no control, cost Harland and Wolff £1 million.

1978 was the worst year of the recession, exacerbated by the fact that the owners of the *Coastal Corpus Christi* were referring alleged defects to arbitration. It was suspected that they wanted to delay delivery until they could legally reject the ship. Arbitration dragged on till 1980 and also involved the *Coastal Hercules*. Smaller ferries for the Irish Sea brought some money in, as did the contract for the new Foyle Bridge at Derry. The engine works was seriously underemployed, making only three main units in 1978.

It was now the turn of the Wilson government to try to enforce a pay policy, and industrial relations took a nasty turn. Wages issues were not resolved till early 1979, and even then there were difficulties. When Margaret Thatcher became Prime Minister in May that year she affirmed that she would let private enterprise expand while cutting state expenditure. The prospect of losing pay constraint was more than compensated for by her decision to impose cash limits on the amount of debt a company could incur. It looked as if the yard workers might have better wages, but they might not have an employer to pay them. Thatcher was reluctant to subsidise failing industries, meaning that there was greater difficulty for Harland and Wolff in maintaining a reasonable flow of work. The Conservative instinct was that if a firm couldn't make a profit building ships it should try to make a profit building something else.

Certainly the future of shipbuilding was not looking very rosy. The only order that came in during 1979 was for another ferry, and it looked as if there would be only one ship on the order book by the end of 1980, a liquid petroleum gas tanker. If it had not been for the fact that arbitration on the *Coastal Corpus Christi* and *Coastal Hercules* was given in Harland and Wolff's favour, the future would have been very bleak indeed. Wage demands continued to be more than the firm could meet, and four hundred redundancy notices were issued in January in the hope that this would moderate this pressure. An unforeseen consequence was that some skilled workers lost confidence in the firm and left to work elsewhere.

Changes in the exchange rate meant that Japanese shipyards could increase their prices by 30 per cent and still offer better value to customers than their European rivals. Now, uncertain of the future of shipbuilding in Europe, the EEC put limits on the amount governments could pay to compensate public undertakings for losses and put hurdles in the way of any increase in capacity in European yards. Thatcher's government thought the problem with Harland and Wolff was that it had a poor record for delivering on time, and if it could do no better it could take the consequences. Against this background of mistrust, Sir Brian Morton retired in October 1980. The only vessels launched during the year were, once again, ferries, the smallest output by the firm since the depression in the 1930s.

The second half of the 1970s had seen a reduction in violence from a peak in 1976. That year saw a petering out of the Constitutional Convention. The Unionist majority bulldozed through a final report on a constitution that ignored the SDLP. The British government rejected this and faced up to the reality of an extended period of direct rule. The lack of political movement left the stage open to paramilitaries of both persuasions. The IRA killed ten Protestant workers near Bessbrook in response to attacks on two Catholic families in south Armagh by the UVF. The cold-blooded nature of the IRA killings, in which the one Catholic worker was separated out and told to 'run up the road,' caused a security crisis. More soldiers were brought in, and the SAS was deployed for the first time.

Violence continued through the summer. There was particular revulsion in August when soldiers shot the IRA driver of a car, which then careered into the Maguire family, killing three of the children. A movement called the Peace People was formed almost spontaneously, crossing the political divide, but this eventually disintegrated in recriminations, like many other initiatives. It could be said that the organisation sank under the weight of expectations.

A tougher attitude to security came in with a new Northern Ireland Secretary, Roy Mason, and a new head of the RUC, Kenneth Newman. They introduced specialised interrogation centres for terrorist suspects. They also increased the numbers in the RUC and UDR, which then took over many of the roles of the army. 'Special category' status was finally ended, but the first IRA man sent to the Maze after the change refused to wear prison uniform and wrapped himself in his blanket instead.

The death toll in 1977 dropped from the 307 of the previous year to 98. Included among these were victims of paramilitary feuds, which recurred regularly. Paisley tried a rerun of the UWC strike but got only limited support, and it collapsed in the face of stout opposition from the government. Fault

lines continued to show within unionism, and in local government
elections in May six different unionist parties were represented. Roy
Mason announced that there was to be another increase in the numbers of
the RUC and increased use of the SAS.

After a quiet January in 1978, in February the IRA fire-bombed the La
Mon Hotel outside Belfast, and twelve people were burned to death. The
European Court of Human Rights had said that Britain had been guilty of
the 'inhuman and degrading treatment' of internees in 1971, and Amnesty
International accused the RUC of malpractice in its treatment of suspects,
but few Protestants treated these accusations seriously in the face of such
atrocities.

In March, republican prisoners in the Maze stepped up the prison
dispute by refusing to 'slop out' their cells and smearing their excrement
on the walls. Once again, Protestants had no sympathy, even when the
numbers involved rose to 250. There were hopes that a new De Lorean car
factory in Dunmurry would make a real difference to unemployment rates.

There were few signs for hope in 1979. The IRA ignited bombs over much
of Northern Ireland on New Year's Day. In March it killed the British
ambassador to the Netherlands and the following day laid on another
bombing spectacular in Northern Ireland. At the end of the month the
INLA, a doctrinaire republican breakaway group, succeeded in assassinating
the Conservative Party spokesman on Northern Ireland, Airey Neave, within
the grounds of the Palace of Westminster. In May a general election brought
Margaret Thatcher to Downing Street and a relatively unknown Humphrey
Atkinson to Northern Ireland. The violence was not over yet, and on one
day in August a bomb killed Lord Mountbatten while he was boating off his
holiday home in County Sligo, while another in County Down was used in
an ambush to kill a civilian and eighteen soldiers, including the commanding officer of the 1st Battalion of the Queen's Own Highlanders. These spec-
taculars led to a huge increase in sectarian murders of Catholics.

In the field of politics, this was the year of the first elections to the
European Parliament. Ian Paisley topped the poll, closely followed by John
Hume. Towards the end of the year Humphrey Atkins published a white
paper proposing a constitutional conference. The SDLP voted against it,
leaving Gerry Fitt, who wanted to attend, in a minority of one. He had
been following an increasingly separate path from SDLP thought anyway,
and he now resigned from the party, the leadership of which was taken
over by John Hume.

The constitutional conference came and went in 1980, leaving nothing
in its wake. It had been boycotted by the Unionist Party, whose leader
claimed it had been 'booby-trapped by an Irish dimension' that had been
introduced as bait to encourage the SDLP to attend. This was an alarming
development from a unionist point of view. Margaret Thatcher met the

head of the Irish government, Charles Haughey, the bogeyman from the arms trial. This meeting led to the launch of studies to look at ways Britain and Ireland could co-operate in matters of security and the economy. There was one worrying development, although it did not seem so at the time. A group of republican prisoners went on hunger strike, but it was called off in December. Apart from that, the death toll for the year was eighty-six, the lowest for any year since 1970.

This was followed by the year of the hunger strikes. In January, Bernadette McAliskey and her husband were shot by the UDA. As Bernadette Devlin she had been one of the leaders of the early civil rights marches. Both of them survived, but in a revenge attack Sir Norman Stronge, the ageing former speaker of the Stormont Parliament, and his son were shot dead by the IRA, who then blew up his house.

The hunger strikes began on 1 March and continued till ten men had died. The first of the strikers, Bobby Sands, complicated matters by being elected to Parliament while in prison on hunger strike. He died in May, and other deaths followed. Huge crowds attended the funerals, and as police traffic and crowd control were seen as aggressive by mourners, many developed into riots. In a mirror image of some of the political funerals of the late nineteenth century, Protestants wondered how respectable Catholics could turn out to the funerals of criminals. The hunger strikes were only called off in October, when a Catholic priest urged the mothers of those whose sons were taking part to intervene once the son went into a coma and to ask for medical aid.

Sinn Féin had done well out of the hunger strikes and began to look like a political force. At its conference the tactic of 'a ballot paper in one hand and an Armalite in the other' was adopted. The Rev. Robert Bradford, a Unionist MP who was an outspoken supporter of the death penalty, was killed by the IRA. Paisley looked for another 'third force'. The first of the 'supergrass' informers appeared. Although few were ever convicted on the testimony of these people, their existence increased the sense of unease among all paramilitaries, traditionally sensitive to 'traitors' within their midst.

At the shipyard, market trends elsewhere showed that orders were again being placed for tankers and bulk carriers, and the Harland and Wolff management hoped that some would eventually come their way. The continuing use of cash limits, however, meant the firm had very little financial leeway, and it looked as if the building programme would have to be held back to stay within them. Exploring possible areas for diversification showed no realistic options, and the continuing presence in the yard of expensive consultants while staff and steelworkers were being made redundant was not good for the morale of a work force that had shrunk to less than seven thousand.

In November 1982 the government appointed John Parker chief executive of Harland and Wolff. The appointment was welcomed on Queen's Island, as Parker had started there on the design team straight from university. Latterly he had been deputy chief executive of British Shipbuilding. He took office in February 1983 and obviously had a major task on his hands. One bulk carrier was on order, there were negotiations with Blue Star Line for some medium-sized cargo ships, and there were a few preliminary enquiries. Other than repairs and refits, that was it. Parker told his managers that he laid great stress on accountability, planning, and the application of new technology. He sent sales teams to the Far East and put pressure on the Ministry of Defence for orders for fleet auxiliaries.

Parker's main concerns were to begin meeting delivery dates and to make Harland and Wolff more competitive. He cut the work force again, this time to 5,500. Managers no longer supervised the work of different trades but took responsibility for individual zones. This system was extended into the technical department. Parker wanted to establish technical contacts with foreign shipbuilders and to broaden the range of products. Although the company preferred to build a series of ships to the same design, it was happy to take on conversions for the Ministry of Defence and one-off designs, like the swops (single-well offshore production system) vessel for BP, which could move around marginal sub-sea oil wells, gathering oil rather as a bee gathers nectar. It would have a capacity for 42,000 tonnes of oil. In the case of the Ministry of Defence conversion, Harland and Wolff was to buy a suitable vessel and then convert it into a ship suitable for training helicopter pilots and transporting Harrier jets. It chose a container ship, the *Contender,* which had been part of the task force for the Falklands War. The never-ending search for diversification brought in an order for aircraft boarding bridges for Terminal 4 at Heathrow Airport, London.

A few weeks before the first Blue Star ship, the *English Star,* was due for delivery, sparks from a welding torch set fire to rags and some insulation that had become soaked with oil. Although there were no serious casualties, the engine room was gutted. In spite of this, the ship's naming ceremony went ahead on time.

Tom McCluskie was back working in Harland and Wolff by this time. The skills he had picked up in the motor industry were enough to get him a job as a technical administrator in the hull drawing office. It was his job to see that the detailed construction drawings produced in the office were approved by the regulatory bodies: the Board of Trade Marine Surveyor's Department and Lloyd's Register of Shipping. As their priorities were not always the same as those of the owners, and the traditional method of sorting these out in the shipbuilding industry was by confrontation, the interpersonal skills that McCluskie had learnt in the motor trade were invaluable. By being diplomatic where possible and bloody-minded when nothing else worked, he usually found it was possible to achieve a compromise. This ability to deal with problems without causing a crisis brought him to the notice of his managers, and he was promoted to senior administrator within a few years. The result was that some of his colleagues began showing signs of resentment. When his work resulted in his being appointed chief administrator, one colleague in particular could not contain his bitterness, and he caused unrest among the administrative staff. Worse, he was refusing to accept McCluskie's authority. When the rival was told by the chief technical manager, in McCluskie's presence, that he could accept the situation or resign, the rebellion was over. The lesson, as far as McCluskie was concerned, was that there was no way round the 'them and us' culture of Harland and Wolff.

From his position in middle management, McCluskie was uniquely positioned to see the various initiatives imposed by the government. His view, like that of most of the work force, was that the succession of experts and consultants brought in were more concerned with making as much money as possible for themselves, and in as short a period as possible, in case someone saw through them. Many of them stayed at the best hotels in Belfast, had generous expense accounts and were flown home, often to Scandinavia, at the weekend. It was infuriating to be told by these people that the method of working in the yard was wasteful and antiquated and that it was the fault of the workers that Harland and Wolff could not produce ships 'efficiently and economically'. Local expertise acquired in a lifetime of work was disregarded, and many of the shipyard's most talented employees left in disgust, either retiring or moving to other jobs. Replacements were appointed who had no experience in shipbuilding and who did not last long when the reality of the job became apparent to them.

It seemed that change was taking place for the sake of change. Even the company's trade mark was changed, as being outdated. The main entrance and reception area was given a renovation that replaced marble with Formica and wood panelling with wallpaper. A new carpet in light grey was installed; to avoid wear and tear, the personnel director forbade employees the use of the front entrance. But they continued to use their traditional entrance, and in a few weeks the carpet was filthy. While the senior management chose to fight battles that they could not win, they were bound to cause deterioration in industrial relations without having anything to show for it; worse, every time they lost this sort of confrontation, what authority they had was being diminished.

Other problems occurred when managers were assigned duties that were beyond their ability. Harland and Wolff's home-grown managers had come through a rough education on the shop floor and were chosen more for their ability to get work done by a recalcitrant work force than for their diplomatic skills. When a decision was taken at the highest level to try to negotiate a co-operation agreement with the Kawasaki shipyard in Japan, with the idea of taking advantage of methods that could regenerate Queen's Island, one of the most technically capable of Harland and Wolff managers was chosen as project liaison director. Unfortunately, no-one had investigated his ability to handle alcohol, and, according to McCluskie, at the dinner meant to welcome them he insulted his guests and ridiculed their ability to teach Belfast anything useful about shipbuilding. The project floundered, never to recover, and production methods went on as usual.

McCluskie and his colleagues watched as the general workers stopped caring. Continuing changes to the structure of the company and the introduction of one method of work only to have it replaced within a short time meant that more work was being expended on accommodating change than on building ships. There was general relief when the news came that John Parker was coming back. He had been one of the youngest naval architects in the history of the company and was, in the eyes of many, almost a reincarnation of Thomas Andrews of *Titanic* fame. Then, as if determined to cancel out the wisdom of Parker's appointment, the government appointed another Scandinavian consultant, Per Nielsen from Denmark, as deputy chief executive. Hackles were raised among the management when they discovered that Nielsen's salary was being paid directly into a trust in the Channel Islands.

In spite of Parker's best efforts, the annual losses continued to grow, reaching £75 million in the year 1986/7. This was more than the government could sustain. It had sunk £1 billion in the company in twenty-two years; the reduced work force meant that the impact on the Northern Ireland economy of closing the firm would not be as great as it might once have been. It was announced that it would sell the firm. When it turned out that the only realistic bidder was Fred Olsen of the Norwegian shipping firm Fredrik Olsen and Company, for whom Per Nielsen had worked, conspiracy theorists among the workers began to recall strange decisions made in the past and wondered whether this was the culmination of a long-lived plot. Certainly the government was determined to get rid of this liability, and Olsen soon realised this and insisted on conditions. He offered £1 million for the assets of the firm, even though the book value of Harland and Wolff was £93 million. The government had to write off £625 million of debt and guarantee him against any claims or liability that might come the way of Harland and Wolff if the deal went ahead. Finally, Olsen wanted a development grant of £20 million to be made available as soon as he took over the company. If all these conditions were met he would pay £12 million: £6 million straight away and the rest in instalments. The government agreed, although it retained £400 million of the debt and gave only £160 million in new loans.

Then Olsen produced his final condition. He would pay if the work force showed its commitment to the firm by investing in it, making it 'their' company. His offer was that 51 per cent of the shares would be in the hands of the workers. In reality, he had his own appointees on the board whose shares would total 5 per cent of the issue; these, taken with his own 49 per cent, guaranteed that his would be the final word. Each worker was told the minimum number of £1 shares he was expected to buy: manual workers 500, junior management grades 1,000, senior management 2,000. The fact that Parker, trusted by the workers, was part of Olsen's consortium gave them confidence. In fact many workers bought more, and Olsen got a rebate of almost £3 million of his original expenditure almost immediately. To show his own commitment, his shipping concerns ordered $150 million in new oil tankers.

Olsen reorganised Harland and Wolff by making it into a holding company and splitting it into its constituent parts. He then set about optimising the company's assets. The pension fund was in a very healthy condition and had actually built up a large cash surplus. Olsen persuaded the trustees to use this to build a bulk carrier that would then be leased to Olsen Shipping. This would guarantee a steady income, although the daily rate was still to be agreed. Because there was no way of predicting what that rate would be in a volatile market, the income might be steady, but it might not be stable. In fact the ship, the *Lowland Trassey,* was finished in 1995 but never succeeded in bringing in a profit to the pension fund, and it was eventually sold to Olsen Shipping at a substantial loss. It sails today as the *Iron Prince,* registered in the Isle of Man.

In the early 1990s Harland and Wolff diversified yet again. It still built tankers and oil rigs, and had a repair subsidiary. In 1991 it got its first order for a ship from outside the Olsen group. There was a separate design subsidiary, which manufactured marine furnishings and marine paint. For the first time it was getting involved in the commercial and residential development of Queen's Island. Per Nielson was now chief executive, and in 1996 he was able to record the firm's first profit in many years, a pre-tax surplus of nearly £3 million.

By now the general outlook for Northern Ireland was starting to look better. After the chaos of 1981, Jim Prior, who had been banished to Northern Ireland by Margaret Thatcher because he was a 'wet', set about gaining the initiative, only to fail because Unionists disliked it and the SDLP, looking over their shoulders at the growing political power of Sinn Féin, rejected it outright. The De Lorean factory went bankrupt in February. Northern Ireland's male unemployment rate went up to 25 per cent. For the middle of the year the Falklands War dominated the news, and the shipyard workers took a vicarious pride in several of 'their' ships, in particular HMS *Fearless* and the venerable *Canberra*, taking leading roles in the task force. There were elections to an Assembly in October. Sinn Féin got 10 per cent of the vote on its first outing, and the Ulster Unionists held the DUP to second place.

There was unrest among Catholics in November when there were two incidents in which policemen seemed to shoot to kill when they could have arrested the suspects. Criticism was silenced in December when the INLA bombed the Droppin' Well bar in Ballykelly, killing seventeen people. In the following spring the Irish government tried to help the SDLP to counter rising support for Sinn Féin by providing an alternative to Prior's Assembly, the New Ireland Forum, meeting in Dublin in May. Just how little effect it had is shown by the fact that Gerry Adams, president of Sinn Féin, was elected member of Parliament for West Belfast in June.

The continually rising vote for Sinn Féin among Catholics was a phenomenon of the 1980s and 90s that concerned unionists and government alike, as it seemed to prove increasing nationalist support for the 'armed struggle'. The change in voting happened because the SDLP had been ignored and sidelined regularly, no matter what proportion of the vote it received. Catholics believed—correctly, as it turned out—that the government could not ignore Sinn Féin. Informers had been used by the police in court cases during the year, apparently with a great deal of success. In November, however, two of them retracted their evidence, while a third was called a liar by a trial judge, who dismissed the cases arising from his evidence.

The early part of 1984 was dominated by controversy about a 'shoot to kill' policy that now seemed to be carried out by the SAS. The RUC brought in John Stalker, Deputy Chief Constable of Greater Manchester Police, to investigate the matter, but it ended two years later in frustration and recriminations. In June a judge acquitted three policemen of the murder of an IRA man. Gerry Adams was wounded in an assassination attempt by loyalists. In October, bombs in Brighton very nearly killed Margaret Thatcher and did kill five people, some of them prominent members of the Conservative Party. Relations between Britain and Ireland reached their lowest point ever when Thatcher indulged herself in a hissy fit after a meeting with Garret FitzGerald, new head of the Irish government, contradicting the statement that FitzGerald had just made. Officials, however, kept meeting and talking.

1985 was not a good year to be a member of the RUC. In the spring with a mortar, and again in May with a landmine, the IRA succeeded in killing fifteen police personnel attached to Newry RUC station. In spite of this, fifty-nine Sinn Féin candidates won seats in council elections in May. In July the rerouting of Orange parades in Portadown led to riots, and scores of people were forced to flee when police homes were attacked by enraged loyalists. A joint Ulster Unionist and DUP working party was set up to respond to an Anglo-Irish Agreement they did not want and that they felt was being drafted over their heads. When the agreement was finally signed in November, unionist outrage was universal. Tom King, then Secretary of State, was assaulted by loyalists outside the City Hall. Shipyard workers marched to Maryfield, where the new secretariat was to be based. Some of them attacked the police on duty. All unionist MPs resigned, to force a series of by-elections that would be fought on the issue. This rebounded on them when a second SDLP seat was gained, by the party's deputy leader, Séamus Mallon.

General nationalist support for the agreement encouraged Sinn Féin to drop its abstention policy. This move left Gerry Adams in undisputed control of the Northern republican leadership. Loyalists persisted in their protests, and there were attacks on the houses of police and of Catholics. The total number of police families attacked by the first anniversary of the agreement was 368.

In 1987 it was the turn of some of the loyalist paramilitary organisations to move towards political involvement. The Ulster Defence Association published a document called *Common Sense*, proposing a devolved, power-sharing government. The leaders of the DUP and the Ulster Unionists got together to draft an alternative to the Anglo-Irish Agreement. Even Sinn Féin published a *Scenario for Peace*. But IRA activity continued. A senior judge and his wife were killed as they crossed the border near Newry, while eight IRA members were killed by the SAS as they prepared to attack Loughgall Police Station. The IRA caused international revulsion when it planted a bomb at a Remembrance Day commemoration in Enniskillen; but that did not stop it, the following month, from killing John McMichael, a leading figure in the UDA and one of the authors of *Common Sense*. Early in 1988 John Hume began a series of talks with the president of Sinn Féin, Gerry Adams. He was condemned at the time for political naïveté, or worse; but it was the first tentative step towards a peace process.

This was a year that saw one of the most violent sequences of events of the Troubles so far. Three IRA members, one of them a woman, were shot dead by an SAS team in Gibraltar. Eye-witness accounts showed that they had been coldly executed. The circumstances of their killing caused great sympathy in Catholic Belfast, and large crowds attended their funeral at Milltown Cemetery. A lone gunman belonging to the 'Ulster Freedom Fighters', Michael Stone, threw hand grenades among the mourners and fired an automatic pistol at those trying to catch him. Three men died and sixty people were injured. The whole incident was recorded on television, including pictures of the police rescuing Stone from an angry crowd that had caught up with him at the nearby motorway.

The sequence of murder still was not complete. During the funeral of one of those killed in the cemetery, two soldiers from the Signals Corps drove their car into the cortege. What happened next was filmed by television cameras and by a military helicopter flying overhead. The crowd was on edge after the Michael Stone incident, and when one of the soldiers fired a shot in the air, the crowd surged over them and dragged them out of the car. They were beaten and then taken a short distance off and shot.

In 1989 the IRA spread its wings and bombed targets in England and continental Europe. There were allegations that the police and military were feeding information to loyalists that was enabling them to kill Catholics. Peter Brooke, the Secretary of State, maintained a policy of trying to lure both Sinn Féin and unionists into talks. A bomb killed Margaret Thatcher's friend and political ally Ian Gow; and the IRA alienated large portions of the Catholic population in October 1990 when it chained three civilians to explosives and forced them to drive to police posts. A three-day IRA ceasefire at Christmas was followed in February by a mortar attack on Downing Street, London, with a bomb falling within fifteen yards of the room where John Major, who had replaced Margaret Thatcher, was chairing a meeting. In spite of this, Peter Brooke pressed on with efforts to get Sinn Féin to the bargaining table.

There was an increase in the number of killings by loyalists as they tried to destabilise any peace initiative involving the IRA. The IRA itself seemed anxious that it should approach any peace talks from a position of strength. In January 1992 it killed eight Protestant workmen who had been working on an army base. It maintained its bombing campaign through-out Northern Ireland and in England, including a 2,000-pound bomb that wrecked the forensic science laboratory in south Belfast. Loyalists responded by increasing their rate of sectarian attacks.

There was an unusual development at the general election in May when Protestants voted with traditional nationalists to elect Joe Hendron of the SDLP to replace Gerry Adams in the British House of Commons.

The last full year of war was 1993. Continuing meetings between John Hume and Gerry Adams—much criticised at the time—were leading inexorably towards a peace formula. Two children were killed in March by an IRA bomb in Warrington, Cheshire. In May loyalists initiated twice as many attacks as did republicans. Negotiations involving the Southern government continued over the summer but were stopped in October when the IRA planted a bomb in the Shankill Road that killed ten people. One of the loyalist retaliations was in the Rising Sun Bar in Gresteel, County Derry, where eight people were killed.

Loyalist violence probably delayed the announcement of an IRA cease-fire, because it made Catholics wonder where their protection would come from if there were no armed republicans. Six Catholics were killed in a bar in County Down in June, and there were calls for retaliation by the IRA. Martin McGuinness, Adams's deputy, said that the current talks were going to establish a complete demilitarisation of Northern Ireland; and on 31 August 1994 the IRA announced a complete cessation of military operations. After testing republican sincerity for a month, loyalists also announced a ceasefire.

It was not the end, of course. There were further killings in the years to come, and much jockeying within the different communities for influence. Indeed it was not till the early twenty-first century that the final obstacles were eliminated and a working Executive—very closely resembling the Executive envisaged at Sunningdale—eventually took office. The pity is that so many people died in that last decade.

It was during this time that the only sectarian murder to take place within the shipyard occurred. Maurice O'Kane, a welder, had worked in the yard from 1969. He had retired in 1989 but had returned temporarily and had only two weeks of his contract left. The UVF shot him in the back, apparently in retaliation for an unsuccessful IRA bomb attack on the Portadown loyalist Billy Wright. The gunman who carried out the attack did not work in the yard, but it seems likely that he had help in identifying his target.

The shipyard struggled on towards the end of the century. At one time it looked as if it might be involved in building a new aircraft carrier for the Royal Navy, but early planning came to nothing. Symbolically, given its history, it began to build bridges, including the Millennium Bridge in Dublin. The last ship built was the *Anvil Point*, subcontracted from a German shipbuilding firm. Repairs and refits are still carried on, and the company continues to be at the forefront of technology, particularly in the field of renewable energy. The greatness is gone, however, and crowds rushing over the bridge to Queen's Island are more likely to be going to watch ice hockey at the Odyssey Stadium than to work in engineering.

The yard has its own memorials, however: the two giant cranes, Goliath and Samson, built in 1969 and 1974. They have looked down for a quarter of a century on a city that has struggled to come to terms with itself. Their shadows have fallen alike on men desperate for change and men who resisted change with all their might. People have looked up to them and wondered about the future. If the cranes knew, they were not telling, but in 2007 one of them, Goliath, was recommissioned after being moth-balled for four years. Perhaps they will have a future after all.

BIBLIOGRAPHY

Bardon, Jonathan, *Belfast: An Illustrated History,* Belfast: Blackstaff Press, 1982.

Bew, Paul, and Gillespie, Gordon, *Northern Ireland: A Chronology of the Troubles, 1968–1999,* Dublin: Gill & Macmillan, 1999.

Blake, John W., *Northern Ireland in the Second World War,* London: HMSO, 1956.

Bruce, Steve, *Paisley: Religion and Politics in Northern Ireland,* Oxford: Oxford University Press, 2007.

Buckland, Patrick, *A History of Northern Ireland,* Dublin: Gill & Macmillan, 1981.

Budge, Ian, and O'Leary, Cornelius, *Belfast: Approach to Crisis: A Study of Belfast Politics, 1613–1970,* London: Macmillan, 1973.

Foster, R. F., *Modern Ireland, 1600–1972,* Harmondsworth (Middx): Penguin, 1989.

Fromkin, David, *Europe's Last Summer: Why the World Went to War in 1914,* London: William Heinemann, 2004.

Holland, Jack, *Hope Against History: The Ulster Conflict,* London: Hodder and Stoughton, 1999.

Kinealy, Christine, and MacAtasney, Gerard, *The Hidden Famine: Hunger, Poverty and Sectarianism in Belfast,* London: Pluto Press, 2000.

Lynch, J. P., *An Unlikely Success Story: The Belfast Shipbuilding Industry, 1880–1935,* Belfast: Belfast Society, 2001.

McAughtry, Sam, *The Sinking of the Kenbane Head,* Belfast: Blackstaff Press, 1977.

McCluskie, Tom, *No Place for a Boy: A Life at Harland & Wolff,* Stroud: NPI Media Group, 2007.

McKittrick, David, and McVea, David, *Making Sense of the Troubles,* Belfast: Blackstaff Press, 2000.

McKittrick, David, et al., *Lost Lives: The Stories of the Men, Women and Children Who Died through the Northern Ireland Troubles,* Edinburgh: Mainstream, 2001.

Maguire, W. A., *Belfast,* Keele: Keele University Press, 1993.

Maguire, W. A., *Living Like a Lord: The Second Marquis of Donegall,* Belfast: Ulster Heritage Foundation, 2002.

Moss, Michael, and Hume, John R., *Shipbuilders to the World,* Belfast: Blackstaff Press, 1986.

Parkinson, Alan F., *Belfast's Unholy War*, Dublin: Four Courts Press, 2004.
Quinn, Raymond J., and Baker, Joe, *Milltown Cemetery: A Brief History*, Belfast: Glenravel Publications, n.d.

INDEX

A Specials, 211, 213, 221
Abercorn Bar, 323
Abercorn Basin, 37, 39
Aberdeen, John Hamilton-Gordon, Earl
  of, 134
abstinence societies, 73, 97
Adams, Gerry, 340, 341, 342
Admiral Scheer, 265–9
Aiken, Frank, 214
aircraft works, 192, 255–6, 257, 260, 273,
  276, 301
airport, 255–6, 302
Al-Alamein, Battle of, 279–80
Albert Crescent, 53
Albert Square, 28
alcohol, 17, 73, 95, 97
Aldergrove, 259, 302
Alexander Graving-Dock, 47
Alhambra, 96
Allen, Charles, 44
Amalgamated and General Society of
  Carpenters, 84
Amalgamated Protestant Associations,
  252
American Civil War, 22–3, 38
American servicemen in Belfast, 277–9
American War of Independence, xiv
Ancient Order of Hibernians, 67, 203
Anderson, Albert, 313
Andersonstown, 289, 302
Andrews, John, 274, 279
Andrews, Thomas, 102, 104, 114, 117, 119,
  139
Anglo-Irish Agreement (1985), 341
Anglo-Irish Treaty (1921), 218–20, 222
Anglo-Irish Truce (1921), 213
Anglo-Irish War, 196, 197, 198–218
anti-aircraft guns, 260

Antrim Road, 88, 271
Anvil Point, 343
Anzio, 282–3
Apapa, 241
apprenticeships in shipyards, 82, 311–13
Aquitania, 124
Arabis, HMS, 259, 281
Arcadian, 193
Ardennes, 285
Ardis, Maggie, 216
Ardoyne, 252, 317, 321
Armagh, 314, 315
arms smuggling
arms trial, 319–20
  Howth, 149–50
  Larne, 145–7
  Arnon Street, 226
artists, 250
Arundel Castle (ship), 234
Ashley-Cooper, Anthony, Lord
  Shaftesbury, 84, 86, 87
Asquith, H.H., 133–4, 141, 143, 145, 147,
  148, 150
Astor, John Jacob, 112
Asturias, 193
Athenia, 261
Atkinson, Humphrey, 334
Atlantic, Battle of the, 261, 265, 274–5,
  280–81
Auchinleck, Lieut-Gen. Claude, 262
Audacious, 121–2, 186
Aurora, 30
Auxiliaries, 196, 208, 209, 213

B Specials, 211–15, 216, 217, 219, 221, 223,
  225, 226–7, 229, 253
  Troubles era, 314, 316, 318
Bainbrigge, General, 28

Baldwin, Stanley, 252
Balfour, Arthur, 134–5, 136
Ballast Board, 26–7, 49
Ballymacarret, 4, 6, 8, 9–10, 15, 81, 211, 215
Bangor, 258, 271, 277, 278
Bank Line, 245
Bank of Ireland, 25
Banner of Ulster (paper), 6, 8, 9–10, 55, 63
Bartlett, Capt. James, 123, 124, 125
Bates, Richard Dawson, 219, 225, 251
baths, 91
battleships, 186–7, 188
  dummy, 185–6, 187, 260
beam shed, 46
Beattie, Jack, 246, 248
Beatty, Rear-Admiral David, 190
Beaverford, 268
Belfast
  pre-1840, ix–xix
  1840s, 1–23, 50–51
  1850–1900, 51–80
  1900s, 81, 84–99
  1914–18, 187–8
  1919–22, 194–232
  1922–39, 237–41, 246–53, 254
  1939–45, 250, 258–65, 269–74, 275–9, 291
  1946–68, 286–310
  1969–1990s, 317–24, 326–7, 329–30, 333–5, 340–43
  capital city, 209
  regional spread, 289, 302–3
  Sundays, 304–5
Belfast (ship), 30
Belfast Brigade, 222
Belfast Castle, ix, x, 86–7
Belfast City Hall, 89
'Belfast confetti', 141, 199
Belfast Co-operative Society, 89
Belfast Corporation, 238, 270, 274, 288, 289
Belfast Guards, 222
Belfast Home Rule Association, 66, 67, 71–2
Belfast Infirmary, 13
Belfast Lough, 24–8, 37, 49, 241

Belfast Morning News, 72
Belfast Presbytery, 248–9
Belfast Protestant Association, 139, 199, 202
Belfast Protestant Working Men's Association, 64, 65–6
Belfast Ropeworks, 41, 249
Belfast Telegraph, 213, 214, 232, 251, 307, 309
Belfast Trades Council, 249
Belgic, 235
Benburb, Battle of, xii
Bermuda (ship), 234
Bibby, James, and Company, 34–5, 36, 37
Biggar, James, 67
Birmingham bombing, 329
Birrell, Augustine, 134
birth rate, 84
Bismarck, 234, 275
Black-and-Tans, 196, 213
Black-out Order, 260
Black Prince, HMS, 259
Blair, Evelyn, 216
Blitz, 269–74, 291
Bloody Sunday (Belfast, 1921), 214
Bloody Sunday (Derry, 1972), 323
Blue Star Line, 336
Blunt, Commander W.F., 109, 110
Bonar Law, Andrew, 135, 140–41, 146, 150, 212
Botanic Gardens, 96
Boundary Commission, 218, 231
Bower's Hill Barracks, 76
bowsprits, 36
Boxhall, Joseph, 113, 118
Boyd, Alexander, 199
Bradford, Rev. Robert, 335
Brew, Major, 183
Bride, Harold, 115
Bright, John, 20
Brighton bombing, 340
Britannic (Olympic class), 40, 111, 120–21, 122–6, 127, 187, 195
Britannic (1930s), 246
British Petroleum, 302
British Shipbuilders Ltd, 234

Brooke, Sir Basil, 279, 287, 293
Brooke, Peter, 342
Brown Square, 58
Browne, Dr Samuel, 92, 93
Bruce, Albert, 166
Bryony, HMS, 281, 282
building berths, 46–7
bulkheads, 104–5
Bull, Sir William, 143
Burgh, William de, ix
Burke, Edmund, 135
Burns, Philomena, 211
Burntollet, 316
Butler, Harriet, 85
Butt, Isaac, 69
Byng, Gen. Julian, 179
Byrne, Alfie, 272

C Specials, 211–12
Caird and Company, 191
Californian, 112–13, 114, 115, 116
Callaghan, Jim, 318
Cambrai, 178–9
Camel, 39, 40
Cameron, Major-General, 220
Campbell, T.J., 250
Campbell, William, 43
Canberra (ship), 299, 300, 339
Carlisle, Alexander, 102, 103, 104, 139
Carnduff, Tom, 250
Carnegie Library, 230
Caroline, HMS, 258
Carpathia, 115, 116, 118
carpenters, 46, 83–4
Carrickfergus, xi, xii, 17
Carroll, Mary Anne, 210
Carson, Sir Edward, 135–6, 137, 138, 141,
  142–5, 146, 148, 150
 First World War, 153
 post-war, 197–8, 202, 209–10
Casement, Sir Roger, 149
Catholic Association, xvi, 70
Catholic Emancipation, xvi–xvii, 50
Catholic Institute, 55, 63
Catholic Young Men's Association,
  66–7

Catholics
 pre-1840, xii–xix
 1840s, 1–2, 6–7, 17–18
 1850–1900, 50–64, 66–78, 97
 1900s, 91, 97–9, 137
 1919–22, 196–7, 198–232
 1923–39, 233, 250–53
 1940–68, 272, 291–3, 304–5, 307–10
 1969–1990s, 313–24, 326–7, 329–30,
  333–5, 340–43
 shipyard workers, 37, 40, 77–8, 98, 196,
  202, 203, 233
  attacked, 141, 199
Cave Hill, 95, 96
Cavendish, HMS, 188, 192
Chamber of Commerce, xiv, 26
Chamberlain, Austen, 135
Chamberlain, Neville, 239
Chichester, Arthur, 1st Marquis of
  Donegall, xiv, xv, 2, 26, 27
Chichester, Sir Arthur, xi–xii
Chichester, Frederick Richard, 86
Chichester, George Hamilton, 3rd
  Marquis of Donegall, 85–7
Chichester-Clark, James, 316–17, 320
Childers, Erskine, 149
cholera, 14–16
Christ Church Protestant Association,
  xvii
Christian Brothers, 63, 73, 99, 238
church-building, 61–2
Churchill, Randolph, 74, 132–3
Churchill, Winston
 First World War, 185, 186, 187, 190
 home rule and, 138, 139–40, 143, 145,
  146
 Northern Ireland state and, 222, 225,
  231, 237, 244
 post-war, 287, 295
 Second World War, 259, 260
Church of Ireland, 63, 66, 201, 304, 305
cinemas, 249–50, 304, 305
City Hall, 89
City Hospital, 290
City Line, 43
City of Cambridge, 43

civil rights movement, 314–16, 322–3
Civil War, 222, 231
Clandeboy O'Neills, x
Clarendon Dock, 26, 29
Clark, Sir Ernest, 231
Clark, George, 43, 145–6
Clark, Lady, 291
Clark, Sergeant, 209
Clifton Street poorhouse, 3
Cliftonville, 206
Clonard, 201
Clones, 221
Coalisland, 314
Coastal Corpus Christi, 332
Coastal Hercules, 332
Coates and Young, 30
Cold War, 301
Coleraine, 313
College of Art, 303–4
College of Business Studies, 304
College of Domestic Science, 303
College of Technology, 99
Collins, Michael, 219–20, 221, 222, 230–31
Columbus, 234
Colville and Sons, 195, 245
Commercial Bank, 25
Commission Club, 48
Common Sense (document), 341
Commonwealth Line, 130
Communist Party, 314
Connell and Sons, 30
Conor, William, 250
Conservative Association, 139
Conservatives, xvii, 64, 65, 66, 71, 73, 79, 132–3, 134–5, 139, 143, 233, 319
Contender, 336
Convery, Fr Patrick, 72
Convoy HX84, 266–9
Cooke, Rev. Henry, 4, 50, 57, 58
Coome's foundry, 76
Corkey, Robert, 291
Corporation Island, 5
Corporation Square, 28
Corporation Street, 16, 218
corvettes, 259, 274, 281

cotton industry, 21, 25
Countess of Caledon, 30
Court Ward, 288, 289
Craig, Alfred, 210
Craig, Sir James (Lord Craigavon)
    home rule, 136–7, 142, 148, 150
    1920s, 202, 205, 209, 211, 212, 217, 227, 230, 231
    Anglo-Irish Treaty, 218–19, 220, 222
    Craig–Collins pacts, 221, 225, 231
    1930s, 248, 250, 252
    1940s, 258
Craig, Sir John, 242–4, 294
Craig, William, 315, 316, 323–4
cranes, 46, 47, 256–7, 259, 300, 343
Crawford, Frederick Hugh, 145–6, 217
Cregagh, 289
Crolly, Archbishop William, 4, 50, 95
Cromwell, Oliver, xii
Crozier, Lieut-Col. Frank Percy, 155, 156, 158, 163, 164, 167, 168
Crumlin Road, 208, 288, 317
Cullen, Cardinal Paul, 51–2, 61
Cuming, George, 193, 194, 195
Cunard Line, 32, 38, 40, 100, 130
Cupar Street, 206
Curragh Mutiny, 147
Curran, James, 75
Currie, Austin, 314

Dargan's Island see Queen's Island
Davison, Sir Joseph, 251
D-Day, 283–4
death rate see mortality rate
de Cobain, Samuel Wesley, 78
Denvir, Bishop Cornelius, 50, 51
department stores, 89
depression (1920s–30s), 233–57
Derry, 197, 238, 270–71, 278
    Troubles, 313–14, 315–16, 317, 322–3, 326
Despard, Captain, 183
de Valera, Éamon, 210, 219, 220, 252, 279, 307, 308
Devenney, Samuel, 317
Devereux, Walter, Earl of Essex, x–xi
Devlin, Bernadette (McAliskey), 316, 335

Devlin, Joseph, 134, 203, 210, 212, 222, 223, 250
Devlin, Paddy, 326
Devoy, John, 72
Dillon, John, 134
Divis Street, 230, 303
Dixon, Archbishop Joseph, 51
Dixon, Thomas, and Sons, 191
Dolly's Brae, 2, 19–20
Donald, Thompson, 237
Donegall, 1st Marquis of, xiv, xv, 2, 26, 27
Donegall, 2nd Marquis of, 84–5
Donegall, 3rd Marquis of, 85–7
Donegall Place, 85–6, 208–9
Donegall Quay, 28, 30, 230
Donegall Road, 216, 217
Donegall Street, 252, 323
Dönitz, Vice-Admiral Karl, 275, 281
Dorrian, Bishop Patrick, 60, 61–3, 71
D'Oyly-Hughes, Capt. Guy, 262
draughtsmen, 45, 102
dreadnoughts, 186–7
dredgers, 26–8
Drew, Rev. Thomas, xvii, 2, 11, 52, 53
Droppin' Well bar, 340
Drummond, Thomas, xviii
Dublin bombing (1974), 329
Duddy, John, 67, 71
Duff Cooper, Sir Cosmo, 118
Dufferin Dock, 273
Duffin, Patrick and Daniel, 209
Duke of Argyll, 298
Duke of Lancaster, 298
Dundonald, 289
Dunkerque, 263–4
Dunleath, John, 87
Dunne, Reginald, 230
DUP (Democratic Unionist Party), 321, 340–41

Eagle, HMS, 293–4
Eagle's Wing, 29
Earl of Dublin, 37
East Yard, 192, 195–6
Easter Rising (1916), 196

education, 50, 51, 63, 73, 99, 238–9, 291–3, 303–4
Education Act 1944, 291–2
Education Act 1968, 304
Edwards, Joe, 325
El-Alamein (Al-Alamein), Battle of, 279–80
elections
    1921, 209–10
    1938, 252–3
    1945, 287
    1969, 316
    gerrymandering, 314
    voting system, 198, 237–8, 305–6
electricity, 238
Elizabeth II, Queen, 296–7
engine and boiler works, 47, 242–3
English Star, 336
Enniskillen bombing, 341
entertainment, 95–7, 249–50, 304, 305
Episcopalians, 63
Ervine, St John, 250
Ervine, Tommy, 158, 168
Essex, Walter Devereux, Earl of, x–xi
Ewart's mill, 78, 271
exports (1916), 187–8

Fair Head, 272–3
Falklands War, 339
Falls, 289
Falls Road, xix, 50, 51, 57, 67, 69, 76–7, 98, 200, 201, 205, 207, 214, 217, 252
    bombed, 272
    Troubles, 317, 319, 321
Famine, Great, 5–16
Faulkner, Brian, 306, 320, 321, 324, 327, 329
Fearless, HMS, 339
Fegan, Captain, 267
Fenians, 62, 66, 72, 99
Ferguson's motor works, 230
ferries, 295–6, 302, 332
    disaster (1953), 296
Ferris, Det-Inspector, 210
fever, 11–16
Fever Hospital, 11–12, 13

Finaghy, 289
First World War, 121–7, 153–93
  lead-up, 150–52
  Olympic and *Britannic*, 121–7, 186, 187
  Ulster (36th) Division, 154–84
  war at sea, 121–7, 185–93
  Western Front, 156–84
Fisher, Lord John, 186–7
Fitt, Gerry, 306, 309, 310, 319, 327, 334
fitting-out basin, 47
FitzGerald, Garret, 340
Fitzgerald, Gerald, Earl of Kildare, x
Flight of the Earls, x, xi
Flood, Major-General, 227
'folk religion', 60–61
forges, 46–7
Formidable, HMS, 257, 258
Forrester, George, and Company, 39
Fort St George, 129
Fox, Freddie, 215
France, Allied invasion of, 283–4
Franco, 253
Franz Ferdinand, Archduke, 151–2
Freeland, Sir Ian, 318
French, Sir John, 147
Friar's Bush Cemetery, 13–14, 57
Fulton, Dr, 240
Furious, HMS, 272
Furniture Trades Union, 192

Gallaher's factory, 249
Gallipoli, 123–4, 172, 173, 187
gantries, 101
Garmoyle, Pool of, 24, 26
gas
  in houses, 91
  on ships, 39
George V, King, 134, 213–14, 250
George VI, King, 250
Georgic, 38, 263
Germanic, 40, 195
gerrymandering, 314
Gibraltar, IRA deaths, 341
Gilmartin, Constable, 208
Gilmore, Patrick, 204
Gladstone, W.E., 73–4, 79, 132, 133

Glengormly, 289
Glitra, 189
Glorious, HMS, 187, 188, 192, 261–2
Gloucester City, 269
Goliath (crane), 300, 343
Gordon, Constable, 226
Gough, Gen. Hubert, 176–7, 178, 180
Government of Ireland Act, 205
Gow, Ian, 342
Graf Spee, 261, 265
Grand Opera House, 96, 97
Grand Ulster Unionist Convention
  (1892), 79
Grant, William, 288, 289
graving-docks, 26, 37, 47, 107
Gray, James, 242
Great George's Street, 204, 208, 250
Greencastle, xiv
Grey Point, 259
Griffith, Arthur, 140
gun-running
  arms trial, 319–20
  Howth, 149–50
  Larne, 145–7

Haddock, Capt. Herbert, 122, 186
Haig, Field Marshal Douglas, 176, 177,
  179
Haig, Major, 150
Hall-Thompson, Samuel, 293
Hamilton-Gordon, John, Earl of
  Aberdeen, 134
Hanna, Rev. Hugh, 53–4, 55–6, 67–8, 76,
  77, 78
Hannahstown, 67–9
Harbour Commissioners, 27, 29, 30, 37,
  139, 192, 196, 255–6, 265, 301–2
Harbour Corporation, xiv
Harbour Police, 233
Harell, David, 149
Harland, Sir Edward, 31–5, 41, 42, 75
Harland and Wolff
  1862–1900, 34–43, 45, 48, 77–8
  1900s, 81–4, 139
  1914–18, 185–6, 187, 188, 190–93
  1919–22, 194–7

1922–39, 233–4, 235–7, 241–6, 253–7, 258
1939–45, 258, 259, 265, 269, 271, 273,
   276–7, 283
1946–70, 293–5, 297–301
1970s–present, 311–13, 324–6, 327–8, 330,
   331–2, 335–9, 343
apprenticeships, 82, 311–13
Catholic workers, 37, 40, 77–8, 98, 196,
   202, 203, 233
  attacked, 141, 199
evangelical meetings, 139
nationalised, 324
Olympic and Titanic, 100–130, 186, 195
sold to Olsen, 338–9
tonnage (1890s), 43
tradition, 311–13
workers, clerical, 83
workers, conditions, 40, 42, 48, 82–4,
   90–91, 194–5, 311–13
workers, injuries and cover-ups, 82, 312
workers, skilled, 47–8, 83–4
workers, unskilled, 82–3, 199
workforce, 41, 42, 43, 81–4
Harrison, County Inspector Richard,
   208, 225, 227
Hart, John, 116
Haslett, James Horner, 73
Haughey, Charles, 319–20, 335
Hawke, HMS, 109–11
Hayes, Capt. Bertram, 110, 123, 126–7,
   128, 129
Head Line, 44, 266
Health, Ministry of, 289–90
Health Service (NHS), 290
Healy, Tim, 134, 136
Heath, Edward, 320, 321, 324, 329
Henderson, James, 70
Henderson, Tommy, 248, 274
Hendron, Joe, 342
Herdman Channel, 265
Hersing, Lieut. Otto, 189
Heytesbury, Lord, 5
Hibernia, 29
Hibernians, 67, 203
Hickson's shipyard, 30–31, 33–4, 42
High Street, 16

Hill, James, 20
Hill, Samuel, 158
Hitchens, Robert, 118
home rule, 66–7, 69–79, 132–50
  First Home Rule Bill, 75, 132–3
  Second Home Rule Bill, 79
  Third Home Rule Bill, 138–43, 148, 150
Homeric, 195
Hope, John Kennedy, 171
Hoppe, Iver, 326, 328, 330
Horton, Admiral Max, 280
hospitals, 13, 229, 240–41, 290
housing
  1850s, 17
  1900s, 91, 93–4
  1920s–30s, 207, 239–40
  1940s–60s, 288–9, 302–3, 314
  discrimination, 314
Housing Committee, 239–40
Housing Trust, 288–9, 303
Howth gun-running, 149–50
Hughes, Bernard, 99
Hume, John, 309–10, 326, 334, 342
hunger strikes, 335

industrial relations, 42, 83–4, 194–5, 197,
   243, 249, 276–7, 327–8
infant mortality, 289
INLA (Irish National Liberation Army),
   322, 334
Inman Line, 38
International Maritime Marine
  Syndicate, 48
International Mercantile Marine
  Company, 101, 130, 242, 243
internment, 232, 320–21, 323, 331
IRA (Irish Republican Army)
  Anglo-Irish War, 196, 197, 203, 205,
   207–11, 213–18
  1920s, 221–2, 226–7, 229–32
  1940s, 259
  1960s–90s, 319–21, 322–3, 326–7, 329,
   333–5, 340–43
IRB (Irish Republican Brotherhood), 62,
  148–9
Irish (10th) Division, 154

Irish (16th) Division, 153–4, 174–8, 183
Irish Independent, 221
Irish National League, 72–3
Irish News, 195, 198, 210, 212, 231, 232, 251
Irish Party, 71, 73, 132, 133–4, 136, 149, 196
Irish Volunteers, 149–50, 153–4
iron industry, xii, 28–9, 31, 34
Iron Prince, 339
Ismay, Thomas, 37–8, 100, 101, 102, 103, 104, 106, 107, 108, 113–14
Italy, Allied invasion of, 282–3

Jaffe Centre, 292
James II, King, xii–xiii
Jarvis Bay, 266, 267–8, 274
Jellicoe, Admiral John, 122, 190
Jenkins, Roy, 329
John XXIII, Pope, 306, 308
Johnston, William, 1, 65–6, 76
joiners' shop, 45
Joiners' Union, 233
Jones, Admiral John Paul, xiv
Juan Perón, 295
Jutland, Battle of, 189–90, 258

Kane, Rev., 78
Kempster, J.W., 139
Kenbane Head, 266, 267, 268, 270
Kennedy, Henry, 251
Kennedy, John F., 306
Kesselring, Gen. Albert, 282
Kildare, Gerald Fitzgerald, Earl of, x
Kilroot, 259
King, Tom, 341
Kinnaird Terrace, 223–4
'kitchen houses', 93, 303
Kitchener, Lord, 153, 155, 161
Korean War, 295, 297
Kyle, James, 76
Kyslant, Lord, 130, 241–2, 253

Labour Party, 198, 202, 238, 239, 253, 287, 305, 306
Lagan, Frank, 322–3
Lagan, River, ix, 24–7, 29, 30
  Lagan Navigation, 28

La Mon Hotel, 334
Larne, 258, 265, 295–6
  gun-running, 145–7
Laurentic, 244
Law, Andrew Bonar, 135, 140–41, 146, 150, 212
Lawson, Captain, xi
Leahy, Bishop John Pius, 61
Lemass, Seán, 307
Lemon Street, 53
Liberals, xvii, 64, 65, 73, 75, 79, 132, 133–4, 136, 138–41
lice, 289
lifeboats, 103–4, 115, 116–18, 119, 120, 299
Lightoller, Herbert, 116
Linen Hall, xiv, 2
linen industry, xiv, 21–3, 25, 90, 187, 202, 248, 249, 276, 293
Lisburn, 203
Liverpool (ship), 122
Lloyd George, David, 97, 133
  First World War, 175, 176, 193
  partition and, 197, 205, 213, 215, 217, 218, 219, 222, 225, 231, 234
Loans Guarantee Act 1922, 234–5, 241, 244
Local Government (Ireland) Act 1919, 198
lock-outs, 42, 83
Logue, Cardinal Michael, 140
Londonderry *see* Derry
Londonderry, Lord, 238
Long, Walter, 135, 146
Loreburn, Lord, 144
Lowland Trassey, 339
Loyal Charles, 29
Loyalist Association of Workers, 327
Lusitania, 100, 101, 103, 108
  sinking of, 155, 189
Lynch, Jack, 317, 319
Lynch, Liam, 222
Lynx, HMS, 37

McAliskey, Bernadette (Devlin), 316, 335
McAllister, Minnie, 76
McAteer, Eddie, 307
McAughtry, Mart, 270

McAughtry, Sam, 94
McCann, Alexander, 137
McClure, Thomas, 65
McCluskie, Tom, 311–13, 336–8
McConnell, John, 58, 59
McCormack, James, 76
McCrory, Joseph, 226
McCullagh, Sir Crawford, 252
Mac Curtáin, Tomás, 198, 203
MacDonald, Ramsay, 239
McFadzean, Billy, 165
McGuinness, Martin, 342–3
McGurk's bar bombing, 322
McGurk's grocery, 201
McIlwaine, Rev. William, 7, 53
McIlwaine and McColl, 44
McKean, Dr William, 142–3
McKee, Billy, 319
McKenna, Bernard, 226
Mackie, James, and Sons, 98, 200–201,
   276, 301
McKinney, Edward, 223
McKinney, Maggie, 215
McLaine, Alexander, 30
MacLay, Sir Joseph, 191
MacLellan, Brig. Patrick, 322–3
McLintock, Sir William, 245, 246
McMahon, Owen, 223–5
McMichael, John, 341
Macmillan, Harold, 299, 306
McMullen, William, 246
MacNeice, Louis, 250
MacNeill, Eoin, 149
McNeill, Ronald, 142
Macready, Gen. Nevil, 214
MacRory, Cardinal Joseph, 203, 206, 210,
   213, 250
MacSwiney, Terence, 206
Magennis, Sir Conn, xi
Magheramayo (Dolly's Brae), 2, 19–20
Maidan, 268
Majestic, 42, 129
Major, John, 342
Malcolm, Dr Andrew, 11, 13, 15–16, 21
Mallabar, John, 324–5
Mallon, John, 226

Mallon, Séamus, 341
Malone, xi, 81
Malta, 282
Manchester Guardian, 197
Marrowbone, 204, 205, 227
Marshall, Capt. A.T., 193
Mason, Roy, 333
Mater Hospital, 229, 290
Matthew, Sir Robert, 303
Maudling, Reginald, 319
Maudsley, Sons and Field, 39
Maultsaid, Jim, 158
Mauretania, 100, 101, 103, 124
Maxwell, Brig. Arthur, 246
May, Edward and Anna, 85
May Street, 53, 85
Maze Prison, 333, 334, 335
Methodists, 304
middle class, 87–9
Midgely, Harry, 274
Midland Bank, 255, 256
Millfield, 204, 221
Milner, Alfred, 148, 150
model shop (shipyard), 45
Monaghan, 221
   bombing (1974), 329
Monck, General George, xii
Mopan, 267
Morgan, John Pierpont, 100–101, 107
mortality rate
   1850s, 21
   1930s, 240
   1940s, 289
Morton, Sir Brian, 331–2, 333
Mountbatten, Lord, 334
Mountbatten, Prince Louis
   (Battenberg), 186
Mountcalm, 186
Mulholland, Andrew, 11
Mulholland, Thomas, 21, 25
Munro, General Robert, xi–xii
Murdoch, William, 113, 116
Musgrave Channel, 49, 192, 196, 325
Musgrave Shipyard, 255, 257, 300
music halls, 96
Myrina, 300, 324

Napier, Admiral Sir Charles, 192
Napoleonic Wars, 21, 25
Narvik, 261–3
Nasser, President Gamal, 298
Nation (paper), 224
National Amalgamated Union of
  Labour, 83
National Health Service, 290
National Shipyards, 193
Nationalist Party, 210, 250, 253, 287, 307,
  309, 314
Neave, Airey, 334
Newman, Kenneth, 333
News Letter, 8, 10, 17, 194–5, 221, 251
Newtownards Road, 200, 201, 204, 210,
  211, 216, 249, 319
  in Blitz, 269
New York (ship), 112
NICRA, 314–16, 322–3
Nielson, Per, 338, 339
Nixon, District Inspector John, 208, 209,
  213, 225, 226–8
Nomadic, 101
Normans, ix
Northern Bank, 25
Northern Ireland Civil Rights
  Association (NICRA), 314–16, 322–3
Northern Ireland Polytechnic, 304
Northern Star (paper), 66
Northern Star (ship), 300
Northern Whig, 8, 9, 201, 238
Northumberland Shipping, 234
North Yard, 44–7, 255
Norway, 261–3
Nugent, Major-Gen. Oliver, 157, 165, 167,
  171
Nutts Corner, 302

O'Brien, Lucius, 289
Oceanic (1870), 38, 40, 80, 102
Oceanic (1927), 244
Oceanic II, 43
Oceanic Steam Navigation Company, 243
O'Connell, Daniel, xvi, xvii, xviii, 70
  effigy burnt, 56–7, 58
O'Connor, Rory, 231

O'Duffy, Eoin, 222
O'Hanlon, Rev. W.M., 16–17
O'Hare, Jack, 229
oil refinery, 302
O'Kane, Maurice, 343
Oldpark, 204
Olsen, Fredrik, and Company, 338–9
Olympia Palace, 96, 97
Olympic, 100–111, 115, 119–23, 126–31, 186,
  195
O'Neill, Sir Brian MacPhelim, x–xi
O'Neill, Major Hubert, 323
O'Neill, Terence, 306–7, 309, 313, 315–16
O'Neills, Clandeboy, x
Opera House, 96, 97
Orange Order
  pre-1840, xv–xvii, xviii–xix, 95
  1840s, 6–7, 17–20
  1850–1900, 50, 52, 56, 63–5, 70–71, 74,
    76, 79
  1900s, 144
  1914–18, 173
  1919–22, 197, 198, 215
  1930s, 251–2
  1960–80s, 308, 309, 317, 319, 340
O'Reilly, Mary, 76
Ormeau Bakery, 249
Ormeau House, 86
Ormeau Road, 218, 223
O'Sullivan, Joseph, 230

P&O Line, 32, 235, 242, 299
Paget, Gen. Sir Arthur, 147
paint shop, 45
Paisley, Rev. Ian, 54, 305, 307, 308
  Troubles era, 314, 316, 321, 333, 334, 335
Parker, John, 336, 338–9
Parliament Buildings, 248, 250
'parlour houses', 93
Parnell, Charles Stewart, 69, 71–2, 73, 79,
  134, 136
partition, 138, 218–19
Party Processions (Ireland) Act 1850, 64,
  66, 71
Passchendaele, 176–8
Pathfinder, HMS, 189

Patterson, William, 246
pawnbrokers, 94
Payne, Charles, 193
Peace People, 333
Peel, Sir Robert, 5, 7
penal laws, xiii
Penelope, HMS, 255, 256, 258, 262, 277, 283
pension, old-age, 94
People's Democracy, 316
Percy Street, 272
Phillips, John (Jack), 113, 114, 116
Pioneer Total Abstinence Association, 97
Pirrie, Capt. William, 41
Pirrie, Lady, 241
Pirrie, Lord William, 26, 27–8, 39, 41–2,
    48, 79, 87, 129, 194–7, 233, 235–7
  control over shipyards, 235–6, 242, 243
  death, 236–7
  First World War, 185, 186, 187, 188,
      190–93
  home rule and, 138–9, 140
  Olympic and *Titanic*, 101, 102, 104, 105,
      107, 114, 119, 186
Pitman, Herbert, 118
Pius IX, Pope, 61
platers, 46, 196
Plumer, Gen. Hubert, 174, 178
Pollack Dock, 265
poorhouses, 3
Poor Law, 3–14, 94, 246–7, 248–9, 288
population (1950s–70s), 302
Portadown, 340
Pound, xv, xvii, xviii, 8, 18, 50–51, 98
  riots, 52–3, 54, 57–9, 67–8, 75, 77
poverty
  1840s–1850s, 3–17, 21
  1900s, 93–4
  1919, 196
  1920s–30s, 207, 237, 240
  1940s, 287–90
Powell, Major-Gen. Herbert, 154, 155
Powerful, HMS, 293
Presbyterians, xiii, xiv, 54, 56, 63, 142,
    304, 308
Princess Victoria, 296
Prior, Jim, 339

Progressive Unionist Party, 252
prostitution, 95
Protestant Telegraph, 308
Protestants
  pre-1840, xiii, xiv–xix
  1840s, 1–2, 6–7, 17–18
  1850–1900, 50, 51–60, 63–71, 74–9, 95
  1900s, 91, 97–9, 137
  1919–22, 196–7, 198–232
  1923–39, 233, 250–53
  1940–68, 272, 291–3, 304–5, 307–10
  1969–1990s, 313–24, 326–7, 329–30,
      333–5, 340–43
Provisional IRA, 319–21, 322–3, 326–7,
    329, 333–5, 340–43
public boards, 313
Pusey, Robert, 118

Q ships, 189
Queen's Bridge, 27
Queen's College, 2, 87
Queen's Island, 27, 30–31, 34, 37, 41, 48,
    82, 95–6, 196, 294, 300–301
Queen's Quay, 28, 91, 215
Queen's Square, 28
Queen's Street, 216
Queen's University, 87, 290

RAF (Royal Air Force), 258–9, 264, 277,
    278
Ragged School, 63
Railway Hotel murders, 207–8
Rangitiki, 267, 268
rationing, 261
Rattigan, Terence, 135
Rebbeck, Dennis, 324
Rebbeck, Frederick, 242–3, 253–4, 255–7,
    259, 293, 297–8, 299–300
rebellion of 1641, xi
Redmond, John, 134, 136, 140, 144, 145,
    148–9, 154
Redmond, Rev. John, 201–2
Rees, Merlyn, 329, 330
Reform Act 1868, 64
Registration Scheme, 260
Reina del Mar, 297

Reina del Pacifico, 294
Republican Clubs, 314, 315
Republican Labour Party, 306, 309
Ribbonmen, xv, xviii–xix, 19–20
RIC (Royal Irish Constabulary), xviii, 60,
 75–6, 78, 209, 217, 225
Richardson, Gen. Sir George, 144
riots and violence
 1800s, 52–3, 56–9, 67–9, 74–9
 1900s, 141–2
 1919–22, 197, 199–232
 1926–35, 246, 249, 250–53
 1960s, 308, 309
 1960s–90s, 317–19 *see also* Troubles
Ritchie, Hugh, 30
Ritchie, William, 29–30
Ritchie and McLaine, 30
riveters, 46–7, 298, 299
 pneumatic, 193
Rochdale, Lord, 331
Roden, Lord, 2, 19
Ropeworks, 41, 249
Rostron, Capt. Arthur, 118, 119
Rowe, George, 114, 115, 117–18
Royal Army Medical Corps, 159
Royal Belfast Hospital for Sick Children,
 241
Royal Inniskilling Fusiliers, 154, 180–81,
 279, 282
Royal Irish Fusiliers, 180, 182–3, 282
Royal Irish Rifles, 155–6, 180–81, 182–3
Royal Mail Group, 191, 241, 243, 244–6,
 254
Royal Mail Steam Packet Company, 130
Royal Maternity Hospital, 241
Royal Ulsterman, 263
Royal Ulster Rifles, 283–4, 295
Royal Victoria Hospital, 241
RUC (Royal Ulster Constabulary), 212,
 225, 227
 Troubles era, 318, 320–21, 327, 333, 334,
 340
Runciman, Walter, 245, 246
Rupert Stanley College, 292, 304
Russell, Lord John, 7, 14

sailors' conditions, 40
sails, square-rigged, 36
St Matthew's Church, 204, 216, 220, 229,
 319
St Patrick's Church, 269
St Peter's Cathedral, 61–2
Saint-Quentin, Battle of, 180–84
St Vincent de Paul, 51, 78, 206, 239, 247
saloons, 96
Samson (crane), 343
San Demetrio, 268–9
Sanderson, Harold, 128
Sands, Bobby, 335
Sandy Row, xv, xvii, xviii, xix, 18, 65, 289
 riots and violence, 52–3, 54, 56–9, 68,
 75–7, 204, 327
Sarajevo, 151–2
SAS, 333, 340, 341
Saunderson, Col. E.J., 74
sawmill, 47
Scapa Flow, 261–2
Scheer, Rear-Admiral Reinhard, 190
Schomberg, Frederick, Duke of, xiii
schools, 50, 51, 63, 73, 99, 238–9, 291–3,
 303–4
Schwab, Charles, 186
Schwabe, G.C., 34, 35, 38
Schwaben Redoubt, 161–72
Scotstoun, 244
SDLP (Social Democratic and Labour
 Party), 319, 320, 326, 327, 329, 333, 334,
 339, 341
Sea Quest, 300
Second World War, 250, 258–85
 American servicemen in Belfast, 277–9
 Blitz, 269–74, 291
 VE day, 286
 war at sea, 259–60, 261–3, 264–9, 274–5,
 277, 280–82
sectarianism
 pre-1845, xv–xix
 1840s, 1–2, 6–7, 17–18
 1850–1900, 52–3, 56–9, 67–9, 74–9
 1900s, 141
 1919–22, 196, 197, 199–232
 1923–39, 233, 250–53

1960s, 308, 309
1969–1990s, 313–24, 326–7, 329–30,
    333–5, 340–43
shipyards, 37, 40, 77–8, 98, 196, 202,
    203, 233
    attacks on Catholics, 141, 199
Seely, J.E.B., 147
settlement of Belfast, ix
sewers, 15–16, 24, 92–3, 241
Sexton, Thomas, 73
Shaftesbury, Lord, 84, 86, 87
Shankill, 75–7, 78, 200, 205, 289, 303
'Shankill Butchers', 326
Shankill Road, 68, 69, 271, 309, 317, 318,
    322, 326, 342
Shaw, George Bernard, 137
Shaw, Savill and Albion Line, 299
Shell, 332
Shipbuilders' Employers' Federation, 83
shipbuilding
    pre-1850, 28–30
    1850–1900, 30–49
    1900s, 81–4
    1914–18, 185–6, 187, 188, 190–93, 194
    1919–22, 194–7
    1922–39, 233–4, 235–7, 241–6, 253–7, 258
    1939–45, 258, 259, 265, 269, 271, 273,
        276–7, 283
    1946–70, 293–5, 297–301
    1970s–present, 311–13, 324–6, 327–8, 330,
        331–2, 335–9, 343
    apprenticeships, 82, 311–13
    Catholic workers, 37, 40, 77–8, 98, 196,
        202, 203, 233
        attacked, 141, 199
    decline, 324–6, 327–8, 330, 331–2, 335–9,
        343
    industrial relations, 42, 83–4, 194–5,
        197, 243, 249, 276–7, 327–8
    operations of shipyards, 45–8
    tradition, 311–13
    workers, conditions, 40, 42, 48, 82–4,
        90–91, 194–5, 311–13
    workers, injuries and cover-ups, 82, 312
    workers, skilled, 47–8, 83–4
    workers, unskilled, 82–3, 199

workforce, 41, 42, 43, 81–4
    see also ship design
ship design, 39, 196, 299
    corrosion, 41
    battleships, 186–7, 188
    battleships, dummy, 185–6, 187, 260
    engines, 35–6, 42–3, 102–3
    engines, diesel, 190, 243
    gas lighting, 39
    lifeboats, 103–4, 119, 120, 299
    Olympic and Titanic, 100, 101, 102–7,
        119, 120, 130, 186
    passengers, 39, 106–7, 130
    safety, 103–5, 119, 120
    sails, 36
shipwrights, 83–4, 191
Shipyard Labour Department, 191–2
shops, 89, 90
Shore Road, 289
Short Brothers, 256, 276, 277, 301
Short Skyvan, 301
Short Strand, 199–200, 201, 207, 208, 211,
    215, 216, 319
Sidney, Sir Henry, ix
Sinclair, Maynard, 296
Sinclair, Thomas, 79, 142
Sinn Féin, 196, 197, 198, 202, 206–7, 210,
    217, 222
    Troubles era, 314, 330, 335, 339–40, 341,
        342
Sirocco Works, 98, 202, 249, 276, 301
Sisters of Mercy, 51, 63, 290
Skillen, Brigid, 228
Sloan, Thomas, 139
slipways, 36, 101, 294
Smiles, Walter, 296
Smith, Charles Dunbar, 139
Smith, Capt. E.J., 107, 109, 110–17, 119
Smithfield, 8, 15, 50, 59, 93, 288, 289
    poorhouse, 3, 4
Smyth, Col. Gerald, 198, 199, 203
social hierarchy, 84–95
socialism, 202
Society of St Vincent de Paul, 51, 78, 206,
    239, 247
Solemn League and Covenant, 142–3

Somme, Battle of the, 156–73
Southern Cross (cargo ship), 44
Southern Cross (liner), 300
South Yard, 44, 47, 235, 255
Spallin, William, 226
Special Branch, 320–21
Special Powers Act 1922, 225, 232
Spence, Gusty, 309
Spiro, Bruno, 145, 146
Springfield, 77
Springfield Road, 200, 205, 208, 210, 217
stagers, 82
Stalingrad, 280
Stalker, John, 340
Stanhope Street, 226, 227
Stanhope Street Further Education
  Centre, 292
Star Line, 44
steel, 42
Stephens, James, 62
Stephenson, George, 31, 33
Stewart, Hugh, 164
stock market crash (1929), 247
Stone, Herbert, 115
Stone, Michael, 341, 342
Stormont, Parliament Buildings, 248,
  250
strikes
  1884, 42
  1919, 194–5, 197
  1926, 243
  1932, 249
  1940s, 276, 277
  1974, 329–30
Stronge, Sir Norman, 335
submarine warfare
  First World War, 188–9, 190, 191
  Second World War, 261, 265, 274–5,
    280–81
Suez Canal crisis, 298–9
Sundays in Belfast, 304–5
Sunningdale Conference, 327, 329
Swanzy, Oswald, 203
Swatara, 12–13
Swilly, Lough, 121–2
Symons, George, 118

Talbot, Richard, Earl of Tyrconnell, xii
Tallents, Sir Stephen, 231
tankers, 294, 300, 332
'tartan gangs', 320
Teelin Head, 44
Templemore, Lord, 27
Teutonic, 42–3
Thatcher, Margaret, 332, 333, 334–5, 339,
  340, 342
theatres, 96–7
Thompson and Kirwan, 30, 33, 34
Thompson, J. and J., 44
Thomson, J. and G., 32–3
Tiger's Bay, 269, 270
timber yard, 45
Times, 197, 198, 204
Tirpitz, Admiral, 188
Tisdall, William, xiii
Titanic, 82, 101–4, 111–20, 126
Tobruk, 279
trade unions, 83–4, 192, 193
Traffic, 101
trams, 89
  routes worsen violence, 200
Trewellard, 268
Troubles, 314–24, 326–7, 329–30, 333–5,
  340–43
tuberculosis, 93, 240–41, 274, 289, 290
Turner, George, 226
Twaddell, William, 230
Tyndall, William and Robert, 31
typhus, 12–14, 16
Tyrconnell, Richard Talbot, Earl of, xii

u-boats
  First World War, 188–9, 190, 191
  Second World War, 261, 265, 274–5,
    280–81
UDA (Ulster Defence Association), 326,
  329, 341
UDR (Ulster Defence Regiment), 318, 322,
  333
Ulaidh, ix
Ulster, partition of, 138, 218–19
Ulster Bank, 25, 34
Ulster Catholic Association, 70

Ulster Constitution Defence Committee, 308
Ulster Day, 142–3
Ulster (36th) Division, 154–84
Ulster (49th) Division, 171
Ulster Examiner, 66
Ulster Loyalist Anti-Repeal Union, 74
Ulster Monarch, 263
Ulster Prince, 263
Ulster Protestant Defence Association, 65
Ulster Protestant Volunteers, 308, 314, 316
Ulster Shipping Company, 44
Ulster Solemn League and Covenant, 142–3
Ulster Special Constabulary, 211–15, 216, 217, 219, 221, 223, 225, 226–7, 229, 253
  Troubles era, 314, 316, 318
Ulster Unionist Association, 250
Ulster Unionist Council, 209, 219
Ulster Women's Unionist Council, 291
Ulster Workers' Council, 329–30
Unemployed Workers' Organisation, 246
unemployment
  1920s–30s, 237, 246, 253, 254, 246–7, 248
  1940s, 258, 274
  1960s, 301, 314
Union, Act of (1801), xv, xvii, 17, 50
Unionist Party, 135–47, 148, 197–8, 209–10, 252–3
  post-war, 287, 291, 305, 306, 307, 320, 324, 329, 334, 340–41
United Ulster Unionist Council, 327
UVF (Ulster Volunteer Force), 144, 197, 204, 207, 212, 217
  First World War, 153, 154, 173
  formed, 144
  gun-running, 145–7
  post-war, 309
  Troubles, 322, 343

vagrants, 11
Vance, Gilbert, 4, 6
Vanguard, 324
variety halls, 96
Vickers Ltd, 256

Victoria (ship), 29
Victoria, Queen, 1–3
Victoria Channel, 27–8, 30, 48, 256
Victoria Street, 16
Victoria Yard, 255, 257, 294
Vindicator, 8
voting system, 198, 237–8, 305–6
  gerrymandering, 314

Walker, George, 211
Walker, Rev. George, 317
Wallace, Col. R.H., 142, 144
Walsh, Joseph, 226
War Shamrock, 191
water supply, 16, 91–2, 241
Watson, William, 53
weavers, 21–2
Weir, Andrew, and Company, 235, 236, 242
welding, 294, 298, 299
welfare state, 288, 290
Welin, Axel, 103
West, Harry, 316, 329
whiskey, 97
Whitehouse, 141
Whitelaw, William, 327, 328
White Star Line, 38–40, 42–3, 48, 80, 100–131, 195, 242, 243, 244
Whittaker, Dr Henry, 93
Wilde, Oscar, 135
Wilding, Edward, 235, 236
William III (William of Orange), xiii
Willowfield, 251, 327
Wilson, Harold, 306, 315, 321, 332
Wilson, Sir Henry, 230–31
Wilson, Rev. Isaac, 57
Wilson, Walter, 39, 41, 42
Winchester Castle, 243
Winslow Boy, 135
Wolff, Gustav, 34–5, 37–8, 41
women, in workforce, 83, 91
Woodburn, J.B., 287
Woods, Séamus, 222
Woods, Major, 171
workhouses, 4–5, 11–12, 13, 94–5, 241, 246, 290

working class, 89–95 *see also* poverty
Workman, Frank, 43
Workman Clark, 43–8
    1914–18, 187, 188, 193
    1919–22, 196, 199, 204
    1922–35, 234, 253, 255
    closed, 234, 255
    workers, conditions, 40, 42, 48, 82
    workers, skilled, 47–8
Wright, Billy, 343

York Street, 77, 204, 207, 215, 216, 218,
    220, 221, 249, 252
    in Blitz, 271–2, 273

York Street Mill, 21, 249, 271–2
Young, Sir Arthur, 318
Young Citizen Volunteers, 154, 155, 156,
    158, 160–72
Young Ireland, 62
Young Men's Christian Association, 63
Young Philanthropists, 290
Ypres, Battle of, 174–8

zinc, in shipbuilding, 41